The Ticos

THE TICOS

CULTURE AND SOCIAL CHANGE IN COSTA RICA

Mavis Hiltunen Biesanz
Richard Biesanz
Karen Zubris Biesanz

LYNNE
RIENNER
PUBLISHERS

BOULDER
LONDON

Published in the United States of America in 1999 by
Lynne Rienner Publishers, Inc.
1800 30th Street, Boulder, Colorado 80301

and in the United Kingdom by
Lynne Rienner Publishers, Inc.
3 Henrietta Street, Covent Garden, London WC2E 8LU

Library of Congress Cataloging-in-Publication Data
Biesanz, Mavis Hiltunen.
  The Ticos : culture and social change in Costa Rica / Mavis
Hiltunen Biesanz, Richard Biesanz, Karen Zubris Biesanz.
     p.   cm.
  Includes bibliographical references and index.
  ISBN 1-55587-724-9 (alk. paper). — ISBN 1-55587-737-0 (pbk. :
alk. paper)
  1. Costa Rica.   I. Biesanz, Richard.   II. Biesanz, Karen Zubris.
III. Title.
F1543.B563   1999
972.8605—dc21   98-7422
                                                                          CIP

British Cataloguing in Publication Data
A Cataloguing in Publication record for this book
is available from the British Library.

Printed and bound in the United States of America.

The paper used in this publication meets the requirements
of the American National Standard for Permanence of
Paper for Printed Library Materials Z39.48-1984.

5   4   3

Contents

Illustrations

Maps

Photos

Preface

In this book we examine a people that has intrigued us for most of our lives. In *Costa Rican Life* (1944), Mavis and her husband, John, described a green, apparently peaceful country of 800,000 people—with its underlying unrest over poverty and stagnation—that would soon erupt in civil war. In the late 1960s and the 1970s, Mavis and her son Richard and daughter-in-law Karen studied the prospering, optimistic Ticos of the welfare state. Hardly had *Los costarricenses* (1979) and its condensed version, *The Costa Ricans* (1982), appeared when the economic crisis of 1979–1982 brought wrenching changes. Eventually we decided to write the present book, in which we trace the evolution of Costa Rican culture and institutions from pre-Columbian times through the late 1990s.

Our methods have been eclectic. They include interviews with Costa Ricans from many backgrounds, daily attention to the country's mass media, and many hours of observation in diverse settings from coffee groves to the Legislative Assembly, including stays of up to seven months with families in several communities. Decades of residence in Costa Rica have provided insight even when we were not playing a social scientist role (e.g., when Karen and Richard's first daughter was born in San José in 1966 and when John was buried in a small-town cemetery three decades later). Of equal importance to us are the insightful writings on Costa Rica by domestic and foreign social scientists, journalists, and novelists.

No observer can offer a totally objective description even of a small and relatively homogeneous country such as Costa Rica. Whether the observer is native or foreign (all three authors grew up in the U.S. Midwest), her cultural background, sex, age, and class position, among other things, influence the questions she asks and how she interprets the answers, as well as how others present themselves to her. And at times, researchers encounter the Hawthorne effect (the social science analogue, perhaps, to physicists' Heisenberg principle): the very attempt to observe a phenomenon may change it. When, for instance, Richard declined offers of illegally distilled *guaro de caña* at a drinking party, hoping to preserve his liver as well as a clear head and civil tongue, his refusal cast a distinct chill on others' conversation. (His subsequent acceptance thawed it but blurred his memory of the talk.)

Many people have helped correct some of these biases, sharing with us their expertise from research or from their own experiences. Others have provided financial, material, and moral support. Special thanks to Michael Snarskis, Sandra Castro, Oscar Herrera and family, Arturo Morales, Leda Montoya, Jovita Hernández, John Biesanz, Barry Biesanz, Sarah Blanchet, Ricardo Vargas, Roberto Salóm, Gravelí Morales, Victoria Esquivel, Roberto Murillo, Carmen Mena, Miguel Salguero, Jorge Chávez, Rafael Angel Calderón, Juan Carlos Vargas, Rafael Mora, Efraín Chacón, Clotilde Fonseca, Etelgive Chinchilla, Eugenia Ibarra, Ricardo Lankester, and Rolando Villega.

We are grateful to Richard Tardanico, Zayra Méndez, Irma González, María Eugenia Bozzoli, Peter Brennan, Alfredo Aymerich, Katia Arroyo, Juan Jaramillo, Eugenio García, and Carmen Naranjo for their insightful comments on several chapters; to David Higgins for maps; to Ingrid Holst, Sarah Blanchet, Sylvia Boxley, Luís Ferrero, Fernando Acuña, Julio Laínez, and the staff of Editorial Universidad Estatal a Distancia (EUNED) for photographs; and to Diane Hess for her keen editorial eye.

— 1 —

The Land
and the People

C OSTA RICANS ARE PROUD OF THEIR SPECIAL COUNTRY. In 1949 it became the first in the mainland Americas to abolish its army—a fact that many Ticos, as Costa Ricans call themselves, attribute to their tendency to settle disagreements peacefully through dialogue and compromise. They boast of 93 percent literacy and, when they had an army, liked to tell visitors, "We have more teachers than soldiers." Their life expectancy is the highest in Latin America thanks to years of government spending on clean piped water, vaccinations, nutrition, and health education as well as to a health insurance program that covers almost everyone.

For half a century Costa Rica's presidents have come to office through honest elections. The incumbent party rarely wins—largely a consequence of Ticos' reluctance to let any one person, party, or other group become too powerful.

Costa Rica's long history of peace, stability, and emphasis on education has attracted numerous foreign investors. This reputation, along with the country's great natural beauty, also attracts over half a million tourists each year. Those who stay for more than a few weeks will find that much of its reputation is well deserved. They may also learn about the country's problems, for Ticos do not hesitate to complain as well as boast to a trusted listener.

The third smallest country in the mainland Americas, Costa Rica has an area of 51,000 square kilometers (20,000 square miles), or twice the size of Vermont. It is located in the narrow isthmus of southern Central America between Nicaragua and Panama. Its maximum length from northwest to southeast is 484 kilometers; its minimum width from the Pacific Ocean to the Caribbean Sea, 119 kilometers.

Despite its small size, Costa Rica has an enormous range of topography and climates. Though it lies only ten degrees north of the equator, temperatures vary greatly from sultry lowlands to cold mountaintops. Rainfall and humidity vary with nearness to the coasts as well as altitude and the direction

1

Map by David Higgins

Map by David Higgins

of prevailing winds. These climatic variations help explain the great diversity of Costa Rica's flora and fauna. So does its "strategic position near the junction of two great continents, biologically quite different, from each of which it has received large contributions."[1]

Mountain ranges run the length of the country like a backbone. One volcanic range, the Cordillera de Guanacaste, begins in the Northwest near Nicaragua and connects with another, the Cordillera de Tilarán. This range runs southeastward and meets the volcanic Cordillera Central, which ends near the center of the country. Five of the 112 volcanoes in these ranges were active in 1998. A higher nonvolcanic range, the Cordillera de Talamanca, runs from the country's center to its southeastern border and on into Panama and Colombia. Much of it is still covered with virgin cloud forests of live oaks up to 600 years old. Its highest parts, treeless, tundra-like paramo, have frost but no snow.

As in all of Central America, the Caribbean slope (or Atlantic slope, as Ticos call it) is mostly gradual and gentle, the Pacific slope mostly steep and hilly. In the Northeast near the Caribbean and in the southwestern lowlands are some of the primary forests that still cover about a quarter of the country's area despite extensive clearing for pasture and farming. A few patches of tropical dry forest remain on hills in the Northwest; there are also flat areas covered with great expanses of cotton and dry rice fields and cattle pasture—forested until a century ago.

Two out of three Ticos live in the Valle Central, or Central Valley; they are especially concentrated in the relatively flat Meseta Central, or Central Plateau. The Central Valley is formed where the two chief mountain ranges, the Cordillera Central and the Cordillera de Talamanca, nearly meet. Altitudes on the valley floors range from about 600 to 1,500 meters.

The Valle Central is not, strictly speaking, a valley any more than the Meseta Central is a plateau, but both terms are traditional and, in everyday speech, interchangeable. The Meseta is actually two small sections of the Central Valley roughly between Alajuela on the western side of the mountains and Cartago to the east. In and near the Central Valley, as well as in the valley of El General to the southeast, the rugged and fragmented terrain strongly affects who interacts with whom. The slopes are a patchwork of forest, cropland, and pasture; the lush green valleys are laced with streams.

Located at the juncture of two tectonic plates, Costa Rica experiences frequent earth tremors, which range from imperceptible shivers through *sacudidos* (shakings-up) and *temblores* (tremblings) to full-blown *terremotos* (serious quakes). Although the National University's seismograph detected 3,000 tremors in 1991, residents felt very few; only one was a *terremoto;* it caused serious damage along the Caribbean coast.

Weather varies with altitude, time of year, and exposure to ocean winds. Daytime temperatures in the Central Valley range from 60° to 85°F, averaging about 75° (23°C), and tourism promoters rhapsodize about "the land of eternal spring." But it is sometimes so chilly, especially in the evening, that sweaters and blankets are welcome.

Costa Rica has a modified version of a monsoon climate. In most regions there are two fairly distinct seasons, called *invierno* and *verano*, whose usual English translations as "winter" and "summer" are misleading. Rainfall varies greatly from the constantly humid Caribbean slopes to Guanacaste with its long and severe dry season. In much of the country *invierno*, the rainy season, lasts from May to November. Sunny mornings are usually followed by overcast skies and a brief downpour, or perhaps by a thunderstorm or rain that may continue all afternoon.

About mid-November strong north winds usher in the dry *verano* for the Central Valley and the Pacific slope but bring more rainy spells to the Caribbean side of the mountain watershed. Most wooded areas stay green all year, but during *verano* pastures turn brown, dust blows from fields and dirt roads in central and western Costa Rica, and smoke fills the air as farmers burn stubble and brush. Although many prefer the dry season, during its final warm months they grow as eager for the first downpour as the parakeets flying overhead in screeching flocks—pleading, say the Ticos, for the rains to begin.

Rain is so much a part of Costa Rican life that Ticos use at least eight words to distinguish various types, from *pelo de gato* (misty "cat's fur") and *garua* (drizzle) to an *aguacero* (downpour) and a *temporal* (steady rain lasting several days, most common in September and October). Rain replenishes the water supply, irrigates crops, feeds the rivers that supply hydroelectric energy and in a few areas are the only travel routes, and frequently results in destructive flooding.

Costa Rica has long been a botanist's paradise. There are more varieties of plants in this tiny land than in all of the United States east of the Mississippi: over 1,500 distinct species of trees and over 6,000 kinds of flowering plants, including 1,000 species of orchids.

Animal life is also profuse. Some 830 species of birds have been identified, more than in all of North America north of Mexico. The National Biodiversity Institute estimates that Costa Rica is home to 350,000 species of insects. Acre for acre the lowland rain forests support a greater variety of animal and vegetable life than any other area of the earth's surface.

Naturalists lament that Costa Rica is no longer the paradise of a few decades ago. Nearly a third of the nation's territory is protected—at least on paper—in public and private parks and reserves. But many forests have been reduced to shreds and patches; giant trees have been felled and burned to make pasture and banana plantations; and in hilly areas, soil erosion has soon followed. Bird and animal populations have dwindled along with their shelter. Twenty-six species of animals were on the endangered list in 1996. During the 1980s one species, the famous golden toad of Monteverde's cloud forests, vanished from the area and is now reportedly extinct.

Destruction of much of the land's original beauty and ecological balance is only one of many problems Costa Rica shares with other so-called third world countries. Arable land is inequitably distributed and inefficiently used. The population grows faster than economic resources, and this growth places a tremendous strain on the environment. Despite a much lower birth rate than that of most developing countries, Costa Rica tripled in population between 1950 and 1985 thanks to a sharply falling infant mortality rate and by 1998 had 3.5 million inhabitants.

Like many of its neighbors, Costa Rica long depended on world markets for a few agricultural products (chiefly coffee and bananas) and has had little power to influence the terms of that trade. Like them, Costa Rica piled up huge foreign debts by defaulting on soft loans from international financial organizations. And like them, soon after a world economic crisis became acute in 1980, it had to bow to the dictates of these creditors to save its credit rating and remain eligible for further loans.

The budget cuts and reforms demanded by the World Bank, the International Monetary Fund, and the Inter-American Development Bank have been wrenching and controversial. On the one hand, the economic growth rate climbed steadily for some years, thanks in part to the wider variety of exports demanded by these lenders. On the other hand, the wealthiest 10 percent have benefited most from this growth. Cutbacks have been deepest in health, education, and welfare programs.

Although many Ticos now complain of pervasive unease and anxiety, Costa Rica is still noted for its remarkable stability. It is a peace-loving nation with honest elections and a comparatively high quality of life. This stability is often attributed to the relative cultural homogeneity of its people.

Since 1990, when the United Nations began to compare more than 150 nations by various human development indices, Costa Rica has ranked consistently high. In 1995 it was judged to have the highest quality of life in Latin America and ranked twenty-eighth in the world in terms of life expectancy at birth (seventy-eight years for women, seventy-four for men), educational level, and real per capita income.

In comparison with most other Latin Americans, the majority of Costa Ricans are physically and culturally very much alike. Most are descendants of both Spanish colonists and indigenous peoples; many also have some African ancestry. Most would be called *mestizos* in, say, Mexico. But few Ticos use this or any other term that acknowledges their mixed ancestry; most see themselves as white.

Regardless of social class and other differences, such as the greater extroversion of lowlanders compared to their Central Valley cousins, most Ticos share similar ways of thinking, acting, and feeling. Roman Catholicism is the official religion and, to varying degrees, that of eight Ticos out of ten. Although the Roman Catholic Church enjoys a constitutional position as the state religion, the Catholic majority is proud of its lack of fanaticism. Almost everyone speaks a non-Castilian Spanish rich in archaic expressions and words as well as words adopted long ago from the various Indian languages.

The capital, San José, and the national government dominate almost all aspects of life even in remote areas: education, health services, the mass media, political administration, religion, the fine arts, provisions for water and electricity, and commerce. This centralization also fosters homogeneity.

But the boundaries of Costa Rica have never been closed to outside influences. Since the early nineteenth century, people of many nationalities have come as immigrants or permanent residents—particularly Chinese, West Indians, Nicaraguans, Germans, and Italians. From 1870 to 1920, between 20 and 25 percent of the population growth could be attributed to immigration; after 1920 its effect was minor. Then in the 1980s many thousands of refugees from Nicaragua and El Salvador entered Costa Rica, and many have remained.

When we refer to "Ticos" or "most Ticos," we generally have in mind the politically and culturally dominant *mestizo* (in Ticos' own eyes, white) majority. Ticos of all classes, political parties, and regions share a sense of national identity. They believe they have a unique way of life and a distinctive national character. They may explain an action by saying, "We Latinos are like that" but are far likelier to say, "We Ticos are like that." They feel set apart from (and superior to) their Central American neighbors not only because of the lighter skin of the average Costa Rican but also because of cultural differences. They often say something is *muy tico*—very Costa Rican—and assert proudly, "I'm as Tico as *gallo pinto*," referring to a favorite dish of rice and beans. They constantly measure proposed—or even accomplished—changes according to how well they fit their "idiosyncrasy" and "the national reality." Decisions must be made "*a la tica*." This means, above all, that they must not violate their most cherished values: democracy, peace, the family, and education.

Surrounded as they have been by military dictatorships, Ticos are keenly aware of and apprehensive of threats to their democratic tradition. They often mention freedom as their greatest blessing. They also profess the essential equality and dignity of all human beings. Ticos loathe arrogance and expect people in high places to act *humilde* (humble). A public speaker citing his own accomplishments may refer to himself as "this servant" rather than "I." There is an easy give-and-take between boss and employee. Except when the occasion clearly calls for coat and tie, presidents typically go about in sports clothes or shirtsleeves and are addressed by their first names or nicknames, preceded by the respectful title *don*.

The values of liberty, dignity, and equality include an insistence that Costa Rica, though small, is a sovereign nation with the right to make its own decisions.[2] Ticos express great concern for the nation's image abroad. They were exuberant when President Oscar Arias won the Nobel Peace Prize in 1987 for his efforts to promote peace in Central America and when the Costa Rican soccer team defeated Scotland in the 1990 World Cup. When swimmers Sylvia and Claudia Poll win Olympic and other international medals and when Costa Rican–born astronaut Franklin Chang makes still another space flight, Ticos no longer feel that they live in a forgotten backwater.

Costa Ricans have long considered their country a peaceful haven in a violent world. They speak of their Nicaraguan neighbors as prone to violence and boast that even today their own president can mingle freely with a crowd. Schoolchildren rather than soldiers parade on patriotic holidays and line the streets to welcome visiting dignitaries.

The constitution declares that the family is the natural base of the society and it is the duty of the state to give it special protection. Most Ticos prize family ties, and many confine intimate friendship to relatives.

Costa Ricans see formal education not only as the best means of achieving material progress but also as a condition of democracy. Framed school diplomas adorn humble homes, and parents urge children to show visitors their school notebooks. University graduates with professional degrees often introduce themselves by using their own graduate titles and address others by their titles. Many Ticos distinguish, however, between formal training in skills and knowledge on the one hand and actual behavior on the other. They consider a rude or graceless person *mal educado* no matter how much schooling he or she may have had.

These dominant values guide behavior. The value of peace, for example, is expressed in various ways. Raised voices are seldom heard, fights rarely seen, and Ticos will nod or say "*sí*" even when they don't mean it simply to avoid conflict. Few Ticos express great hatreds or passions. Anthropologist María Bozzoli considers her typical compatriot a fence-sitter. "He says, '*Quien sabe?*' (Who knows?), '*Tal vez*' (Maybe), '*Mas o menos*' (More or less). He doesn't want to commit himself." Playwright Melvin Méndez agrees: "People in other countries can be categorical. Not Ticos. We beat around the bush to avoid saying 'No,' a syllable which seems almost rude to us, and rather than hurt someone, we say one thing and do another."[3] A young Cuban immigrant comments, "Ticos are so polite, but rarely open or sincere."

This *sí pero no* (yes but no) attitude allows Ticos to find ways out of difficult situations by means of compromise. Decisionmaking *a la tica* means constant bargaining in an effort to avoid conflict, even though the problem may not really be resolved. Decisions are postponed indefinitely and, once made, may never be implemented. Some Ticos scorn this behavior as *palanganeo,* evoking an image of riding the waves unsteadily in a *palangana,* or basin, tilting from side to side, getting nowhere. Others call it achieving consensus.

The saying "Each in his own house and God in all" indicates the high value Ticos place on *convivencia*, or peaceful coexistence. They often refer to their nation as a family. In their relations with others, Ticos want above all to *quedar bien* (pronounced kay-DAR bee-EN), to get along and make a good impression in an encounter, to appear amiable. Their use of diminutives is often an attempt to *quedar bien* by expressing affection or softening a word or assertion. "I will get your *facturita* [little bill]," says a salesperson. The desire to *quedar bien* often wins out over other values, such as keeping one's word. (A university professor told us, "You North Americans are insulted when someone calls you a liar. We Ticos are not.") It is easier to promise to do something *ahorita* (in a little while) or *mañana* and thus avoid possible friction at the moment than it is to tell someone that it cannot be done soon or perhaps ever.

The masked gunmen who trapped Supreme Court magistrates in the court building for several days in 1993, demanding ransom, were assumed at first to be Colombians involved in narcotics traffic. When their speech betrayed them to be Ticos, wrote Dery Dyer, editor of the *Tico Times*,

> we suspected the jig would soon be up. . . . It's one thing to be up against an unknown, unpredictable menace represented by anonymous masked men of undetermined nationality; it's quite another when you know you're dealing with a couple of *majes* [ordinary guys] from Tres Ríos. . . . Costa Rican cultural *idiosincrásia* is so strong, it . . . supplied the government with its most powerful weapon to use against them. Once unmasked, [the kidnappers] deflated like leaky balloons, reverting almost immediately to their Tico selves.
> . . .
> The members of the "Death Commando" were real terrorists as long as nobody knew who they were. Once their identities were revealed . . . the kidnappers found themselves facing the dreaded disapproval of family, friends and countrymen. They wrote a letter pleading for understanding: Guillermo, they explained, was desperate to get a liver transplant he believed he needed, but they would never have hurt their hostages. They pleaded for their families', friends' and society's forgiveness and apparently felt they had regained the right to re-enter its loving embrace: outcasts no longer, they were Ticos among Ticos, civilized, peaceful and gentlemanly. So thoroughly had they slipped back from terrorist into Tico mode that they ended up trustingly laying down their weapons and walking wide-eyed into a police trap.[4]

And how did they acquire those weapons? By convincing the local police chief—a friend and neighbor—that they wanted to practice target shooting and maybe do a bit of hunting. If it occurred to the police officer that the guns they asked for were a bit heavy, he handed them over anyway—because he, too, wanted to *quedar bien*.

Rituals such as the proper ways of greeting and leave-taking govern much interaction. Men shake hands, pat shoulders, and perhaps embrace;

women, or a man and a woman, embrace and pat shoulders, perhaps touch cheeks and kiss the air. They ask after one's health and that of the entire family. Similar queries and salutations begin and end phone conversations.

There is something specific to say in almost every situation. Upon first seeing another member of the household early in the day, the standard question is "¿Cómo amaneció?" (How did you awaken?) and the standard reply—even when untrue—is "Bien, por dicha" (Well, fortunately). The visitor approaching an isolated rural house shouts "Upe!" from a distance. Upon entering a house, the visitor asks permission—"Con permiso." Whether leaving for Miami or the supermarket, one is wished a good journey accompanied by God. Flowery language and compliments are common even in business letters. (When Richard wrote a letter to a University of Costa Rica dean requesting a library card, a Tico friend, finding it overly curt, rewrote it with the proper compliments, thus tripling its length.) These rituals ease interaction and give Ticos their reputation for politeness and friendliness.

Properly followed, social rituals take time. In Costa Rica, time takes a backseat to courtesy and enjoyment. Despite the clockbound programming of TV programs, school sessions, and working hours, many Ticos still have a rural sense of time.

Emphasis on dignity and courtesy often takes the form of saving face for others as well as oneself. Ticos rarely accept blame for mistakes and usually take care not to embarrass others, especially in public.[5]

Though fond of jokes about national shortcomings, Ticos very seldom tell jokes on themselves as individuals. They are *delicados*—easily offended. The criminal code provides a prison sentence of ten to fifty days for one who by word or deed offends a person's "dignity or honor." Face-saving is so important that the sentence is far heavier if the slander is committed in public.

When one Costa Rican feels insulted by another, the desires for face-saving and for peaceful coexistence may be at odds. Fifty years ago, a man might have challenged the offender to a duel—with fists, not guns or swords—on a date months in the future. "By the appointed time," says a small-town dentist, "tempers would have long since cooled, and the two would meet and shake hands. If both simply showed up, the honor of both was preserved." In today's rapidly changing society, customary solutions to such dilemmas are fewer.

A Swiss-born psychologist sees his adopted country as underdeveloped not solely because of dependency on and exploitation by richer and more powerful countries but also because of the prevailing "culture of the *pobrecitico*" (the poor little thing). In this paternalistic culture, says Pierre Thomas Claudet, people seldom develop assertive, autonomous personalities. They are pitied much like helpless children simply because they are expected to accept responsibility and cope with the normal problems of life. In many conversations one hears the word *pobrecito* applied whether the person is sick, pregnant, hung over, suffering unrequited love, tired, working at a job, studying . . . or because this person *must* study, work, get up early, walk, cook, take an exam, do a task; or because he or she got a bad grade, was punished, was scolded. . . . Not only is the person a *pobrecito* but also *salado* [unlucky] because he didn't get away with ignoring the rules: he is caught copying, fined for driving drunk, got the current cut off for not paying the electric bill, arrived late, overslept, lost a job, had to do extra work.

[People brought up in the culture of paternalism and commiseration] are invited to perceive themselves and others as "victims" of their situations, duties and obligations. Furthermore, this phenomenon serves as a shield to justify not assuming the responsibility and discipline of vital personal, family, social and work situations.[6]

Claudet may be too sweeping in his judgments; nonetheless the term *pobrecito* is often used in much the way he describes it, as we saw in the story of the Supreme Court kidnapping. When we confronted an attorney who had defrauded us, he told us that his judgment had been impaired by a recently discovered brain tumor. Another attorney to whom we mentioned this howled with laughter. "That's a classic excuse—that and 'My mother is dying.' He wants you to think he's a *pobrecito*."

Ticos greatly value individual liberty. Some note a "negative attitude toward all forms of association and collective enterprise" except for the circus aspect of politics and the similarly superficial emotions aroused by soccer. And even so, "the Tico is such an individualist that he plays soccer only by a miracle."[7] Individualism, say social critics, often means selfish concentration on personal and family affairs and an unwillingness to cooperate or to sacrifice for the common good. In recent years the phrase "Mmmmmimporta a mi?" has entered common parlance. "What does it matter to me?" shrugs off responsibility and justifies lack of involvement. A strong strain of resistance to law goes along with the belief in individual liberty. This tendency is especially evident on streets and highways. Anonymous behind the wheel, free of pressure to *quedar bien*, many Ticos drive recklessly, both fatalistic and confident that they can get away with breaking laws. Either *padrinos* (patrons in high positions) or a charming smile will work, especially if one is clearly of high social standing. Traffic cops, many hope, can also be bribed to overlook infractions.

One of the strongest social controls among Costa Ricans is fear of what others will say. They are quick to gossip about others, especially if they are different in some respect, but are afraid to become subjects of gossip. It is safer, therefore, not to make friends because your confidences may be repeated. Signs in some public buildings ask people to avoid malicious gossip; clergymen preach against it.

Choteo—mockery—keeps people in line without confrontation or violence. "We don't chop off a person's head," Ticos say; "we lower the floor he is standing on." Cartoons often depict a smiling speaker quite unaware that a saw is cutting a circle around his feet and that any moment his pride will suffer a fall. Young men ridicule others' blunders with choruses of falsetto hooting.

Choteo ranges from friendly irony to rancorous attacks. If it is done with humor it is very effective and may even be appreciated by its targets. It may also discourage ambition and imagination. Costa Ricans, say some social critics, want to keep everyone on the same mediocre level; they envy someone who excels and pity anyone who falls below the common level as a *pobrecito*.

Along with conformity go conservatism and caution. Not only are Ticos reluctant to accept change but they are suspicious of large-scale organized planning. Columnist Julio Rodríguez often writes that doing things *a la tica* means "little by little, now and then, and half way."

Such conformity and conservatism are supported by fatalism. Many Ticos believe they must be resigned to the will of God and habitually add the phrase "si Diós quiere" (God willing) to any mention of plans, even something as simple as "I'll see you tomorrow." Death, they believe, comes only at the preordained moment, and therefore one must be accepting and resigned.

One is born either lucky or unlucky. But one can help one's luck by making the right connections—with God and the saints through prayer, with good witches who help thwart evildoers, and especially with relatives and "godfathers" who have wealth or political clout. In a small society where "everyone is everyone else's cousin," personal contacts are often more important than merit.

Costa Ricans tend to be formalistic and legalistic as well as conservative. They pass laws, create agencies and institutes, and hold meetings and symposiums to "solve" problems—often only symbolically. "Saying is more important than doing, announcing than acting," says writer Carmen Naranjo.[8]

Although these generalizations about Costa Ricans are subject to many qualifications and exceptions, we see these common values and norms reflected in such institutions as the family, education, government, and religion, as well as in the class system.

Many deep-seated cultural patterns clash with what some Ticos see as the traits of a developed society. In the minds of other, more tradition-oriented Ticos, moral and spiritual values are eroding as cars, VCRs, and trips to Disney World become the measures of people's worth. Individualism and liberty, they add, are threatened by the tyranny of the job and the clock. (*Hora tica* means perhaps an hour or two after the appointed time; *hora americana* or *hora exacta* means punctually.) Some observers also see a far greater emphasis on work, planning, and enterprise, especially among the middle class, since the 1940s. And cooperation is evident in many associations and community projects as well as in the growth of arts demanding teamwork such as dance, symphonic music, and theater. As the society grows more complex and new subcultures emerge, old social rituals no longer apply in many situations, and confusion and anxiety follow.

Despite all the changes of the past half-century, numerous observations made in the 1940s—and even in the 1850s—still apply today. In Chapter 2 we discuss the origins of today's Costa Rican society and culture, tracing both changes and continuities with the past.

Notes

1. Alexander F. Skutch, *A Naturalist in Costa Rica* (Gainesville: University of Florida Press, 1971), pp. 7–8. See also chapter 17 for his description of the various ecological zones.

2. Familiar with both Arabic and Costa Rican cultures, Arabist Margaret K. Nydell described their many similarities to us (personal communications, 1984–1986). Many colonists came to Costa Rica from southern Spain, dominated by Arabs for centuries. Among the common values of the two cultures are emphasis on dignity, honor, and reputation; the desire to create a good impression on others; loyalty to one's family; dislike of solitude; sensitivity to criticism; the tradition of personal appeal to authorities for exceptions to rules; and fatalism. See her *Understanding Arabs: A Guide for Westerners*, 2nd ed. (Yarmouth, Maine: Intercultural Press, 1997).

3. Quoted in Elsa Morales C., "Con el tico en el alma," *Perfil*, April 24, 1989, pp. 60–61.

4. Dery Dyer, "Terrorism, Tico Style: Or, the Need to 'Quedar Bien,'" *Tico Times*, May 7, 1993, p. 2.

5. Peggy Barlett, *The Use of Time in a Costa Rican Village* (San José: Associated Colleges of the Midwest, 1969), pp. 68–69.

6. Pierre Thomas Claudet, *La cultura del pobrecito* (San José: Editorial de la Universidad de Costa Rica [EUCR], 1992), pp. 27–28.

7. Abelardo Bonilla, "Abel y Cain en el ser histórico de la nación costarricense," in Luis Ferrero, ed., *Ensayistas costarricenses* (San José: Lehmann, 1971), p. 281.

8. Carmen Naranjo, *Cinco temas en busca de un pensador* (San José: Ministerio de Cultura, 1977), p. 105.

— 2 —

History

COSTA RICAN HISTORIANS HAVE LONG TRACED their country's democratic traditions to colonial times. Because there were few precious metals or Indians, they argued, Spanish settlers were forced to till the soil as independent subsistence farmers rather than becoming feudal lords who exploited native peoples and the gold and silver they mined. Thus there developed a rural classless democracy of peace-loving white farmers who greatly valued freedom and family. This, in a nutshell, is the long-accepted version of colonial history.

Archaeological studies as well as recent research into the 500 years of the European presence have led contemporary historians to revise this *leyenda blanca*, or "white legend," as Theodore Creedman calls it.[1] They assert that it downgrades indigenous peoples, ignores their cruel treatment by the colonists, and exaggerates the whiteness of Costa Ricans. Its core, honoring "a small democracy of small farmers," has, however, long served as the unifying myth of the nation and is still taught in schools and repeated in patriotic speeches.

Pre-Columbian Cultures

Humans have lived in what is now Costa Rica for at least 11,000 years. The earliest inhabitants, small bands of hunters and gatherers, left behind stone spearheads that attest to more than just their age: Some of them, the Clovis points, are a North American invention, and others, the Magellan type, are of South American origin. They show that the region was both a bridge and a filter for human cultures.

Two millennia ago the region clearly contained two main culture areas, one largely Mesoamerican (that is, Middle American, from Mexico south into Central America), the other reflecting South American influence.[2] Some 400,000 to 500,000 people, according to recent research, were probably living in the area that is now Costa Rica—mostly in the Central Valley and in the northwest—when Columbus landed in 1502. This research overturned the long-held belief that the indigenous population was tiny.

13

Pre-Columbian ceramic vessel (Hector Gamboa, reprinted from Biesanz et al., Los costarricenses, *[San José: EUNED, 1979])*

Only a fairly large population could have built the hundreds of residential sites identified in recent decades and created the thousands of intricately worked artifacts found, along with embalmed bodies, in ancient burial mounds. These artifacts also attest to the movements of migrants and traders into the area through centuries of pre-Columbian history.[3]

When Columbus arrived in this area, there were an estimated nineteen chiefdoms. Though their members spoke different languages and differed in social structure, they communicated among themselves in Huetar, the language of the Central Valley's inhabitants.

Archaeological data show that the Mesoamerican culture, strongly influenced by the Mayas and Aztecs, reached into western Costa Rica through trade, migration, and conquest. The people of la Gran Nicoya, the northwestern area that now includes Guanacaste Province, lived in towns with central plazas and grew corn, beans, and sunflowers as well as squash, gourds, cotton, and the cacao pods they used as money. Religious rites resembled those farther north, although there was less human sacrifice. The calendar, paintings, and games also showed strong Mayan and Aztec influences. So did ceramic, gold, and jade artifacts as well as stone sculptures such as elaborate three-legged rimless *metates* for grinding corn.[4]

Their societies, like those of the Aztecs and Mayas, were rigidly stratified. A *cacique,* or warrior chieftain, governed with a council of elders and shared high status with priests and nobles. Lesser chiefs in outlying communities paid tribute to the principal *cacique*, who led a standing army. The lower strata—the great majority of the population—were peasants, artisans, and slaves taken as prisoners of war.

South American influence was evident among the seminomadic peoples living in eastern and southern tropical forests. Though they, too, raised corn, they also cultivated cassava and other tubers and peach palms, using each not only for food but also for drinks—both fermented and nonalcoholic. They also chewed coca, a custom usually associated with Andean cultures.

The inhabitants of drier regions of the central highlands erected, on stone foundations, large, round stockaded dwellings where hammocks were hung for three or four extended families. Remains of hundreds have been located, and the few that have been excavated reveal towns similar to those in northern South America with their cobbled streets and causeways, plazas and sophisticated aqueducts and drainage systems. Some South American motifs appear in stone statuary and monochromatic ceramics decorated with incisions and holes. Supported by shifting cultivation (slash-and-burn farming), hunting, fishing, and the gathering of wild foods in the hinterlands, the permanent residents of the largest towns were mostly artisans, priests, and nobles.

Why did the chiefdoms, with their food surplus and occupational specialization, apparently not build ceremonial centers as monumental as the Mayan ones of Tikal and Chichén-Itzá? Archaeologist Michael Snarskis estimates that such a center would have required at least 50,000 inhabitants and that the shifting agriculture of the region was not adequate to suport a population this large.

Furthermore, war was endemic. Each chiefdom was an extended clan whose members could be mobilized for war. Why? Water was never an object of strife in this part of Middle America, as it was in desert areas farther north. But each group coveted slaves, territory, sources of rock and clay, control of traditional roads and paths, and key points on trade routes.

Snarskis speculates that when a disaster such as a major volcanic eruption weakened a group, it became easy prey for enemies. At Playa Hermosa in Guanacaste a seven-inch layer of volcanic ash suggests that such a catastrophe occurred about 1,000 years ago.

Archaeologists are sure that vegetation and soil still cover many ceremonial centers similar to El Guayabo on the slopes of Turrialba Volcano, a site abandoned for unknown reasons about a century before the arrival of the Spaniards. Excavation thus far indicates that even lacking huge stone temples, aboriginal cultures were more complex and sophisticated than many had believed.[5]

Unlike the Mayas, however, the area's inhabitants (like those throughout South America) left no written records. Their symbolic themes are repeated in many ways and in many art forms—the feathered serpent, the snarling jaguar, birds, and frogs, for example—but are not subject to analysis as are hieroglyphs and alphabetic writing.

Perhaps most mysterious are the stone balls found only in Costa Rica. Almost perfect spheres of granite or other stone, they weigh from a few kilograms to over 7 metric tons and measure from 10 centimeters to over 2 meters in diameter. A team from the National Museum headed by archaeologist Ifegenia Quintanilla has arrived at several conclusions: The spheres originated in the Diquis Delta in southwestern Costa Rica in about A.D. 300 and production was at its peak between A.D. 800 and 1200, when there were large population centers in the area.

But what do they mean? Were they boundary markers? Parts of a calendar? Signs of power? Although archaeologists have several hypotheses, the stone spheres remain as mute as the statues of Easter Island.

European Contact and Conquest

On September 18, 1502, on his fourth and final westward voyage, Christopher Columbus landed at Cariay, now Limón, on the Caribbean, and stayed eighteen days to repair his ships. He called the aborigines *indios* because he remained convinced he had reached his original destination, the East Indies.

For the next sixty years, Spanish expeditions stayed close to the Pacific seashore. Mud, dense forest, and steep mountains made the highlands almost inaccessible from the Caribbean side. Exploring the Nicoya Peninsula on the Pacific side in 1522, Captain Gil González was given so much gold that the Spaniards came to think of this area as "the rich coast," and by 1539 the territory between Panama and Nicaragua was officially known as Costa Rica. But Spaniards found much more gold in Guatemala, which they made Spain's administrative center for Central America.

Several coastal settlements established after González's exploration were destroyed by pirate raids and by rivalries among the Spaniards. By 1560 many thriving colonial cities had been founded in other parts of the Americas, and the royal representatives in Guatemala thought it high time to explore and colonize the interior of Costa Rica. King Philip II promised any future colonists that they could divide the *indios* among themselves in *encomiendas*—groups of families that would work as slaves a certain number of days a year for two generations or pay tribute; the masters in turn were obliged to "protect and Christianize" these families.

In 1561 an expedition founded Garcimuñoz in the western Central Valley (today's Rio Oro de Santa Ana area). The following year Juan Vázquez de Coronado was named head of the governing council. With his companions he explored the Central Valley and in 1564 moved the residents of windswept and sterile Garcimuñoz to Cartago, the first permanent settlement.

As the 500th anniversary of Columbus's first arrival in the Western Hemisphere on October 12, 1492, approached, controversy about the meaning of this event became heated. Was it a "discovery"? Only from the Europeans' point of view. An "encounter"? That implies a meeting of persons or groups of more or less equal power. Historian José Solano sees the event as a clash or collision:

> Although our pre-Columbian ancestors received the visitors courteously at first, when they comprehended their true intentions they decided to fight and defend what by right belonged to them. Nor was it a confrontation of the "old" world and the "new," but rather of two opposed worlds.
> The badly named "Discovery of America" is no more than the tragic moment . . . in which were lost to history societies and cultures thousands of years old: labor networks, ways of ordering the world and explaining chaos, ways of feeling and thinking, languages and wisdoms.[6]

Protesting the emphasis on ties with "Mother Spain" in the celebration of October 12 as decreed by a 1968 law, three other Costa Rican historians wrote in 1993:

> The contact of Europeans and the indigenous peoples who had inhabited this continent for thousands of years before the arrival of the Europeans, has been presented to many generations of Costa Ricans in terms of false and simplistic dichotomies: civilization/barbarism, light/darkness, Christianity/paganism. Similarly, school texts . . . have affirmed that the origins of our nationality and our identity are found only in Spain.[7]

Soon after publication of their book, the Legislative Assembly passed a law changing "The Day of the Race" to "The Day of the Cultures" in recognition of Costa Rica's multicultural legacy.

The Colonial Period

Costa Rica, the Cinderella of Spanish colonies, was taxed, scolded, ignored, and kept miserably poor. An isolated and neglected province of the captaincy general of Guatemala, it was unable to raise enough revenue to pay its own administrative expenses. Its clergy was subordinate to the bishop of León in Nicaragua, who rarely visited. Partly because of this isolation, a distinct society concentrated in the Central Valley slowly evolved and became the nucleus of the Costa Rican nation.

The Spaniards were able to destroy the social organization of many Indian societies by curtailing the power of their *caciques* and imposing leaders picked by the colonists.[8] They were less successful in establishing the *encomienda* system: The Spanish Crown had put many restrictions on this system by the time Costa Rica was colonized. And many Indians died of diseases brought by the Spaniards, were shipped to Peru as slaves, or fled to remote forests.[9] The first *encomiendas* in 1569 allotted several hundred Indian slaves to each landowner. Within a century, many landowners had only three, and family farms became the norm.

Spanish colonization reduced the number of Indians in Costa Rica to 2,000 in four centuries. The very few who remained in or near early Spanish settlements were segregated into *pueblos de indios*. The Huetares of the Central Valley were easily subdued, but enslavement and disease nearly exterminated them before long.[10] Survivors mated with the colonists or their African slaves and blended over the centuries into the general *mestizo* population. (In the absence of mines and large-scale agriculture, there were probably no more than 200 African slaves at any one time. Some were domestic servants; many others, unsupervised in small Caribbean-coast cacao plantations—whose owners remained in the highlands—escaped.)

The aborigines had lived in harmony with the environment for centuries, though they did alter it—clearing small plots in order to farm, for instance, and planting some areas with trees that yielded a nutritious, milky sap; huge descendants of these trees can still be seen today. Spanish patterns of settlement and land use (which still persist) were very different. The colonists' iron implements cut down trees much more quickly than had the Indians' stone and wooden tools. Cleared tropical forest land, with its thin topsoil, is good for only two or three plantings. Whereas the Indians would let an area revert to forest after a few harvests, the colonists often used the now-impoverished land as pasture. Most farmers had both cattle and crops, but already in the early colonial period landowners in sparsely populated areas preferred ranching to crop agriculture because it demanded much less labor.[11]

When Irazú Volcano erupted and covered Cartago with ashes in 1723, this capital consisted of only seventy houses of adobe and thatch, two churches, and two chapels.[12] There was no doctor, no druggist, no sale of food. Even the few artisans were usually farmers as well. Most colonists lived in or near small highland farming villages and came to town only on festival days. The poorest colonists, who had by then settled farther west in the Central Valley, seldom came even then.

The poverty and dispersion of the colonists disturbed civil authorities because taxes were hard to collect; religious authorities were concerned because the colonists did not fulfill their obligations as Catholics. In 1711 the bishop of León, dismayed by low attendance at mass, commanded the colonists to build churches, and three years later he decreed excommunication for all who had failed to do so.[13] But they were slow to comply—perhaps, some historians think, because most had no suitable clothing to wear to church.

The colony was tranquil in part because it was poor. Mineral wealth—a bone of contention in other colonies—remained undiscovered. Although land was readily available, by the eighteenth century most colonists had only family labor to work it. The tiny settlements were isolated from one another by heavy rains, broken terrain, and lack of roads. Finally, Costa Rica was remote from other colonies, which were often the scene of raging disputes. In 1809 Governor Tomás de Acosta, like his predecessors since 1648, reported that everyone still lived near a subsistence level. Compared to most other Spanish colonies, Costa Rica was indeed poor. But historian Carlos Monge Alfaro saw in the humble colonial farmer, with his love of liberty and autonomy, the foundation of Costa Rican democracy. Each farm, he wrote in a text used in schools through many editions, was

> a small world in which the family was born and raised far from other farms. Their simple life, without ambitions or desires, gave the inhabitants a rude, mistrustful, very individualistic character. They were without exception peasants who had to till the soil for their food; as a result Costa Rica became a rural democracy. Unlike other Spanish colonies, Costa Rica had no social classes or castes, no despotic functionaries who looked down on others, no powerful creoles owning land and slaves and hating the Spaniards, no oppressed mestizo class resentful of the maltreatment and scorn of the creoles.[14]

This view of colonial history is still glorified in newspaper editorials, presidential speeches, and civic ceremonies. In 1992, for example, the minister of planning lauded the democracy and equality of colonial farmers as the foundation of today's democratic nation and exhorted today's Costa Ricans to emulate their ancestors: "simple, frugal, hard-working and egalitarian."[15]

This conventional version of history ignores the distinctions of wealth and power that existed. It ignores, too, the enslavement of Indians and Africans and the enforced racial segregation of Central Valley residents. It also exaggerates the isolation of colonial farmers, most of whom, says historian Lowell Gudmundson, lived in small villages rather than on lone homesteads.[16]

Toward the end of the eighteenth century and the beginning of the nineteenth, there was more movement toward larger settlements. San José, prospering from its tobacco industry and mule trade, was especially attractive. As towns grew and surrounding lands were occupied, many landless people founded hamlets and villages on frontier lands rather than become peons. The formation of the republic in the nineteenth century was, as we shall see, impeded by the strength of community loyalties.

The Emergence of a Nation

Despite Spain's neglect, few of the 65,000 inhabitants of Costa Rica actively sought independence. Though aware of the independence movement in neighboring colonies, Costa Ricans were taken by surprise when they learned

in October 1821 that the independence of all Central America had been proclaimed in Guatemala on September 15. The councils of the four largest
Meseta towns—Cartago, San José, Heredia, and Alajuela—met separately
and each declared its independence from Spain. Representatives of the four
towns then met and agreed to remain neutral toward one another "until the
clouds of the day disappear." This is often cited as the classic instance of the
Tico tendency to postpone decisions.

Division and conflict marked the first years of the republican era.
Nicaragua, Guatemala, and Mexico all sought to dominate the new nation.
And each of the four towns, as independent as the city-states of ancient
Greece, claimed the right to be the capital. On other issues they formed two
factions that were to clash for years. The conservative and aristocratic leaders
of Cartago and Heredia joined forces against the progressive and republican
leaders of San José and Alajuela, and their differences sometimes erupted
into armed confrontations.[17] Victorious in a battle in the Ochomogo Hills near
Cartago, the republicans moved the capital to San José in 1823.

Costa Rica joined the Central American Federation that same year. In
1824, when Guanacaste-Nicoya asked to be annexed to Costa Rica rather
than remain part of strife-torn Nicaragua, the federation approved, but spo-
radic disputes over the province flared up between the two countries for
decades.

In 1825 those Central Americans eligible to vote (on the basis of property)
chose a congress to draft a federal constitution, which proclaimed freedom of
thought and abolished slavery in the region. It left to each state the right to establish its own head of government, congress, supreme court, and army.

By 1838, however, the federation existed in little more than name. Costa
Rica withdrew and declared itself a sovereign state, which would nonetheless
"continue to belong to the Central American family." Attempts to form closer
ties persist to this day, as does Costa Rica's ambivalence about them.

Costa Ricans had long since organized their own government. In 1824 an
elected congress chose Juan Mora Fernández as the first chief of state. Mora
offered rewards to anyone who would open up roads and ports or other means
of promoting industry and commerce. The first newspaper appeared shortly
after his reelection in 1829.

Costa Rica was not yet a unified nation but "a group of villages separated
by narrow regionalisms."[18] Braulio Carrillo, who ruled as a heavy-handed
dictator from 1835 to 1842, imposed measures favoring national unity. He established an orderly public administration without lining his own pockets and
replaced the anachronistic Spanish laws with legal codes patterned after those
of France. His other great accomplishment was to promote coffee production.

The first coffee plants cultivated in Costa Rica were little more than
botanical curiosities. Ticos preferred to drink chocolate or *aguadulce* (raw-
sugar water). But coffee was a modish drink in Europe, and Costa Rica's lo-

cal governments, and later the national government, encouraged its cultivation in hopes of a new source of prosperity. They gave plants to the poor, decreed that every homeowner plant a few trees near his or her house, exempted growers from tithes, and offered free land to anyone who would plant coffee on it.

Most Ticos, however, were reluctant to wait five years for trees to mature; they saw no market in a land where only mule trails connected the highlands to the inadequate port of Puntarenas on the Pacific, and there was no access to the Atlantic except around Cape Horn. Nonetheless, some began to grow and export coffee, and in 1830 an export line to Chile was established for reexport to Europe.

Then on Christmas Day, 1843, Captain William Le Lacheur of England sailed into Puntarenas harbor in search of cargo, and in San José he found growers willing to trust him with their unsold coffee. Two years later he returned with pounds sterling. Thus began a flourishing trade with England that made Costa Rica, with its scant 80,000 people, the most prosperous nation in Central America. European iron stoves soon replaced the three stones on which cooking pots had been set; an increasing number of homes acquired window glass, mirrors, and other imports bought with coffee profits.[19]

"The grain of gold" became the crop nearest to Costa Rican hearts and pocketbooks. Even today, despite a sharp decline in coffee's importance to the economy, groves of low, glossy-leafed trees decked with fragrant white blossoms in April and red berries in December cover much of the Central Valley and other regions.

Costa Rica had several advantages over its isthmian neighbors in building a large-scale coffee export business. There were no rival products to claim time, energy, and investment and few surviving Indians to claim coveted lands. The Central Valley, where most Costa Ricans lived, offered the ideal combination of altitude, temperature, rainfall, and volcanic soil for producing prime coffee.

By the end of the century the heart of Costa Rica was almost entirely given over to coffee. It was harvested in the dry season and piled into carts that teams of oxen and mules pulled down the new road to Puntarenas.

The importance of coffee growing to the formation of Costa Rica lay not in new wealth alone but also in its distribution. The many small farms of the Central Valley were well suited to coffee, which requires intensive labor and returns profits on even a small share of the product. Thus small farmers, carters, and relatively well paid peons all shared in coffee prosperity.

Small growers, however, could not finance processing, transport, and shipping. Fortunes were amassed by those who could. They bought coffee from small farmers, processed it, and arranged for export and international finance. The *cafetaleros,* or coffee elite, were the leaders—and in some ways the owners—of the country for the next century.[20]

Despite the success of coffee and Carrillo's other achievements, opposition to his autocratic rule was bitter, especially outside San José. In 1842 Carrillo's enemies invited General Francisco Morazán of Honduras, former president of the Central American Federation, to use Costa Rica as a base for fulfilling his dream of restoring a regional union. Morazán accepted and exiled Carrillo. But a military draft and direct taxes made him even less popular than Carrillo had been. Five months after the general entered the country he was captured and executed during an uprising.

In 1847 Congress named as the first president (rather than chief of state) twenty-nine-year-old José María Castro, who had earned a doctorate of law from the University of León, Nicaragua. In the interim administration of his predecessor, Castro had inaugurated the University of Santo Tomás and established a newspaper; one of his first acts as president was to found a high school for girls. He believed that ignorance is the root of all evil and that freedom of the press is a sacred right—risky stands to take in a land "moved by personal and family interests and passions."[21] In 1849 the coffee barons used the army to force his resignation and replaced him with his vice president—Juan Rafael Mora, a leading coffee planter.

Costa Rica was still torn by local rivalries when Mora took office. In his first term, with his popularity slipping, Mora dissolved the rebellious Congress and rigged new elections in his own favor. Had it not been for a U.S. invader, William Walker, he would probably not have been allowed to finish his second term. Walker was responsible for "the most transcendent event" in Central American history—more important, says one historian, than independence from Spain.[22]

Like many of his compatriots, Walker believed it was the manifest destiny of the United States to control other peoples. Soon after his arrival in 1855 with his army of filibusters, he controlled Nicaragua and its armed forces. Cornelius Vanderbilt, who owned various enterprises in that country, threatened to oust him. Just when Walker was becoming desperate, a group of southern U.S. slaveholders offered him support on condition that he institute slavery in Nicaragua. Although once an abolitionist, Walker accepted. Hoping to hand over the weak nations of Central America to his supporters as part of a confederacy of southern American states, he invaded Guanacaste in March 1856.

The Costa Rican envoy to Washington had informed President Mora of Walker's designs, and in February the Legislative Assembly authorized military action against Walker. Costa Ricans of all social classes (and later, other Central Americans as well) responded enthusiastically when Mora called up an army of 9,000 men, which he led in ousting Walker from Costa Rica. A U.S. blacksmith helped the Ticos "forge their simple tools into arms," in the words of the national anthem, and Captain Le Lacheur's ships carried soldiers up the coast toward the Nicaraguan border.

In Rivas, Guanacaste, a big farmhouse served as Walker's stronghold. According to legend, Juan Santamaría, a drummer boy from Alajuela, ran up and torched the roof before dying in a hail of bullets; he was eventually exalted as a national hero. His feat and the victory it helped bring about are celebrated every year on April 11. The main airport is named after him.[23]

Returning soldiers brought home a deadlier invader than Walker's army—cholera. In 1856 and 1857 it killed 27,000 of the 110,000 Costa Ricans.

Although Walker did not again invade Costa Rica, he threatened other parts of the isthmus until 1860, when he was executed by a Honduran firing squad. His inadvertent role in Costa Rican history was to help unite its people during their National Campaign.

"Don Juanito" Mora, the victorious president, reached new heights of popularity. But his arbitrary actions and favoritism toward friends and family soon earned him many enemies; wealthy Ticos objected to his creation of a national bank and his family's virtual monopoly of the coffee market. Then as now, Costa Ricans resisted having the same people in power over long periods of time, and when Mora rigged the 1859 elections to ensure himself a third term, his opponents, with the army's help, toppled and exiled him.

The political struggle was confined to a few extended families. Class tensions were minimal because, as we saw earlier, the many small coffee growers enjoyed modest prosperity and, thanks to the scarcity of labor, peons were comparatively well paid. But by the mid-nineteenth century the power of the *cafetaleros* was already apparent. Political enemies and allies alike were often relatives or in-laws and nearly all were members of the coffee elite. Mora's successor, for example, was his brother-in-law and, like Mora, a member of a wealthy coffee-growing, -processing, and -exporting family. During the 1860s even the military men who helped make and topple presidents, or assumed the office themselves, were either members of this class or took orders from it.

Militarism was part of the national culture from the time of the 1856–1857 National Campaign until well into the twentieth century. After 1893 teachers, for the first time, outnumbered soldiers, though the size of the army also continued to increase for the next quarter-century. Militarism declined in the three decades before the abolition of the army in 1949—primarily, says historian Astrid Fischel, because the country's elite finally felt able to control the masses ideologically through the expanded school system.[24] Although military service was obligatory, the standing army was small. Young men who had not chosen a military career were called to active duty only during border disputes; it was easy to call up a substantial force because young Ticos considered it their patriotic duty to respond.

After a successful coup in 1870 Colonel Tomás Guardia held power—in and out of office—until 1882. Like Braulio Carrillo, he used dictatorial power not only to punish his enemies but also to promote the nation's progress. He replaced the constitution with a new one that remained in force until 1948. He levied high taxes and spent revenues on education, public health, and transportation, including the Atlantic Railroad, which he envisioned as a powerful unifying symbol of national progress.[25] He also used a loan from England—the beginning of a foreign debt that still plagues Costa Rica—to finance this railroad. His arguments—greater efficiency and accountability—for having private contractors rather than the state construct it are familiar ones today. Guardia negotiated a contract with John Meiggs, a U.S. engineer who had built railroads in the Andes. In 1876 Meiggs's nephew, Minor Cooper Keith, gradually assumed control and contracted for one stretch after another of the railroad.

Malaria, yellow fever and dysentery, lack of fresh food, and the difficulty of securing Costa Rican laborers all impeded progress. Keith recruited Chinese and Italians and finally completed the job with the aid of thousands of West Indians—and at a cost of 5,000 lives.

Built to transport coffee from the Central Valley to the Caribbean coast, which would cut three months and much expense from the trip to Europe, the railroad led to the development of another product even more dependent on foreign investment and foreign markets—bananas. Costa Ricans had been growing bananas in small quantities near the Caribbean coast since 1874. With the railroad, the banana venture quickly attracted both foreign capital and government support. Exports increased from 100,000 stems in 1883 to ten times that in 1890, when the railroad was finished. No export tax was levied until 1909.

The coffee oligarchy that ran the nation thus helped create the country's other leading export. The railroad continued the transformation of the subsistence economy of the precoffee era to a specialized commercial-agricultural one largely dependent on powerful foreign nations—increasingly the United States rather than Great Britain. As historian and geographer Carolyn Hall puts it, "Ironically enough, it was after achieving political independence [from Spain] that Costa Rica developed a typical colonial economy . . . based on exporting one or two primary products and importing a wide variety of manufactured products and raw materials."[26] Thus it once again became dependent on other countries.

Although the *cafetaleros* had supported building of the railroad, they were reluctant or unable to invest in the banana industry, an enterprise that demanded a huge capital outlay in the undeveloped Caribbean region: transportation systems, drainage, and facilities for housing, schooling, and health care. Nor were the coffee barons concerned about protecting their own country's banana growers, who might have rivaled their power.[27]

The banana-producing areas of Limón Province, therefore, began as isolated enclaves under foreign control—chiefly that of the Boston-based United Fruit Company—and remained so for decades.

Toward Electoral Democracy and Social Reform

From its inception Costa Rica was a republic, but not a democracy. No leader had been freely elected by all the people; no opposition group had won an election; no group had admitted losing one. The constitution provided for division and balance of powers and for protection of basic human rights but not for popular elections.

The 1880s brought far-reaching changes. During Guardia's dictatorship a group of young men met to discuss political ideas. Many had studied in Europe or Chile and returned to Costa Rica as champions of a secular state, universal education, and popular elections. After Guardia's death in 1882 they ushered in a new stage in Costa Rican history—a shift to "liberal" democracy.

The parties that formed around prominent members of this group, however, were based on personal charisma rather than on programs and ideologies. Violence, electoral fraud, and the elite's monopoly of power persisted during the decades of their influence. But a free press increasingly guided public opinion, and Costa Ricans became accustomed to hearing critical discussions of ideas as well as of individual candidates.

In the 1880s liberal governments secularized the cemeteries, passed laws allowing divorce and civil weddings, expelled both the Jesuits and Bishop Bernardo Thiel—accusing both of lusting after power—and closed the church-dominated University of Santo Tomás. They proclaimed that primary education should be not only free and obligatory, as provided in the 1871 constitution, but also secular. They also abolished the death penalty. Although Bishop Thiel's exile was brief and Catholic doctrine has been taught in public schools since 1940, the other reforms have remained in place.

In 1889, for the first time, the election was not rigged by the government, and both presidential candidates sought the popular vote. Propagandists for both parties spoke to rural villagers as they left church. As election day neared, President Bernardo Soto imposed his own candidate. On November 7, fired up by young orator Rafael Iglesias, angry peasants marched on San José with sticks and knives. Soto could easily have routed them with government troops but did not want to be responsible for bloodshed. He resigned and named an interim president, during whose term peaceful elections were conducted. For the first time a large number of ordinary Costa Ricans had insisted on their right to choose their leader. All but one of twenty-six presidents since then have been elected, although the right to vote was long restricted to literate, landowning males.

Democracy's growth suffered setbacks. The new president, José Joaquín Rodríguez, turned dictatorial in the face of bitter conflict between the liberals and the Catholic Union Party, headed by Bishop Thiel. Rodríguez, ignoring the courts, suspended civil liberties, closed opposition newspapers, and arrested his opponents, each of whom pleaded a writ of habeas corpus before the Supreme Court. Its president, thirty-one-year-old Ricardo Jiménez, freed them almost as soon as they were arrested.

After the Congress censured him in 1892, Rodríguez dissolved Congress and exiled or imprisoned a number of journalists, congressmen, and other citizens. Ricardo Jiménez declared the dissolution of Congress a mortal blow to the constitution and resigned from the Supreme Court.

As the 1893 elections approached, Rodríguez restored constitutional guarantees but was so alarmed by Bishop Thiel's pastoral letter urging just wages for laborers and artisans that he maneuvered to ensure that neither the liberals nor the Catholic Union Party won.

His handpicked successor was Rafael Iglesias, the young orator who had been the power behind the throne. Iglesias soon began construction of a railroad linking the Pacific to San José (and thus to the Caribbean as well). He also opened the splendid National Theater, financed in part by contributions (more or less voluntary) from *cafetaleros* as well as ordinary citizens but mostly by an import tax. Like the electric lighting and streetcars inaugurated in San José in 1884, the theater reinforced the economic and cultural dominance of the capital, still evident today. But Iglesias felt blocked by his compatriots' "conservative and fearful spirit, attachment to the letter of the law, indecisiveness and lack of practical sense."[28] Consequently he ignored public opinion and pressured Congress to approve a constitutional amendment by which he could be reelected. His opponents did not even participate in the 1897 election.

When political unrest led to conspiracies and assassination attempts, Iglesias had his enemies flogged in public. Accused of tyranny, he declared that the violently critical newspapers had turned the people against him. Toward the end of his term, his opponents among the elite united behind Bernardo Soto as their choice for president. Nonetheless, when Iglesias suggested a compromise candidate, Ascensión Esquivel, they capitulated in one of the agreements or "transactions" so frequent in Costa Rica even today.

Despite general rejoicing when he took office in May 1902, Esquivel was hampered by an economic crisis. The price of coffee had dropped sharply, and it was necessary to import corn and beans for the fast-growing population, which had nearly tripled in fifty years to over 340,000.

A heated campaign for the next term included five contenders, three of whom joined forces against the front-runner in the primaries, Cleto González, for the final election. Believing the public order to be in danger, Esquivel exiled all three. González took office on May 8, 1906, amid great political unrest because he had been imposed on the people.

Don Cleto, however, soon pacified them with his respect for law and popular opinion and his promotion of public works and public health. He was succeeded by Ricardo Jiménez, who also won the hearts of the Ticos over many years of public service.

Don Ricardo changed the electoral system so that the voters chose the president directly instead of merely choosing electors. If no candidate had an absolute majority, Congress was to choose between the two with the largest share of votes. But presidents, including don Ricardo, continued to alter election results to favor their chosen successors.

Nor was Jiménez's innovation observed in the 1914 election, in which two of the three candidates resigned; instead of naming the third, Congress declared him ineligible and chose Vice President Alfredo González Flores to serve as president, though he had not been a candidate at all. Costa Ricans believed in honest popular elections but had not yet achieved them.

After his inauguration in 1914, González faced a decline in revenue and a rise in debts because of World War I. An admirer of U.S. president Woodrow Wilson, he considered the tax system the root of the government's financial problems. Revenues were negligible because the coffee elite had kept taxes indirect and regressive, and both import and export tax revenues declined with the wartime drop in trade.

Unwilling to follow the usual practice of taking out foreign loans, González proposed an income tax. Large planters and businessmen—backed, he later asserted, by foreign oil companies—arranged his ouster in a 1917 coup by Minister of War Federico Tinoco and his brother Joaquín.[29] After an election in which he was the only candidate, Federico Tinoco's status had constitutional support.

Once entrenched, the Tinocos filled the jails with political prisoners and clamped rigid controls on the press. Costa Ricans might have tolerated an ineffective government, but they repudiated one that restricted liberties they had come to expect. Schoolteachers (mostly women) and high school students set fire to the pro-Tinoco newspaper's plant. When the government sent troops against them and fired into the U.S. consulate, where some had taken refuge, the public was thoroughly alienated. In August 1918, when a coup seemed imminent, the Tinocos fled to Europe.[30]

The next three presidents tried to stabilize a country in financial chaos with shaky international relations and little domestic order. Then Ricardo Jiménez was elected for a second term in 1924. He had defeated the first candidate of an ideological party in Costa Rican history—General Jorge Volio, whose Reformist program included "Christian socialist" ideas he had adopted in Europe.[31]

Don Cleto and don Ricardo between them occupied the presidency for twenty of the years between 1906 and 1936. They personified the "liberals of Olympus" who laid the foundations of Costa Rica's electoral democracy. Except for the Tinoco era, those decades are now generally considered more democratic and tranquil than any previous period.

Tranquility also meant perpetuation of the status quo and lack of concern for the poor. These presidents limited the state's economic role primarily to building roads and schools. During the 1930s depression, electoral fraud (particularly in congressional elections), the exploitation of workers on banana plantations, and the influence of fascist and communist ideas disturbed this illusory tranquility. Young lawyer Manuel Mora founded a communist party, the Bloc of Workers and Peasants, and led a strike of banana workers in 1934—the first large-scale strike in the nation's history.

León Cortés, who succeeded Ricardo Jiménez in 1936, was less protective of civil liberties. In the midterm elections Mora's party won a seat in Congress. Cortés, whose sympathies (like those of many other Costa Ricans before Pearl Harbor) were with the Nazis, dissolved the Electoral Tribunal and did not allow the congressman to be seated.

Though Jorge Volio had been defeated in 1924, he had made many Ticos more receptive to socialist ideas. Costa Rica's abysmal poverty was compounded by a 27 percent increase in population (from 516,000 to 655,000) between 1930 and 1940.[32] Former president Rodrigo Carazo (1978–1982) recalls

> that bucolic Costa Rica without social benefits or adequate public services. . . . The crisis of the '30s had completed the process Rodrigo Facio called "the peonization of the *campesinos*" by the concentration of wealth and property in the hands of the few, especially the *cafetaleros.*
>
> I knew the Costa Rica of social injustice. A country of people without shoes or teeth, without a university, with scarcely half a dozen high schools.
>
> I experienced the Costa Rica of the *gamonal* [well-to-do farmer] who gave a house along with a job, thus becoming the owner of the peon's family.
>
> . . . It was a Costa Rica without a limit on working hours, in which children also worked like grownups; [where] infant mortality was like that in the rest of Latin America . . . and life expectancy was barely more than 40 years.
>
> I saw the sick ask for hospital attention as charity. . . . Workers had no vacations, no dismissal notice, no severance pay. . . . A Costa Rica without social guarantees.[33]

The 1940s: A Decade of Turmoil

These problems, as well as government attempts to solve them, led in the 1940s to events that divided the nation, eroded the power of the coffee elite, and started Costa Rica on the path toward becoming an industrialized welfare state. The decade and its climax, the civil war of 1948, mark a great turning point in Costa Rican history.

One decisive event was the declaration of war against Germany and Japan the night of December 7, 1941—before the U.S. Congress met the next day and formally declared war. (This declaration was primarily symbolic.

Political leaders of the 1940s: Manuel Mora, Mons. Victor Sanabria, Teodoro Pic-
*ado, Rafael Angel Calderón Guardia, and an unidentified officer (*La Nación,
reprinted from Biesanz et al., Los costarricenses *[San José: EUNED, 1979])*

Only a few Costa Ricans fought in World War II, enlisting in Allied armies.)
Under a pact drawn up in Rio de Janeiro, the various states of the Americas
had agreed to support any one of them attacked by a non-American power.
President Rafael Angel Calderón Guardia, furthermore, had secretly agreed
with President Roosevelt that Costa Rica would help defend the Panama
Canal in case of war. This alliance resulted in financial aid and in such projects as the Inter-American Highway.

Dr. Calderón, elected in 1940, instituted a health insurance program for
urban workers patterned after Germany's and Chile's, as well as the Labor
Code and Social Guarantees, which established for all workers a minimum
wage, an eight-hour day, a six-day week, and the right to organize; protected
them against arbitrary dismissal; and made collective bargaining mandatory
in labor-management disputes. The president also secured passage of a law
allowing the landless to acquire title to unused land by cultivating it. These
measures would have been difficult to pass without the support of Archbishop
Victor Sanabria.

Calderón won the admiration of workers and of some members of the
growing urban middle class, which stood to benefit most from his establishment of the University of Costa Rica (UCR) in 1940. But landowners and
businessmen felt that these programs improved the workers' lot at their expense. Fiscal disorder and widespread government corruption intensified

their opposition. Needing supporters, Calderón agreed in 1942 to an alliance with Mora's communist party (now called Vanguardia Popular). The fact that the Soviet Union was an ally of the United States in World War II lent the party some respectability. Although this alliance won Calderón support in some sectors, it further alienated farmers, who felt it threatened their traditional way of life.[34]

Another source of persistent attacks on *calderonismo* was the Center for the Study of National Problems. Founded in 1940 by a small group of law students, the center attracted idealistic young middle- and upper-class professionals, students, and white-collar workers. They advocated government-led development programs but opposed Calderón's alliance with the communists. They were also alienated by Calderón's "personality cult," by corruption in his administration, and above all, by electoral fraud. "Electoral purity," though rarely a reality, had long been held sacred in Costa Rica, and the center's members saw their group as a major defender of this value. Like other anti-Calderón Ticos, they were angered by the deceptions that ensured the victory of the government candidate, Teodoro Picado, in the 1944 election.

Largely a puppet of Calderón, whose immediate reelection was prohibited by the constitution, Picado maintained the National Republicans' ties with the communists. Calderón hoped to regain the presidency in 1948, and all through Picado's term he waged an electoral campaign against a strange new coalition called simply the Opposition.

In 1945 the Center for the Study of National Problems merged with Acción Demócrata, a group of mostly young middle-class men, to form the Social Democratic Party. It was headed by José ("Pepe") Figueres Ferrer, a coffee and sisal grower whose 1942 radio broadcast attacking Calderón had made him, for two years, the country's first political exile since the Tinoco era. The center contributed the ideological element and Acción Demócrata the political and fiscal savvy. The Social Democrats entered an electoral coalition with Cortés's personalist party, which was committed to a reactionary economic program, and with another personalist party clustered around Otilio Ulate, publisher of the daily *Diario de Costa Rica.* One purpose—the defeat of Calderón—united oligarchic elites, idealistic reformers, and ambitious activists. Calderón's continued alliance with Vanguardia Popular guaranteed support for Figueres's party in the postwar United States, now obsessed by fears of international communism.

The Opposition made honest elections the central issue of the 1948 presidential campaign, in which Ulate ran against Calderón. Though the press charged Picado's government with tyranny and oppression, it actually remained free "to the point of license; newspapers were permitted to print even outrageous personal attacks against the president."[35] Freedom of assembly and the independence of the courts were respected under President Picado;

the army of 300 poorly trained and equipped men led by nonprofessional officers could not have upheld an oppressive government.

When the Congress, dominated by *calderonistas*, voted to annul the election apparently won by Ulate, Figueres declared war on the government. After six weeks of fighting and over 2,000 deaths, President Picado and Father Benjamín Nuñez, emissary of the victorious Figueres, signed a peace treaty that guaranteed a general amnesty and provided for indemnities to all victims regardless of their affiliation. Mora's influence was responsible for a clause stating that "the social rights and guarantees of all employees and workers will be respected."

The treaty, says historian John Patrick Bell, prevented far worse bloodshed, followed the customary Costa Rican pattern of pacification and compromise, and provided a basis for continuity.[36] But Figueres, though pledged to honor Ulate's election, wanted a sharp break with the past. He believed that if Ulate took office little would change. Only he should be the architect of a "second republic," which would benefit from the same careful planning that had distinguished his military campaign. On May 1 he and Ulate signed an agreement by which a junta headed by Figueres would govern for eighteen months. During this time a constitutional congress would ratify Ulate's election as president.

During its brief tenure, the junta issued 834 decrees-laws, which Figueres still insisted thirty years later "transformed everything." Two of them permanently alienated Figueres's wealthiest former allies—nationalization of the banking system and a forced contribution of 10 percent of their wealth by owners of more than 50,000 colones worth of private property (a levy successfully applied only to bank deposits).

According to *calderonistas* Mavis met in Panama in 1949, the junta that governed directly after the war violated the peace terms by carrying out reprisals against the losers. Some members of the two losing parties were imprisoned or sent into exile for speaking out against the junta, and their goods were confiscated by courts outside the regular judicial system. Critics and political opponents were fired from both government and private positions and prevented from teaching in or graduating from the university.[37]

The Constitutional Congress, whose forty-four members included only four *figueristas*, would not even discuss the draft of a new constitution presented by a junta-appointed committee. Instead, in 1949, the Congress modified the constitution under which government had been carried on since 1871. But it also incorporated changes prompted by the events of the 1940s. It abolished the army, outlawed the communist Vanguardia Popular, and barred former presidents from reelection for eight years after leaving office. (Amendments in the 1970s removed the ban on Vanguardia Popular and limited presidents to one term during their lifetimes, except for those who had held that office before the amendment. Thus Pepe Figueres could run for a third term.) The new charter provided for civil service rather than a spoils system for government employees. It gave the executive less power and the legislature more than was usual in Latin America. It established the Supreme Electoral Tribunal as an independent guarantor of fair elections. Not only did it extend the franchise to women and illiterates but it also conferred full citizenship on the children of West Indian immigrants by providing that anyone born in Costa Rica was automatically a citizen. Finally, it provided for "autonomous institutions" (public corporations resembling the Tennessee Valley Authority) to take over basic services such as banking and public utilities.

An ironic consequence of the period of junta rule was general acceptance of Calderón's reforms, which no longer seemed radical when compared with the junta's. These "social guarantees" soon came to be regarded as Costa Rican traditions.

Calderón, fearing personal reprisals, fled to Nicaragua and later to Mexico. He retained many supporters, however, and continued to work for a return to power. The junta quashed an attempted coup and an invasion from Nicaragua headed by Calderón with Nicaraguan president Anastasio Somoza's support. A similar attempt in 1955, during which Nicaraguan planes bombed San José, was repulsed by an army of 6,000 volunteers, including high school youths, with the aid of the Organization of American States. Calderón was allowed to return to Costa Rica and ran unsuccessfully for president in 1962; he died in 1970.

The Legacy of 1948

Idealists on both sides during the civil war were convinced that they were fighting for fair elections. *Calderonistas* thought they were also defending social reforms; *figueristas*, that they were also fighting corruption and communism.

This bloodiest event in Costa Rican history left deep wounds that took decades to heal. It broke up families and alienated friends and neighbors. For four decades political campaigns played upon the old loyalties and antagonisms.

What did the fratricide of 1948 really accomplish? It restored (some say it established) the honesty of elections. No administration has come to power by force since 1948. Figueres honored his agreement to cede power to Ulate after eighteen months. It is generally agreed that elections since then have been honest. Every four years, with two exceptions, the presidency has alternated between two main parties—the National Liberation Party (PLN) founded by Figueres in 1951, and an opposing coalition of other parties, which finally formed the stable Partido Unidad Social Cristiana (PUSC, or Unidad) in time for the 1990 election.

Bell sees as the most important results of the conflict

> a rededication to the maintenance of civil government, the peaceful transfer of power from one popularly elected candidate to another, and a perfecting of the electoral process. . . . The bitterness engendered by the whole process of the revolution proved anew to the Costa Rican people that, even though representative government can be slow and unresponsive, it is an effective safeguard against government excess.[38]

The victories of Rafael Angel Calderón Fournier in the presidential election of 1990 and of José María Figueres Olsen in 1994 showed that their paternal surnames had not lost their magic. But fifty years earlier, who could have predicted the Inauguration Day ceremony of May 8, 1994, when the presidential sash was peacefully transferred from Dr. Calderón's son to Pepe Figueres's son?

Since 1948

Pepe Figueres and the PLN were largely responsible for the direction of Costa Rican society for three decades. They "consolidated the reform program of the previous eight years by moving the center of controversy farther to the left."[39] The *cafetaleros* and merchants who had long dominated the country now had to yield much of their power to a growing middle class and a government bureaucracy committed—at least in theory—to social justice achieved through a welfare state and to attracting foreign capital to industrialize the country.[40] The services sector grew while the agricultural sector shrank. And although the population doubled between 1954 and 1974, per capita buying power more than doubled, reaching $1,514 in 1978 and rising faster than inflation.[41]

PLN policies and the trend toward big government prevailed until the early 1980s; PLN's conservative opponents were unable to reverse them even when they controlled the executive branch of government. The state steadily grew more powerful and more expensive. By 1979, every fifth worker was a government employee, and by official figures, the public sector accounted for a fourth of the gross national product—by some estimates, about half.

Economist Juan Manuel Villasuso sees the nation's history from 1950 to 1980 as divisible into three stages according to the role of the state:

1. During the first twelve years, the "developmentalist" stage, the government was concerned chiefly with building a physical and social infrastructure. Numerous new public agencies built roads, airports, and seaports and produced and distributed electrical power, potable water, and telephone ser-

vice. At the same time, government hospitals, clinics, and schools were established all over the country.

2. By the late 1960s and the early 1970s it was apparent that many people remained poor and neglected. Attempting to extend the benefits of development to them, the government created the Program of Family Assignments and the Mixed Institute of Social Aid, thus assuming the role of the "paternalist state."

3. Government continued to expand under the "entrepreneurial state" beginning in the mid-1970s. Because the private sector was unable or unwilling to invest in socially beneficial projects that require large capital outlays, government officials decided the state should do so. And thus the state grew larger—and more bureaucratized, politicized, inefficient, and corrupt—but not more productive.[42]

All three stages were financed by borrowing—an old habit, as we noted earlier, of the nation's leaders. (Ricardo Jiménez once said, "If the Costa Ricans could buy the British fleet on the installment plan, we would.") Huge debts to international lenders led to a fourth stage, structural adjustment.

The world economic crisis of the early 1980s hit Costa Rica hard, and all three functions—development, welfare, and enterprise—faltered. Between 1980 and 1982 per capita buying power declined 40 percent as annual inflation rose from 18 percent to 82 percent, and the public debt tripled.[43] By 1981 Costa Rica suspended debt payments to most of its creditors and requested assistance from the World Bank and International Monetary Fund.

Its international creditors insisted that to qualify for further loans and for soft terms on settling defaulted loans, Costa Rica's government (like other governments in a similar situation) would have to stabilize and privatize the economy. The state was required to minimize its control of industry, business and finance, and even social services and to encourage foreign investment, production for export, and open competition in a free-market global economy. It was also required to drastically reduce government spending. The many opponents of structural adjustment saw this extreme version of free-market economics as a return to the law of the jungle.

But the economic crisis left no alternative to compliance. Even PLN presidents Luís Alberto Monge (1982–1986), Oscar Arias (1986–1990), and José María Figueres (1994–1998) were forced to bow to these demands in order to keep their governments solvent. Although the goals agreed to in the first two PAEs, or structural adjustment pacts, were reached only in part, the steps taken toward reaching them greatly affected Costa Rican society.

Despite their traditional optimism, many Ticos now express uneasiness about their economic future. Economic trends and prospects are difficult to untangle from government and politics. In the next two chapters we examine both in more detail in the light of cultural and social history.

Notes

1. Theodore Creedman, *Historical Dictionary of Costa Rica* (Metuchen, N.J.: Scarecrow Press, 1977), p. x.

2. Michael Snarskis, "La vertiente atlantica en Costa Rica," *Vínculos*, Vol. 2, No. 1, 1976.

3. The first metal pieces to appear were gold artifacts shaped by the lost-wax process. Metallurgy was a South American invention, appearing in the Andes as early as 1000 B.C. and in Costa Rica from A.D. 200 to 500. Panamanian and Costa Rican gold pieces have been found as far north as Chichén Itzá, Yucatan. Olmec jade, in turn, was carried south, appearing in Costa Rica between 300 B.C. and A.D. 1000. Archaeologist Michael Snarskis, interview, March 2, 1993. Much of this section is based on his information.

4. Michael Snarskis, "The Archaeology of Costa Rica," in Suzanne Abel-Vidor et al., *Precolumbian Art of Costa Rica* (Detroit: Harry N. Abrams, in association with the Detroit Institute of Arts, 1981), pp. 15–18. See also Snarskis, "The Archaeological Evidence for Chiefdoms in Eastern and Central Costa Rica," in Robert D. Drennan and Carlos A. Uribe, *Chiefdoms in the Americas* (Lanham, Md.: University Press of America, 1987), pp. 105–117. Also Eugenia Ibarra, *Las sociedades cacicales de Costa Rica* (San José: EUCR, 1990).

5. Carlos Aguilar, *Guayabo de Turrialba: Arquelogía de un sítio indígena prehistórica* (San José: Editorial Costa Rica [ECR], 1972).

6. José Solano A., "Encuentro o choque de culturas?" *La República*, January 19, 1993, p. 16A.

7. Omar Hernández, Eugenia Ibarra, and Juan Rafael Quesada, *Discriminación y racismo en la historia costarricense* (San José: EUCR, 1993), pp. 14–15.

8. Eugenia Ibarra Rojas and Elizet Payne Iglesias, "De las sociedades cacicales a la sociedad colonial," in *Costa Rica en el siglo XVI* (San José: Editorial Universidad Estatal a Distancia [EUNED], 1991), p. 25.

9. Marc Edelman, "Land and Labor in an Expanding Economy: Agrarian Capitalism and the Hacienda System in Costa Rica, 1880–1982," Ph.D. Dissertation, Columbia University, 1985, p. 33.

10. See Marcus Guevara Berger and Rubén Chacón Castro, *Territorios indios en Costa Rica: Orígenes, situación actual y perspectiva histórica* (San José: García Hnos., 1992).

11. Carolyn Hall, *Costa Rica: A Geographical Interpretation in Historical Perspective* (Boulder: Westview, 1985), p. 84.

12. Tatiana Lobo gives a vivid and historically accurate picture of colonial Cartago in her 1992 novel *Asalto al paraíso* (San José: EUCR, 1992).

13. One popular explanation for this laxity is that many colonists were in fact Sephardic Jews who had fled the Spanish Inquisition and were only nominal converts. Historian Carlos Meléndez refutes this notion on the basis of genealogical research; there were a few Sephardic Jews in Mexico and the rest of Central America, but there is no evidence that any migrated from Spain to colonial Costa Rica. Interview, February 25, 1994.

14. Carlos Monge Alfaro, *Historia de Costa Rica*, 14th ed. (San José: Trejos, 1976), p. 192.

15. Carlos Vargas Pagan, "La igualdad democrática," *La Nación*, April 3, 1992, p. 18A.

16. Lowell Gudmundson, *Costa Rica Before Coffee: Society and Economy on the Eve of the Export Boom* (Baton Rouge: Louisiana State University Press, 1986), pp.

25–32. See also Gudmundson, *Estratificación socio-racial y económica de Costa Rica: 1700–1850* (San José: EUNED, 1978).

17. Two different interpretations of this alignment are those of Samuel Stone, who sees the residents of San José—rebellious smugglers in the colonial era—as having a different lifestyle from the traditionalists of Cartago and Heredia: *La dinastia de los conquistadores: La crisis del poder en la Costa Rica contemporánea* (San José: Editorial Universitaria Centroamericana [EDUCA], 1975), pp. 251–256; and Rodolfo Cerdas Cruz, who sees Cartago and Heredia as the nucleus of a conservative agricultural-export bloc and San José and Alajuela as interested in commerce and imports. The first wanted simply to replace colonial government with that of the vested interests created in the old regime; the latter wanted a change to a liberal democratic regime: *La crisis de la democrácia liberal en Costa Rica* (San José: EDUCA, 1972), pp. 25–29.

18. Monge, *Historia*, p. 192.

19. Carlos Meléndez, *Historia de Costa Rica* (San José: EUNED, 1991), p. 106.

20. Stone, *La dinastia*, p. 39.

21. Monge, *Historia*, p. 204.

22. Clinton Rollins, *William Walker* (Managua: 1945), quoted in Enrique Guier, *William Walker* (San José: Lehmann, 1971).

23. Steven Palmer, "Sociedad anónima, cultura oficial: Inventando la nación en Costa Rica, 1848–1900," in Ivan Molina Jiménez and Steven Palmer, eds., *Héroes al gusto y libros de moda* (San José: Porvenir, 1992), pp. 169–205. Palmer says that Juan Santamaría was not hailed as a hero until three decades later when, in 1885, Guatemalan dictator Justo Rufino Barrios threatened to unify Central America by force. About that time the Costa Rican government, while planning a mobilization against the threat, reprinted an article lauding Santamaría in its official paper. Though Costa Rican troops never fought Barrios, who had been defeated by Salvadoran troops, beatification of Juan Santamaría continued and helped Costa Ricans to think more in terms of their nationality rather than their locality.

24. Astrid Fischel, *Consenso y represión: Una interpretación sociopolítica de la educación costarricense* (San José: ECR, 1990), p. 202.

25. Carmen Murillo Chaverri, *Identidades de hierro y humo: La construcción del ferrocarríl al Atlántico 1870–1890* (San José: Editorial Porvenir, 1995), p. 29.

26. Hall, *Costa Rica,* p. 111.

27. José Luís Vega Carballo, "La evolución agroeconómica de Costa Rica: Un intento de periodización y síntesis (1560–1930)," *Revista de Costa Rica,* No. 9, April 1975, pp. 19–70.

28. Monge, *Historia*, p. 241.

29. Alfredo González Flores, *El petróleo y la política en Costa Rica* (San José: Trejos Hermanos, 1923).

30. A widely applauded novel describes the Tinoco era: Daniel Gallegos's *El pasado es un extraño país* (San José: rei, 1993).

31. Marina Volio, *Jorge Volio y el Partido Reformista* (San José: ECR, 1974).

32. See John Biesanz and Mavis Biesanz, *Costa Rican Life* (New York: Columbia University Press, 1944); and John Patrick Bell, *Crisis in Costa Rica* (Austin: University of Texas Press, 1971), ch. 2, "The Social Question."

33. Rodrigo Carazo Odio, "Garantias sociales: Medio siglo," *La República*, August 30, 1993, p. 21A.

34. Bell, *Crisis,* p. 46.

35. Ibid., p. 45.

36. Ibid., p. 215.

37. This was corroborated by several interviews with Professor Corina Rodríguez, a leftist writer, between 1949 and 1977. See also Bell, *Crisis*, p. 158.

38. Bell, *Crisis,* p. 161.

39. Ibid., p. 160.

40. Stone, *La dinastia*, pp. 328–329.

41. SIECA (Secretaria de Integración Económica Centroamericana), *Series Estadísticas Seleccionadas de Centro America y Panamá,* November 1973, Cuadro 190, p. 359.

42. Juan Manuel Villasuso, "La reforma democrática del estado costarricense," in Villasuso, ed., *El nuevo rostro de Costa Rica* (San José: Centro de Estudios Democráticos de América Latin [CEDAL], 1992), pp. 409–422.

43. Jorge Rovira M., *Costa Rica en los años 80* (San José: Editorial Porvenir, 1987), pp. 43–45.

— 3 —

Economy

IN SAN ANTONIO DE ESCAZÚ, FIFTEEN MINUTES from the traffic snarls of San José, a farmer guides his painted oxcart loaded with sugarcane to the old family *trapiche* (small sugarmill). He unyokes the oxen and with the help of two brothers sets an ox to turning the millstones. As the cane is crushed, its juice pours into a vat over a fire of coffeewood and dried cane stalks. It is boiled down and poured into molds, soon to appear as cylinders of coarse brown sugar at the corner *pulpería* (general store).

An hour's drive away, trucks and tractors loaded with cane pull into line at one end of a large building. The cane disappears into a complex of pipes and computerized machinery. At the other end of the building, granulated white sugar fills plastic bags printed with a brand name to assure supermarket shoppers of reliable quality. About a third of the mill's sugar will be exported.

Like other relics of the traditional agricultural economy, *trapiches* and *pulperías* are disappearing. Many Costa Ricans welcome—with some reservations—the changes that modernization involves: more city jobs, more diversions, more schooling, more *things*. The need for development has been an article of faith since 1950.[1] By 1995 some asked whether Costa Rica—with its $9 billion ($2,700 per capita) gross domestic product and with only a fifth of its labor force still employed in farming—should still be considered a third world country, a question underscored by the recent withdrawal of USAID and reduction of the Peace Corps presence.

In the 1940s Costa Rica was still overwhelmingly agricultural. Coffee was still king. Bananas were cultivated in enclaves far from the Central Valley. Industry was typified by a match factory where workers dipped each match by hand. Store inventories turned over slowly. They included few manufactured products, mostly imported and expensive. Mired in this stagnant economy, many young Ticos saw a bleak future even for university graduates. Their frustration led some to join Pepe Figueres's rebellion in 1948 and to promote the sweeping changes that followed, many in the name of economic development.

Economists once thought that countries had to go through a marked phase of industrialization before the service sector could become dominant.

In the United States, for instance, a farmer's son might have built houses or automobiles, and his granddaughter might have become a stockbroker or counselor. But in Costa Rica a farmer's child might well become a bureaucrat and never do industrial labor at all.

But if she does work in industry, it is likely to be agroindustry—the processing of agricultural products. For this reason and because of the historic importance of agriculture, we first consider the land as the basis of the economy.

Land Use and Land Distribution

How land is used and shared is basic to the amount and distribution of wealth in any society, particularly in one still largely dependent on agriculture.

"Our soil is so fertile that a stick will grow," Costa Ricans have long boasted. Living fences—rows of young trees flourishing from fresh-cut branches stuck in the ground—seem to bear them out. To the trained eye, however, the diversity of Costa Rica's vegetation indicates a wide variety of soils and conditions. Productivity depends largely on the suitability of land for a farmer's crops and methods.

Tropical soils are not generally fertile; most nutrients are found in the forest canopy, not in the thin layer of topsoil. Nonvolcanic mountain soils are especially poor. The coastal lowlands would be relatively fertile if properly drained, but they are difficult to work: Near the surface lies hard clay. Half the country's soil, in fact, is clay.

Unsustainable land use began with Spanish colonial farmers. Unlike the indigenous peoples, whose shifting cultivation had sustained them for many centuries with minimal deforestation, the colonists used the same land year after year, as their forebears had done in Spain. Forests were considered the enemy, covering the real resource, the soil. Until recently a squatter earned certain rights over land if he cut down trees, thereby *limpiando*—cleaning—it. Even today, deforested land usually commands a higher selling price, although, as we noted in Chapter 2, it is usually good for only two or three crops before it becomes pasture. In 1950, 75 percent of the country's surface was still covered with forest; by 1990, only 23 percent. The unprotected topsoil is soon eroded by rain, wind, and cattle, followed by drought and the displacement of people. Between 1980 and 1989 the country lost about 2 billion tons of soil, and in 1995 about 43 percent of the country was affected by moderate to severe erosion.

All through the nineteenth century anyone could settle on frontier land. The open frontier and small population kept farm wages high, slowed the concentration of land, and helped distribute coffee wealth widely. Small landowners also worked as peons on larger farms, and it was wiser for larger landowners to pay good wages and not buy up small farms than to push their workers into leaving for the frontier and making new farms of their own.

This situation prevailed into the mid-twentieth century. Then the population exploded and land prices soared. The safety valve of the open frontier vanished. Many newly landless and land-poor *campesinos* (country dwellers) now worked mainly as low-wage agricultural peons. And many gave up and moved to towns.

Yet the myth of a small country of small landowners persists. Certainly land is more equitably distributed than in some Latin American countries, where most farmworkers are virtual serfs on great feudal estates. But neither is Costa Rica a Switzerland or Finland of well-subsidized small farmers who eat well and sell their surplus crops to satisfy other needs.

More than half the landowners in Costa Rica own less than 10 hectares (1 hectare = 2.4717 acres), adding up to no more than 5 percent of agricultural land. Even more significantly, 37 percent of landowners have *minifundios*, farms of less than 2 hectares; and all their holdings together compose less than 1 percent of agricultural land. Yes, there are many small farmers. But their plots are too small to satisfy the basic needs of a family and make full use of its labor.

At the other extreme are *latifundios*, large farms—mostly cattle ranches that need few workers per hectare. In 1993, 3.5 percent of farms were larger than 200 hectares, and 2.8 percent of landowners owned almost half (47 percent) of farmland.[2]

Between these two extremes are numerous medium-sized farms. About two farms out of five have 5–50 hectares. Usually dairy farms or truck farms on fertile soil, they are the most productive per hectare of all farms. Like the smallest farms, they rely heavily on manual labor, at times nonfamily, and simple tools.

Thousands of *campesinos* own no land at all. Their numbers have grown with Costa Rica's population increase and because nearly all land is now in private hands or in state-protected parks and reserves. Like *minifundistas*, they work for larger landowners.

Between 1961 and 1996 government agencies (currently IDA, the Institute of Agricultural Development) provided 75,000 landless families with small plots, often purchased from large landholders.[3] Early in the program, these plots averaged 20 hectares; then, as both available land and government resources dwindled, so did the size of the parcels: down to 3 hectares in 1995.

These new landowners are often pioneers. On the trail to one IDA hamlet we visited in 1992 our horses were knee-deep in mud. We found a small group of settlers gathered to discuss their problems. They were building a school on their own. But they lamented the lack of roads, technical advice, credit, and social services—all officially part of the IDA program. Some had worked in the Central Valley and were familiar with available technology.

Now, like the early colonists, they work hard growing a nontraditional and unfamiliar crop, cardamom, under strange and difficult conditions and barely manage to subsist. In a society that has encouraged rising expectations, they may feel even poorer than did the established subsistence farmers who predominated in the precoffee era and served to create the myth of Costa Rica as a democracy of small farmers.

Coffee

The myth of small farmers dominating agriculture has been sustained in large part because most coffee farms are small; 92 percent of coffee farmers own less than 5 hectares, too few to need hired hands.

Ticos have long believed that coffee is good for them and their country. Primary school children in the 1940s learned to read with "Coffee is good for me. I drink coffee every morning." In 1998, Coffee Institute of Costa Rica ads extolled the health benefits of caffeine and described coffee as "the true aphrodisiac." Says columnist Julio Rodríguez:

> Coffee has meant to our development and the formation of our culture and our democracy, in the economic sphere, what the Christian faith has represented in the spiritual sphere and education in the transmission of knowledge and values. Those flowering coffee trees and that admirable and devout ritual of the harvest following the school year describe a luminous part of our history. Were they to disappear, they would take with them a large part of our soul.[4]

Although coffee occupies only about 2 percent of agricultural land, it was long vital to the national economy—a third of the labor force once depended directly or indirectly on its cultivation. Said early-twentieth-century president Ricardo Jiménez, "The best Treasury Minister a government can have is a good coffee crop." From 1840 to 1890 coffee was virtually the only export, later rivaled only by bananas. With increasing agricultural diversification, industrialization, and tourism, coffee's importance has declined. In 1986 it accounted for about 35 percent of export earnings; in 1995, only 16 percent.

Growers have little recourse against price fluctuations. Occasionally producer nations agree to hold back a certain portion of the crop to keep prices higher. They have formed cartels such as the Association of Coffee Producing Countries that set quotas for each member country. The Costa Rican government has often helped growers when the crop or the market has failed. In 1992, when coffee prices dropped to the lowest level in twenty-five years, the generally laissez-faire Calderón Fournier administration gave subsidies to all growers.

Coffee pickers at the end of the day (Mavis Hiltunen Biesanz)

This price drop, like previous ones, hit small producers the hardest. Many could not repay their debts and sold their land to urban developers. Others abandoned their groves and left to work on banana plantations. Many, however, hung on; they could not imagine turning to another crop and felt confident that better times must come again—and they did, in 1994 after frosts hit Brazil's coffee crop. Every year one sees new coffee groves.

But the demand for coffee is relatively inelastic, whereas supply continues to increase as new producers like Angola and Vietnam enter the market. At the same time world consumption per capita is falling. Consuming countries like the United States and Germany balk at paying high prices. Add the abandonment of the international quota system in favor of a free market and Costa Rica, which seldom supplies more than 3 percent of the world's coffee, finds itself at a great disadvantage. The history of coffee will probably continue to be, as it has always been, a roller coaster of rags to riches and back again.

Bananas

Whereas coffee has been the darling of the nation, the banana industry has been vilified as the root of foreign domination, labor exploitation, and, more recently, destruction of the environment. But as a major employer and source of government revenue from export taxes, it has also been treated warily and has even been encouraged to expand operations. Since 1975 Costa Rica has ranked second only to Ecuador in volume of banana exports, and in 1994 it provided 20 percent of the world supply. Nearly a third of Costa Rica's export earnings come from bananas—twice as much as from coffee.

Large companies dominate the banana industry for several reasons: Only a large-volume operation handled with great efficiency can make a profit on the easily spoiled fruit. Cutting, shipping, and marketing must be well coordinated to bring bananas to the table at a desirable stage of ripeness. There are many risks: floods, hurricanes, blights, delays in loading, and strikes. Because demand is relatively inelastic, the amount shipped must be carefully controlled.

Plantations of the United Fruit Company, founded in 1899, were managed by North Americans for the profit of U.S. shareholders. Most laborers came from Jamaica and other Caribbean islands. Already familiar with banana farming and accustomed to heat and humidity, they had another important advantage: They spoke English with their bosses.

From 1905 to 1917 United Fruit was Costa Rica's chief exporter. It was also the "Octopus"—the symbol of "Yankee imperialism"—deservedly, says Thomas P. McCann:

> [It was] a new form of business enterprise: the multinational company
> . . . in many instances more powerful and larger than the host countries in

which it operated. . . . United Fruit bought protection, pushed governments around, kicked out competition, and suppressed union organization.

[In the host countries] the United States Government and the Octopus whose interests and policies that government nurtured were seen as one and the same: brutal, monolithic, oppressive.[5]

By 1926 "independent" producers, many of them Ticos, grew 75 percent of the bananas exported. Still, the company controlled loading, shipping, and marketing and could set its own price for producers' bananas. The stems of an uncompliant producer would be rejected as defective.

Costa Ricans now play an important role in most phases of the banana industry as producers, executives, and laborers. But big foreign-based multinational companies—mostly U.S., English, and Colombian—still dominate; they produced 60 percent of banana exports in 1992 and charged smaller growers for their services as exporters.

Since 1978 successive administrations have promoted the industry's expansion. Between 1980 and 1994 the land devoted to bananas almost doubled, to some 49,000 hectares. But many Costa Ricans insist that whereas coffee contributes to economic development, banana companies impede it: They take profits to their home countries and destroy rain forests in their relentless expansion. Moreover, economist Juan Carlos Cruz told us in 1992:

> They employ only one or two people per hectare after a farm is productive. It takes a lot of land to make a banana farm productive, not like coffee. Coffee creates entrepreneurs; bananas create peons. It's mainly the multinationals, not small producers, that benefit in the banana industry. When times are hard for coffee growers, they increase production. But when they're hard for banana companies, they simply abandon a region and leave a lot of poverty behind.

Coffee has been a focus of national pride, but bananas still symbolize imperialism and dependency. Coffee is associated with the beautiful Central Valley and "white" Ticos; bananas with hot, dangerous lowlands and "undesirable" Nicaraguans and blacks (the latter still widely seen as foreigners). (A 1997 Labor Ministry study found, however, that Ticos composed only 25 percent of coffee pickers; the majority were Nicaraguans.) Writes sociologist Francisco Escobar:

> In the Meseta Central, the middle class and those in government look toward the banana lands with fear and gradually erect a barricade of prejudices and police repression instead of a patriotic concern to defend [workers'] rights and solve the economic and social problems generated by the banana industry. We don't consider the workers and their families who suffer there to be Costa Ricans.[6]

The two industries, however, are alike in many respects. Both are subject to natural disasters and international events. In both, a few large firms have controlled exports and profits and exercised great influence over government. The demand for both is inelastic, and producers and exporters have tried to control prices—more successfully in the case of bananas than of coffee. Many Ticos have long urged that for all these reasons the country should produce a wider variety of exports.

Agricultural Diversification

Much of the initiative for diversification came from coffee and banana exporters. Planted in rice and African oil palm—largely by United Fruit as banana profits dropped during the 1960s—the southern Pacific coast became one of the richest agricultural regions. Coffee exporters likewise began to promote diversification rather than expansion of coffee groves as a hedge against the uncertainties of the market.

The biggest—and most disastrous—step toward diversification of the two-crop economy was taken in the 1960s and 1970s, when many Ticos, encouraged by foreign demand and investment as well as plentiful U.S. aid and World Bank loans channeled through their own government, invested heavily in beef cattle.

In 1973 and 1974, ranchers received 26 percent of the credit accorded by the Central Bank—more than industry and crop agriculture combined. For a time, recalls Alvaro León, rural development expert for the Costa Rican Ecological Association, "it was easier to get a loan for cattle than for a house." By 1975 there were nearly as many cattle as people in Costa Rica.

Enthusiasm waned in the 1980s. U.S. fast-food chains ordered less beef as North Americans became more cholesterol conscious. This declining demand was fortunate for Costa Rica. The conversion of forests to pasture was blamed for persistent drought in many areas. Some ecologists claimed that a ton of soil had been eroded for every pound of beef produced. Ranching had also forced many peons out of work, since it requires only one cowhand in an area that once employed sixteen farmworkers.[7] But Ticos still see cattle as a profitable and prestigious investment: Over two-thirds of agricultural land (and 40 percent of the national territory) was pasture in 1994; only 7 percent was devoted to crops.

Rice, corn, and beans, called the basic grains, are the traditional staples of the Costa Rican diet. Even in San José's working-class suburbs corn is grown in many vacant lots or backyards, often interplanted with beans.

Beans and corn, being labor intensive, once provided much employment. They grow in many areas and yield two crops a year. The government began to subsidize production of all three crops in 1974, providing improved seeds, herbicides, and other technical assistance and guaranteeing prices as well as

Planting black beans in June for September harvest in San Antonio de Escazú
(Ingrid Holst)

compensation for losses. Production, particularly of rice, greatly increased. But prices were at times among the highest in the world and could be guaranteed only by levying heavy duties on imported grain.

Since 1985 the government, under terms of the structural adjustment pacts, has completely reversed this policy. In free-market theory it is economically sounder to import—tax free—any foods that foreign farmers can produce more cheaply. Costa Rican farmers are now encouraged to produce the more lucrative nontraditional products for export. Coffee and bananas—

along with meat and sugar, now also considered traditional products—accounted for only 43 percent of export earnings in 1995. Small coffee and basic-grain farmers whose profits have vanished are urged to plant citrus or mango trees, flowers, ornamental plants, fruits and vegetables, cardamom and macadamia nuts, as well as such foods as plantains, chayotes, and yuca for export. The many small farmers who still grow corn, beans, or rice no longer get easy credit or guaranteed prices.

Small farmers have benefited far less from the new crops than have large, often foreign, investors, who get most of the state's agricultural credit and technical assistance. This credit, moreover, shrank from 61 percent of all government credit in 1983 to 9.5 percent ten years later; almost half went to the banana industry.

Cooperation Among Farmers

Small farmers, often described by urban Ticos as stubbornly individualistic, actually cooperate in many ways. It is common for two or more relatives or friends to work a borrowed field or pasture—perhaps in exchange for keeping it free of weeds—and to share the profits or losses. Or they may sharecrop, one supplying the land and seeds, the other the labor. The owner of a pickup truck taking his own produce to a farmers' market in town may, for a small fee, take a neighbor and his produce along; thus both bypass the middlemen whom farmers describe as *chorizeros* (swindlers). And farmers have long cooperated to build roads, bridges, and schools and to bring water and electricity to their communities.

Since 1949 many farmers have developed their own formal cooperatives ranging from savings and loan associations (the most common) to consumer and producer co-ops. Most milk is provided by the huge Dos Pinos co-op; co-ops account for nearly half of coffee production. A large coffee co-op may have its own processing plant and give members credit for farming and construction as well as low rates on life insurance, private medical care, fuel, and a wide range of supermarket items. Government banks have provided credit and technical assistance to co-ops, particularly during PLN administrations. Under the privatization policy, the giant public-sector CNP, the National Production Council, transformed its retail outlets for farm products into co-ops.

But Ricardo Vargas, an authority on co-ops, told us in 1994:

> Small growers produce so inefficiently that they don't make much profit even as co-op members. And the state often starts a co-op without studying markets, so many co-ops fail. Remember what happened recently in San Pablo, when hundreds of angry members looted the supermarket that their failing coffee-growers' co-op had organized? You can expect a lot of that to happen in the next few years if the number of co-ops keeps growing faster than the state's ability to bail them out.

Industry, Government, and Structural Adjustment

For more than a century beginning in the 1840s, Costa Rica depended on agricultural exports for both hard currency and the products it could buy. Because even then Costa Ricans preferred imports to domestic products, most industries that developed in the nineteenth century soon withered. Every fall in coffee prices meant a drop in imports or a greater trade deficit and renewed calls for industrialization and agricultural diversification.

In some countries, such as the United States, the mechanization of agriculture displaced many farmers and created a labor pool for industrial growth. Industry (including construction) has grown substantially in Costa Rica since the 1960s and employed slightly more people than did agriculture in 1996—about 23 percent of the labor force. But this growth was not a result of agricultural mechanization, for most farming was (and remains) labor intensive. It was population growth and the cattle boom that swelled the migration of unemployed *campesinos* to San José, thus creating not only a labor supply for entrepreneurs but also electoral support for the creation of new jobs.

By joining the Central American Common Market (CACM) in 1963, Costa Rica greatly increased the duty-free zone for its industrial exports. But industrial investment was put on hold by the economic crisis of 1979–1982. The crisis resulted from several setbacks occurring in quick succession: sharp price increases in imported petroleum as OPEC (Organization of Oil Exporting Countries) nations withheld much of their production, a substantial decline in CACM trade due to civil wars in Nicaragua and El Salvador, recession in developed countries and consequent reduced demand for Costa Rican exports, runaway inflation, and higher interest rates on the foreign debt.

Some of these factors were global and affected many other "developing" countries as well. To such lending institutions as USAID, the International Monetary Fund (IMF), the World Bank, and the Inter-American Development Bank, the crisis meant that these countries were less able to pay the interest on their considerable debts and were less attractive prospects for future loans. Seeing an opportunity to convert the world's many state-managed and protectionist economies into free-market systems, they made the first of several structural adjustment agreements with debtor governments. In return for rescheduling interest payments on past debts and providing conditions for further loans—at extremely low interest rates of 4 to 5 percent—these lenders, as we noted in Chapter 2, required major increases in production and exports to generate foreign exchange, currency devaluation, reduction of import tariffs, the privatization of many state agencies, and reductions in public spending. For Costa Rica, these last two requirements implied especially great changes. The state had long been the major employer and, through its dozens of public corporations, the agent most responsible for industrial development.

In 1985 President Monge signed the first structural adjustment pact (PAE-I) as a condition of further loans. A second followed in 1989 and a third in 1994.

Corporación Costarricense de Desarrollo (CODESA), the giant of public corporations, had been created in 1974 to unite under one government agency all the productive activities the private sector was unwilling or unable to perform and eventually included forty enterprises. Unwieldy and wasteful, it was a principal source of conflict between the government and private industry. Its dismantling and the privatization of its member industries under PAE-I began in 1985; USAID financed a plan to sell the companies to private buyers or to cooperatives. With the sale of its cement and fertilizer industries in 1993 after much debate, the privatization of CODESA was almost complete. By then it had left the central government in debt to the Central Bank for some $115 million.

Despite increasing privatization—in industry, banking, education, postal services, and many other activities—the state remained heavily involved in the economy in 1998. The Central Bank frequently devalued the colón. Government ministries and autonomous institutions still held much of the responsibility for developing infrastructure: hydroelectric energy, petroleum refining, ports and roads, and purification and distribution of water. The Labor Ministry was responsible for enforcing workers' legal rights and, together with industrial and union representatives on the National Salaries Council, for setting minimum wages and salaries in 200 categories of occupations. The Ministry of Economy fixed maximum retail prices for many essential items. Employers were required to pay health insurance premiums to the Social Security Fund.

In 1985 business leaders got financial support from USAID to create a private-sector agency they hoped would attract foreign industries. This was CINDE, the Coalition of Incentives for Development. Its rationale for industrial development, unlike that which prevailed in the 1960s and 1970s, was not to decrease reliance on imports but rather to earn hard currency through exports. This currency would pay for imports as well as service the mounting foreign debt and, under the PAEs, help make the nation eligible for further loans. Even so, in 1994, 78 percent of industrial production (mostly processed food, cigarettes, and furniture) was consumed in Costa Rica.[8]

The government, too, offers many incentives to foreign companies, such as a twelve-year tax exemption on industries operating within any of several free-trade zones and training for workers already touted as highly literate. Costa Rica's political stability is also attractive to foreign investors.

Most of Costa Rica's industrial products are typical of countries lacking iron ore and petroleum and just emerging from an agrarian economy: Processed foods and textiles predominated in the 1980s and 1990s. Multinational drug and electronics companies have also made considerable investments. Intel's microprocessor plant, opened in 1998, was expected to account for two-thirds of Costa Rica's exports by 2001. Encouraged by CINDE, the textile industry expanded from 14,000 workers in 1986 to 43,000—a third of the industrial labor force—in 1996. In some years textile exports have brought more foreign exchange than have bananas. Only Italy, Canada, and South Korea export more. Textile companies, however, invest little in infrastructure or in development of workers' skills; most jobs are routine, low-paying, and unstable.[9]

Small Costa Rican–owned industries—the great majority have fewer than fifty workers—are numerous, but many fail or are sold to foreigners as import duties are reduced and as multinationals, based mostly in the United States, build factories in Costa Rica. (Other major investors are Canadians, South Koreans, Taiwanese, Germans, Dutch, British, Mexicans, Nicaraguans, Colombians, and Panamanians.) Local industries tend to lack efficient marketing and sales programs, as well as postsales services such as warranties. Long dependent on state subsidies, tax exemptions, and protective tariffs, they had little incentive to invest in research or studies of consumer preferences. With the removal of such props under PAE demands, many local businesses are in no shape to compete even though various trade agreements allow most Costa Rican products to enter the United States, Mexico, and Europe duty free. And just as Costa Rica's coffee is often sold as the better-advertised Colombian product and Costa Rican macadamia nuts are marketed as Hawaiian, so, too, much of the excellent software produced in Costa Rica is bought by U.S. firms and resold under their own labels.

The United States bought almost 40 percent of the country's exports in 1995; the European Economic Community, another 31 percent. Central America's purchases accounted for most of the rest.

Services

As in many other countries, Costa Rica's service sector has grown much faster than its industrial sector, accounting for 65 percent of the GNP in 1995 versus industry's 20 percent and for 54 percent of the labor force.

Commerce and finance accounted for about half the service sector's earnings in the mid-1990s. Commerce involves deals ranging from the corner grocer's sale of loose cigarettes to multimillion-dollar import orders.

Ticos have always enjoyed buying and selling, especially buying. They have long described themselves as "spending more than we earn"—largely on imported luxuries. In the mid-nineteenth century, shortly after the initial coffee boom, Ticos spent five times as much on imported wines, cognac, and fine clothing as on imported machinery and tools. Easy credit (at high interest) still makes this possible, and often the only advertised price is the monthly payment. Huge malls, offering mostly imported goods, proliferated in San José's suburbs in the 1990s. Even in the countryside peddlers sell imported (slightly used) U.S. clothing on the installment plan.

Banking

Until 1949, banks were nearly all private and owned by U.S. citizens. When President Alfredo González Flores founded a state bank in 1914, he alienated bankers, who joined U.S. oil companies and wealthy Ticos in toppling him and closing the bank in 1917. But nationalization of the entire banking system was a key element of the PLN program three decades later—essential, party leaders argued, to ensure that credit be given according to criteria of social responsibility, not simply profit. Thus many small- and medium-sized farmers got low-interest loans from state banks. These banks helped fund health, education, transportation, cooperatives, and rural development. They were given exclusive rights to checking accounts and time deposits, and the Central Bank governed monetary policy.

Opponents of the nationalized system have always charged that it was inefficient and wasteful. Many clients agreed; in 1992, for example, it took three weeks for a check from Guanacaste to clear in San José and months to clear a U.S. dollar check. It was almost impossible to fire incompetent bank personnel, who enjoyed the rights and privileges of all public employees. And credit approval was often dependent on political connections because each bank's directors always included four members of the party in power and three of the opposition party.

In 1994 the collapse of the Banco Anglo-Costarricense, founded in 1863 and incorporated into the nationalized system under PLN, strengthened the critics' case. The board of directors—recent political appointees without banking experience—had made huge unsecured loans based on political favoritism. Charged with misuse of government funds, members of upper-class families were imprisoned for the first time. The bank's losses left the national treasury with a deficit of some $136 million—to be covered by the public in the form of more bond issues, taxes, inflation, high interest rates, and devaluation. Said the comptroller general, "It's high time we start running state banks as banks rather than as political playthings."

The first major step toward privatizing banking had come during the Monge administration (1982–1986) with a law permitting the development of private commercial banks, a change imposed by USAID as a condition for new loans and grants. By 1996, in the wake of the Banco Anglo scandal, private banks were permitted to perform all the functions of state banks (though their assets were only one-fifth those of the state banks). And the World Bank continued to oversee monetary policy, as it had since 1985.

Defenders of a nationalized banking system see total privatization as an obstacle to development. Says journalist Martha Honey,

> Historically, the goal of the state banks was to use their resources for the egalitarian development of the entire country. However, the state banks are now forced to compete with the private banks, which are much less willing to finance projects that, despite their social benefit, may involve high risks or low profitability. Therefore, state banks have also become reluctant to make small, risky, or potentially difficult-to-collect loans, particularly to small farmers and entrepreneurs. Instead, both government and private banks now exhibit a bias toward bigness even though, economists say, Costa Rican farmers have a relatively good repayment record compared with large growers or cattlemen.[10]

Tourism

Costa Rica's natural beauty, great biodiversity, and fishing and surfing, as well as its reputation for peace and stability, make it a popular vacation spot for North Americans and Europeans. For twenty years, tourism was in third place as a source of foreign exchange, after coffee and bananas. It climbed to first place in 1994, employing one in ten members of the labor force and providing 28 percent of foreign exchange and almost 8 percent of the GDP.

Euphoria was general; the annual number of tourists, 750,000 in 1994, would be sure to reach a million a year, and prosperity would climb steadily. Hotel builders were encouraged by government tax exemptions. The less optimistic warned that Costa Rica was not ready for mass tourism and that, ready or not, such tourism was not necessarily a good thing.

By 1995 it was apparent that the critics were right. Hotels had been overbuilt and some were nearly empty much of the time. Other aspects of infrastructure—many of them the same ones that retard industrial growth—had not kept pace with tourism. The main airport was inadequate and inefficient. Roads had deteriorated from overuse after the government lowered import duties on used cars. Tourism, like so many other potential sources of wealth, suffered from lack of planning.

Nor do all tourist dollars go to Ticos. As with the nation's industrial growth, foreigners have made most investments and hence most profits. One visitor notes:

> Our travel plans were made through a Montreal-based charter company— $2,600 to them. We rented a car through a car rental agency in San José— $600 to them. We rented a small beach house from an American we never met—$720 to him. . . . We spent $200 on fruit and vegetables at a local vendor, about $50 on gasoline and another $100 on local handicrafts. We also paid a housemaid $50 to help with cleaning. . . . Adding this means that out

Costa Rica's natural beauty is a prime tourist attraction (Mavis Hiltunen Biesanz)

of a total expenditure of $4,320, less than 10 percent went to the local community where we actually spent our time.[11]

Tourism entrepreneurs are largely North Americans and Europeans. A frequent complaint is that *gringos* own most coastal property and charge such high rates at their hotels that few Ticos can afford them, making them feel like aliens in their own country. A familiar story on both coasts is that of the farmer who sells his land to a foreigner and remains in the locality. There his children work in construction or make beds or wait on tables at tourist lodges while foreigners and Ticos from the capital manage the business. Says a historian, "Costa Rica is no longer the Eden where there are more teachers than soldiers, but the country where waiters are better paid than teachers. . . . Will the Costa Rica of the year 2000, then, be the land of an army of waiters?"[12]

Many Ticos complain, too, that large resorts attract thieves, prostitutes, drug dealers, and entertainment falsely presented as authentic national folklore. Anthropologist Carmen Murillo says that with massive tourism, "our folk culture becomes a commodity, and the foreign visitor receives a simplistic, commercialized, out-of-context version of our culture, which projects a false image of the quality of our people. The faces of our people are erased and only things remain."[13]

Ecology

Mass tourism endangers the very environment that attracts tourists in the first place. The construction of huge coastal resort complexes has violated conservation laws and reduced the habitats of monkeys, birds, and other wildlife popular with visitors. Alvaro Ugalde, a founder of the national parks system, warns that Costa Rica's reputation for ecological awareness is threatened by such projects; if the country doesn't live up to its "green" image, he says, tourists will stop coming.

At the same time small eco-friendly tourist enterprises are prospering all over the country.[14] Unlike the sprawling resorts that may destroy estuaries, forests, and beaches, these are not seen as a threat to Ticos' cultural identity or, if properly managed, to the natural environment. Indeed, they can have the opposite effect. Many Ticos are delighted that so many foreign tourists prefer rice and beans to Rice Krispies for breakfast, are curious about local customs, try to learn some Spanish, and would rather stay with a local family than in a large hotel. And as one tourism entrepreneur, a former rancher, says, "Tourists come here to see birds and monkeys, not cows." Tourism has, indeed, been a major reason for private as well as public-sector reforestation.

But visitors expecting Costa Rica to be an ecological Eden are dismayed by evidence of past and current deforestation—among the highest rates in the world; by the profligate use of pesticides; by rivers clogged with garbage and sewage; and by San José's serious air pollution. Even those who had visited the country a decade earlier see striking evidence of Costa Rica's 2.25 percent annual population growth.

Many private organizations—foreign and national, commercial and non-profit—are taking steps to reverse unsound policies. Some have bought endangered forest or wetlands. A few, including Costa Rica's largest supermarket chain, have recycling programs. Many have provided incentives for conservation such as giving solar panels to landowners in exchange for a written agreement not to develop their land for a certain number of years or teaching farmers to raise crops without chemical pesticides or herbicides. (Organically grown foods now bring high profits both in Costa Rica and abroad.)

The state, too, has made some efforts to sustain and improve the environment. Since the 1970s it has created numerous parks and biological reserves; in 1998 these covered nearly one-third of the national territory. The public-sector Costa Rican Institute of Electricity has begun to tap the geothermal power so abundant near the surface of this volcanic country. The Ministries of Education and Natural Resources involve schoolchildren in planting trees. In 1996 the Refinadora Costarricense de Petroleo (RECOPE), the state refinery, began providing unleaded gasoline. Now, all motor vehicles have to pass an emissions test before receiving the newly required "eco-sticker." Coffee-processing plants, though still a major source of water pollution, have largely complied with strict new waste-disposal laws. Although many praiseworthy conservation laws are only spottily enforced and state officials have sometimes colluded with banana companies and mass tourism developers in destroying forests and mangroves, the constitution's Article 50, which guarantees Costa Ricans the right to a healthful and ecologically balanced environment, is somewhat more than an idealistic gesture.

Work

Some Costa Ricans still fit the image of the "simple peasants" whom the national anthem extols as the typical sons of their noble fatherland. *Campesinos* are still praised in official speeches as the backbone of the country—and perhaps rightly so. When we ask rural Ticos how they amuse themselves, the most frequent answer is "work." In her unpublished journal of a year in a rural highland area in the early 1990s, Sandra Shaw says, "We have never seen people work so hard." Her Tico neighbors would, if necessary, work from dawn to dusk and beyond, in organized fashion, like an assembly line when building a road or like automatons as their machetes flashed unceasingly in the cane field. "They never complain except perhaps to say with a smile, 'Muy duro' [very hard]."

Many Ticos say, nonetheless, that most of their compatriots are lazy and inefficient. "Nicaraguan immigrants now harvest most of our coffee and sugar," they point out. They are especially critical of urban Costa Ricans, who, they note, are encouraged to work as little as possible by the fact that many jobs are obtained, and presumably kept, more through connections than merit; by state paternalism, which makes it expensive to fire an incompetent worker; by professional guilds that restrict competition; and by the numerous holidays that Ticos are very reluctant to give up. The director of the movie *1492,* filmed in Costa Rica, was puzzled when local extras, even after signing contracts for the twelve-hour days normal in filmmaking, refused to work such long hours.[15] And a Costa Rican businessman complains, "Mediocrity prevails in every profession. On almost any legal document, for instance, you can expect at least one major error." In our experience, he is correct.

Still, few Ticos rate their jobs only according to income and prestige; nor are these always necessary or sufficient work incentives. Also important is how interesting a job is, how competent one feels in meeting challenges, and whether one is salaried, paid hourly, or self-employed. An elderly mason we met showed evident pride in his skill at making and painting tombs, and a young farmer bragged about his skill in driving muddy roads. Self-employed farmers, fishermen, taxi drivers, seamstresses, *pulpería* owners, and private-

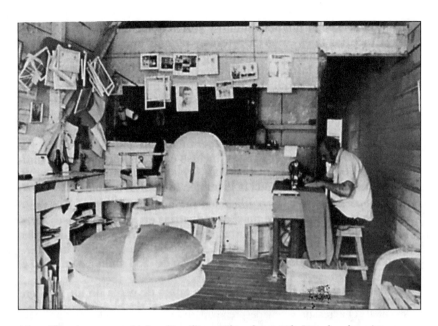

Many Ticos have several jobs; this village tailor also cuts hair and makes picture frames (Sylvia Boxley de Sassone, reprinted from Biesanz et al., Los costarricenses *[San José: EUNED, 1979])*

sector artisans and professionals frequently work ten- to fifteen-hour days and take pride in the amount and quality of their work.

The Labor Code and Social Guarantees of 1943 tacitly acknowledged that labor relations in city and country alike were becoming more impersonal, based increasingly on formal contracts. Although both originated with President Calderón Guardia (1940–1944), they were greatly expanded and strengthened under PLN administrations. They "are in a large degree responsible for the social peace that the country has enjoyed for the last 40 years," wrote *Tico Times* editor Dery Dyer in 1994.[16]

In return for full-time work (five days a week for eight hours a day or six hours for rural peons) employees today are supposed to receive not only a minimum wage and social security benefits (health care, disability benefits, and pensions) paid for mostly by their employers but also a large Christmas bonus and substantial severance pay if fired after working three months or more. The Ministry of Labor and the Social Security Fund are quick to investigate workers' complaints. Pregnant women and new mothers are entitled to four months off with pay and an hour a day for breast-feeding.

Many employers, however, fail to comply with these requirements, and not all workers dare to complain. Many say they fear losing their jobs or cannot take time off to file a complaint. This is especially true, says a Labor Ministry inspector, of the young, poorly educated single mothers who account for two out of five textile workers. They often work long hours at below minimum wage. They can't afford to quit, and it takes time, money, and baby-sitters to pursue a complaint or look for another job.

Unions have existed since 1916, when European immigrants organized artisans in Puntarenas. In 1921 the new General Confederation of Workers called a general strike that achieved an eight-hour day and a 40 percent pay hike for many workers, but it was soon absorbed into Jorge Volio's ill-fated Reformist Party.

The new communist Bloc of Workers and Peasants won some concessions for banana workers in a 1934 strike. Ever since then employers—and many workers as well—have labeled almost any union activity as communist-inspired. Fear of communism continues to divide workers and weaken the labor movement.

This is especially true in the private sector, where in 1995 unions represented only one worker in sixteen as compared to three out of five public employees. (Four out of five strikes between 1988 and 1993 involved public employees.)[17] One reason is a widespread distrust of private-sector unions; many workers see union officials as corrupt and self-seeking, likely to make secret deals with owners and managers. Those who do join private-sector unions tend to prefer small single-industry unions over confederations, which they consider too impersonal and unaccountable.

Fear of reprisal against organizers also discourages union membership. "Anyone suspected of wanting to start a union would be fired right away," says a textile worker; we have heard similar comments from many others. Even the once-strong banana workers' unions have collapsed.

Private-sector workers increasingly prefer *solidarista* associations to unions. Described by founder Alberto Martén in 1947 as a Costa Rican solution to labor problems, these are basically savings and loan associations financed by payroll deductions and encouraged by employers as well as foreign lenders. In the private sector *solidaristas* far outnumber union members. Although many workers appreciate the low-interest loans, critics charge that *solidarismo*, while remaining firmly under management control, misleads workers into thinking they will eventually share the business's profits.[18]

Far better financed and more effective than labor unions or *solidarismo* in promoting their members' interests are the twenty-two *colegios* (guilds) of professionals: lawyers, doctors, architects, dentists, journalists, engineers, accountants, and others. *Colegios* have the legal right not only to regulate who may practice their profession but also, in many cases, to sell special stamps that must be affixed to contracts.

Estimates of the unemployment rate in the 1990s varied between 4 and 7 percent; some estimates do not count those who give up looking for work that

suits them. Economists agree, though, that the underemployed—those who work fewer hours than they would like to or in jobs not up to their qualifications—are far more numerous and have been since at least the 1940s.[19]

Among the underemployed are many of those who work in the "informal economy"—the estimated 22 percent of the labor force (1995) not officially recognized and hence not even minimally protected by labor laws. Their numbers have greatly increased since the crisis of the early 1980s. They range from self-employed street vendors, unlicensed ("pirate") taxi drivers, garbage-dump scavengers, and drug dealers to those who shine shoes, guard cars, or bag and carry groceries at supermarkets for tips. *Hormigas* ("ants") make regular trips to Panama, Miami, or free-trade zones such as Golfito, bringing back untaxed goods to sell to friends and coworkers. Many work for others "off the books" in restaurants, small factories, bed-and-breakfasts inns, family-owned *pulperías*, small construction sites or farms, or as maids and baby-sitters for less than the minimum wage and without their employers paying the required social security taxes. Workers outnumber jobs, and many willingly accept such terms. Says a small farmer, "I need peons much of the time, but I can't afford to pay minimum wage and social security. So I don't hire anyone who insists on them."

Female heads of households, who need work that can be combined with caring for small children, make up a large share of this sector. So do children, many of them school dropouts; those between ages twelve and nineteen make up one-eighth of the total labor force; thousands more are even younger.

Many with regular jobs moonlight; a civil servant or teacher may sell clothing or raffle tickets to neighbors and colleagues; a secretary or store clerk may be an after-hours call girl. A popular term for the attempt to make ends meet by looking for small jobs on the side, even if they pay poorly, is *camaronear*. A *camarón* is literally a shrimp. One man shrugged, "It's small, but it's better than nothing. People shrimping in a river don't find a lot in any one place, but one here, another there." Many of those without regular jobs do nothing but *camaronear*. We know one who works as a free-lance karate teacher, massage therapist, carpenter, and bartender.

In a university professor's office a graduate student told us about the increase since 1980 in the number of Ticos who *polaquear*—peddle things to people in homes and offices, often on credit. (The verb comes from *polaco*, the term for Eastern European Jewish immigrants of the 1920s and 1930s who made a living by peddling door-to-door.) While we talked, one student brought in a painting he hoped to sell to the professor; another peddled coffeemakers. Meanwhile, the professor touted her own new book to everyone who entered. Many of the new *polacos*—with no ethnic implications—are middle-class people whose salaries buy less with devaluation and inflation.

One big business is clearly not "on the books"—the laundering of drug money, which may involve hundreds of millions of dollars annually. It is

Textile factory (Ingrid Holst)

widely believed that this money is used to build hotels, malls, and urban residential complexes. Money laundering is said to be easier since the government relaxed currency regulations under structural adjustment. The laws make it difficult to prove guilt, and by mid-1995 only two persons had been convicted.

In the formal economy, even in businesses managed by Ticos, culture shock—on both sides—can impede productivity. Many textile workers feel that they are treated like machinery: Each stage of operations in making an article of apparel is regulated by whistles, conversation is prohibited, and managers rarely mix with workers even during coffee breaks.[20] Managers find it hard to convince workers of the need for discipline, punctuality, and precision. A former director of the Chamber of Textiles says, "In the international market half a centimeter is half a centimeter; sometimes a whole shipment is returned because it is off just a tiny bit."[21]

The Chamber of Textiles has proposed conferences to teach foreign investors how Costa Rican culture affects work. Sensitive about personal dignity, Ticos are not ready to admit mistakes or to forgive a scolding or correction made in the presence of others. They want to be recognized as individuals with the courteous rituals common among Ticos. They want above all to *quedar bien*, to make a good impression in the face-to-face encounter of the

moment even if it means pretending to understand an unclear directive or promising to fulfill it when they know they can't or won't. One saves face for an employee by asking matter-of-factly, "It's not finished yet, no?" rather than "Haven't you finished it yet?" But this works better with a single employee than in a factory where the work of many must be coordinated.

Summary and Conclusion

Long dependent on a few agricultural exports, Costa Ricans' prosperity fluctuated along with world markets for these crops. Abject poverty, however, was less common than elsewhere in Latin America, thanks to abundant land, scarcity of labor, the paternalism of employers, and, after 1948, the welfare state. Agricultural diversification, beginning in the 1950s with the cattle boom, made Costa Rica less vulnerable to declines in world coffee and banana prices, but the conversion of forest and farmland to pasture was to have grave social and ecological consequences.

The industrialization fostered by the Central American Common Market in the 1960s and 1970s was hailed as a step toward greater economic diversity and national self-determination. The Costa Rican government borrowed heavily from international lending agencies during these decades, largely to help finance the expansion of the public sector. Supporters of this expansion argued that public-sector programs involving banking, infrastructure, health, education, housing, and welfare would not only improve living conditions for many Costa Ricans but also promote social and political stability, thus making the country more attractive to investors. Critics saw the state bureaucracy with its maze of poorly coordinated agencies, complex regulations, and monopoly of many essential activities as an obstacle to development.

This debate grew more heated after 1985, when the government signed the first of several structural adjustment pacts (PAEs) with international lenders. The pacts require substantial increases in exports, reduction of import tariffs, and the privatization of many state agencies. Their supporters insist that they have made local businesses and industries more competitive, brought inflation under control (9 percent in 1993 versus 27 percent in 1990), and trimmed a costly and often obstructionist government bureaucracy. The loans Costa Rica has received as a result of the PAEs have, lending agency officials say, been put to good use—agriculture, for instance, is far more diversified. All this, they insist, has resulted in the prosperity evident in new shopping malls, high-rise buildings, cars, posh residences, tourist resorts, jobs for thousands of workers employed by multinational firms, reduced inflation, and, by 1995, a trade surplus of $165 million—the first since 1934.

Critics of structural adjustment reply that the pacts have mostly benefited the already-affluent few and hurt everyone else. The withdrawal of government aid to small basic-grain farmers was one reason for the widening gap. Another was the PAEs' insistence on measures that hit the urban poor and working class hardest, such as fee hikes for electricity and water and an end to subsidies for bus companies and for certain staple items, particularly food, whose prices have soared. Poverty clearly increased between 1992 and 1996 as the population grew faster than production, resulting in increased unemployment (6.2 percent, up from 4 percent) and a probable rise in underemployment. Meanwhile, inflation increased once again, to 13 percent in 1995, falling two points by 1997.

The free-trade and growth-through-export models agreed to in the PAEs have led to further problems for Costa Rica. Pressure to increase exports has resulted in environmental destruction—for example, old-growth forests are cleared to expand heavily sprayed banana plantations. The cost of restructuring is often prohibitive for growers of unfamiliar export crops and for local industrialists hard pressed to compete with the flood of less-expensive imports unleashed by declining tariffs—especially when they must pay 30 to 40 percent interest on loans. Large multinational companies with more capital, technical know-how, and access to markets have benefited most.[22]

Most seriously, say PAEs' opponents, the pacts have reduced Costa Rica's sovereignty and weakened its cultural identity. The foreign firms that have invested there partly because of changes wrought by PAEs exert much influence on the government. The heavily advertised goods they sell further undermine Ticos' pride in their own products and capabilities. The new laissez-faire policy toward basic-grain farmers has made Costa Rica much more dependent on imported food and thus more vulnerable to food shortages. And the PAEs allow international lenders to "manage" Costa Rica to some degree—to approve the government's budget and economic policies, for instance, and to determine whether it may negotiate with other foreign lenders.

Since any administration, regardless of party affiliation, is dependent on foreign loans, the PAEs have contributed to the growing (and accurate) popular belief that the two leading parties have become very similar. This, in turn, is one reason many Costa Ricans have become skeptical about the legitimacy and effectiveness of their systems of government and politics, institutions we discuss in the next chapter.

Notes

1. We recognize that modernization and development are not universally regarded as desirable goals. We use them to mean a cluster of trends that usually go together: industrialization, urbanization, and secularization.

2. *Rumbo*, April 20, 1993, p. 36, citing a report of the Project for Agricultural Institutional Reform and Sector Investment.

3. Interview with IDA official Tamaris Arrieta, December 2, 1996.

4. Julio Rodríguez, "En vela," *La Nación*, July 2, 1992, p. 15A.

5. Thomas P. McCann, *An American Company: The Tragedy of United Fruit* (New York: Crown, 1976), p. 160.

6. Francisco Escobar, "Fruta dulce, bananal amargo," *Rumbo*, November 1, 1994, p. 5.

7. Irene Aguilar and Manuel Solís, *La elite ganadera en Costa Rica* (San José: EUCR, 1988), p. 5.

8. Silvia Lara, Tom Barry, and Peter Simonson, *Inside Costa Rica* (Albuquerque: Resource Center Press, 1995), pp. 43–44.

9. Ibid., p. 47.

10. Martha Honey, *Hostile Acts: U.S. Policy in Costa Rica in the 1980s* (Gainesville: University of Florida Press, 1994), p. 92.

11. Letter to the editor, *Tico Times*, January 31, 1992, p. 2.

12. Juan Rafael Quesada Camacho, "Educadores o meseros?" *La República*, n.d. [1993].

13. Quoted in Elberth Durán, "Turistas presionan la cultural nacional," *La República*, March 22, 1993, p. 2.

14. To locate some of these, see Beatrice Blake and Anne Becher, *The New Key to Costa Rica* (Berkeley, Calif.: Ulysses Press). This excellent guidebook, updated yearly, emphasizes lodgings that "have a low impact on the environment, support the local economy, and promote the best of local culture."

15. Melanie Gruer, "Film Director Says Costa Rica 'Needs Experience,'" *Tico Times*, March 27, 1992, p. 35.

16. Dery Dyer, Editorial, "Deja Vu in the Banana Zone," *Tico Times*, May 20, 1994, p. 2.

17. Ivan Molina and Steven Palmer, *Costa Rica 1930–1996: Historia de una sociedad* (San José: Porvenir, 1997), p. 35.

18. Manuel Rojas Bolaños, "The Solidarismo Movement," in Marc Edelman and Joanne Kenen, eds., *The Costa Rica Reader* (New York: Grove Weidenfeld, 1989), p. 158.

19. John Biesanz and Mavis Biesanz, *Costa Rican Life* (New York: Columbia University Press, 1944), p. 165.

20. Carlos Sandoval García, *Sueños de la vida cotidiana: Trabajadores y trabajadoras de la máquila y la construcción en Costa Rica* (San José: EUCR, 1997), pp. 75, 84.

21. Patricia Letton, "Ticos no llenan expectativa de textileros," *La Nación*, March 2, 1992, p. 8A.

22. Karen Hansen-Kuhn provides a scathing criticism of their effects in "Sapping the Economy: Structural Adjustment Policies in Costa Rica," *Ecologist*, Vol. 23, No. 5, September-October 1993.

— 4 —

Government
and Politics

TICOS HAVE LONG PRIDED THEMSELVES on their democratic system. Their pride is justified in many ways. Costa Rica has no standing army, guerrillas, or political prisoners. All citizens eighteen and older (except convicted felons) are required to vote, and most do. There is great freedom of expression and assembly. The legislature and courts limit the actions of the president, who is peacefully replaced every four years, usually by the opposition party's candidate. The constitution provides for clear separation of executive, legislative, and judicial powers.

Why, then, have Costa Ricans in recent years, while remaining profoundly attached to principles of peace and democracy, become increasingly cynical about both the effectiveness of their government and the legitimacy of their political system?

The Structure of National Government

Delegates to the convention that drafted the current constitution in 1949 wanted no recurrence of events such as those that had led to civil war the year before. Conservatives feared that Pepe Figueres would continue the pattern of strong presidencies dating back to 1870. Social democrats such as Figueres feared a legislature with control of electoral processes, like the one that had approved fraudulent elections in the 1940s. These fears are reflected in provisions for weakened powers of both branches of government. Political scientist Olivier Dabene describes the resulting pattern as "semi-presidential and semi-parliamentarian," an ideal framework for compromise, lacking a clear, strong center of decisionmaking.[1]

The public sector includes such a bewildering maze of agencies that it is often difficult to know who is responsible for making what decisions—and who actually does make them. And therefore, it is easier to understand why

65

some decisions are slow to be made and why many others are made only symbolically, if at all.

For fear of concentrated power, the constitution places strict limits on presidential and congressional terms. It limits the president to a single four-year term, and the fifty-seven *diputados* (legislators) are elected for four years and can be reelected only after at least one term out of office.

The Presidency

The president, a major symbol of national unity, commands the police and acts as chief of state on ceremonial occasions. He gives direction to national policy through his influence on public opinion and his close ties with the ministries. Through the Ministry of Planning he coordinates government programs (to the extent they are coordinated at all) and allots their budgets. His power is checked to some extent by other branches of government, by public employees' unions in the very bureaucracy he heads, and by his concern for public opinion.

The Legislature

The Legislative Assembly has the power to pass, amend, and repeal laws and to impose taxes. Before international agreements and foreign loans negotiated by the executive branch can take effect, the legislature must ratify them by a two-thirds majority.

The legislature—which the constitution designates as the principal power in government—checks the executive branch through its power to amend the budget submitted by the president and to appoint the comptroller general, who must approve public expenditures before their release and thus (in theory, at least) prevent the executive branch from overspending its budget. The legislature also considers many administrative issues such as the licensing of cab drivers.

The collaboration of the legislature with the president is essential to any fundamental change. In situations such as the economic crisis of 1979–1982 when the legislature cannot be counted on to act swiftly, the president issues executive decrees. He may then be charged with abusing his office. (Fear of such charges, say some observers, keeps most presidents from issuing many decrees of great scope.) The number of decrees has declined since 1981, but in 1990 they still outnumbered laws by roughly four to one.[2] Since 1980, most laws, too, have originated with the president as bills requiring legislative approval. And even when the legislature has exercised its right of censure, as it did in 1996 when President Figueres's minister of public security led an illegal police demonstration outside the Legislative Assembly building, the president typically refuses to dismiss the censured official. The constitution, concludes one political scientist, "is obsolete in calling the legislature the principal power."[3]

The constitution states, "The power to legislate resides in the people, who delegate it, by means of the vote, to the Legislative Assembly." But leaders of both major parties, headed by their presidential candidates, decide who goes on the ballot and in what position. Since voters choose a party, not individual candidates, for the legislature, and *diputados* are seated according to their party's share of the vote and their own places on the ballot, the legislature is, in Rodrigo Fournier's phrase, not elected but *selected* and thus is not truly representative. This provision makes it less likely that a member of a minority ethnic group, the far left, or the working class can become a legislator.[4] It also means that *diputados* have no promises to keep to their constituents, only obligations to party leaders. And the president's power to allocate or withhold pork-barrel funds to *diputados* gives him considerable influence over legislators in his own party, who get the lion's share of them.[5]

The ban on immediate reelection, however, weakens party discipline, as it was meant to; a president is sometimes at odds with legislators of his own party. It may also weaken *diputados'* image as public servants. True, John M. Carey found that legislators typically spend most of their time meeting with constituents from areas assigned to them by their parties (usually discussing local rather than national needs).[6] But they are widely believed to be interested primarily in making contacts that will help their business or professional careers when their brief term ends. Polls have repeatedly found that the Legislative Assembly has the lowest credibility of all national institutions; and we have heard, for decades, comments like this one from a street musician whom we asked about the whereabouts of his usual accompanist: "That guy's like a *diputado*. He thinks he should make a whole lot of money for working just half an hour a day."

A minority-party *diputado* told us that he was frustrated by the partisan wrangling that had held up legislative approval of major foreign loan offers so long that these offers were withdrawn. He also pointed out, however, when Richard shadowed him for most of a thirteen-hour day in 1993, that many legislators work much harder for their constituents than most Ticos believe.

The Judicial System

The twenty-two magistrates of the Supreme Court of Justice are chosen by a simple majority of the legislature. The constitution, tacitly regarding the judicial system as above suspicion, provides for few checks on its power. Free of executive control, the court is also fairly independent of the Legislative Assembly, since magistrates' terms are not concurrent with those of legislators and are automatically renewed every six years unless the legislature decides otherwise, which seldom happens. The Supreme Court names judges of the civil and penal courts in each province as well as of minor courts in some cantons. The legislature has also created courts specializing in juvenile, family, labor, agrarian, fiscal, and traffic issues, as well as a constitutional court, the Sala IV. There were some 200 judges in 1998.

The Supreme Electoral Tribunal

The "fourth power," the autonomous Supreme Electoral Tribunal, oversees the formation and functioning of parties, the course of electoral campaigns, and the actual voting and counting of votes. Three magistrates are appointed by the Supreme Court for six-year terms, one every two years to minimize partisanship. Two others are appointed a year before each election.

Autonomous Institutions

The 1949 constitution also provides for the autonomous institutions, or public corporations, discussed in Chapter 3. Each is charged with a function once left to private agencies or to central and local government, if it was performed at all. Among the largest are CCSS, the Social Security Fund; the Costa Rican Institute of Electricity (ICE), in charge of electricity and telecommunications; RECOPE, which imports, refines, and distributes petroleum; and the state banks. PLN administrations created most of these agencies—over 200 by 1980. Their autonomy has eroded since the president was given power to appoint or dismiss their chief executives and to require that they buy bonds from the chronically indebted central government. More than half of them have been dismantled and privatized or must compete with private agencies as a condition of structural adjustment pacts. Still, the remaining *autónomas* accounted for slightly over half of all public employees in 1995 and spent over four-fifths of all public-sector funds.

The Scope of Government

By any measure, little Costa Rica still has big government. One out of seven people in the labor force in 1996 was a public employee. The government included twenty-four ministries and seventy-three autonomous and semiautonomous institutions. It also included eighty-one municipalities, though the budgets and functions of these once-powerful local governments (which we will discuss in Chapter 6) are dwarfed by those of national government.

Government has a finger in almost every pie. Not only is it the sole legal liquor manufacturer, as it has been since 1852, and the chief banker, as it has been since 1948, but it also produces and distributes electricity, provides telephone service, monopolizes the sale of insurance, subsidizes housing, supports symphony orchestras, builds roads, transplants hearts, and promotes tourism. It spends a larger share of its budget on health and education than do most other countries. It looks, to some extent, after the welfare of children, the elderly, the indigent, and the disabled. It makes itself felt at every turn, not in the manner of a police state but as a bureaucratic giant that must be dealt with in order to own and drive a car, cut a tree, leave the country, build a shed, bury a body, buy or sell, employ or be employed.

Some public-sector agencies have gone far toward achieving their original goals. Public health programs have helped increase life expectancy since the 1940s; the Costa Rican Institute of Electricity has made electric current and telephone service available to almost all Ticos; the National Institute of Apprenticeship (INA) trains thousands of workers each year in marketable skills.

But long before PAE-I, the first structural adjustment pact, many Costa Ricans believed the public sector, especially the *autónomas*, had become too large, too wasteful, and uncoordinated.[7] After JAPDEVA, a government *autónoma,* took over the Atlantic Railroad, for example, service was slower than it had been around the turn of the century; a loaded freight car took ten days or more to get from Limón to San José (an eight-hour run), and no one seemed to know where it was at any given time. JAPDEVA fell under the axe of structural adjustment, and the once-proud railroad system has been shut down.

Although most central government workers since 1953 have been protected by a civil service system designed to replace political patronage, the spoils system dies hard. To be sure, the days are gone when a new president could replace all opposition employees with his own supporters. But new jobs can be created, and there are ways around civil service procedures. The losing party in any election, despite its ritual complaints of political persecution when many of its members lose government positions, must make it clear that its supporters will also be rewarded if it wins four years later. Thus recent presidents have found it politically difficult to comply with the PAEs' requirements to reduce the government payroll.

Growth in an agency's size often defeats its alleged purpose. Two recent administrators of Instituto Mixto de Ayuda Social (IMAS), created in 1971 to meet the needs of the poorest Costa Ricans, found that only 20 percent of their budget went for this purpose; the rest was spent on salaries. And Dr. Guido Miranda, former director of the Social Security Fund, the country's largest bureaucracy, charges that when this agency grew from 17,000 employees in 1978 to 23,000 in 1982 as a way of reducing unemployment, the agency had to cut maternity and other medical benefits.[8]

The great size of the public sector has still other consequences. The officially neutral bureaucracy has become the largest pressure group in the country, and one of the strongest. Employees of some *autónomas* enjoy vacation and other bonuses, three raises a year, and subsidies for food, weddings, childbirth, and their own burial as well as those of family members. Public-sector unions' demands for higher pay, shorter hours, and greater fringe benefits are backed by their ability to cut off important services. The constitution prohibits public-sector strikes; still electrical workers, postal employees, and social security doctors and nurses as well as teachers and government office workers often threaten to strike and sometimes do; of 127 strikes between 1988 and 1993, 104 took place in public-sector agencies.[9]

Costa Ricans complain that most government employees are slow, inefficient, and rude. Facilities are too centralized, say residents of outlying provinces, who often have to spend time and money on trips to San José to get simple matters attended to. A teacher's appointment must be processed through eight agencies. In the 1990s thousands of motorists waited nearly four years for metal license plates; they had to renew the flimsy paper ones on their windshields every year. The long delay was blamed on a bidding war and court battles about who should distribute the plates. Often one office after another disclaims responsibility and sends the supplicant to still another. "We have a Minister of Agriculture, a Minister of Agrarian Development, and a Minister of Regional Agricultural Development. Who's in charge of the agricultural sector?"[10] It is also easy *not* to make decisions and to block a decision almost anywhere in the paper jungle. "Come back tomorrow" is a standard request. Many foreign entrepreneurs, bewildered by such delays, decide not to invest in Costa Rica.

The Party System

Traditionally, coalitions of extended families among the elite informally agreed on a candidate to run against that of another such group or compromised with their rivals on a candidate. They acted, in effect, as political parties.

In the 1920s and 1930s the first ideological parties appeared: Volio's Reformists and Mora's communists. But *personalismo* remained important. The appeal of Calderón Guardia's Partido Republicano, which won the 1940 and 1944 elections, came from both its "Christian social" ideology and Calderón's charisma. After his defeat by the *figueristas* in the 1948 civil war, the two sides formed parties that have dominated politics ever since; even the Catholic Church, which has far higher credibility, has much less power.

The seven provinces play only one important role—as electoral districts for the legislature, whose fifty-seven seats are allotted according to population and redistributed after each decade's census if population shifts make this necessary. (Within each province, seats are allotted according to the proportion of its vote for each party.) Thus a legislator does not represent any specific canton within the province, and minor parties are encouraged to try for congressional seats even when they have no hope of electing a president. (Because 40 percent of the vote is necessary to elect a presidential candidate, one of the two large parties always wins the presidency.) It is easy to split one's vote because separate ballots are issued for the presidency, the legislature, and the municipal council. It is also easy to form new parties, and those that win 5 percent or more of the vote in one election usually reappear four years later because they can claim a proportionate share of the campaign subsidies provided by the government.

Founded in 1951, PLN, the Partido Liberación Nacional of the victorious *figueristas*, espoused a "social democratic" ideology for the next thirty years:

> PLN presented itself as the heir of the Costa Rican democratic tradition it had fought to defend; it not only respected and adopted the social reforms of Dr. Calderón Guardia, but carried them further; it appeared as the country's liberator because its 1948 victory meant the defeat of corruption, disorder, fraud and the influence of Communism—that subversive imported ideology; it had a nationalist project of a mixed economy leading to development, liberty and social justice.[11]

During these three decades, PLN—the majority party in the legislature until 1990—promoted the nation's political stability, largely by means of the favors it could grant through a growing bureaucracy in an expanding economy. By the 1990s, structural adjustment had restricted this ability, and the party itself was unstable; some losers in the 1994 party primaries withheld support during José Maria Figueres's winning presidential campaign. And during his administration, deep fractures in the party were evident.

For these same thirty years, PLN's chief opponent was a coalition formed only to back a candidate before each election. Despite several official changes of name, it has always been called *calderonismo*. Since 1984 this opposition has been officially recognized as an "institutional" party—Partido Unidad Social Cristiana (PUSC). This means that it automatically qualifies for the ballot at election time and need no longer build a coalition to oppose PLN every four years.

Whereas both parties espouse capitalism, PLN leaders have traditionally supported state intervention to ensure decent living standards for all Ticos. The *calderonista* opposition, by contrast, has traditionally opposed big public spending (ironically, since its founder instituted such landmark reforms as social security and protection of workers' rights).

Most voters show little interest in platforms and say that they vote for the candidate rather than the party. Even party loyalists seem more interested in who can do them favors than in ideology. Others vote against whichever party is currently in power either for fear it might become too strong or out of resentment that it did not, say, build a road near their farm or give their son a government job.

Since it became imperative for any administration to adopt structural adjustment policies, ideological differences have become even less important to voters. PLN policies have, since 1982, moved far closer to those of PUSC. Although PUSC has far more openly championed structural adjustment, PAE-I and PAE-II were both signed by *liberacionista* presidents. Since 1982, the two parties have "co-governed," says Luís Paulino Vargas. "In effect, they act like one party with two heads, never like two ideologically different parties. This has made it possible to go ahead tranquilly with progressive privatization of banking, gradual destruction of the small farmer and the slow dismantling of the basic social services of health and education."[12] Vargas's point was confirmed by several 1995 meetings between President Figueres and former president Calderón, in which these leaders of the two rival parties evidently reached agreement on several privatization measures.

Many voters, disenchanted with both parties, think their leaders want the same thing—to get in and get theirs—and they see little difference in their policies once in office. In a 1994 poll, 58 percent of respondents considered it necessary to form a third party; of these, 61 percent said they were willing to help form one. Most adults voted in that year's elections, but many told us they were planning "to shut my eyes and vote for the lesser of two evils"—a statement we had also heard in past election years but never so frequently. A 1996 poll found that 41 percent had no party preference, up from 28 percent in 1988.

Nonetheless, although minor parties continue to win a few seats in the legislature and on municipal councils, the choice of president has been increasingly limited to two candidates. In 1974 minority parties got 26 percent of presidential votes; four years later, only 6 percent; in 1994, less than 2 percent. This trend reflects the increasing consolidation of PUSC as well as the decline of the left. The presidential aspirations of minor parties are balked by a self-fulfilling prophecy: Voters believe a minority party has no chance of winning; they don't vote for it, so it doesn't win.[13] The mass media contribute to this vicious circle by focusing almost exclusively on the two major parties.[14]

Still, small parties may influence decisionmaking. They may act as gadflies and publicly call major-party leaders to account when they stray too blatantly from their avowed principles of social justice and the common good. They can also block decision and action when big-party legislators are at odds or tip the balance toward one position or the other. In 1994, for example, the sole *diputado* of the Cartago Agricultural Union demanded favors for his province before agreeing to vote regularly with PLN and give it a solid majority. And the record number of minority-party *diputados* elected in 1998 forced both big parties to woo them.

Campaigns and Elections

Every four years, voters cast ballots for the next president and two vice presidents, fifty-seven legislators, and local officials for all eighty-one municipalities. Scheduled elections have been interrupted only twice since 1889—in 1917 and 1948. And since 1949 suffrage has gradually been extended to a larger share of the population—women, eighteen-year-olds, illiterates. Nearly 2 million Ticos—almost two-thirds of the population—were eligible to vote in 1994.

The two major parties choose their presidential candidates in nationwide primaries. A precandidate who can pay for publicity has an advantage, and party leaders expect contributions from those who want a place on the party's congressional slate. No control exists over private contributions, whose sources and amounts are known only to party officials. (In some cases, this secrecy is preferred because donors give to both major parties; in others, many allege, because the money comes from foreign or national drug lords.) Six months before the election the president gives the Supreme Electoral Tribunal (TSE) power to call on the Civil Guard in case of any violation of electoral laws, and the TSE announces the formal beginning of the campaign. As Election Day approaches, motorists sound their horns in codes representing their favorites' names. On Sundays, children stand on sidewalks and roadsides to wave party banners at passersby. Friendships may cool because of political differences, and fistfights, normally rare, break out in bars and on streets.

With the major parties' tacit agreement on most important issues and restrictions on certain kinds of propaganda (such as poll results, accusations of communist sympathies, and appeal to religious beliefs), personal appeal is all the more important. Candidates try to visit every community at least once. They give speeches, shake hands, smile, and eat the inevitably proffered tamales. Costa Ricans will overlook a great deal in candidates they like but will not forgive arrogance. Although major candidates are usually wealthy, no candidate who fails to seem folksy and humble is likely to succeed. One technique of personal appeal is identified with Pepe Figueres—the deliberate use of *campesino* idioms and manners to attract rural votes. At a 1969 rally in a highland village, we heard don Pepe—a known teetotaler—jokingly accept an offer of a drink "as long as it's *chirrite* [moonshine]." In recent campaigns both major parties have hired U.S. advertising firms to polish their candidates' images. During the 1986 campaign, advisers to Oscar Arias sent him to a special "clinic" in New York to improve his overly proud appearance on TV.

Ticos complain that campaigns are increasingly dirty, that "the recent campaign was the worst ever." But campaigns have seldom, if ever, been conducted at a high level of courtesy and seriousness. In 1909 candidate Rafael Iglesias was called a scarecrow and a comedian who "has a pact with the devil and will attack the innocent, hard-working, virtuous girl that is Costa Rica."[15] In 1923 Ricardo Jiménez was accused of "smelling of cockroaches"; in 1931, of being a puppet of the hated foreign monopoly Electric Bond and Share.[16]

The TSE and Catholic clergy pleaded that the 1994 campaign stick to public issues, and both parties promised to comply. But personal attacks in the mass media, on posters, and in anonymously printed flyers far overshadowed any discussion of platforms. PUSC propaganda capitalized on rumors that as a young police cadet Figueres had murdered a small-time drug dealer and on his supposed military training at West Point. (The infighting of pre-candidates before the PLN primaries had given PUSC plenty of ammunition.) Silhouettes of Figueres's profile showed him wearing devil's horns. PLN in turn repeated accusations that PUSC candidate Miguel Angel Rodríguez had sold tainted meat to the United States and engaged in other shady business deals.

Both parties also engaged in a practice not seen since the 1940s—vote buying. In 1928 and in 1944, says one critic, parties handed out meat, shirts, blankets, and money. When his supporters complained about the opposition's doing so, Ricardo Jiménez replied, "If they kill one cow, we'll kill two." In those days, "politicians bought votes with money from the pockets of the rich. Today they buy them with taxi licenses, housing subsidies, and student subsidies, which come from the pockets of all wage-earning Costa Ricans."[17] In 1994 the two major parties promised a variety of individual or family subsidies (amounting to as much as $5,000 per family) for housing, schooling, food, and light bills and distributed certificates to be redeemed if their candidate won. Campaigners made these promises openly, face-to-face, seeking out poor people at home or inviting them to party headquarters.

Election Day, the first Sunday in February every fourth year, is a major public holiday. No liquor may be sold from the previous Friday night to Tuesday morning. By Sunday, the TSE has distributed ballots to the hundreds of schools that serve as polling places. Members of local electoral boards, whose status is honorary and unpaid but obligatory upon appointment, arrive long before the polls open at 5 A.M. to arrange the tables and set up booths for secret voting. A pollwatcher from each party may be present. Teenagers dressed in party colors are on hand to usher voters into the proper room. Although voting is, says the constitution, "a primordial and obligatory civic function," there is no punishment for failure to vote. About 80 percent of eligible voters participated in 1986, 1990, and 1994, and only 71 percent in 1998—the lowest turnout since 1956.

Children "vote" each election year (Sarah Blanchet)

Having done their civic duty, voters are free to join the *fiesta cívica* of excited people of all ages honking horns, waving banners and balloons, throwing confetti, or working for their party, perhaps transporting sympathizers to the polls.

The major parties depend for the bulk of their votes on hard-core loyalists. But enough Costa Ricans "switch colors," enough consider themselves nonpartisan, and enough new voters are added every four years to make the outcome of most elections hard to predict. PUSC candidate Miguel Angel Rodríguez's winning margin in 1998 was 2.5 percent, only slightly larger than his predecessor's 2 percent margin in 1994.

Elections reaffirm the pride of Ticos in their system. By Inauguration Day, the second Sunday in May, resentments among friends and neighbors of opposing parties have all but disappeared, the few party flags still fluttering over buildings have faded, and power peacefully changes hands. Many, however, have a sense of letdown. "After each election—the only opportunity to exercise democracy," says a journalist, "we fall again into defeatism and impotence, feeling, perhaps, that all the campaign promises will soon be forgotten."[18]

But most political decisions are based neither on campaign promises nor on the formal rules written in the constitution and in codes and laws, including international agreements. Unwritten cultural values and norms also guide—or block—decisionmaking and action.

Cultural Patterns and Government Functions

Fear of monolithic power, as we have seen, is responsible for limits on elected officials' terms, for the decentralization of decisionmaking power, and for voters' reluctance to keep one party in the presidency for two or more consecutive terms. These policies do work against a concentration of power; they also have unintended consequences.

Term limits waste expertise, make it impossible for a legislator to build a career on his or her voting record or a president on his accomplishments, and may actually increase the corruption they supposedly discourage. Roads are built conveniently close to the houses and farms of high officials. Because the president may serve only one term, no fear of defeat in any future election enters his calculations.

Frequent alternation of parties is very costly: The labor code provides that almost all the appointees who must leave when a new party comes in are eligible for severance pay. Alternation of parties and the ban on reelection also work against effective planning. Postponing action "until the clouds of the day clear"—Costa Ricans' response to the news of their independence from Spain—is still, some Ticos say, a classic excuse for avoiding any hard decision. Grand plans are usually filed away; piecemeal solutions are hastily improvised when a problem is on the verge of exploding. Instead of a complete overhaul of the inequitable tax system, for example, one specific tax is levied to meet one urgent problem, another when a new crisis looms.

Political actors cut red tape by going through informal channels. A bureaucrat may speed up someone's pension payment because of personal sympathies, family ties, or a bribe. A president may ignore constitutional checks, as did President Figueres in his 1994 decision to bypass the legislature and the courts and quickly deport several accused bank robbers to their native Venezuela.

Some unwritten norms and values make government more effective and responsive; others have the opposite effect. Compromise is still common, as it has been all through Costa Rican history. A tempest may be raging on the surface with both sides flinging charges and countercharges in the mass media and other public forums. Behind the scenes, meanwhile, a deal is being worked out that saves face for all concerned. We observed far more cordial bipartisan cooperation as well as genuine attention to experts' testimony, for instance, in legislative committee meetings than in sessions of the full legislature, which are broadcast on radio.

The emphasis on consensus and compromise, however, may actually impede real solutions to problems. Consensus is often achieved at the expense of decisiveness. Economist María Elena Carvajal observed in 1992 that President Calderón Fournier "is very Costa Rican when it comes to settling political problems—he shies from definitive acting in his desire to offend nobody, with a resulting indecision that has affected the nation's economic policies."[19]

Another means of keeping the peace, but one that also works against effective decisionmaking, is the symbolic solution to a problem. Costa Rica is often called a nation of laws and lawyers, and to call anything *muy legal* is high praise. But many laws, unsupported by a realistic plan or by resources for enforcement, are simply evidence of good intentions. This is an old pattern: Colonial laws prohibiting cockfights and the production of contraband liquor were unenforced, as was, soon after independence, an 1828 law requiring all children to attend school. Then, as now, many extremely detailed legal codes were on the books.[20]

Symbolic solutions satisfy the formalistic, legalistic outlook common among Costa Rican leaders. They meet to discuss a problem in committees, seminars, and workshops; proclaim the correct solution; pass a law or create a new agency; and presto! the problem is considered solved. One example is the Ministry of Health's program of preventing HIV by distributing condoms to prostitutes who appear for their mandatory monthly checkup. Each gets twenty-four—far fewer than most need. Likewise, writes novelist and columnist Anacristina Rossi, "Natural resources are unprotected not for lack of laws but because of the disorderly and incoherent proliferation of regulations and the lack of coordination and harmony among the agencies charged with applying them."[21] Lack of enforcement also breeds disrespect for laws: although all unlicensed ("pirate") cab drivers work illegally, for instance, the law is so little enforced that in some communities the Association of Pirates operates openly.

Political Participation and Power

Cynical though they are, Costa Ricans appear far better informed about politics and government and more interested in them than are citizens of many other countries, including the United States. Political cartoons and jokes take up far more space than any other form of humor in the leading newspapers. Many see politics as a game and elections as colorful fiestas enjoyed by all ages. It is easy, in this small country, to know some of the players, including the president, who moves about easily and informally. (Without making any special effort, we have met all but one of the presidents since 1942.) Although direct access to the president is no longer as easy as in the 1980s, when President Monge's pocket was picked in downtown San José, security is still so lax that many Ticos boast, incorrectly, that their president has no bodyguards.

The most common mode of political participation is asking public officials for personal and group favors. Nearly all Ticos, from the elite to the poor, try to use connections—friends, relatives, acquaintances, and those who may owe them favors. Their clout, of course, varies enormously with the number and power of such connections. This pattern dates back to the days when extended families were in effect political parties and employer-employee relationships were quasi-familial. A peon appealed to his employer, the employer in turn to the party leader who counted on him to deliver votes. With population growth and modernization, family networks have unraveled a bit and work relationships have become much more impersonal. But patronage is still important and power, still personalized.

Today, however, it is party connections that count most. Daunted by bureaucracy, a Tico seeks a friend or relative—often a government official—to cut red tape. Officials at all levels of government are besieged by people seeking personal or community favors. A cabinet minister, for example, finds long lines of people gathered outside his or her house every day. Community residents wanting a road, church, or soccer field—or a scholarship for their child—ask *diputados* for a share of the pork-barrel funds that the president allots to them.

The new style of patronage, like the old, works against class consciousness and solidarity. It both reflects and reinforces Ticos' individualism. Dabene finds the only truly class-conscious groups of Ticos at opposite ends of the social ladder—"the banana proletariat" (whose unions, as we saw in Chapter 3, have recently lost most of their power) and the governing elite, or "directing class."[22]

Members of the elite, regardless of party, are overwhelmingly urban, male, middle-aged, and upper- or upper-middle class. Analyzing the backgrounds of ministers, legislators, and Supreme Court justices between 1948 and 1974, Oscar Arias found that most were already in the upper class when they got their first political post—94 percent of ministers and 60 percent of *diputados*. No ministers and only three *diputados* came from the lower class. The rest were middle class.[23]

Prominent public officials tend to be both highly educated and wealthy: President Figueres Olsen's cabinet included several PhDs from Yale and Harvard. The era of the *cafetaleros* is long past. Says a sixty-year-old business manager and professor, "I see a new mix of state and private power. Many high officials are members of the new managerial class who have used their political connections to great advantage. A lot of ministers are financiers, bankers, or business people. And I know many industrialists and people in business and agribusiness in sub-ministerial posts."

Costa Ricans remain proud of their honest elections, but most are aware that the two major parties are now very similar. Several political scientists agree that, however honest, elections seldom offer real choices. Dabene, for example, believes that far from having a real choice, voters are simply betting on the outcome of a "dispute among friends."[24]

If there are no ideologically opposed elites struggling for power but rather similar groups with different party labels, how do they continue to dominate the political scene? The answer lies at least partly in the attitudes of Ticos themselves. Faith in the system—general acceptance of it as legitimate—helps uphold the power of the elite. Most Ticos are probably unaware that they are subject to a continual "ideological bombardment" that assures them they live in the best of all countries—that there is no other as democratic, peaceful, and beautiful or any as concerned with its citizens' welfare.[25] Presidential speeches, campaign oratory, editorials, school lessons, and celebrations all stress these themes, as they have since the late nineteenth century.

The Costa Rican preference for peace and compromise also helps keep the elite in power. Pepe Figueres once accused Ticos of being as docile as sheep. They prefer to let scandals die and are not easily aroused to passionate defense of a position or cause or to organized protest against injustice and incompetence. Even in 1948 only a small percentage of Ticos took an active part in the civil war or the events that led to it. Most, however much they grumble privately, continue to leave political action to the government and to rival party leaders, just as did past generations. But when their personal interests are clearly involved, Ticos often do take action. In 1995 the Ombudsman's Office, created by the legislature in 1993, received more than 20,000 complaints, mostly from poor women alleging neglect or mistreatment by public employees or overcharging by public corporations, for example, on water or electricity bills. Although it has no enforcement power, the office can recommend changes. It has had some immediate successes such as persuading the Health Ministry to close several noisy dance halls and a pig farm polluting a river and getting women who had been fired because of pregnancy either reinstated or paid severance.

The Ombudsman's Office may help make government agencies more accountable: On several occasions after it publicized complaints within such agencies about such formerly taboo topics as sexual harassment or their discrimination against cohabiting couples, the Legislative Assembly extended citizens' rights in those areas. Or it may become yet another paternalistic escape valve, resolving individual complaints—or giving the impression that someone in government is doing something about them—without changing policies or procedures. Indeed, the Ombudsman's Office charged in 1996 that several government agencies—which it named—had refused to abandon their illegal activities; for example, the public-sector National Insurance Institute was overcharging poor people for homeowner's insurance.

Many Costa Ricans also try to influence government through pressure groups. These may be as evanescent as pairs of students painting political graffiti on walls or as permanent and structured as chambers of commerce, as confident as these chambers of commerce or as desperate as landless *campesinos* squatting on uncultivated property, as peaceful as signers of a petition for a constitutional amendment fixing a percentage of the government budget for higher education or as violent as villagers throwing rocks and shouting down officials trying to explain why their community should be the site of a new metropolitan garbage dump. Group pressures are often far more influential than the votes of their individual members.

Since personal contacts between government officials and members of elite groups are frequent in tiny Costa Rica, these groups hire no permanent lobbyists. Business groups are especially powerful. Not only does the membership of many companies' boards of directors overlap, it also includes directors of autonomous institutions, *diputados*, and central government officials.[26]

During the early 1980s with the government on the verge of bankruptcy, associations of merchants and manufacturers persuaded President Monge to sign PAE-I. At the same time, landless *campesinos*—less able to peacefully occupy unclaimed land than were earlier generations in a much less crowded country—were feeling more powerless and becoming more radicalized. Since then mass land invasions have led to violent confrontations between squatters and police. In 1993, 256 different organizations were in line to apply to the Institute of Agricultural Development, demanding land for 45,000 families—a sign of the size of this pressure group but also of its fragmentation.

Between these two extremes of power is the buffer zone of the great majority of working- and middle-class Costa Ricans. Most of them belong to no pressure group at all, hoping instead to improve their own lives through education and family and party connections. (The powerful public-sector employees' unions are a major exception, as are the professional guilds.) Aside from squatters, *campesinos*—small farmers and farmhands—are often considered politically inert. In comparison to some other groups, they do appear conservative and inactive. It is a mistake, however, to label them all apathetic and indifferent. John Booth found in the 1970s that they were far more active in community organizations than were city dwellers.[27] Our interviews confirmed that this was still true two decades later.

But rural people have the least political clout of any Costa Ricans. (Arias found that only 4 percent of ministers and 6 percent of legislators between 1948 and 1974 had rural backgrounds.)[28] And they are aware of this. In a survey of three villages, two-thirds said elections had no impact on their problems.[29] Associations of small farmers have repeatedly failed, partly because their members produce too little to have much bargaining power. Their feeling of impotence and their relative lack of organization, leadership, and formal education reinforce one another and help keep *campesinos* comparatively powerless.

Residents of small rural communities and of poor urban barrios sometimes organize protests of government inaction or of steep price hikes for food and basic services—problems that have increased with cutbacks of state subsidies under the PAEs. Road construction and maintenance, water systems, schools, clinics, and recreational facilities, especially those outside the metropolitan area, lag far behind needs and promises. Community leaders present a list of their needs when a president, minister, or legislator visits them. If they are not given what they ask for, they may take stronger measures. For several days in 1993 residents of Parrita and Quepos blocked their vital Pacific coast road, which had remained unpaved year after year.

During the same year, residents of a highland village repeatedly complained about the stench from a fishmeal factory and petitioned for the plant's removal. Impatient with slow legal procedures and indifferent bureaucrats, 3,000 villagers broke onto its grounds one night and burned it down, resisting police efforts to restrain them. Three years later, residents of a Guanacaste village blockaded a road and burned two buses in hopes of persuading a Legislative Assembly committee to recommend that their district be given cantonal status.

Young people may be most visible at such events, but most young Ticos, even university students, show little interest in politics. In 1974, when eighteen-year-olds could first vote in a presidential election, 25 percent of all absentees would have been eligible to cast their first vote. Most nonvoters in 1994 were between the ages of eighteen and twenty-nine.

Costa Rican women have, on the whole, less interest in politics and far less power than men. Most wives follow their husbands' political preferences without question; when they differ, it is cause for comment. Major political groups are directed almost exclusively by men. Parties have women's auxiliaries that usually meet separately.

Yet Ticas have generally been much more interested and active in politics than have women in most other Latin American countries.[30] Many expressed strong convictions of their own long before they had the vote, which they achieved in 1949 after fifty years of struggle.[31] Women, joined by high school students, marched against the Tinoco dictatorship in 1918. They have demonstrated for honest elections, against establishment of a Soviet embassy, and in favor of a revised family code and of measures to protect themselves and their children from domestic violence. Although women have not yet organized permanent pressure groups and in 1997 held only about 10 percent of electoral positions, both major parties seek the votes of women, whose turnout is as high as men's.

In recent years a few women have been cabinet ministers, ambassadors, and members of the boards of autonomous institutions such as the Social Security Fund. Two have served as vice presidents in PLN administrations. José María Figueres's second vice president, Rebeca Grynspan, who has been called the most powerful woman in Costa Rican history, was an influential adviser on economic and social-welfare policy. Both 1998 candidates had two women vice-presidential candidates on the ticket. And winning presidential candidate Miguel Angel Rodríguez created a Ministry of Women's Concerns.

Autonomous institutions, central government ministries, and public corporations also act—quite aside from their employees' unions—as pressure groups. They compete for power and financing and use TV and radio spots and full-page newspaper ads to convince legislators and the public that their farsighted policies are indispensable to national progress.

Corruption

Many Ticos insist that their society today is corrupt from top to bottom and that the hunger of politicians, financiers, and contractors for *chorizos* (swindles—literally "sausages") is emulated in a host of ways by less powerful people. A reporter wrote a newspaper account of his visit to a store to buy a pair of trousers. The salesclerk suggested he take three pairs to the fitting room, choose one to pay for, wear another under the one he wore when he entered, and return the third as unsuitable—and, of course, split the gains with the clerk.[32] Accounts of a "good *chorizo*" are greeted with guffaws. A young cafe owner in a small town says:

> Practically everyone steals or cheats. Employees assume their bosses are thieves, so they don't mind stealing from them. A government employee who doesn't take bribes is likely to be fired, since others in his department are afraid he'll report them. It costs so much to send kids to school, and they're always saying, "Buy me this! Buy me that!" And whatever we have, we want more; if we have a car, we want a better one. *Chorizos* are the only way.

Politicians are often alleged to receive illegal campaign funds or to misuse lawfully donated funds. Customs officers and traffic policemen are widely believed to demand bribes to overlook real or bogus infractions; we can confirm that this is true of many police officers.

Corruption also springs, as we noted earlier, from the rigidity of bureaucratic rules: A Civil Registry official, for example, cannot legally approve or even study a document until she is sure it has all the required stamps, tax receipts, and signatures, and it may pass through the same hands any number of times—unless, of course, client and bureaucrat tacitly agree that there *is* a shortcut.

Luxurious houses and cars may be financed by tax evasion in the private sector or corruption in the public sector. They may come from the astronomical severance pay and pensions claimed, often long before normal retirement age, by government officials adding up their years in teaching, civil service, the legislature, ministries, and ambassadorships ($13,000 a month in one much-publicized case in 1994). Beneficiaries point out that such pensions are perfectly legal. Many Ticos protest, nonetheless, that they are unjust in a poor nation. But they protest *a la tica*, in newspaper essays and letters as well as in proposed reforms with little chance of passage among legislators dreaming of their own future rewards.

Strong anticorruption measures are occasionally taken. In 1996, for instance, the minister of environment and natural resources, René Castro, dismissed his agency's entire Forestry Department, acknowledging that many employees had long demanded bribes to ignore illegal logging. In that same year, customs inspectors came under much closer scrutiny, and the posts of honorary consuls, many of whom had been accused of corruption, were all abolished. Corruption is more visible in some administrations than in others. And a 1997 study by a nonprofit group, Transparency International, reported less influence peddling in Costa Rican government than anywhere else in Latin America.[33] Still, says columnist Julio Rodríguez: "There it [corruption] is, serpentine, encrusted in the convolutions of public administration and the private sector. Its power is colossal. It mobilizes dormant desires, stalled procedures, productive projects. It is the lubricant of the system, to the point where the honorable citizen, if he does not play the game, loses out."[34]

The News Media

Costa Ricans were long accustomed to slow-arriving news and swiftly spreading rumors. Now the latest news, mingled with advertising and propaganda, blares from radio and TV sets everywhere and arrives on the doorstep in the daily papers or on the computer screen.

Newspapers are widely read. Since the 1830s there has been, during most periods, little government interference with what they print, although a public agency may stop advertising in a paper that displeases its directors.

Editors are more fearful of offending advertisers than of libel suits, which, though frequent, seldom succeed. Most media are owned and managed by the business elite, who are also the chief buyers of advertising time and space. Most shareholders and board members of the leading daily newspaper, *La Nación*, also belong to commercial, industrial, and agricultural pressure groups; and the paper clearly reflects these groups' interests, as do the major TV and radio stations and magazines owned by the same corporation.[35] Its chief rival, *La República*, attracts much less advertising but has become nearly as pro-business, along with the PLN, which it generally supports.

Politicians both fear and court the media. Government agencies and ministries, universities, banks, and the legislature woo journalists by such means as lavish Christmas parties. But politicians also pressure media owners to punish employees who reveal damaging information about them.

Asked in a 1992 survey to cite limitations to freedom of the press they had encountered, reporters said they had been threatened and insulted by public employees and private organizations and censored by the companies they work for. Because their right to keep their sources secret is no longer protected by law, a growing trend toward investigative journalism has slowed down. Freedom of the press suffered a further blow in 1994 when the Supreme Court forbade the media to identify "any person or entity" being investigated for a crime.

Journalists often editorialize in the process of presenting news. Residents of the town of Esparza demonstrated violently when the government first decided to dump San José's garbage nearby. When they calmed down and accepted it (for a while) two news anchors on the most popular TV channel praised them for acting "as Costa Ricans should."

Street Crime and the Police

Costa Rica was long so tranquil that lone policemen walked their beats carrying only nightsticks—and screwdrivers for removing the license plates of illegally parked cars. But by the 1970s, we heard many Ticos, especially in San José, complain about the rise in crime and violence. In the 1990s such complaints—fueled by frequent news reports of bank robberies, muggings, and several kidnappings and drive-by murders—were constant. They are increasingly well founded. The reported homicide rate doubled between 1950 and 1994 from 2.9 to 5.8 per 100,000 population and rose to 7.6 in the next two years. Burglary is so common that rich and poor alike hesitate to leave a house or business unguarded. Those who can afford it resort to window grills, high fences, dogs, alarm systems, and hired guards for protection. By 1993 private guards outnumbered the police.

Gun ownership became widespread after the civil wars of the 1970s and 1980s in El Salvador and Nicaragua, when arms for both sides were funneled through Costa Rica; many remained in the country and more were brought in by refugees. Many Costa Ricans now buy handguns for protection, and a growing number, impatient with the slow responses of police, use them on intruders.

Official data once confirmed the belief, still popular, that most street crimes are committed by foreigners, especially Nicaraguans and Colombians. This scapegoating is no longer valid; 96 percent of those convicted of such crimes in 1993 were Costa Ricans.

Just as they blamed movies for fostering immorality in the 1940s, so Ticos now call television "a school for delinquency," one that promotes both violence and *consumismo*—a desire to live, by whatever means, like the wealthy people shown in commercials and imported programs.

Drugs are also widely blamed as substances that many addicts will kill to obtain and that make people crazy and violent. (All illegal drugs from marijuana to crack are usually lumped together in such explanations, whereas alcohol—far more widely abused—is rarely mentioned.) Cocaine (including crack), heroin, and marijuana flow through coastal ports, through the Panamanian border on the Pan-American Highway, through the main airport, and through airstrips where smugglers bound from Colombia to Florida refuel; much of it is now unloaded in Costa Rica.

In recent years, decreased spending on public education and the widening breach between rich and poor have enlarged the underclass, responsible for much of the crime. A primary school dropout, for example, cannot enter a trade school and may leave home to scrounge a living on the street. There he may join a criminal gang such as those that terrorized the San José area in the early 1990s. In groups of eight or so, they suddenly surrounded a passerby and demanded money and valuables at knifepoint. Their methods earned them the name *chapulines,* or grasshoppers.

"Good people have to live behind bars and criminals run loose," Ticos complain. "Where are the police?" There were about 13,000 police in 1995, most of them in two agencies. Three out of four worked in the Civil Guard, whose members patrol urban areas, often walking in pairs. The other sector, based in small communities, was the Rural Assistance Guard, whose main responsibility for decades has been to act as public servants—to help build schools, clinics, their own police posts, and simple jails; distribute school supplies and election materials; administer first aid; and radio the police helicopter in emergencies.

Security forces—a total of ten agencies responsible to four different ministries—also include such special units as the Coast Guard, the Traffic Police, the Presidential Guard, the elite corps of Military Police, the San José Municipal Police, the narcotics squad, detectives, and the Public Reserve Force.

Police receive little training or pay, and as many as a third resign every year. When an election produces a change of party, police jobs are given as rewards for party loyalty, even for merely allowing a party banner to fly above an aspirant's house. Even the minister of public security—the country's top cop—is almost always a civilian with no police experience. Thus there is little continuity or efficiency in security services, and few checks on police corruption.

Any hint of reforms in the direction of a well-trained career police force has long been rejected as *militarismo.* This fear is somewhat justified by the military training (in the United States, the Canal Zone, Israel, and Guatemala) not only of the Public Reserve Force and narcotics squad but also of many members of the Civil Guard, who wear olive drab and camouflage uniforms and whose military ranks (from corporal to colonel), abolished by President Arias, were restored by his successor. The Coast Guard's twenty boats are armed with 50-millimeter weapons. (It is largely financed and directed by the U.S. Drug Enforcement Administration and charged mostly with patrolling coastal waters in search of drug traffickers; it has caught very few.)

Police tactics today are frequently at odds with Ticos' democratic, peaceful self-image. The once unarmed rural police still have many duties besides crime control but, like the Civil Guard, have carried pistols and even submachine guns since the early 1980s and occasionally use them in confrontations with squatters, striking workers, presumed drug traffickers, and protesters. Routine Civil Guard and OIJ (Office of Judicial Investigation) investigations, even questioning about petty theft, sometimes involve beatings and such tortures as applying electricity to the testicles.

During its first month in office (May 1994) the Figueres administration was severely criticized for its handling of a banana strike, when riot police shot and wounded workers blocking a road, and for a one-day police roundup of 350 San José street children, most of whom had no criminal record and had done nothing wrong, according to the Costa Rican Human Rights Commission.

That month, however, Figueres also placed the Civil Guard and Rural Guard under a single command and called for the eventual creation of a permanent professional police force that would be phased in over twelve years. Police would no longer owe their jobs to party color. He also provided for professional nonmilitary training of career police officers with an emphasis on human rights instruction. Special training sessions are now held for crisis management, domestic violence, and negotiation with aggressors.

The Court System

Judges, especially those of the Supreme Court, were long respected, even revered. Although little conflict has been evident between the judiciary and the other branches of government, the courts have done much to enforce constitutional checks on presidential power, such as guarantees of suffrage and of freedom of expression, assembly, and worship as well as constitutional prohibitions on ex post facto laws, exile, and capital punishment. But even judges, like other government officials, are increasingly perceived as dishonest.

The judicial system has long functioned according to the Spanish model, a close copy, in turn, of the Napoleonic code, which does not include trial by jury. In criminal cases a judge or a panel of up to three judges serves as investigator, prosecutor, and defender as well as judge. All parties, but not the general public, may attend court hearings.

Once arrested, criminal suspects have a right to trial within six months. Many, especially juveniles, are released within hours despite strong evidence of guilt. Hundreds of others are imprisoned for years, some for suspicion of crimes punishable by as little as a month in jail. Of those declared innocent of the charges against them in 1991, 30 percent had been in prison for a year and a half.[36]

Why do such violations of due process happen? Court calendars are congested. Most courts are closed for a long Christmas-through-January vacation. Evidence-gathering remains at a low technical level. Sometimes those involved do their best to keep a case from coming to trial: In 1992, for example, legislator Rodrigo Gutiérrez cited the case of a woman kept in jail five years for complicity in an abortion; her jailers, he said, did not want it known that she had been tortured.

A litigant may appeal a decision to a higher court, or the court may transfer the case instead of passing sentence itself. Many cases drag on for years, says the president of the Supreme Court, because the law allows many appeals and presentation of irrelevant documents, and lawyers "fight over absolutely everything they can."

Civil cases tie up the courts far more than do criminal ones. So many people are involved in lawsuits that, as an early-twentieth-century president remarked, a safe conversational opening in Costa Rica is, "How's your case coming?" In 1994 the Supreme Court established centers of mediation and arbitration as a means of reducing court loads for minor civil cases. Mediators are largely retired judges and lawyers; arbitrators are designated by business, labor, and professional organizations.

One branch of the Supreme Court—the Constitutional Court, or Sala IV—created in 1989, was supposed to provide rapid justice for victims of unconstitutional laws or actions. Many see it as a defender of individual liberty against an often arbitrary state and a corrective to the slowness of other courts. Soon many Ticos used the new court as a threat—perhaps against an employer who reprimanded an employee, a landlord who raised the rent, a policeman who issued a traffic ticket, or a bureaucrat who told a client once too often that his file had been mislaid. Other judges consult the Sala when they want to be sure some decision they are about to make is constitutional; *diputados*, when they think some project to be presented to the legislature might run into problems of constitutionality.

Access to this court was made so easy, and its authority so broad, that it, too, soon acquired a huge backlog of cases. This backlog, combined with the fact that Sala IV routinely suspends a law or procedure in a pending case, has often slowed down decisionmaking and action. For months, and sometimes for over a year, the Sala has, for example, prevented the Ministry of Health from confiscating allegedly unsafe food or drugs, the police from conducting searches and seizures, drunk drivers from being given Breathalyser tests, and the municipality of San José from opening a much-needed new landfill. Many feel, therefore, that the court has contributed to the maddeningly slow pace of needed action and change.

Others believe that Sala IV, like the new Ombudsman's Office, would not be so overloaded if public administration were more efficient and caring and people in general less frustrated. "For the great majority of Costa Ricans," however, "the Constitutional Court has been . . . an escape valve that lets us continue to believe in our democracy."[37]

Lawyer Ricardo Lankester offers yet another explanation for Sala IV's heavy caseload. The 1949 constitution, he says, was an unrealistic hybrid of the 1871 constitution and the *liberacionistas'* social democratic ideology. Thus the only way many laws or policies could be enacted was to ignore it— one reason many Ticos now advocate a new constitution with fewer, broader, and more flexible provisions.

Government Income and Expenditures

"A government is like the head of a family," says an elderly *campesino*. "If it does poorly, everyone suffers. We have become very developed but only by going deeply into debt. And now we will suffer because of it." A cabdriver echoes his words: "The government is like a poor family, always borrowing, leaving projects half-finished, digging one hole in order to fill another." A prime example of such fund juggling, noted earlier, is the central government's growing habit of borrowing from "autonomous" agencies. Indeed, the 1996 internal debt of $3.7 billion, though almost identical to the foreign debt, caused far more concern among Costa Ricans, due perhaps to its far more rapid growth, and led President Figueres to propose such controversial measures as the sale of a major state bank as well as some beaches (all of which had been public). In a pattern evident since 1982, each new president complains that his predecessor has left the public coffers empty, imposes austerity measures during his first two years, then attempts to restore his popularity by a spending spree in his last two years. This then provokes a new fiscal crisis.[38]

About three-fourths of central government funds come, however, from indirect taxes such as those on sales and imports. Since all consumers pay the same percentage on purchases, those least able to pay are hit hardest.

Employers are required to pay corporate income taxes, payroll taxes, and Social Security Fund premiums for their employees. Although taxes on personal salaries increased by 70 percent between 1985 and 1990, businessmen and private-sector professionals paid only 5 percent more. According to tax authorities, only 12 percent of doctors, dentists, engineers, and architects declared income for 1992–1993. Revenue is further reduced by legal loopholes and deductions and by the ease of tax evasion in a country where white-collar crime is largely ignored. "Costa Ricans seem to have created a culture in which cheating the tax collector is an act to be celebrated," says a former minister of the economy. Nearly 90 percent of income taxes and 65 percent of sales taxes, by one estimate, go unpaid, mostly by big business. In 1994 alone these unpaid taxes amounted to more than twice the fiscal debt.[39]

Property taxes account for even less tax revenue—about 3 percent in 1996. This policy of very low property taxes, often uncollected, encourages people to build luxurious houses and hang on to uncultivated land rather than invest in productive enterprises.[40] There is no tax on foreign-source income and only a 1 percent tax on capital gains.

Even when tax revenues are high, expenditures outrun them. (This is an old story. A large deficit is so typical of the annual budget that President Daniel Oduber called it "as normal as a rainy day.") The central government pays interest on past loans with new loans. Debt service accounted for 38 percent of the 1994 budget.

Autonomous agencies, such as the Social Security Fund, that "lend" money to the central government (mostly by obligatory purchase of bonds) can do little to ensure repayment. Debts on foreign loans, another major source of revenue, are another matter. The government's desire to qualify for further loans, as we have seen, has been the main reason for its agreement to structural adjustment pacts.

International Relations

Costa Rica has long emphasized three values in its relations with other countries: national sovereignty, neutrality, and peace. In recent decades another theme—concern for its image abroad—has become increasingly important. Like individual Ticos, the nation wants to keep its dignity and to *quedar bien* with everyone.

These values often conflict with one another. Ever since independence, for example, Costa Rica's relations with other Central American countries have vacillated between isolation and cooperation. Costa Rica has signed many of the hundreds of trade agreements among these countries; its presidents and foreign ministers have attended numerous regional conferences on issues ranging from energy-grid interconnection to sustainable development. But national concerns still rank far ahead of regional solidarity, and Costa Rica's concern over its fiscal deficit led it, in 1995, to raise tariffs on imports from other Central American countries above the agreed regional tariff.

Economic ties with large, prosperous nations have been crucial to foreign policy for over 150 years: first the coffee trade with Britain, then the power of U.S. banana interests, and currently the demands of international creditors. Relations with the United States became crucial after the 1914 opening of the Panama Canal and during the U.S. Marines' occupation of Nicaragua between 1912 and 1934. They became even more important when U.S. funds built the Pan-American Highway during and after World War II. The United States is Costa Rica's principal trading partner, its biggest source of foreign aid and tourism dollars, and, for good or ill, the strongest foreign influence on its government and its popular culture.

Since the abolition of its army in 1949, Costa Rica has acquired an international reputation as a peaceful country, enhanced by the award of the Nobel Peace Prize to President Oscar Arias for his role in ending wars in El Salvador and Nicaragua. Its spokesmen are listened to respectfully in international forums such as the United Nations and the 1992 Earth Summit.

Relations with Nicaragua have long been troubled by dictatorship, civil war, and the constant furtive flow of destitute Nicaraguan immigrants seeking work. The Organization of American States (OAS) supported Costa Rica in 1955 when, as we noted in Chapter 2, armies of Nicaraguan president Anastasio Somoza, a friend of the exiled Calderón Guardia and bitter personal and ideological enemy of President Pepe Figueres, abetted an invasion by *calderonistas;* Costa Rican youths flocked to join defending forces and turned them back under air cover provided by the OAS. From then on most Ticos hated the Somoza dynasty, and after revolution broke out in 1978 many approved of the support given the rebellious Sandinistas by the Carazo administration (1978–1982).

In November 1978 Costa Rica severed diplomatic relations with the Somoza government and expropriated the dictator's land in Guanacaste. Some Costa Ricans severely criticized their government for violating neutrality and objected to allowing Sandinista forces to train in the northern jungles near the border, but most were jubilant over the Sandinistas' 1979 victory. Relations with the new government were cordial at first. But many Ticos soon grew anxious about having as their neighbor a Marxist state with ties to the Soviet Union and Cuba.

Costa Rica's sovereignty and neutrality were soon repeatedly violated not only by Nicaragua but also by the U.S. government. Relations with the United States became difficult; Costa Rica's presidents in the 1980s dealt with the problem in different ways.

In 1981 Rodrigo Carazo reversed his policy of nonalignment and adopted the anti-Sandinista rhetoric of the Reagan administration. His successor, Luís Alberto Monge (1982–1986), wavered in actions and statements between neutrality and belligerence toward Nicaragua, depending on his audience and what he expected of it. Citing the nation's tradition of peace, which made it a "spiritual power," in 1983 he issued the Declaration of Perpetual, Active, and Unarmed Neutrality, "a model of ambiguity and not a decision," never made law.[41] It was unrealistic in view of Ticos' fear of Marxism and growing U.S. insistence that Costa Rica support the Nicaraguan counterrevolutionaries (Contras). After 1984, under pressure from Costa Rican business and industrial groups, Monge tilted toward the U.S. position. With Monge's tacit compliance, high U.S. officials, including the ambassador to

Costa Rica, arranged to build a secret landing strip for Contra planes in the thinly populated northern zone and to train Contras on Costa Rican territory.

This shift in foreign policy, along with the adoption of free-market economic policy, was in effect "something of a quid pro quo for critical economic support."[42] Declaring Costa Rica a "showcase for democracy," the Reagan and Bush administrations poured more than $1 billion into the country. Between 1983 and 1985 alone, this aid amounted to over a third of the government's operating expenditures.[43] At one point only Israel was receiving more U.S. aid per capita. Much of it financed military training and equipment for Costa Rican police. A great deal went to private-sector banks, universities, and other institutions in hopes of destroying public-sector agencies and creating a more favorable climate for U.S. investment.[44]

Monge's successor, Oscar Arias (1986–1990), took a more independent stance. Accusing Monge of having violated Costa Rica's neutrality, he refused to cooperate with the United States in fighting the Nicaraguan government. When U.S. ambassador Lewis Tambs left in 1987, he was forbidden ever to return on the grounds that he had tried to arm the Nicaraguan Contras in northern Costa Rica and had violated Costa Rican neutrality.

In the 1990s U.S. aid was cut drastically as Central America became more peaceful. Several points of friction remained. One was the problem of nonpayment for land expropriated from U.S. owners, which after seventeen years was finally submitted to the International Center for the Settlement of Investment Disputes for arbitration in March 1995.

Another problem came from an unexpected source—organized labor. In 1988 Costa Rican union leaders, spurred by the AFL-CIO and threatened by structural adjustment and the rise of *solidarismo*, documented abuses before the International Labor Organization (ILO). In 1991 the ILO study commission concluded that Costa Rican workers were unprotected against reprisals for union activity. AFL-CIO leaders pressured the U.S. Department of Commerce to revoke Costa Rica's privileged trade position on the grounds that union organizers are routinely fired and strikers blacklisted—a violation of Costa Rica's own labor code. Ironically, this repression had been encouraged by USAID and by international (largely U.S.-based) lending agencies.

While these and other violations of Costa Rica's sovereignty anger many Costa Ricans, their anger is softened by their admiration for many aspects of U.S. culture and by such enterprises as student exchanges and scholarships, road- and bridge-building projects by U.S. Army engineers, and many small-scale efforts by groups of U.S. and Costa Rican citizens, such as the Minnesota sister-cities project.

Though the United States looms very large in Costa Rica's foreign affairs, its relations with other countries are increasingly important. The governments as well as nongovernmental agencies of many other countries—notably Japan, Taiwan, the Netherlands, and Canada—give technical aid and grants for ecological projects, industrial and management training, and health care. Summit conferences of various blocs, bargaining over export quotas, and other involvements help explain why this tiny country has a relatively large foreign service: ambassadors and consuls in forty-nine countries in 1997.

Summary and Conclusion

Costa Rica is hailed worldwide as a model democracy. Ticos themselves are proud of their long history—particularly evident in the past half-century—of fair elections, high voter turnout, and absence of military influence. Post-1948 reforms, such as the creation of numerous autonomous institutions, further limited executive power and promoted political stability while bringing prosperity to some and decent living conditions to many more.

But many of these same reforms have also limited government effectiveness and long-term planning, fostered corruption, and drained national resources into a huge, poorly coordinated bureaucracy. When the state has acted decisively, it has usually done so because of pressure from upper-class interest groups, striking civil servants, international creditors, or foreign governments, chiefly that of the United States.

In recent years, government has lost not only much effectiveness but much of its legitimacy as Ticos' faith in their political institutions has waned. Their doubts and anxieties, expressed repeatedly in polls and casual conversation and shown in the growing reliance on handguns and private guards, may be in part a reaction to disappointed expectations under structural adjustment after three decades of the welfare state. We heard far fewer Ticos boast about "our classless democracy" during the 1980s and 1990s than in earlier decades.

Cynicism about politicians' motives, long common in Costa Rica, has grown, and many people say public officials grow rich at the public's expense. "Things are getting worse all the time" is a frequent lament, as is "There's no real choice between parties any more." Recent polls show that the government agency with the most credibility is Sala IV, the Constitutional Court, which has often stymied the actions of other branches of government.

Given such perceptions of the ineffectiveness and corruption of government and the consequent erosion of its legitimacy, President Figueres's 1995 declaration that Costa Rica had become ungovernable seems less of an exaggeration.

We share, nonetheless, some of Olivier Dabene's optimism about the future of Costa Rican democracy:

It would seem that the system knows how to profit even from crises to reinforce its stability. This may seem paradoxical in a country that we have described as almost at a complete standstill. But this immobilism affects only the implementation of public policies, while democracy is fostered by many other elements of a symbolic, cultural, and even religious nature.

In Costa Rica, democracy is carefully protected. It is cared for like a machine. . . . And it is maintained as a conversation is maintained—by means of perpetual discourse or propaganda which is very audible in a small country and believable because it is based on the historical heritage. The world of representations is a substitute for reality and democracy is lived by the Costa Ricans in the symbolic or religious order of things. . . . The collective belief . . . is the firm basis [of democratic institutions].[45]

Dabene might be more pessimistic today than he was in the mid-1980s. But Ticos' own growing despair about their government and political systems indicates, we think, that they continue to judge these systems by democratic ideals.

Notes

1. Olivier Dabene, *Costa Rica: Juicio a la democrácia* (San José: Facultad Latinoamericana de Ciencias Sociales, 1992), p. 356.

2. Carlos José Gutiérrez, "Cambios en el sistema jurídico costarricense," in Juan Manuel Villasuso, ed., *El nuevo rostro de Costa Rica* (San José: CEDAL, 1992), p. 370.

3. Alberto Salóm E., "Donde está el primer poder?" *La Nación*, May 20, 1994, p. 15A.

4. George Guess, "Narrowing the Base of Costa Rican Democracy," *Development and Change*, Vol. 9, No. 4, 1978, pp. 599–609. The Partido Liberación Nacional proclaimed in 1997 that its own legislative candidates would be more democratically chosen in all future elections.

5. John M. Carey, *Term Limits and Legislative Representation* (Cambridge: Cambridge University Press, 1996), p. 107.

6. Ibid., pp. 112–113.

7. Charles Denton, *Patterns of Costa Rican Politics* (Boston: Allyn & Bacon, 1971), p. 42; and Ronald Fernández Pinto, "Estabilidad y subdesarrollo: Un análisis preliminario de la burocrácia en Costa Rica," *Revista de Ciencias Sociales* (UCR), No. 11, April 1976.

8. Cited in Juan Jaramillo Antillón, *Salud y seguridad social* (San José: UCR, 1993), p. 523.

9. Ivan Molina and Steven Palmer, *Historia de Costa Rica* (San José: EUCR, 1997), p. 111.

10. *La República*, May 12, 1994, p. 11B.

11. Dabene, *Costa Rica,* p. 312.

12. Luís Paulino Vargas Solís, "Las dos cabezas de un partido único?" *La República*, June 19, 1993, p. 15A.

13. Jorge Rovira M., "El nuevo estilo nacional del desarrollo," in Villasuso, *El nuevo rostro,* p. 453.

14. Silvia Lara, Tom Barry, and Peter Simonson, *Inside Costa Rica* (Albuquerque: Resource Center Press, 1995), p. 13.

15. Larissa Minsky and Alvaro Alvarado, "Metamórfosis de las campañas políticas" (quoting *La Prensa Libre* of August 18, 1909), *La Nación*, September 6, 1992, *Revista Dominical*, pp. 6–11.

16. Alberto Cañas, "Chisporroteos," *La República*, September 18, 1993, p. 21A.

17. Juan Rafael Quesada Camacho, "Se compran votos!" *La República*, December 6, 1993, p. 27A.

18. Editorial, "Reflexión al nuevo gobierno," *La República*, February 16, 1994, p. 18A.

19. *Tico Times*, January 17, 1992.

20. Eva María Guevara, Raimundo Quesada, Damaris Salazar, Clotilde Benavides, and Alfredo Aymerich, "Vida cotidiana en la colonia, 1680–1821," Lic. Thesis in History, UCR, October 1994, pp. 190, 268.

21. Anacristina Rossi, "Desea usted saber que pasa con las leyes?" *Rumbo*, July 20, 1993, p. 6.

22. Dabene, *Costa Rica*, p. 115.

23. Oscar Arias, *Quién gobierna en Costa Rica? Un estudio de liderazgo formal en Costa Rica* (San José: EDUCA, 1976), p. 53.

24. Dabene, *Costa Rica*, p. 181. See also Robert Hervey Trudeau, "Costa Rican Voting: Its Socioeconomic Correlates," Ph.D. Dissertation, University of North Carolina at Chapel Hill, 1971, p. 192; and Jorge Enrique Romero Pérez, *La social democracia en Costa Rica* (San José: Trejos, 1977), pp. 170–171.

25. Dabene, *Costa Rica*, p. 156.

26. Teresa Quirós M. and Jorge Vargas C., "Camaras empresariales en Costa Rica," Lic. Thesis, Universidad Nacional Autónoma (UNA), 1985.

27. John A. Booth, "Democracy and Citizen Action in Costa Rica: The Modes and Correlates of Popular Participation in Politics," Ph.D. Dissertation, University of Texas at Austin, 1975. See also his "Political Participation in Latin America," *Latin American Research Review*, Vol. 14, No. 3, 1979, p. 38.

28. Arias, *Quién gobierna*, figs. 46–48.

29. Leslie Anderson, "Alternative Action in Costa Rica: Peasants as Positive Participants," *Journal of Latin American Studies*, Vol. 22, February 1990, pp. 89–113. Two of the villages were in Limón Province, whose residents have—justifiably—long felt especially neglected, but we frequently heard similar comments from small farmers in the Meseta Central.

30. Charles D. Ameringer, *Democracy in Costa Rica* (New York: Praeger, 1982), p. 14.

31. Macarena Barahona Riera, *Las sufragistas de Costa Rica*, Lic. Thesis, UCR, 1994, p. 151.

32. Mario Leyton Rojas, "La contracultura del chorizo," *La Nación*, October 5, 1992, p. 18A.

33. Reported in *Tico Times*, August 8, 1997, p. 16.

34. Julio Rodríguez, "Setiembre de 1993," *La Nación*, October 5, 1993, p. 15A.

35. Daniel Camacho, *La dominación cultural en el subdesarrollo* (San José: ECR, 1983). See also Willy Soto, *La manipulación de la información* (San José: Alma Mater, 1985).

36. Roberto Vargas Fallas, "El sueño de la justicia pronta y cumplida," *Aportes*, May 1992, pp. 6–8.

37. Carlos Arguedas, "Un país de ensueño," *La Nación*, June 22, 1992, p. 14A.

38. Lara et al., *Inside Costa Rica*, pp. 56, 58.

39. Alberto Salóm, "Porqué seguimos atrampados?" *Rumbo*, March 20, 1995, p. 14.

40. Miguel Rojas, "Evasión fiscal," *Aportes*, September 1992, pp. 12–13.

41. Dabene, *Costa Rica,* p. 274.

42. Richard Alan White, *The Morass: United States Intervention in Central America* (New York: Harper and Row, 1984), p. 217.

43. Marc Edelman and Joanne Kenen, eds., *The Costa Rica Reader* (New York: Grove Weidenfeld, 1988), p. 189.

44. Martha Honey, *Hostile Acts: U.S. Policy in Costa Rica in the 1980s* (Gainesville: University of Florida Press, 1994), pp. 97–132. See also Lezak Shallat, "AID and the Secret Parallel State," in Edelman and Kenen, *The Costa Rica Reader*, pp. 221–226.

45. Dabene, *Costa Rica*, p. 389.

— 5 —

Class and Ethnicity

COSTA RICANS' LONG-STANDING BELIEF THAT they are a traditionally egalitarian people of European descent has been seriously challenged in recent decades.

When Costa Rica is compared to colonies in which a few European families exploited large numbers of indigenous or African slaves to work mines and plantations, this claim is understandable. In the mid-nineteenth century, foreign visitors noted that even beggars made their rounds on horseback.[1] And most Ticos do look "whiter" than their neighbors to the north and south.

As we noted in Chapter 2, however, even in colonial times Ticos were not as equal in wealth, power, or privilege—or as "white"—as depicted by the "white legend." We now look more closely at class and ethnic stratification.

Class and Ethnicity in the Colonial Period

The wealthier Spaniards headed for the most promising territories in the Americas—those with the most Indians and the richest mines. The *hidalgos* (aristocrats) who came to Costa Rica, by contrast, were largely of Spain's poorer nobility. Arriving (with a few African slaves) to conquer and Christianize the indigenous tribes, they soon set the scene for both class distinctions and interracial mixing.

The Spanish Crown conferred special privileges on *hidalgos*, who controlled the territory from the start.[2] They were the only settlers who could serve on Cartago's municipal council. As other towns were founded these aristocrats named their sons and sons-in-law to municipal office. Their African slaves worked their cacao plantations while Indian serfs raised their food.

Despite colonial *hidalgos'* pride in their noble status and their pure Spanish blood—which in Spain had meant no Moorish ancestors and in America meant no Indian or, especially, African forebears—interracial mixing was "impressively rapid."[3] Very few Spanish women came to Costa Rica in the

97

early colonial period; hence, informal unions between Spanish men and Indian and black women were common.

A 1700 census found 19,293 nonindigenous inhabitants, of whom only 2,416 were classified as Spaniards. (Indians were not enumerated.) Few Spanish migrants arrived during the remainder of the colonial era. Most nonindigenous residents of the colony, then, were *mestizos*. And "the part-Black population . . . increased continually throughout the colonial period; from 170 individuals in 1569 . . . to 8,929 [or 1 out of 6] by 1801."[4] But even these "mixed-bloods" spoke Spanish, practiced Catholicism, and adopted other elements of Spanish culture.

Biological amalgamation and cultural assimilation were not, however, accompanied by residential and social mixing. Cartago neighborhoods were segregated according to degree of "racial purity." As the Indian population dwindled because of disease and shipment to Peru, black slaves were taken to Guanacaste to work the cattle ranches. Many colonists of mixed African and European ancestry migrated voluntarily to Guanacaste, hoping to encounter less discrimination there. Many of them, too, worked on ranches; others farmed, hunted, and fished.[5]

By the late eighteenth century status distinctions had become much less sharp. The fathers of poor "white" girls, whether or not they could claim noble ancestry, often gave the girls in marriage to somewhat wealthier persons of mixed ancestry or to illegitimate sons of *hidalgos*. Children sired by masters with their slaves or servants were often tacitly recognized as part of the master's family and eventually married people of similar status in other families.

Most of today's Costa Ricans inherit from their colonial ancestors this mixture of European, Indian, and African ancestry. After five decades of research, University of Costa Rica geneticists Bernal Morera and Ramiro Barrantes declared in 1995 that almost all Costa Ricans are *mestizos* with varying combinations of the general population's mix of genes: 40–60 percent white, 15–35 percent Indian, and 10–20 percent black.[6] The mix varies according to region and socioeconomic status.

Whereas racial distinctions were blurred by the late colonial era—the late eighteenth and early nineteenth centuries—class distinctions were somewhat sharper, though less so than in other Spanish colonies. As noted in Chapter 2, the majority of colonists—subsistence farmers—had far less prestige, power, and wealth than the families claiming aristocratic ancestry.

In 1800 about 20 percent of the "Spanish" population of the four main towns were *hidalgos,* most of whom resided in Cartago and Heredia. Throughout the colonial era, Cartagans felt they controlled the destiny of the colony. The old elite families (few of whom by 1800 could legitimately claim pure Spanish blood) monopolized political power and continued to do so after independence from Spain.

Independence and Coffee Power: 1821-1940

The twenty-eight most influential members of this intermarried and tightly knit elite signed the Act of Independence; twenty-three of them were close relatives.

Whatever else they were, most of the elite were also merchants. Abundant land and a scarcity of landless peons meant that land was not a major source of wealth or prestige. But trade, even retail trade, was.[7] A German traveler noted in about 1830: "On market day the President of the Republic does not disdain to cut some yards of gingham for a peasant. . . . Behind the improvised counters there are officials, captains, and majors selling nails and scissors; magistrates of the Supreme Court sell cotton socks; lawyers find buyers for underwear."[8] This same elite retained its power after the 1840s through control of the new coffee trade. But the coffee boom did not change Costa Rica from the mythical rural democracy of small landowners to a semifeudal society of land barons and peons.

True, the biggest coffee planters soon owned processing plants, controlled access to credit and export markets, and monopolized political power. Paid in advance by their European customers, exporters in turn contracted with smaller growers for their harvests and loaned them part of the agreed-upon price, at high interest rates, for their expenses.[9] The coffee elite consolidated their landholdings through intermarriage and through foreclosure on loans, which turned some peasants into peons.

But small growers remained numerous and by the mid-1800s constituted a middle class.[10] The fact that coffee was an appropriate crop for the small farmers already settled in the Central Valley is probably more significant for the stability of Costa Rican democracy over the past 150 years than is the settlement pattern of colonial days.

Although they had many other economic interests besides coffee, nineteenth-century members of the upper class, largely descended from the colonial *hidalgos*, were called the *cafetaleros*. Different factions of this elite competed for political power but usually united to further their common interests. They controlled taxes, granted themselves exemptions and subsidies, and spent government revenues on roads and railroads that would facilitate shipping.

Especially in the first decades of coffee export, owner and worker mingled at cockfights, baptisms, and harvest feasts. As late as the 1940s, many *cafetaleros* managed their farms and processing plants themselves and had direct contact with their laborers. As they became absentee landlords, however, the tastes and lifestyles of the more affluent nineteenth-century planters diverged toward urban and European ways. Many traveled to Europe and educated their sons abroad; they embraced European arts as well as fashion and cuisine. Anyone with pretensions to "culture" spoke French. *Cafetaleros* living in the capital were now more likely to take their wives and children to formal dances and concerts than to join their workers at cockfights when they visited their farms.

When the first rich coffee planters died, their most capable sons or sons-in-law usually inherited their holdings, and the others had to seek wealth and prestige elsewhere. Many studied for the professions, especially law and medicine. They tended to be less conservative than those who stayed on the land, more open to new ideas and change.[11]

As the elite became ever wealthier in the mid-nineteenth century they insisted ever more strongly (and, as we have seen, often falsely) on their "pure European stock" and ridiculed their rivals with racial epithets. Official portraits showed some presidents as lighter-skinned than they really were.[12]

Though the elite were reluctant to marry down, coffee enabled many Costa Ricans to climb socially. The few who went from rags to riches typically began with a small farm and perhaps an oxcart transport business, later investing in more farms and eventually in processing plants.[13] But only after their children acquired foreign degrees and upper-class lifestyles were they accepted by the elite.

As the needs of government and commercial interests for well-trained employees grew during the nineteenth century, the government opened several high schools in and near San José, and their graduates joined the older middle class of small businessmen and professionals such as teachers. At the same time the number of urban workers and craftsmen also grew.

Income alone was not the major source of prestige, for an artisan might earn more than a higher-ranking teacher. Class position was also determined by occupation, educational attainment, and lifestyle. (A teacher, unlike an artisan, considered a domestic servant essential to his status.)

The leading personage in Central Valley villages was the *gamonal*, a well-to-do landowner who still lived as simply as he had before he prospered and continued to work alongside his peons, who respected him not only for his wealth but also for his maturity, honesty, and common sense. Because his workers voted as he did, the *gamonal* was much courted by politicians from the capital, beginning with the 1909 election, when two descendants of Juan Vázquez de Coronado vied for the presidency and one of them, Ricardo Jiménez, went to all the *gamonales* on the Meseta with promises to decentralize government and thus enhance their power.

Residents of large towns outside San José distinguished between *la clase social* and *la clase obrera*. As anthropologists noted in 1942, the *clase social* included wealthy planters, businessmen and professionals, municipal officials, teachers, and white-collar workers. The *clase obrera* (working class), also called *el pueblo* (the people), included rural and urban laborers, artisans, vendors, servants, and other manual workers. Residents of San José distinguished three classes. Members of the upper class, set apart by both lineage and wealth, had little contact with the small businessmen, intellectuals, and white-collar workers of the middle class, and even less with the lower class.[14]

Although family background was still important—especially in choosing a spouse—wealth, occupation, and education also weighed heavily. Clothing was a much clearer sign of status than it is now; perhaps half the Ticos went barefoot all or much of the time.[15] Another clue to status, valid for a century or more, was whether a family had servants or potentially were servants.[16]

The picture of class structure in the nation as a whole rather than just the Central Valley was more complex. Just as the coffee barons had been obliged to share power with British financiers, so the banana trade and the Atlantic Railroad further diluted the power of the *cafetaleros,* who relinquished much of it, willy-nilly, to U.S. companies around the turn of the century. At the same time, at the other end of the social scale, a new proletariat of Afro-Caribbean immigrants was growing; its members were long confined to the Caribbean coastal enclave of the United Fruit Company.

By the 1940s many middle- and upper-class Ticos insisted that theirs was a classless society, a claim that we still heard occasionally in the late 1960s.[17] This claim—made by people who in most respects seemed quite aware of status differences—resulted perhaps from the indistinct boundaries between the urban middle and upper classes as individual fortunes rose and ebbed; from the fact that degrees of wealth, power, and prestige did not always coincide; and from the middle class's access to such status symbols as imported clothing.

Rising Expectations: 1948–1978

Middle-class Ticos' economic frustrations, however, were largely responsible for the 1948 civil war. The economy was stagnant because the wealthy descendants of the early coffee barons were reluctant to risk investing in new enterprises.[18] The middle class—especially urban professionals and small businessmen—had little power and saw little chance of advancement unless the country began to industrialize. Many saw hope for such change in Pepe Figueres's Army of National Liberation. *Calderonistas* and communists were also eager to break the status quo, but they stressed a more even distribution of wealth rather than increased production. Some *cafetaleros* joined each side; many others felt that both sides threatened their interests.

Leaders of the victorious Partido Liberación Nacional (PLN) claim that they achieved the aims of both groups—modernization and social justice. Their party, they say, democratized the society by giving more people a share of both wealth and political power, at least until the economic crisis of 1979–1982. Indeed, the mass education, industrialization, and social welfare policies and the growing bureaucracy promoted by the PLN raised the general level of living and created new opportunities for many Ticos. The myth of classlessness gradually gave way to the myth that Costa Ricans were all middle class.

For three decades after 1948, more Costa Ricans rose than fell from their parents' social class. Many children of working-class parents attained middle-class status (as nurses, teachers, office workers, accountants, etc.) thanks to the expansion of schooling and of the public payroll. And as the country became more urban and industrial, many who would otherwise have been domestic servants or farm laborers like their parents instead got factory or construction jobs; learned a trade at the public-sector National Institute of Apprenticeship; or became sales clerks, waiters, or cabdrivers. Able to buy many things their parents had never dreamed of, they fully expected their children to climb even higher on the social ladder.

In 1950, according to one study, roughly 12 percent of Ticos formed the middle class; by the late 1970s, some 28 percent. They served as a "mattress" between the upper and lower classes, preserving social and political stability.[19] Even during the era of rapid development, however, upward mobility remained impossible for at least a quarter of all Ticos. Those living in remote areas lacked access to schooling; many who migrated to the city in hope of a better life found themselves struggling for mere survival. During those decades, however, government health services, schools, potable water, and help to the indigent spread to much of the country. Electricity, telephone service, and television reached ever farther. Government housing projects helped relieve the pressure of rapid urban growth.

Changes Since 1981

Expansion of the middle class ended with recession in 1979, followed in 1981 by sharp devaluation of the colón in 1981 and accompanying inflation, which continued at a slower rate well into the 1990s. (In early 1979 the rate of exchange was 8.6 to the dollar; by mid-1998, 255.) Real wages and salaries fell by 40 percent between 1979 and 1982. The number of poor families doubled from 1980 to 1983. Middle-class Costa Ricans suddenly felt poor, too.

Although salaries began to recover some of their lost buying power by 1984, the average Tico's income bought less in the mid-1990s than in 1978. In 1980 the median middle-class salary was three times that of a laborer. By 1983 it was only 2.5 times as much, and in 1992, barely double. It was not that the lower class had gained buying power but that the middle class had lost it.[20] Once-secure civil servants who had expected one promotion after another and retirement on a comfortable pension now felt uncertain even about job security, as the PAEs demanded austerity and reduction of the public payroll. A university degree no longer served as a virtual guarantee of a public-sector position.

Some professionals and technicians entered the competitive private sector, seeking opportunities in tourism, banking, the agroexport industry, and telecommunications. More family members, especially wives, entered the job market for the first time.

Many tried to stretch their salaries by moonlighting and by the coping strategies of *polaquear* and *camaronear,* described in Chapter 3. A teacher who had given up his car and now sold used clothing door-to-door in his free time to stretch his salary told us in 1992, as have many other Ticos since then, "The middle class is disappearing." At the same time, many sacrificed to patronize private schools and doctors as public education and the public health system deteriorated.

Not only have devaluation and inflation reduced the buying power of wages and salaries but the tax system has become ever more regressive. From 1983 to 1990 the share of government tax revenues from indirect taxes rose from 47.2 percent to 71 percent, demanding most from those least able to pay. At the same time revenue from direct taxes (such as income and corporate taxes) fell from 44.4 percent to 18.7 percent.

Signs of great poverty and considerable wealth have both increased: Lines of washing along the edges of bridges betray the presence of abysmally poor families living below. Nearby stand new high-rise condominiums and shopping malls fringed by luxury cars. The distance between the top and bottom of the social pyramid has, according to some studies, grown dramatically. In 1973 the richest 16 percent of Costa Ricans received an average income sixteen times greater than the poorest 10 percent, reports Martha Honey. By 1990 the share of the top tenth was thirty-one times greater.[21] CEPAL, the UN Economic Commission for Latin America, reported that this inequality continued to increase in the early 1990s. Only those in the top 10 percent of the pyramid grew wealthier.[22]

Estimates of the extent of poverty depend on the criteria of measurement and often on the bias of the researchers. Government reports based on the ability to supply a family of four with the official "basket of basic needs" usually place poverty at below 20 percent of the population and declare that it has declined under the current administration.

Likewise, a study funded by USAID insists that the incidence of poverty was lower in 1994 than in 1980 and that income distribution had become slightly more equal. It attributed these changes mainly to a stronger private sector, a decrease in the percentage of the labor force working on farms, smaller households, and an older and better-educated labor force.[23]

Statistician Wilburg Jiménez paints a gloomier picture: About 40 percent of Ticos, he believes, live in some degree of poverty. He further calculates that some 250,000 families—a third of the population—cannot supply the basic necessities.[24] A confidential study leaked from within the Labor Ministry found that these neediest Costa Ricans increased from 21 percent of the population in 1987 to 28 percent in 1992.[25]

Whichever estimate is correct, poverty is, say many, a time bomb—not because the poor face outright starvation but because they are increasingly resentful of the enormous gap in living standards and opportunities between themselves and wealthier Costa Ricans. And the middle class feels squeezed into a "sandwich" rather than a cushion, fearful of slipping downward, less confident of rising.[26]

In 1996 sociologists at the University of Costa Rica described a pyramid of four social classes with two out of three Costa Ricans in "the lower class."[27] We prefer to conceive of a five-level pyramid that corresponds fairly closely with theirs except for this largest category, which many Ticos think of as two fairly distinct classes: the working class and the lower class. Otherwise their model and ours are very similar.

What criteria determine class standing today? Although a few old upper-class families are now active in banking, commerce, or industry, most such families still focus on coffee production and ranching—and on politics.[28] Although they trace their ancestry to the conquistadores, they would be ridiculed by most Ticos if they boasted about this. They now interact with newly rich industrialists and business owners who have no such "old family" ancestry; many are, in fact, the children of Jewish, Italian, or Lebanese immigrant merchants. Both of these strata, together with the families of wealthy executives and professionals and the directors of state bureaucracies, compose an upper class that, according to the 1996 study, includes 4.5 percent of the population.

The upper-middle class includes bureaucrats and professionals of slightly lower rank or wealth, university professors, those industrialists and landowners who lack the wealth and family background to claim elite status, and the new managerial class. The latter emerged in the 1960s and 1970s, when the government began to attract foreign entrepreneurs by means of various subsidies and incentives, and has grown in size and influence in the free-market economy of recent years.

The lower-middle class includes white-collar workers, small-business owners, and poorly paid professionals such as nurses. Some teachers fit into this category, but family connections or a spouse's occupation or income would place others at a higher level. Many Ticos would also place fairly prosperous small farmers in this class. Together, according to the University of Costa Rica study, the families in these two strata make up a middle class that includes about 30 percent of Costa Ricans.

Many members of this class, especially those who work in the private sector, still hope for upward mobility. They depend more on connections and on individual effort (work, study, thrift) than on organization to achieve such private goals as a scholarship, a higher-ranking civil service job, or a government loan. Consequently, they feel little class identity and are slow to join pressure groups of any kind. Bureaucratic employees (including teachers), who often call strikes to achieve their common goals, are the only highly organized middle-class groups.

Low-paid manual and service workers with fairly steady employment are widely considered working class: construction and factory workers, private guards, waiters, cabdrivers, domestic servants, self-employed artisans, urban and rural peons with steady jobs, and small landowners whose farms yield little more than family subsistence. Many work ten-to-fifteen-hour days. Like the middle class, most try to provide as much schooling as possible for their children; place a high value on independence, dignity, and respectability; and fear slipping into the lower class. Many, in fact, see themselves as part of the middle class and are sometimes considered as such by other Ticos.

Sporadically employed urban peons, landless rural peons, and many single mothers and their children are often described as lower class. At the very bottom in prestige in this class are small drug dealers, street vendors, bootblacks, beggars, thieves, garbage-dump scavengers, and prostitutes. In the 1990s, landless rural laborers seemed to fare as badly as urban beggars.

Interaction and Status

Although social class largely determines one's choice of friends, as well as whether one addresses another by the familiar *vos* or the more formal *usted*, easy give-and-take among people of different status is embedded in Costa Rican culture. An elderly bar owner in one highland village comments, "People here, even the richest, act *humilde* [self-effacing, humble]." Much like nineteenth-century coffee planters with their peons, members of today's upper class often assume an air of camaraderie with subordinates. They may change their speech patterns when joking with a street vendor or beggar—who, in turn, may maintain eye contact and show little deference. Observes Dabene, "Frequent contacts with *el pueblo* [the common people] diminish social distances. . . . One must not forget that in Costa Rica, a [small] country . . . the bootblack may perfectly well be the cousin of his banker or entrepreneur client."[29]

Anthropologist Paul Kutche, however, sees a recent change in class attitudes and interaction. As late as 1974 ranchers and farmers told him they had to treat workers as equals because unhappy workers could find other bosses or could migrate. But the closing of the frontier and growing economic uncertainty have changed this, and by 1990, jobs were scarcer, bosses could treat employees more arrogantly, and employees had to tread carefully in order to survive. . . . During my first visit people on the street all might have been yeomen farmers, judging by their proud but simple demeanor. By 1990 the poor no longer spoke quite so much like fully enfranchised people. Public cynicism and the assumption that people with power and wealth were corrupt had increased a great deal.[30]

Likewise, sociologist Carlos Sandoval, in his 1996 participant observation study of construction workers, noted that they typically chose the backseats on public buses. In a similar study of textile *máquilas*, he saw almost no interaction between workers and managers in factory cafeterias or on buses.[31]

How do Ticos judge one another's social class and perhaps demonstrate or try to impress others with their own? Dress is no longer the reliable indicator of class status it was through the 1940s, when half the population went barefoot. Now all but the poorest children wear polished shoes and clean, carefully ironed garments on Sundays and special occasions. Most little girls of the working class, in fact, wear frillier dresses than those of higher status, who are likely to wear colorful shorts, tops, and sandals. And although middle-class office workers often dress down on Friday, working-class employees are more apt to dress up. Sandoval notes that young working-class males, unable to afford such status symbols as cars, may spend three weeks' wages on a pair of Reeboks or Nikes.[32]

With public schooling available to everyone, private schools and university degrees have long been steppingstones to higher status. The mother of five children who attend the prestigious Lincoln School told us in 1996, "My husband's salary just keeps us going; mine pays the children's tuition. It's an investment. They will mingle with the right people and some day they will get to be somebody." A foreign degree, especially from the United States or Europe, is highly prized. But as more Ticos have acquired advanced degrees, the prestige value of an academic or professional title has declined, and a degree, however necessary, is no longer sufficient to guarantee a good job.

In little Costa Rica one reliable clue to status has long been one's family. Unlike North Americans, who ask, "What do you do?" new Tico acquaintances may ask each other's first and second surnames. These are, says journalist Peter Brennan, "like a roadmap to Costa Rican society," revealing "whether the family is one of the oldest in the country, or is well-connected politically"[33]—or, we would add, at least socially respectable. At all levels of the social pyramid, a favorite topic of conversation, especially among women, is the interweaving of kinship ties.

Children once learned this roadmap early, especially in upper- and upper-middle-class families. "When I invited my playmates home," recalls an upper-class woman of sixty-five, "my mother grilled them. 'What family do you belong to?' She wanted to know both surnames. Then what school they attended. That way she could tell if they lived in a good neighborhood."

As the society becomes more complex and impersonal, surnames have become less important, at least to the young, who often introduce themselves by first name or nickname only. Image is sought. "It used to be easier to know who belonged in our circle," says a man in his thirties. "We all went to the same club, the same beach, the same school. Now there are two main classes: the 'Miami' and the nobodies. A certain crowd is totally Miami culture. Those who don't belong may brag to their friends about a trip to the beach or a fishing lodge, and often mention the newest mall; they make up most of it." Going to the beach on holiday "like everyone else" is such an important status symbol to many teens and young adults that even those who dislike camping may pitch tents on the sand and eat food brought from home. Those who can afford hotels and restaurants may sneer at the campers behind their backs as "egg-eaters."

Many Costa Ricans decry the growing importance of image. "No matter how corrupt, a person can rise in social status if he can afford to project the right image, and knows how to carry it off," agree the members of a writing workshop. The trend to large impressive houses and gardens, satellite dishes, and cellular phones (many of them fake) is deplored as evidence of the increase in *consumismo,* which critics see as an effort by *plásticos* (plastic people) to *aparentar* (appear)—that is, to claim high status. *Aparentando* is also facilitated by credit cards and installment plans (which carry high interest rates) and often by the presence of several wage earners in one family, as well as by the new attitude that debt is not shameful. Many poorer Ticos, with similar motives, skimp on food in order to buy stylish clothing for themselves or their children. An upper-class man in his thirties told us in 1996,

> My parents are shocked by the huge mansions people are building these days. When I was a child they still considered a small house, unimpressive from the outside, quite adequate. The real "cachet" was indoors among books, paintings, and other signs of good taste and education. We had to speak only French at dinner, observe the rules of etiquette such as perfect table manners, and never leave the house without being well groomed and properly dressed.

Social psychologist Gabriel Coronado and sociologist María Eugenia Pérez of the Universidad Nacional interviewed members of the urban middle class in 1990. Eighty-seven percent of respondents put possessions highest on their list of perceived needs. At the top of this list were their own house, a car, and household appliances.[34]

A disdain for manual labor persists in urban areas, especially among those concerned about projecting a middle-class image. A naturalized citizen from Canada says of his teenage son, brought up in Costa Rica: "He's typically Costa Rican. He'll paint the house if I ask him to, but he'll scrub and scrub afterward so there's no evidence of it. That's the same attitude I overheard in a group of local teachers. A colleague was fixing a typewriter, and they asked her, 'Why are you doing that? Why not get someone to do it?'" The construction peons with whom Sandoval worked were anxious to conceal their "low, dirty" jobs from new acquaintances, just as they frequently lied about what neighborhood they lived in.[35] In smaller communities, such an image is harder to project, and the attempt to do so may be ridiculed. Several taxi drivers in one small town laughed at the pretensions of another driver who, wanting his daughters to grow up as "ladies," would not allow them to ride buses.

Rural Stratification

The hard manual labor that is part of everyday life in rural areas is no doubt one reason many urban Ticos feel superior *to maiceros* (hicks; from *maíz*—corn). (Residents of San José even applied this term to President Oscar Arias, a native of the town of Heredia, simply because he was not a *josefino*. Urban *diputados*, too, may speak of their rural colleagues this way behind the latters' backs.) Rural Costa Ricans, by contrast, still place the high value on manual labor that anthropologist Victor Goldkind noted in the 1960s and still think most urban employment—especially office work—is greatly overpaid and is not really work at all.[36] They also place much less emphasis on conspicuous consumption than do villagers and city folk. Even young *campesinos* are likely to mention work along with family and health when asked what is most important to them.

Fifty-six percent of all Costa Ricans lived in rural areas in 1992. But 70 percent of the poor were rural, and 55 percent of rural families were poor, according to a study by the Inter-American Development Bank. In the late 1960s we often heard poor Ticos say, "God made the poor. There are some of every kind, and we must be content." Fewer are now resigned to poverty as God's will. As the pressure to acquire land becomes greater, many *campesinos*, as we noted in Chapter 4, join associations and demonstrate for fairer treatment. They may invade private land held by absentee owners, often in militant bands of squatters.

In their members' interactions among themselves rather than with outsiders, some rural communities appear almost classless. Villages and rural areas made up of family farms have long been the most egalitarian communities in Costa Rica. Small landowners, as noted, often work alongside their peons. Says a rural carpenter, "They have known each other since childhood and gone to school together. Landowners take pride in how well they treat their peons. Both are respected according to how hard they work." Likewise, rural people often lend each other money on easier terms than banks would provide. They swap favors, often quite casually, and a visitor may help a neighbor with chores.

The higher class in more densely populated—and more stratified—rural areas includes landowners who employ peons, municipal government officials, the school director and teachers, the parish priest, and local businesspeople. Most of these people live in their canton's central village; consequently, the lion's share of the state's pork-barrel funds for rural cantons goes to such villages. Villagers refer to people in outlying hamlets as *gente de campo,* or country folk. (They in turn are lumped in that category by residents of larger towns.)

As rural communities have become less isolated and as land has become scarcer, class distinctions there have approached the urban pattern. Landowners may send their children to high school and even to a university or to work for a time in the United States, thus enhancing their own prestige in the community while weakening their identification with it. They are now also more likely to seek out friends or commercial amusements in a large town and less likely to share their wealth with poorer kin.

Visiting and mate selection, too, tend to follow class lines. Says a high school boy in a highland village, "Girls here are more impressed by what a boy has in his pocket than in his head." And a sixty-five-year-old small farmer in a nearby hamlet comments, "Both rich and poor greet each other when they pass. But each has his own friends." This comment encapsulates an old truth about social class in Costa Rica: Although one's class position has profound effects on lifestyle and opportunities, it is downplayed in most face-to-face interaction, where the desire to *quedar bien* is paramount.

Racial and Ethnic Minorities

Although most Ticos, as noted earlier, have indigenous and perhaps African as well as European ancestors, few consider themselves *mestizos;* the term is rarely heard. A Costa Rican with evidence of some black or Indian ancestry but Latino cultural traits is usually seen as white.[37]

Even though the 1801 census listed fewer than one in ten as being of entirely Spanish ancestry, by 1850 "whiteness" had become part of the national self-image propagated by the elite. This image included political stability and widespread landownership as well. By the end of the nineteenth century, it also embraced literacy, civilization, and democracy—all traits that were emphasized as praiseworthy contrasts to neighboring countries.

Pride in Costa Ricans' whiteness lingers today. Only recently has mention of it disappeared from tourist literature. TV and newspaper ads use a disproportionate number of very light-skinned models; beauty contestants, especially finalists, are markedly whiter than most Ticos; many are blond.

Many other Central Americans accuse the Ticos of "thinking they're Tarzan's mother"—that is, of feeling superior, in part because their skin is lighter. Indeed, Costa Rican soccer fans often taunt their Central American opponents as *indios*. And many Ticos refer to Centroamérica as if it did not include Costa Rica, usually comparing the region unfavorably to their own country.

Most Ticos are aware of, and often overestimate, the cultural and physical differences between themselves and the most conspicuous minorities— Indians, blacks of West Indian ancestry, Nicaraguans, and Chinese. Although they give lip service to tolerance, many consider members of these groups not only different but also inferior.

Indians

Costa Rican Indians have never been a homogeneous group. The 400,000 or so aborigines living in the area in 1502 belonged to many societies, distinct both politically and culturally. Today's 30,000 Indians—about 1 percent of Costa Rica's population—include members of eight societies. Almost all live as subsistence farmers in seventy-five communities within the twenty-two officially designated Indian reserves, which compose about 6 percent of the national territory.

As we saw in Chapter 2, the feudal *encomienda* system did not flourish in Costa Rica. Though vestiges of slavery survived until 1812, the typical highland colonist perforce became the small farmer now praised as the basis of today's democracy. He had no Indian peons, since most surviving Indians had fled to forests far from Spanish settlements. Many of those who remained in the Central Valley were forced out when coffee transformed the national economy and their land was expropriated. In 1841 Braulio Carrillo "abolished the system of communal Indian territories, supporting and legitimizing the continual usurpations the Indians of the central region had suffered during the expansion of coffee lands."[38]

The twentieth century brought more invasions of Indian lands. Beginning in 1909 the Chiriquí Land Company, a subsidiary of United Fruit, deforested much of the Talamanca Valley near the Caribbean coast, thereby destroying the hunting-gathering economy as well as the traditional leadership structure of its Bribri and Cabecar inhabitants. Indians who did not sell their lands for the pittances the company offered were met with violence and legal chicanery abetted by government officials. Many reacted by sabotaging plantations and railways and eventually fleeing higher into the steep and infertile Talamanca mountains. After heavy floods in the 1920s, the company abandoned the area, and Indians slowly began to return and rebuild. But "important cultural patterns such as [matrilineal] clan structure, collective labor and use of the native languages began to give way to nuclear and patrilineal family structures, salaried work, and the Spanish and English languages."[39]

As the agricultural frontier disappeared and new roads gave outsiders access to the reserves in the 1950s and 1960s, *campesinos* seeking farms invaded Indian lands. Says anthropologist María Eugenia Bozzoli, "Until a few decades ago all Costa Ricans, including the Indians, thought of land as an inexhaustible resource. That's not true any more, and land disputes have become common."[40]

Church and state both exerted authority over the Indians. Catholic priests, for example, insisted on burial in consecrated public cemeteries rather than clan burial grounds. The state refinery, RECOPE, seeking petroleum during the 1973 world oil crisis, was welcomed by some Indians as a source of development and a bridge to the rest of the world. But most saw the company as a further threat to their environmental and cultural integrity, and a Committee in Defense of Indian Rights was soon formed in every community. RECOPE destroyed indigenous traditions far more than did the Spaniards or the Chiriquí Land Company, according to geographer Victoria Villalobos and anthropologist Carlos Borge.[41] It ended isolation from mainstream Costa Rican society and introduced a monetary economy, private property, consumerism, and new and unhealthful dietary habits.

Today, invasion of the Indian reserves by squatters, banana companies, gold prospectors, and timber poachers continues; tourism promoters have also made incursions. And outside agencies, foreign and governmental, by selecting residents other than traditional leaders as conduits for funds, have, however unintentionally, provoked conflict within the reserves.

Villalobos and Borge summarize both change and continuity among the Indians of Talamanca:

> Talamanca . . . travels in boats with outboard motors; keeps up with the news of the world through radio and television; studies in elementary and high schools and in universities; cuts trees with a chainsaw; drinks cold beer; attends Christian services; dances rancheras, salsas, rap and reggae; exports plantains. Its young people like name-brand clothes and drink chicha from plastic glasses; they have electric light and they want computers.
>
> But they are also healed by the Awa; bear the mother's surnames; know to which clan they belong and whom they may marry; respect the norms and rules regarding their relation to the forest; respect their elders; their traditional leaders continue to guard the Indian seed. And they continue to consider themselves the center of the universe—an ethnocentrism that has allowed them to resist all their enemies.[42]

The southern Indians survived by fleeing to almost impenetrable mountains; the Chorotegas of what is now Guanacaste Province were annihilated as a genetically and culturally distinct group. Many of their cultural traits, however, "became part of a 'creole' and *mestizo* culture, as seen in foods,

Guaymí women and child (Mavis Hiltunen Biesanz)

dance, etc. now promoted as 'folklore'" and described in schools and mass media all over the country as Costa Rican traditions.[43]

Costa Rican anthropologists and other social scientists have encouraged mainstream Costa Ricans, as *mestizos*, to value their Indian heritage and to regard contemporary Indians as fellow citizens. And in recent years we have heard more and more Ticos speak not of the "pre-Columbian era" but rather of "our ancient history" and "our indigenous ancestors."

Indians themselves are aware of their losses and their rights. A Bribri woman, age forty-five, told us, "I would like my great-grandchildren to see the wonderful animals I saw as a girl. But they are disappearing." A Guaymí woman addressing the Fourth International Conference of Women in 1993 voiced a common sentiment: "Whites have destroyed the land, water, and woods God gave us to care for. Now we are sentenced to death. Our shamans can no longer find all the medicinal plants they need to cure us. We are losing our language. Soon our customs and culture will be gone. We must teach our kids that we are children of the corn and the sun."

A congressional committee reported in the 1960s that the Indians were miserably poor and exploited and had a high incidence of disease and alcoholism, a low life expectancy, and a high infant mortality rate compared to other Costa Ricans. It urged that they be given full citizenship. Yet not until 1991 did the Legislative Assembly pass a bill declaring that all of Costa Rica's Indians are Costa Rican citizens. Since then they have gradually been issued the ID cards necessary for voting and many ordinary transactions and have been provided access to health care.

Indians are now represented by several associations and by radio stations broadcasting in Indian languages as well as Spanish. They have staged demonstrations and formed a committee that lobbies the Legislative Assembly to require the enforcement of pro-Indian laws.

On Columbus Day, 1992—the 500th anniversary of Columbus's "discovery" of America—President Calderón (who had once stated, on a visit to Spain, that there were no Indians in Costa Rica when Columbus arrived) signed the United Nations Treaty on Indigenous Populations and Tribes. This stands above national laws and guarantees Indians sovereignty over their reserves as well as bilingual education and rights to health care and security. At the same time, the minister of education promised to train teachers in tribal languages and customs. Three years later, under the next administration, a new high school was opened in Talamanca with classes in both Bribri and Spanish.

Some Indian parents complain that their children insist on being considered white. A social scientist who has long worked for Indian rights agrees, saying that many identify themselves as Indians only when they have something to gain, such as scholarships or the right to live on a reserve.

But many Indians see their problems as solvable, not as an inevitable fate to which they should passively succumb. Some add that Indians have much to teach other Costa Ricans about cooperation, herbal medicines, and ecology, which they can do only if their cultures and reserves are protected.

Freddy, age twenty, may indicate the direction of change as well as the possibility of preserving Indian cultures. We found him, during a university vacation in 1991, digging a drainage ditch on a small banana farm with his father, a contract laborer from Guanacaste. As a child, Freddy was never interested in his mother's Bribri heritage. Now in his fourth year of studying computer science at a public university, he finds that his classmates want to know about Bribri culture; so he asks his mother's parents for stories of old times and is trying to learn Bribri. "Many are ashamed to admit they're Indians. I'm not; I'm proud!"

Blacks

Today's "black" Costa Ricans are not descended from the few slaves brought to the colony by early Spanish explorers and settlers. Such descendants were almost completely assimilated by the end of the colonial era. Vestiges of their culture and physiognomy remain strongest in Guanacaste, where black slaves and free *mulatos* worked on colonial haciendas. But those who exhibit these traces are not seen as black or part black; as elsewhere in Latin America, one's *raza* depends more on culture than on ancestry.

Some Afro-Caribbeans came to Costa Rica's eastern shore as early as 1824, intending to stay. They were turtle fishermen and farmers who planted the coast south of Port Limón in coconut palms, marketing the nuts and oil and a few crops such as cacao. For 170 years their descendants were nearly self-sufficient.[44]

Most of today's blacks are descendants of the West Indians, mostly Jamaicans, recruited in the late nineteenth century to work on the Atlantic Railroad. They stayed to work on the new east coast banana plantations and were later joined by newer West Indian immigrants. Many expected to return to their native islands with a sizable nest egg. Loyal to their British heritage in the heyday of the empire, they were content to live apart from the Latinos, whose language, religion, hygiene, and easygoing work habits they despised.[45]

"White" Costa Ricans, too, preferred such segregation. Wages in the banana zone, however, were five or six times higher than those in the highlands, and work was steady year-round. In the mid-1920s work became scarce in the highlands and the east coast was far more healthful—as a result of the efforts of the United Fruit Company—than it had been when the first West Indians arrived. Many highlanders went to work in Puerto Limón, and tension arose between them and the blacks. Conflict focused on access to jobs, treatment on the job, and status in the strict hierarchy of United Fruit Company towns. Ticos resented the blacks, believing they monopolized the higher-paid supervisory, technical, and clerical jobs simply because they spoke English.[46] (In fact, United Fruit managers had found blacks to be trustworthy and hardworking; most blacks were the grandchildren of slaves and thus, says Bourgois, found the company's working conditions more "normal" than did Latinos or European immigrants.)[47] Purcell argues that the company also exploited ethnic tensions: "In fact, the Company imported laborers from different West Indian islands to avoid labor solidarity. Exploiting deep-seated black-Hispanic divisions required little effort. When blacks went on strike, the Company used Hispanic strike breakers and vice versa."[48]

When United Fruit abandoned its blight-ridden Caribbean plantations in the 1930s and transferred its operations to the Pacific coast, it offered to resettle its workers there. But President Ricardo Jiménez, in a 1934 decree, forbade the company to transfer "colored" employees, arguing that relocation would upset the country's "racial balance" and possibly cause "civil commotion."[49] His interior minister added that relocation "would endanger the racial purity of the Costa Rican." The decree was repealed in 1949.

West Indian immigrants and their descendants, according to an estimate based on the 1973 census—the last to ask about racial or ethnic origin—numbered perhaps 35,000 in that year, about 2 percent of Costa Rica's population (down from 4.6 percent in the 1950 census) and 40 percent of that of Limón Province. By 1983 so many had emigrated to the central highlands that only an estimated 29 percent of *limonenses* were black.[50] Few are left of the last immigrant generation, which arrived in the 1930s. These immigrants continued to practice the customs of their home islands and never dreamed that they might stay on and raise their children in the new land. They sent their children to private schools that used Jamaican texts in English and took them to the Baptist and Anglican churches on Sunday. They were indignant over a 1910 law that their children had to attend public schools or pay a fine of ten colones a day.[51]

The first generation of Antillean blacks born in Costa Rica had no country, for they were not recognized as British subjects and Costa Rica denied them citizenship. Forbidden to own land, they often lost their small subsistence farms to whites with bogus documents in Spanish, a language they could not read. Blacks' position improved after the 1948 civil war, during which many had joined the rebel forces of Pepe Figueres, who won their loyalty by speaking English, dancing with them, and kissing their babies. Soon after the war, Figueres decreed that anyone born in Costa Rica had all the rights of citizenship.

From then on blacks began to enter politics, move to San José, attend public schools, and assimilate culturally. The university graduating class of 1957 was the first to contain many black professionals. By the 1970s, thanks in part to a cacao boom, many children of black cacao farmers had entered professions throughout Costa Rica. (Maureen Clarke, José María Figueres's first minister of justice, is a black woman.) Although a leaf fungus later forced many cacao farmers into agricultural wage labor, rural blacks' average income remained higher than that of rural Latinos.[52] Most blacks in Limón Province today work as clerks, artisans, independent farmers, and fishermen; fewer now work for the banana companies.

But prejudice and discrimination persist. The idea that blacks are not really Ticos is often stated or implied. Many "white" Costa Ricans tell jokes depicting blacks as stupid and ugly and consider them good only for sports and music. A 1993 cartoon in *La Nación* depicted blacks as cannibals.[53]

According to black novelist Quince Duncan, the mass media and school texts paint blacks as lazy, criminal, and addicted to drugs rather than as the honest, hard workers that most of them are.[54] (In 1995 we saw several articles in leading newspapers that identified criminal suspects as being "of the black race"; white suspects were not identified as such.)

The Limón tradition has been trilingual, observes Trevor Purcell: A *limonense* would switch from Spanish to standard Caribbean English or to a local Creole dialect of English, depending on the situation. Today fewer speak Limón Creole, but most are fluent in Spanish and in American English (familiar from school, tourism, and TV).[55]

Although most adopt Spanish and other elements of Costa Rican culture as they reach their midteens, they generally remain at least nominally Protestant. Though their interest in reggae and Rastafarianism suggests that many young blacks still feel links to black coastal and island societies of the western Caribbean, they are also increasingly demanding their full rights as Costa Rican citizens, and many insist they are not blacks but Ticos.[56]

Still, black-pride groups have arisen; members protest the lack of black history and culture in school textbooks, and some now teach the subjects to mixed private classes. In 1994 the Association for Afro–Costa Rican Development was established. The voters of Limón Province, offended that the PLN had not put a single black on the 1994 congressional ballot for Limón, gave that vote to the PUSC, although they did support José María Figueres for president because they perceived him to be fun-loving, tough, and confident through many trials—like themselves.[57]

Chinese

Immigrants from China's Canton Province, impoverished by the opium wars, began to arrive in the mid-nineteenth century; many found work as peons and domestic servants of Costa Rican and German coffee growers. The influx soon became so great that an 1862 law forbade immigration of "Orientals." The ban was lifted in the 1870s to supply cheap labor for building the Atlantic Railroad, with contract provisions that once the work was done, the workers would receive passage home. More than 600 Chinese laborers came in 1873; they were paid a fifth of the going wage and made to live and work under miserable conditions; their 1874 strike was among the first in Costa Rica's history.

More Chinese were allowed to enter in subsequent years, but in 1896 the government again prohibited further immigration because "that race is hurtful to the progress of the Republic." Many of those who remained were, in effect, sold as household servants to prominent Costa Ricans. Says sociologist Hilda Chen Apuy, "We can't find descendants of these early immigrants because they lived as slaves and probably died without issue."[58]

In recent decades Chinese have immigrated quite freely; many have sent for their families. Some have achieved remarkable success; for example, a third-generation Chinese, Isidro Con Wong, is a locally and internationally admired painter, and his relatives have founded thriving factories and export businesses; and Hilda Chen Apuy is an internationally recognized authority on Asian cultures.

In 1992 the Chinese numbered about 30,000. They are most conspicuous in small lowland towns, in some of which most retail stores, restaurants, hotels, groceries, laundries, cinemas, and bars are Chinese-owned. In rural Limón Province they act as brokers, buying and selling bananas and other products. Although they have been most easily absorbed into San José, the thirty-five-year-old owner of a Chinese restaurant there says, "It really bothers me that, even though I grew up in Costa Rica, people always call me *la chinita.*" As a schoolgirl, she announced to her parents after the first day of class that she should be called María because her classmates ridiculed her Chinese name.

Ever more numerous in recent years are wealthy immigrants from Taiwan (with which country, unlike the People's Republic, Costa Rica maintains friendly diplomatic and trade relations). Discouraged by high taxes in Taiwan and foreign discrimination against their products and attracted by Costa Rica's stability, many consider Costa Rica simply a helpful stop on their way to the United States or Canada.

Many non-Chinese Ticos complain that the Chinese spend little of their money in Costa Rica but save it in order to send for their relatives. Chinese Costa Ricans consider themselves as more hardworking, responsible, and educated than most of their compatriots.[59]

Although the older Chinese form a tightly knit community, there have long been many mixed marriages, such as the one that produced astronaut Franklin Chang Díaz. Children of these marriages, like most young Ticos of Chinese descent, share language, soccer, religion, and cuisine with their agemates; only their physical features and their studious, obedient habits identify them as different. Cross-cultural influence has not been entirely a one-way street; Chinese restaurants, for instance, are popular even in small towns, and acupuncture is increasingly accepted as a valid medical specialty.

Nicaraguans and Other Latin Americans

Since the late 1970s the great majority of foreign residents have been Nicaraguans. In 1979 some 100,000 were refugees from Somoza's reign of terror—sheltered, despite Ticos' long-standing distrust of *nicas*, by Costa Rica's tradition of political asylum. Many more came during the 1980s and 1990s to escape postrevolutionary chaos and poverty; in 1995, according to one estimate, 475,000 *nicas*, two-thirds of them undocumented, lived in Costa Rica, making up 14 percent of Costa Rica's population.

In 1979 philosopher Constantino Láscaris foresaw that comparatively prosperous Costa Rica would attract "wetbacks" before long and that they would take over the disagreeable work that fewer and fewer Costa Ricans were willing to do.[60] By the mid-1990s, as he predicted, it was mostly Nicaraguans who harvested sugarcane, picked coffee and oranges, and sought jobs as domestic employees and construction workers. Many more, fleeing a country with about 50 percent unemployment, continued to slip across the border to live as subsistence farmers on any scrap of land they considered safe from immigration authorities.

Official policy toward immigrant *nicas* fluctuates between severe repression and partial acceptance. Police periodically round up "people who look as if they could be undocumented aliens." (Nicaraguans tend to be darker than most Costa Ricans, one reason for discrimination against them.) They may then be deported if they lack work permits and other papers. Especially near the northern border, police justify this policy by the high incidence of contagious diseases in Nicaragua and declare that they turn back only those who have tried to enter furtively and illegally.

Contractors are glad, given the shortage of "grunt" labor, to employ *nicas*, who have a reputation as good workers and are unlikely to complain about employers who pay neither the minimum wage nor the required social security premiums. Many Nicaraguans, however, feel like outcasts in Costa Rica. Their children are sometimes not permitted to attend school for lack of legal documentation; except in cases of contagious diseases, health care is occasionally denied them as well. A cabdriver honking at a black cow in the road yelled, "Move it, *nica!*" Said a young male *nica* who came for the coffee harvest, "When I go to a dance hall on Saturday nights and ask girls to dance, they refuse. They are very snobbish."[61]

The popular Nicaraguan ballad "Poor María" depicts both the hope and the eventual disillusionment of many *nicas:* In María's fantasy San José is the place to escape from misery, to get a better house, clothes, and electrical appliances. She finds only misery in a San José slum.[62]

Tens of thousands of Salvadorans also entered Costa Rica during the 1980s, fleeing both guerrillas and government death squads. Many returned at the end of El Salvador's civil war; many others have remained. Anthropologist Tanya Basok found that although middle- and upper-class Costa Ricans distrust Salvadorans as potential leftist agitators and sneer at them as dark-skinned *maiceros* (hicks), they have been well received by the poorer majority, which does not see them as economic competitors.[63] Colombians and Panamanians have immigrated in lesser numbers.

Jews

A few Sephardic Jews immigrated from the Netherlands in the late nineteenth century and assimilated successfully, entering business and, in the third generation, the professions. "Some remember their grandfathers, some don't, and some don't want to," comments a Costa Rican of more recent immigrants with Jewish ancestry.

The first few *polacos*, as most Costa Ricans call Eastern European Jews, fled pogroms in Poland in the 1920s and 1930s; still more arrived as postwar refugees in the late 1940s.[64] Many, as noted in Chapter 3, made a bare living by peddling clothing, notions, and brooms door-to-door; they introduced installment buying, now common in Costa Rica.

Survivors and descendants of these Ashkenazi immigrants now form a highly endogamous colony of some 400 families. Their religious and community life revolves around the Jewish Community Center near downtown San José. Nearly all Jewish children attend the Weizman Institute, where Judaism and Hebrew supplement the required Costa Rican curriculum.

Many older Jews recall the insults and abuse they suffered in public school and insist that because they were born and raised here, no one can make them foreigners in their own country. "It is not necessary to have the surname of a conquistador to be more Tico than *aguadulce*," said a well-known Jewish physician.[65] Anti-Semitism, overt in the 1930s and 1940s, was still evident in the 1960s. We overheard many onlookers during the Holy Week processions in 1968, for instance, identifying Christ's Roman captors as Jews.

Today Jews are prominent in such professions as medicine, law, and engineering; in banking, commerce, and industry (the 1995 president of the Chamber of Industries is a Jew); and in charity organizations. They play increasingly prominent roles in government and politics.[66] The ministers of security and culture in Calderón Fournier's cabinet, Luís and Aida Fishman, are Jews; Luís Fishman is also president of the 1998–2002 Legislative Assembly. Rebeca Grynspan, Figueres Olsen's influential second vice president, and Herman Weinstock, his health minister, are also Jewish. Nonetheless, Jews—who are stereotyped as greedy and clannish—are, like black and Chinese Costa Ricans, still generally not considered "full" or "pure" Ticos.

Other Groups

Beginning in the nineteenth century, immigrants from Germany, England, France, and Lebanon were attracted by coffee prosperity. Many became successful coffee planters and exporters, merchants, ranchers, and industrialists; many of their children married Ticos. Some residential districts of metropolitan San José bear the names of European migrants whose coffee farms gave way to urban development—Rohrmoser and Dent, for example. Despite expropriation of their property during World War II, Germans now have the numbers and resources to support a German-language school, church, newspaper, and cultural center. French influence, as we saw earlier, was especially notable among the upper class during the nineteenth and early twentieth centuries. Although English has long since displaced French among aspirants to high social status, a French school and cultural center flourish.

Although a trickle of Italians entered Costa Rica in the early republican era, not until 1887 did they come in considerable numbers, contracted to help build the Atlantic Railroad. The following year they went on strike. (Most had been active members of a farm laborers' union in Italy.) Of the nearly 1,500 who had come, over half were repatriated in 1889. But Italians continued to arrive for the next half-century, fleeing poverty and bad working conditions. Most became traders and artisans.

In the 1950s a large group of Italian immigrants settled in southwestern Costa Rica and founded the colony of San Vito de Java, where they grew coffee. Many of their descendants, and hundreds of more recent (and more prosperous) Italian immigrants, have settled in San José and in tourist areas.

Italians have assimilated quite thoroughly and moved from shoemaking, railroad building, and coffee growing to urban businesses and professions. They "love Costa Ricans and Ticos are enchanted by Italians. Tico-Italian marriages have been plentiful."[67]

The United States and Canada account for at least 20,000 residents. Most conspicuous of these are U.S. citizens—*gringos*. (This term lacks the negative connotation it has in, say, Mexico, and many long-term residents refer to themselves as *gringos*.) Diplomatic and foreign aid personnel, missionaries, biologists, and businesspeople, as well as ever greater numbers of North American tourists, exchange students, and retirees, have come in recent decades, lured by Costa Rica's climate and natural beauty and by Ticos' strongly pro-Yankee attitudes. (Some Ticos, nonetheless, complain of the preferential treatment often accorded *gringos*. "I would be refused service in a bank if I wore shorts, but you would not," a Tico revealed.) Private English-language schools and two weekly newspapers cater largely to a North American clientele. Many signs in San José and other tourist centers as well as all labels on imported foods are in both English and Spanish. McDonald's, Kentucky Fried Chicken, Pizza Hut, and numerous U.S.-based multinational industries have set up shop.

Central and South Americans, as well as Spaniards, can become citizens after five years' residence if they also pass a test in Costa Rican geography, history, and literature and can read, write, and speak Spanish. They must have two character witnesses. The residence requirement for all others is seven years.

Summary and Conclusion

Ticos' insistence that their respect for equality has deeper historical roots than in most of Latin America is partly correct. But inequalities of several kinds have always existed. Many of the well-to-do downplay the extent of poverty and point to the easy interaction among Ticos of different classes. Although family origins have been declining in importance for at least the past half-century, wealth—or the appearance of wealth—has been ever more avidly sought since the 1920s, largely for the prestige it brings. Prestige also comes with academic degrees and with occupations free of the taint of manual labor.

Recent structural changes in the economy have widened the gap in life chances and lifestyles between the top and bottom of the social pyramid.

Discrimination against ethnic minorities also has a history long ignored by the "white legend." Some Ticos insist that the remedy is to treat all Costa Ricans exactly the same.

Novelist Quince Duncan, by contrast, eloquently states the case for both full citizenship and respect for different cultural identities among minority groups:

> We Costa Ricans are not a monolithic group. Certainly there is a majority with Spanish ancestry, but this majority is . . . culturally and racially mixed. The full incorporation of the *indígena* and the black is in the national interest. This would not be to "whiten" them but to acknowledge their existence, procure for them the greatest possible social justice, respect and appreciate their contributions, give them the same opportunities for development (health, education, housing) as other Costa Ricans have had, and above all to incorporate their contribution as an essential part of our reality.[68]

Notes

1. Carlos Meléndez, *Historia de Costa Rica* (San José: EUNED, 1991), p. 105.

2. Samuel Stone, *La dinastía de los conquistadores: La crisis del poder en la Costa Rica contemporanea* (San José: EDUCA, 1975), p. 73.

3. Lowell Gudmundson, *Estratificación socio-racial y económica de Costa Rica: 1700–1850* (San José: EUNED, 1978).

4. Michael D. Olien, "Black and Part-Black Populations in Colonial Costa Rica: Ethnohistorical Resources and Problems," *Ethnohistory,* Vol. 27, Winter, p. 18.

5. Marc Edelman, "Land and Labor in an Expanding Economy: Agrarian Capitalism and the Hacienda System in Costa Rica, 1880–1982," Ph.D. Dissertation, Columbia University, 1985.

6. Instituto de Investigaciones de Salud, *Caracterización étnica de la población costarricense mediante marcadores genéticos* (San José: UCR, February 1995). See also María Eugenia Bozzoli, Eugenia Ibarra, and Juan Rafael Quesada, El 12 de octubre: *Día de las culturas. Costa Rica: Una sociedad pluricultural* (San José: Asamblea Legislativa, 1996).

7. Quoted in Lowell Gudmundson, *Costa Rica Before Coffee: Society and Economy on the Eve of the Export Boom* (Baton Rouge: Louisiana State University Press, 1986), p. 68.

8. Wilhelm Marr, quoted in Ricardo Fernández Guardia, ed., *Costa Rica en el siglo XIX,* 3rd ed. (San José: EDUCA, 1972), pp. 178–179.

9. Carolyn Hall, *El café y el desarrollo histórico-geográfico de Costa Rica* (San José: ECR, 1976), p. 51.

10. Ibid., p. 88.

11. Stone, *La dinastía,* p. 195.

12. Gudmundson, *Costa Rica Before Coffee,* p. 86.

13. See Hall, *El café.*

14. John Biesanz and Mavis Biesanz, *Costa Rican Life* (New York: Columbia University Press, 1944), pp. 22–23.

15. Ibid., pp. 19–24.

16. Gudmundson, *Costa Rica Before Coffee*, p. 116.

17. Biesanz and Biesanz, *Costa Rican Life*, p. 19.

18. John Patrick Bell, *Crisis in Costa Rica: The 1948 Revolution* (Austin: University of Texas Press, 1971), p. 8.

19. Mylena Vega, Carlos Castro V., Ana Lucia Gutiérrez, and Carlos R. Rodríguez S., *Cambios en la estructura de clases costarricense 1987–1994* (San José: Instituto de Investigaciones Sociales, UCR, 1995).

20. Ibid.

21. Martha Honey, *Hostile Acts: U.S. Policy in Costa Rica in the 1980's* (Gainesville: University of Florida Press, 1994), p. 91.

22. CEPAL, *Panorama social de Latino América, 1994* (San José: CEPAL, 1994).

23. Victor Hugo Céspedes and Ronulfo Jiménez, *La pobreza en Costa Rica* (San José: Academia de Centroamérica, 1995).

24. Wilburg Jiménez Castro, "Mayor pobreza real en 1993," *La República*, January 1, 1994, p. 17A.

25. Silvia Lara, Tom Barry, and Peter Simonson, *Inside Costa Rica* (Albuquerque: Resource Center Press, 1995), p. 70.

26. Vega et al., *Cambios en la estructura.*

27. Ibid.

28. Jeffrey M. Paige, *Coffee and Power: Revolution and the Rise of Democracy in Central America* (Cambridge: Harvard University Press, 1997), p. 24.

29. Olivier Dabene, *Costa Rica: Juicio a la democrácia* (San José: Facultad Latinoamericana de Ciencias Sociales, 1992), p. 93.

30. Paul Kutche, *Voices of Migrants: Rural-Urban Migration in Costa Rica* (Gainesville: University of Florida Press, 1994), p. 212.

31. Carlos Sandoval García, *Sueños en la vida cotidiana: Trabajadores y trabajadoras de la máquila y la construcción en Costa Rica* (San José: EUCR, 1997), pp. 82–84.

32. Ibid., p. 22.

33. Peter Brennan, "Some Questions Are Best Unasked," *Tico Times,* April 7, 1995, p. 21.

34. Gabriel Coronado and María Eugenia Pérez, *La clase media costarricense: Psicologia y organización* (Heredia: Editorial Universidad Nacional Autónoma [EUNA], 1992), pp. 18, 114, 129.

35. Sandoval, *Sueños en la vida cotidiana*, pp. 82–83.

36. Victor Goldkind, "Sociocultural Contrasts in Rural and Urban Settlement Types in Costa Rica," *Rural Sociology,* Vol. 26, 1961, pp. 365–380.

37. Trevor W. Purcell, *Banana Fallout: Class, Color, and Culture Among West Indians in Costa Rica* (Los Angeles: Center for Afro-American Studies Publications, Regents of the University of California, 1993), p. 126.

38. Marcos Guevara Berger and Rubén Chacón Castro, *Territorios indios en Costa Rica: Orígenes, situación actual y perspectivas* (San José: García Hnos., 1992), p. 39.

39. Victoria Villalobos and Carlos Borge, *Talamanca en la encrucijada* (San José: EUNED, 1995), p. 46.

40. María Eugenia Bozzoli, interview, June 26, 1995. See also Bozzoli, "La frontera agrícola de Costa Rica y su relación con el problema agrario en zonas indígenas,"

Anuario de Estudios Centroamericanos, No. 3, 1977, pp. 225–234; and Bozzoli, "La población indígena, la cultural nacional y la cuestión étnica," Paper presented at the Institute of Anthropological Research conference, Mexico City, November 13–17, 1989. Printed in *Cuadernos de Antropología* (UCR) 8, 1990. Also Paula Palmer, Juanita Sánchez, and Gloria Mayorga, *Taking Care of Sibo's Gifts* (San José: Editorama, 1991), p. 9.

41. Villalobos and Borge, *Talamanca,* pp. 53–80.

42. Ibid., p. 2.

43. Guevara and Chacón, *Territorios indios en Costa Rica,* p. 18.

44. Paula Palmer, *"What Happen": A Folk-History of Costa Rica's Talamanca Coast* (San José: Ecodesarrollos, 1977).

45. Quince Duncan, "El Negro antillano: Inmigración y presencia," in Duncan and Meléndez, *El Negro en Costa Rica,* pp. 85–89.

46. Jeffrey J. Casey, "La mano de obra en la industria bananera: Limón entre 1880 y 1940," Paper presented at the Semanario Centroamericano de Historia Economica y Social, Ciudad Universitaria Rodrigo Facio, April 21–23, 1977.

47. Philippe Bourgois, *Banano, etnia y lucha social en Centro América* (San José: DEI, 1994), p. 93.

48. Purcell, *Banana Fallout,* p. 42.

49. Carlos Meléndez, "Aspectos sobre la inmigración jamaicana," in Duncan and Meléndez, *El Negro en Costa Rica,* p. 78. The law appears in *Colección de leyes y decretos,* listed as Article 5, Par. 3, Law 31, December 10, 1934. (Both laws took effect the year following their signing.)

50. Ana María Headley Mollings, "Algunas características de la familia negra en la ciudad de Limón basada en una comparación con la familia blanca," Lic. Thesis, UCR, 1983, p. 185.

51. Rev. Robert Evans, "Introducción a la cultura negra," cited in *La Nación,* August 29, 1993, p. 7C.

52. Philippe Bourgois, "Blacks in Costa Rica: Upward Mobility and Ethnic Discrimination," in Marc Edelman and Joanne Kenen, eds., *The Costa Rica Reader* (New York: Grove Weidenfeld, 1988), p. 164.

53. Arcadio, *La Nación,* July 15, 1993, p. 14A.

54. Quince Duncan in *Rumbo,* May 14, 1992.

55. Purcell, *Banana Fallout,* p. 107.

56. Ibid., pp. 126–129.

57. Roger Churnside, "Limón, el presidente y el PLN," *La Nación,* May 19, 1994, p. 15A.

58. Hilda Chen Apuy, "La minoría china en Costa Rica," *Reflexiones* (UCR Facultad de Ciencias Sociales), No. 3, November 1992.

59. Larissa Minsky Acosta, "Un soplo de Oriente," *La Nación,* March 22, 1992, p. RD14. Also Wendy Schmidt in *Costa Rica Today,* November 5, 1992.

60. Alberto Cañas, "Chisporroteos," *La República,* January 21, 1995, p. 17A.

61. Bret Putnam, "La majestad de los inmigrantes," *La Nación,* January 23, 1994, pp. RD10–11.

62. Eugenia Ibarra, "La pobre María," *La Nación,* May 14, 1994, p. 14A.

63. Tanya Basok, *Keeping Heads Above Water: Salvadorean Refugees in Costa Rica* (Montreal: McGill-Queen's University Press, 1993), pp. 38–53.

64. The origins and consequences of these migrations are discussed in detail in Jacobo Schifter Sikora et al., *El Judio en Costa Rica* (San José: EUNED, 1979).

65. Willy Feinzaig Rosenstein, "Extranjero en mi patria?" *La Nación,* October 13, 1992, p. 18A.

66. Cristina Arias and Mario Bermúdez, "Poder judio," *Rumbo,* December 20, 1994, pp. 6–15.

67. Hubert Solano, "Who Ate That Funny-Looking Green Chicken?" *Costa Rica Today,* April 25, 1993, pp. 6–7. Early Italian immigrants are said to have eaten parrots, assuming they were exotic chickens.

68. Quince Duncan in *Rumbo,* May 14, 1992, p. 31.

— 6 —

Community

Many Costa Ricans identify more with their town or village than with the country as a whole. Many still spend their entire lives in one community, even in the same neighborhood or house. Anthropologist Carmen Murillo describes miners on the slope of Irazú Volcano who work long hours for low wages. "They know they could earn more in the city, but their identity is linked to their village," she says. "They don't know who they'd be in San José."

Ticos who leave their birthplace feel a continuing attachment to it. Juan Carlos Vargas, also an anthropologist, has met many Guanacastecans who, after living for a time in or near San José, were happy to return home. "They see the *patio* outside their house in Guanacaste as the center for work and leisure, even as the center of their lives," he told us. "In the capital they have no such space." University students in the San José area join associations of students from the same region and get together for parties and for excursions "back home."

But community and neighborhood ties are increasingly strained or broken as *campesinos* move to the city and villagers commute to work there. Passing strangers are no longer greeted with an "adiós!" in villages that have become almost as impersonal as the metropolis itself. In 1968 as we watched a drunken woman in one village loudly cursing the police who had arrested her, residents hastened to tell us that she was not a local woman. Today that village is a suburb of San José, and its commuter residents, many newly arrived there, feel no such community pride. Its distinctive traditions, such as a youth's leaving cypress branches on a former sweetheart's doorstep as a sign that he has severed his ties to her, are remembered only by older residents. A generation ago many Ticos still spoke of their native community as "the place where I left my umbilical cord," a reference to the custom of burying the cord by the house where birth took place. Today even rural women give birth in urban hospitals, and both the custom and the phrase have disappeared.

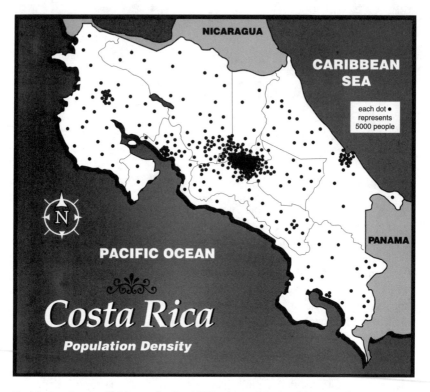

*Population density, 1994; map by David Higgins and Richard Biesanz (based on data
from Departmento General de Estadística y Censos, San José, 1996)*

Distribution of Population

Geographer Carolyn Hall sees Costa Rica's geography as the basis for the
sharp distinction, ever since colonial days, between the more-developed center and the less-developed periphery.[1] Most early Spanish settlements were
located in the fertile and pleasantly cool Central Valley. (New settlements,
notes historian Carlos Meléndez, were typically founded about 10 kilometers
from an older one, allowing a round trip before the afternoon rains.)[2] As the
population grew, subsistence farmers and the landless moved out in all directions. Consequently, those living farthest from the country's center have always been among the poorest Ticos with the least political clout or access to
government services. By the 1950s, after most arable land had been
claimed—and as more and more farmland became pasture—migrants increasingly turned to the San José area. Few industries had yet been developed. The push of rural poverty and unemployment rather than the pull of the
city accounted for the first huge wave of urban growth.[3] But the expansion of

government bureaucracy and industry in later decades made the San José area an ever-stronger magnet for migrants. The 1927 census listed 19 percent of the population as urban—the same as in 1864. By 1990, 54 percent were classified as urban.

Most clearly urban is the San José metropolitan area—the central canton of San José and its ten adjacent cantons, which from the air appear to form one huge city. About a third of all Costa Ricans lived there in 1995.

The Bureau of Statistics and Census also defines the greater San José metropolitan area, which embraces not only these urbanized cantons but also those in the provinces of Heredia, Cartago, and Alajuela and accounted for 51 percent of all Ticos in 1995. Dozens of old towns and villages are now dormitory suburbs whose residents commute to San José or to other suburbs to work, shop, study, and play. Here new concrete-block houses, complete with antiburglary grills and carports, stand amid old adobe and wooden houses, coffee groves, and pasture. Cows wander the streets.

Given this pattern of change, anthropologist María Eugenia Bozzoli finds any classification of communities as urban or rural somewhat arbitrary. Even in remote areas, she points out, there is no longer a sharp distinction. "Talamanca [a mountainous canton on the Atlantic slope, populated mostly by poor Indians and migrants from Panama and Guanacaste], has bus service in the hamlets, two high schools, electricity, running water, and telephones. A few people there own computers, fax machines, and so on."

It is still valid, nonetheless, to make broad generalizations about different types of communities on the urban-rural spectrum, ranging from the metropolis of San José to remote hamlets. Whereas our categories are not found in official statistics, they do correspond to generally accepted usage.

The Metropolis

Like many other Latin American capitals, San José dominates national life. More than half of all Ticos, as we noted, live in its greater metropolitan area. Many commute to work, school, or university there—some from outside the area, others from one suburb to another. For many bureaucratic routines, such as renewing a driver's license, it has long been necessary to go to San José or its closest suburbs, though several regional offices now facilitate some procedures, including tax payments.

Diplomats and multinational corporations, as well as industry and agribusiness, make San José or a suburb their headquarters. Most hospitals and specialists; the main universities, museums, art galleries, and libraries; the National Theater; and the most prestigious private schools are found there. Painters, writers, and musicians gravitate to the city. Good restaurants and nightclubs, country clubs, modern department stores and shopping malls,

*Modern San José skyline with pre-Columbian stone balls (National Museum) in fore-
front (Richard Biesanz)*

and many imported specialties in supermarkets and boutiques are all found
almost exclusively in or near the capital.

Half of the land in the central canton of San José is now occupied by
businesses and another fifth by government facilities, many in buildings that
once housed families. Only a fifth is residential. By 8 P.M. most commuters
and shoppers have gone home. The city's bars, cinemas, brothels, theaters,
dance halls, and restaurants are active then, but many streets are nearly deserted.

In the early 1940s the capital claimed only 70,000 inhabitants, a mere
tenth of the country's population. When its population began to mushroom after midcentury, the metropolitan area grew haphazardly, encroaching on villages and coffee groves with neither planning nor zoning. Streets, the water
supply, and sewage disposal—even cemeteries—were totally inadequate for
future growth.

The population of suburban Alajuelita, for example, tripled during the
1970s and 1980s. Says economist Raul López:

> People moved into half-finished houses, without basic services. Behind
> them came water, electricity, the ministries of Education, Public Works, and
> other agencies, offering an infrastructure of mends and patches. [In these
> new suburbs] the inhabitants suffer a great rootlessness because they do not

identify with the rest of the community. Every day they must go elsewhere to work, to study, to shop.[4]

Garbage disposal, as we noted in Chapter 4, became a major problem for many communities in the early 1990s, particularly for San José. When the capital's dump in suburban Rio Azul overflowed, residents of one distant town after another angrily objected to proposals that their community be the new site for *josefinos'* wastes. (As plastic and other nonbiodegradable substances have become common, streets and roadsides nationwide are increasingly littered with refuse. Despite their personal cleanliness and neat homes, many Ticos have no qualms about littering on public property; until recently signs in some buses requested that passengers throw their trash out the window.)

Traffic is another nightmare. San José was not designed for the 300,000 vehicles that clog its narrow streets each weekday; even a beltway has done little to reduce congestion. Although four-fifths of urban workers commute by bus, buses make up less than 7 percent of the capital's daily traffic. But the state has given low priority to mass transit and, under structural adjustment pressures, lowered import duties on used cars so much in 1993 that tens of thousands were added in a few months. In the central city, cars moved at an average speed of 30 kilometers per hour in 1970; congestion had slowed traffic to 5 kilometers per hour by 1995. Drivers use their horns liberally, and many people report headaches and fatigue from noise and from air as toxic to residents as if they smoked two packs of cigarettes a day.

Many streets in the older parts of San José are still lined with one- or two-story wooden houses, often flush with one another and abutting on a sidewalk, their rooms opening on an enclosed patio. The stroller finds interspersed among them such surprises as stained-glass bay windows, ornamental grillwork, and recently renovated parks adorned with trees—a rarity in newer parts of the city. In some areas nineteenth-century houses have been turned into attractive small hotels and restaurants. And a six-block stretch of Central Avenue is now a cobblestoned pedestrian boulevard.

But one is also likely to see wreckers tearing down charming old buildings to make way for drab, boxy, high-rise office, hotel, and apartment buildings. Vacant lots and rundown little wooden houses and stores with rusty tin roofs also await the developer and the wrecker. Half the buildings of central San José were found in "bad" condition in a 1993 study.

Suburban residential neighborhoods include expensive private homes, government and private housing projects for low- and middle-income families, and squalid shantytowns, as well as older neighborhoods that were villages not long ago. Suburban stores and shopping malls—including a seven-story mall in one suburb—offer many goods and services once available only in downtown San José or not at all.

A rural pulpería *(general store) serves as a wayside stop and social center (Mavis Hiltunen Biesanz)*

The ambivalence about city life shown in Joaquín García Monge's classic 1900 novel *Hijas del campo*, which contrasts the honest, healthful rural folkways with the corruption and sleaze of San José, persists today even among lifelong city dwellers and with ample reason. *Josefinos* visit rural kin to relieve the stress they complain of. "You have to live in a cage because of the crime," say many. The weakness of municipal government, here as elsewhere in Costa Rica, is evident in the thousands of illegal street and sidewalk vendors whose stalls and pushcarts compete with vehicles and pedestrians for space and that successive administrations have tried for decades to remove. It is evident, too, in haphazard construction, potholes, and broken sidewalks, where unguarded holes are sometimes knee-deep. (Like their rural cousins, urban Ticos learn to be careful. A tourist guide says that his North American and European clients frequently stumble on forest trails, but his Costa Rican clients, whether rural or urban, almost never do.)

Few residents identify primarily with the city. Many feel that if anything, they are part of a *barrio* (neighborhood) rather than of the city itself. But constant razing and rebuilding and commuting to work or school, where one's coworkers or classmates may be from many *barrios* or towns, weaken identification even with one's *barrio*. Although a resident of the capital still runs into many acquaintances during a brief stroll, *josefinos* often say they hardly know their nearest neighbors and their friends are widely scattered. Sociologist Jorge Riba notes:

> People used to chat with neighbors in neighborhood *pulperías* [small general stores], barber shops, and shoemakers' shops. They still do in villages. But city people today are in a hurry, and don't know or trust their neighbors as they used to. The first thing to go in urban *pulperías* were benches, because customers had stopped using them. Now the *pulperías* themselves are being replaced by supermarkets, and barbershops by hair stylists, with whom you have to make an appointment. City people now spend more time at home or in private clubs because they're afraid of crime. And new diversions, outside the home, like video arcades or discos so loud that you can't talk, really don't allow for much interaction.

Cities and Towns

The population of San José remains many times larger than that of the other highland provincial capitals—Alajuela, Heredia, and Cartago—but that fact has become increasingly irrelevant to the lives of people in these old colonial rivals of San José as they, along with many smaller settlements, have merged into a single metropolitan region.

The capitals of the three lowland provinces, by contrast, are so distant that most Central Valley residents go there only as tourists, if at all: Puntarenas, a Pacific coast fishing port with an estimated 102,000 people in 1996; Liberia, the inland capital of Guanacaste Province with 41,000 residents; and Limón, the Caribbean port, which had 77,000 residents. These three cities and their provinces are still like neglected poor relations; the nation's wealth, even more than its population, remains concentrated in the Central Valley.

Most cities and towns, including these provincial capitals, are the central districts of populous cantons and are wealthy roughly in proportion to their proximity to San José; well-to-do and influential businesspeople and professionals generally prefer to live within commuting distance of the capital.

As in San José, the centers of other highland cities and towns, usually built on level ground, typically exhibit a Spanish-style grid pattern around a plaza that may contain benches, a fountain, and a bandshell among shrubs, flowers, and trees; public phone booths and a corner taxi stand add a modern touch. Across a street from the eastern edge of the plaza stands the commu'nity's oldest Catholic church, built to no standard pattern, and the prie' house-cum-office. The municipal building, the police station, and a bank ally face the plaza.

On nearby streets are an interurban bus stop; a Red Cross buildir station; schools; government health clinics; restaurants; cafés; billia' small hotel; Protestant churches; offices (often combined with hor'

Commercial street in San José (Richard Biesanz)

tors, dentists, optometrists, beauticians, accountants, surveyors, and lawyers; and stores offering packaged foods, medicines, hardware, and video rentals. An old roofed marketplace, perhaps covering an entire block, shelters many small retail businesses, mainly produce vendors and cafés.

Away from the center, attractive new or remodeled houses are interspersed with rundown old ones and with *pulperías*, bars, small churches, and the local cemetery. Filling stations mark the few highways leading out of town; paved streets become dirt roads at the edge of coffee groves, pasture, or cane fields.

Not long ago the choicest location for a house in large towns and cities was in the center. Some of the more affluent still live there, except in San José, but most now live at the edge of town or in the country. On other fringes of the town are squatters' neighborhoods of scrap-wood and metal shacks.

There is still considerable cooperation within each of a town's *barrios*. Each may have its own development association and soccer team and perhaps its own shrine to the Virgin, the venue of occasional outdoor masses and prayer meetings. Some community spirit is evident during church or school fairs and Holy Week processions. Ticos say, however, that both community and neighborhood solidarity have declined. And even in small towns many people, especially commuters, do not know their next-door neighbors' names.

A few decades ago Ticos talked of differences in personality among the residents of Central Valley cities. Comparative isolation over generations gave each town a distinctive stamp. Heredians were said to be withdrawn and pious, Alajuelans open and merry, Cartagans as proud and cold as their old town, residents of San Ramón inclined to write and enjoy poetry. One still hears some towns described as liberal or conservative.

Such differences have largely vanished because of the homogenizing effects of the mass media and of easy travel and communication. Not only do Heredians, for example, work and shop in the capital, but their town is visited daily by thousands of students attending the National University. For such reasons, many no longer identify with the town they live in, and a fan—or even a member—of Alajuela's soccer team may well live in Heredia or Cartago.

Small Towns and Villages

The typical center of a rural canton is a town or village of under 10,000 people. There are about seventy-five towns and villages of between 5,000 and 10,000 inhabitants, not all of them cantonal capitals, and hundreds more with 500 to 5,000 people. Such communities are primarily trade centers for surrounding rural districts.

A Catholic church, a school, professionals' offices, shops, private homes, and a municipal building surround the central plaza, which may serve primarily as a soccer field. Branch offices of several national government agencies are also found near the plaza; their personnel are far more urban than rural in educational background, outlook, values, and relationships.

Most streets, except those near the plaza, are unpaved and are lined with the homes of small farmers, merchants, artisans, and commuters, as well as with bars and *pulperías*. On a slope above the village is the water reservoir, a metal-covered spring. On a hillside below is the iron-fenced cemetery.

Villages, like the even smaller hamlets and *caseríos*, do not always have official political boundaries. They may center around a church or school and be delimited by roads, by natural boundaries such as rivers, or simply by custom. They are recognized as communities by the consensus of their inhabitants. Sometimes identification with one's neighborhood is so strong that villagers distinguish, say, between Upper Guaitíl and Lower Guaitíl. But soccer rivalries between villages also create a feeling of community within each one. Villagers also boast of successful church fairs or new health centers and may taunt those of a nearby village because their soccer field lacks lights or their church needs painting. The old rivalry between Santa Ana and Ciudad Colón, which occasionally resulted in fistfights, is now confined to soccer matches and to jokes: "When we inaugurated the new cemetery in Ciudad Colón, we had to borrow a corpse from Santa Ana because no one ever dies here."

Refugees from a 1989 earthquake in Puriscal met resistance when they tried to relocate to Ciudad Colón, 20 kilometers away. "We don't want outsiders moving in," said a Ciudad Colón old-timer. Similarly, longtime residents of San Isidro de Heredia, now a suburb of San José, are slow to accept newcomers. Says a commuter businessman in his forties:

> The new people—many of whom are doctors, lawyers, and administrators—are seen as *fuereños* [outsiders] even though most are Ticos. When some of us "new" people started to work to get AyA [the autonomous institution in charge of water supply] to take over the village water supply, many native *isidreños* were resentful. They complained at a meeting of the municipal council, that this was an idea of *fuereños*. It's not a matter of social class; many natives have a fair amount of money; most are small landowners, and have made money selling some of their land. It's that the local people are suspicious of outsiders. We've been here ten years, but it's still hard to be accepted.

Old-timers, in turn, sometimes charge that newcomers isolate themselves. In some Caribbean coastal villages, for instance, new residents may erect barbed-wire fences around their land instead of the more traditional shrubbery that allows others to pass through freely.

The Hamlet

An ever smaller minority of Costa Ricans live in rural communities of fewer than 500 people, either hamlets or the little clusters of houses of related families called *caseríos*.

The widely scattered wooden houses of a hamlet surround a central plaza, usually a grassy square used for soccer. Near the plaza are a school, a *pulpería*, and a tiny wooden church where mass is said by a visiting priest at most once or twice a month; in some communities the school also serves as a church. A concrete *salón comunal* built by the local community development association is a venue for many gatherings from meetings of road-building committees to wedding parties.

Hamlets have no buildings devoted exclusively to government functions. Typically, the only government employees in a hamlet are Rural Guard (who may have no jail) and a teacher, who is often responsible for all six primary grades. Nearly all other residents, perhaps even the *pulpería* owner, are farmers. Many houses, especially in peripheral regions, still lack potable water, electricity, and indoor toilets, though all this is rapidly changing.

Some *caseríos* are so remote even from a hamlet that schoolchildren must walk, bicycle, or ride horseback for an hour or two or in some areas go by boat. In the rainy season, many trails are often knee-deep in mud and creeks, unfordable.

Many hamlets and *caseríos* are now deserted for much of the year or left to women, small children, and elderly men. As work became scarce in most rural areas with the expansion of cattle ranching, many teens and young adults sought work in San José, in banana zones, or in the United States. Says a thirty-eight-year-old woman in a highland *caserío*, "We used to raise food here—corn and beans. There was work for everyone. Now most land is in pasture, and five of my eight siblings have moved to San José to work. I am able to live here only because my husband has a job near the city. He comes home on weekends." A postal clerk in a highland town, where we saw few young adults, showed us that day's incoming letters—nearly all sent from New Jersey by youths who had moved there from surrounding *caseríos*.

Mobility and Communication

New means of transportation have made it easier to commute to work or school or to leave one's birthplace—and to return. The few roads of a half-century ago were often impassable in the long rainy season. Even poor *campesinos* sometimes used the small commercial planes that served many remote areas in the 1930s and 1940s, but most transportation was by foot, horse, or oxcart.

Nearly 6,000 kilometers of paved roads and about six times as much unpaved road now crisscross the country. The Ministry of Public Works and Transportation considers only 1 kilometer of every 20 to be in good condition. Maintenance has been lacking since the economic crisis of 1980. Increased traffic—and, many Ticos say, increased corruption—creates potholes everywhere.

Often built by pioneer settlers in new areas (with or without government help), roads encourage further settlement. Whenever politicians visit a remote area, the first request is for help with building a road.

The interurban bus is the lifeline of the countryside. In some rural areas packages, messages, and even money may be entrusted to bus drivers or passengers, who pass them along to bystanders in the recipient's neighborhood. Neighbors and strangers talk at bus stops and on the bus itself. But in other ways buses, like cars, may limit local interaction. Says a woman in a working-class neighborhood on the edge of the San José area, "Before bus service reached us, people had to walk everywhere and would often stop and talk to neighbors along the way. Not any more."

Whereas cars may be a status symbol for urban Ticos, four-wheel-drive trucks help some farmers market their crops without brokers. Many male office workers and rural schoolteachers commute to work on motor scooters, which can negotiate even steep and narrow foot trails. Farmers of yesteryear could often identify a distant oxcart by the distinctive squeak of its wheels; today they may announce, "I hear Enrique's *moto!*" Many adults and children ride bicycles, often two to a bike, especially in flat coastal areas. Competition with roads, as well as mismanagement, has recently ended both cargo and passenger service on the government-owned railroads that had linked San José with both coasts for a century.

Commercial airline service to peripheral areas has also dwindled as the road network has spread. Yet many landing strips are still used, and small planes still serve some areas where roads do not exist. Passenger jets of many airlines and countries use the main airport near Alajuela; some use the newer international airport near Liberia.

Despite a high reported literacy rate, most Ticos prefer oral to written communication. Messages entrusted to a rural bus driver or passenger are usually oral. Radio and TV are the most popular means of learning the news even where newspapers are available. An elderly farmer who grew up in the steep mountains near the central Pacific coast says that even today *campesinos* there shout brief messages across long distances; each has his own distinctive yell. In the past, he says, one notified neighbors of an emergency with a loud blast on a conch shell.

Continuing this oral emphasis, the public Costa Rican Institute of Electricity has vastly improved and expanded telephone service in recent years. In 1994 there were 320,000 phones, or 14.5 for every 100 inhabitants. Two-thirds—many of them cellular phones—were in the San José metropolitan area. Most Ticos have access to one or more public phones. In small villages where everyone knows everyone else, a bystander may pick up a ringing public phone, hear, "Tell Fulano to call me at 5 P.M.," and relay the message. Nearly all homes have one or more radios, and several stations broadcast death notices and requests that Fulano call Zutano at a public phone number at a specific time.

Now that over 90 percent of homes have electricity, most, even poor ones, have television. Satellite dishes and cable bring in U.S. stations, which are popular among those who can afford them.

In San José and other urban centers, mail is delivered to homes or put into rented boxes at the nearest post office. *Campesinos* may receive mail at a *pulpería*, where a neighbor may pick it up and pass it on. Mailing addresses typically include estimates of distance from well-known landmarks (perhaps long since vanished), and a letter often takes a month even to cross San José. In the early 1990s there were many reports of mail theft by postal employees—one reason bills are usually paid in person. Since the government's legal monopoly on postal services ended in 1992, private courier and express services have been heavily used by those who need and can afford them. Businesses, government agencies, universities, newspapers, and individuals increasingly use e-mail and fax; many now have Web sites on the Internet.

Local Government

In colonial times, the governing bodies of Costa Rica's towns and villages (chosen in elections restricted to male property owners) were its centers of political activity, problem solving, and, to some extent, democratic government, frequently defying royal edicts. Historian Alfredo Aymerich comments: "Since Costa Rica was so isolated that the colonists might not hear an edict until two years after it was issued, they trusted local governments more. Also, the colony was so small that people were used to seeing the governor and other Spanish officials and didn't hold them in awe, just as with our presidents today."

The intercity conflicts of the early republic reflected not only resistance to the dominance of San José and rivalries among elite families but also, says historian Rodolfo Cerdas, the people's attachment to the more direct, more local participation that the municipal regime provided.[5]

In the early nineteenth century, as we saw in Chapter 2, municipal councils were so strong and so rivalrous that dictator Braulio Carrillo took measures to put the national government above local authority. By the late 1860s local government posed so little threat to central authority that the 1871 constitution provided that each canton would be a municipality. It would be responsible for the "free, compulsory and obligatory" education that the constitution also proclaimed and would name a board of education. Municipalities were also in charge of water supplies, streets and parks, disease control, promotion of agriculture and commerce, and civic fiestas.[6]

Later, municipalities once again lost much of their autonomy. As education became more centralized after 1885, local school boards no longer made policy. After 1949 electricity, water, and sewage disposal were increasingly supplied by national *autónomas*, and the social security system absorbed community hospitals once run by local boards. Central ministries were made responsible for police protection.

Local officials say they lost still more jurisdiction during the 1990s, blaming the loss on the far-reaching tentacles of national government under the misleading rubric of "decentralization." This policy transfers many formerly local responsibilities to local branches of autonomous agencies and ministries, whose policies are made in San José and are not coordinated with the municipal government.[7] In 1995 only one out of every twenty-two public-sector employees worked in local government. When, that same year, the national government laid a heavy new responsibility on municipalities—the collection of property taxes—few were ready to discharge this new duty efficiently; many simply asked property owners to provide their own estimates of property values.

Scanty resources are usually blamed for the ineffectiveness of municipal government. Overflowing garbage dumps, nearly all of them municipally owned and managed, provide one example. Most are in open air, on the banks of rivers. Rivers and seacoasts, as a result, are especially polluted in the rainy season. The uncovered sites are subject to few controls; anyone can dump anything there, usually free of charge. In many communities, sidewalks and vacant lots clogged with garbage bags and loose trash testify to the infrequency of pickup as well as to the habit of littering.

Municipal revenues come from such diverse sources as a levy on the slaughter of pigs; stamps for legal papers; and permits to erect buildings, hold serenades, and sell liquor. But, says a forty-eight-year-old councilwoman in a highland village, "not only are these fees small, but supporters of whichever political party controls the council can get away with delaying payments or not paying at all. When this lack of revenue results in poorer services, many other people also refuse to pay local taxes."

Today each of the eighty-one cantons has its own municipal council, elected every four years along with the nation's president and legislature. Each council names a municipal executive. The Supreme Electoral Tribunal determines the size of the council (from seven to nine voting members) on the basis of the canton's population. To represent its interests each district in the canton chooses a delegate, who has a voice in council meetings but no vote.

To get anything important done the municipality depends on specific appropriations voted into the national government budget by the legislature. These accounted for only one colón in a thousand—for all municipalities combined—in the 1993 budget, down from 11 percent of all public funds in 1950. Party politics strongly influence a canton's allotments. It helps if a provincial *diputado* has ties to the canton and belongs to the president's party—and if a majority of council members belong to this same party. When a legislator visits, council members and other community leaders present appeals for funds to help with specific projects. Says the councilwoman we quoted above: "*Diputados* are the intermediaries between the state and the local communities. So council members like me must spend a lot of time with them, making them feel important and fostering their belief that they are the saviors of our community, when what we really need are some services in return for our taxes."

Party politics, it is often charged, affect not only revenues but also the quality of municipal councils. National party leaders nominate candidates for council members as political favors. They tend to regard municipal ballots as relatively unimportant and are not greatly concerned with qualifications other than party color.

The sometimes violent struggles over the site of a new landfill for the metropolitan area, which began in 1992 and were still unresolved in 1998, are not simply over garbage, says political scientist Alberto Salóm, but are a continuation of the historic conflict between local communities and centralized power—now expressed in the municipalities' distrust of national government rather than the reverse.[8]

Community Development

In 1935 Chester Lloyd Jones noted that "community activities are poorly developed except for those centering around the church, the schools, and the recently introduced sports, the chief of which is soccer."[9] Three years later, novelist Yolanda Oreamuno wrote, "We [Ticos] act for ourselves, and very often have no idea what neighborliness is."[10]

As we saw in Chapter 1, Costa Ricans continue to describe their compatriots as self-centered and uncooperative. But Ticos have in fact always been quite cooperative when their interests have coincided. "Costa Rica was built by *turnos* [village festivals]," writer Carmen Naranjo told us. (See Chapter 11, "Leisure.") There is an old rural tradition of neighborhood working bees, whether to build a house, a school, a road, or a church or to harvest a crop. Today, teenage volunteers solicit donations for the local Red Cross or for their high school. Farmers, fishermen, and artisans form co-ops. Urban squatters organize to petition the government for electricity and piped water and for funds to build better houses.

Voluntary associations are numerous in communities of all sizes. Most of the 130 ecological associations existing in 1995 were urban-based. Residents of one San José *barrio* united to save its historic buildings from demolition. An even bigger impetus to urban neighborhood and community organization in recent years has come from the sharp increase in burglary and mugging.

Asked in a 1994 poll what measures would be most effective in protecting them from crime, 50 percent of those answering replied, "Organizations of neighbors." Although such private defenses as watchdogs and handguns are still the norm, a few San José neighborhoods have used block parties to organize successful antiburglary efforts. Neighbors—many of whom had not known one another previously—used their new ties to achieve other common goals as well.

Some 1,500 community development associations existed in 1997, most of them in rural areas and small towns. Though a central government agency such as the Ministry of Public Works and Transportation may help fund or supervise a project, residents must organize to request such help. And even then they are expected to contribute labor as well as most of the funds, which they raise through fairs, raffles, and donations.

The main concerns of most community development associations, as well as of many less formal groups of rural neighbors, are infrastructure and ecology: schools, roads, bus service, and clinics or protection of a watershed from deforestation or pollution. As in larger settlements, the same persons are usually involved in directing several projects. (Though women tend to be very active, project leaders are nearly always men.) And disagreements—often unaired—make many associations short-lived. Nonetheless, group decisions are usually arrived at by discussion leading not to a vote but to a tacit consensus. This avoids confrontations and open conflict and permits people to *quedar bien*, to get along and keep their dignity.

A farmer high on a mountain near Puriscal told us how his and neighboring families improved a trail leading to the nearest road:

> We didn't name a president of a board or anything like that. We didn't ask for government help. We just agreed that on certain days we would get together and work. We did, and it's done. Now our children have to walk only an hour to the bus that takes them to high school in Puriscal. [Probably the small number of families involved made it more likely that everyone would pitch in.]

Summary and Conclusion

Ties to their local community are still important to many Costa Ricans. But unemployment has led many rural Ticos to resettle in urban areas. The expansion—largely chaotic and unplanned—of the greater San José metropolitan area has blurred many community boundaries and widened the long-standing gap in power and wealth between the Central Valley and lowland areas. New means of transportation and communication and fear of crime often reduce interaction among neighbors.

These same forces, however, also link Ticos on a broader scale and in new ways. Many now have friends, relatives, coworkers, and classmates in distant communities. Many now belong to regional and national voluntary associations or to neighborhood-watch groups. And especially in rural areas, the decline of municipal government has made local cooperation all the more essential.

Notes

1. Carolyn Hall, *Costa Rica: A Geographical Interpretation in Historical Perspective* (Boulder: Westview, 1985), p. 96.

2. Carlos Meléndez, *Historia de Costa Rica* (San José: EUNED, 1991), p. 73.

3. Hall, *Costa Rica*, p. 207.

4. Yasmín Ross, "Radiografía del caos urbano," *La Nación,* July 11, 1993, pp. RD9–10, citing economist Raul López.

5. Rodolfo Cerdas, *Formación del estado de Costa Rica* (San Pedro: UCR, 1967).

6. Carlos Araya P. and Priscilla Albarracín, "Régimen municipal y movimiento comunal: Rasgos de su evolución histórica," in *Historia de Costa Rica en el siglo XX,* 3rd ed. (San Pedro: Editorial Porvenir, 1991), p. 135.

7. Ana Cerestina Camacho, "La agonía municipal," *Aportes,* August 1993, p. 5.

8. Alberto Salóm, "Basura y poder político," *Rumbo,* February 28, 1995, p. 21.

9. Chester Lloyd Jones, *Costa Rica and Civilization in the Caribbean* (Madison: University of Wisconsin Studies in the Social Sciences and History, No. 23, 1935; reprint, New York: Russell and Russell, 1967), p. 126.

10. *Repertorio Americano,* 1938.

— 7 —

Housing, Health, and Everyday Living

H AVING DISCUSSED THE HISTORICAL, economic, and political context of Costa Rican life as well as the social structures of class, ethnicity, and community, we now begin to describe that life in more detail. In this chapter we consider two constant concerns of Costa Ricans: housing and health. We also describe a typical weekday in the lives of families of different social classes in urban and rural settings.

Housing

Colonial houses combined Spanish tradition with available materials. Skilled artisans were few, and the colonists, too poor to import tools and materials, used what was at hand. For the adobe walls of their single-story houses they mixed mud with grass or sugarcane waste, trampled by oxen and shaped into large sun-dried blocks put together with fresh adobe for mortar, or packed into an earthquake-resistant frame of *caña brava,* a bamboo-like plant. The walls rested on foundations of stone and wood or rose directly from hard-packed earth. Workmen shaped roofing tiles by patting soft clay over their thighs. Doors and door frames, window frames, bars, and shutters were made of moisture-resistant wood. The few windows, rarely glazed, were closely shuttered at night and during sickness to keep out "harmful" breezes. Floors were of packed earth, hardwoods, or rectangular clay tiles. Walls were usually coated with whitewash with a wide strip of Prussian blue at the base to discourage pecking chickens. A roofed veranda opened onto an interior patio or the front of the house. There the family and neighbors gathered to talk in the afternoon and to celebrate special occasions.

Such houses predominated in the Central Valley and in Guanacaste until the early twentieth century. Few remain. Most Ticos now live in small wooden or concrete-block houses, many of them painted bright pink, green,

Villager relaxing on his veranda (Julio Laínez)

turquoise, or blue. Floors are of wood or tiles; the roof, of corrugated iron, which rusts with time.

Ninety-three percent of all dwellings had running water by 1993, half of them from wells, the other half from government aqueducts. Nine out of ten had electricity. Of every 100 dwellings, thirty were connected to a sewer system; nearly all the rest had septic tanks or outhouses.

A single-story house with wooden or concrete walls shelters the small farmer, artisan, or low-grade white-collar worker. The front door opens on a *sala,* or parlor, where guests are entertained. As in all social classes, special effort is taken to furnish it as well as possible, for appearances are important, and this is the only room that any but intimate callers see. Artificial flowers, china figurines, and family photos crowd wall shelves and adorn a low doily-covered wooden table in the center of the room. Plastic-covered upholstered chairs and a matching sofa are neatly arranged around the table. A television set stands at one end of the room. The women may make their own clothes on a sewing machine in the corner. Religious pictures, school diplomas, family photographs, and brightly colored lithographs deck the walls.

Farther back and invisible from the *sala* are a kitchen, bathroom, and one or more bedrooms. The unscreened glass windows in each room are covered day and night with plastic curtains or venetian blinds to ensure privacy. In towns they are also covered with metal grills to discourage burglars.

An electric or propane stove is found in most Central Valley kitchens, though even there many rural residents also use wood to boil beans and other foods requiring long cooking. Firewood, gathered and chopped by the men and boys, is stacked in a shed and burned in an iron stove that stands on a wooden platform. A kitchen contains a cupboard or two, some wall shelves, a sink with a cold-water tap for washing dishes, and a wooden table for preparing and eating meals. A stone or concrete sink in the shed or on a covered side porch is used for washing clothes and heavy utensils.

The adults' bedroom may contain a double bed with a cotton-stuffed or foam-rubber mattress and pillows. Two or three children sometimes share each bed in other rooms; some may sleep in the *sala*. A wooden dresser, a vanity table, a nightstand, and perhaps a small rug and table lamp are found in each bedroom. A porcelain sink stands outside the bathroom, which contains a flush toilet and a cold-water shower.

The walls of each room are painted in different pastel colors; green is a favorite for the *sala*. At least one overhead lightbulb dangles in each room. In rural areas a wooden or tiled front porch is adorned with flowers, ferns, and other plants in tin cans or boxes, and perhaps with a caged songbird or a parrot or macaw on a perch. Here family members sit on benches to talk and perhaps watch neighbors pass, though many prefer the privacy afforded by trees and shrubs in the front yard. Medicinal herbs and vegetables, especially the easily cultivated chayote squash, which grows on a climbing vine, are planted near the house if space permits. A motor scooter, a bicycle or two, and perhaps an old car may be parked nearby.

Many lowland houses, floored with rough wooden planks, are raised a foot or two off the ground on wooden posts as a protection against floods and snakes and to provide shade for small animals.

The poorest lowland *campesinos*, as well as Indians even in the mountains, often live in small windowless houses of *caña brava*, with dirt floors and roofs of grass or palm thatch. *Caña* may divide the house into two rooms. It may also form, just under the roof, a wide platform for storing food and tools and for sleeping; it is reached by a notched-log ladder. The walls of vertical *caña* allow breezes to pass. Chickens run in and out. Next to the house, an unwalled shelter consisting of a steep thatched roof supported by four log posts may serve as a kitchen and, during the hottest months, as a sleeping area. Some furniture and tools, such as a large wooden mortar and pestle used for hulling coffee and rice, may be homemade.

Prosperous urbanites usually live in one-story cement-block houses, less often in two-story or split-level ones, each with a large, well-kept garden, an iron-barred carport or garage, a paved driveway, and perhaps a verdant inner patio. A high concrete wall, crowned with broken glass or razor wire, surrounds older upper-class houses; newer ones may have grill-covered windows, burglar alarms, and a watchdog or two plus a tiny shelter for a private

House in a metropolitan suburb (Richard Biesanz)

Urban shantytown (Richard Biesanz)

guard. A concrete walk leads to an elaborately carved front door. Inside, a scrolled gilt mirror and shelf decorate an entrance hall.

Sala furniture may be made of beautiful native hardwoods upholstered in showy materials. Family photographs, vases, figurines, pre-Columbian artifacts, and reproductions of famous paintings or originals bought on travels or painted by family or friends decorate the room. A dining table and chairs may occupy one end of the *sala* or the center of a separate dining room. In a more informal room, which usually includes a bar, the family entertains relatives and close friends, watches television and videos, plays CDs, or surfs the Net. Bedrooms, like *salas*, are often ornately furnished. Children may watch TV and play video games there.

The kitchen contains the electrical appliances owned by most affluent families in the Western world, and the bathroom the usual amenities, including a bidet but rarely a bathtub; Ticos prefer showers. A small, sparsely furnished maid's room and bathroom near the kitchen may be used only during the day, as live-in maids are now rare. Near it are a utility room and patio for hanging clothes, used only during power failures, since most such houses are equipped with washers and dryers.

Middle-class houses range between the two types already described. Nearly all have a refrigerator and at least one TV. Most have a device to heat water in the shower head rather than a hot-water tank. Some members of this class remain in the houses they have lived in since they were born, or since marriage; others have realized a dream of moving into a new suburban house. It is far easier to generalize about the housing of the very rich or the very poor.

The dwelling of a poor urban laborer or street vendor is typically in a crowded slum at the edge of town. Some remain standing for years with residents paying rent to a landlord. Others, euphemistically called "informal settlements" in official reports, spring up overnight as squatters build on unoccupied private land at the edge of a town or in a fallow field. Their unpainted shacks are made of boards discarded by sawmills and of corrugated iron sheets used for the roof and for one or more walls. Although floors are made of dirt or broken wooden planks or tiles, most such homes are as neat and clean as conditions permit. Air and light enter through a door left open during the day. Plastic curtains create partitions. In the one bedroom, several people may sleep in each bed, perhaps a set of raised burlap-covered planks. Several may also sleep in the *sala,* where a table and a few wooden chairs may be the only furniture. Pictures of saints adorn the *sala* walls, together with calendar girls, magazine pictures of luxurious homes and smiling blond babies, and newspaper photos of "society" brides or favorite soccer players. A wooden outhouse, sometimes shared with other families, stands in back. Water is taken from a stream or a municipal tap. Electric current for the bare overhead lightbulbs, a radio, and perhaps a TV may be stolen from nearby lines until the state's utility agency wires the houses.

The most frequent answer to the question "What would you do if you were rich?" is "I'd buy a house." About two-thirds of Ticos owned their homes in 1996. The ideal is a detached single-family dwelling with a yard and a garden. But many homes do not fit that description: There is little space between many urban working- or lower-class dwellings, and rising costs and fear of burglary have made condominiums with a shared watchman increasingly common in upper-middle-class San José suburbs (even though their residents, like most Ticos, would prefer less involvement with neighbors than such housing entails). Most of the other third either rented a house, apartment, or room; lived with relatives or (especially in San José) with friends from the same village; or built shacks on land to which they had no title.

Although relatively few sleep in the streets or under bridges, adults who share housing with parents, in-laws, or siblings would generally prefer not to. Like renters and slum dwellers, they have long pressured government for housing grants and low-interest loans.

Since the 1930s, various agencies—state, government-subsidized, and private—have attempted to remedy the chronic housing shortage. Today, those with moderate incomes often seek a fifteen-to-twenty-year mortgage from a national bank or mutual fund. In 1996 such loans usually covered 80–90 percent of construction costs. Interest rates averaged 24 percent and monthly repayment fees were so high that many eligible borrowers lamented that they were unaffordable. A Housing Ministry official told us: "These complaints reflect our national aversion to planning. Very few Ticos save money—for a house or for anything else. But the complaints are also partly justified—and for the same reason. Our short presidential terms don't facilitate national planning either—for housing or for anything else."

Those with incomes too low to qualify for a mortgage may apply for a public-sector *bono*—a small grant to defray repair or construction costs. Few *bonos* are available and much red tape is involved in getting one—unless one has an influential friend or relative or it is an election year.

Because of economies of scale, land and construction costs are lowest in a working-class *colonia,* or housing project, typically designed and built by private firms and financed by both private- and public-sector funds. Each unit has a living-dining room, two or three bedrooms, and a bathroom with toilet, shower, and washbasin. (Middle-class *colonias* contain more varied housing and are entirely financed with private-sector funds.)

A Housing Ministry economist told us that little planning goes into most housing projects. A civil engineer agrees and argues that political factors—especially the desire for working-class votes—rather than technical studies have determined where and how they are built.[1] The concrete walls and floors and corrugated iron roofs are hastily and poorly assembled, following the same design throughout the country, ignoring climatic variations. The rows of identical buildings are formal and rigid. Thin adjoining walls afford little pri-

Public housing project during an electoral campaign (Julio Laínez)

vacy among neighbors. Parks are few. The roads are designed for vehicles, not pedestrians, but bus stops are far apart. When large projects are built, they are spread out in areas cleared of trees, destroying watersheds and costing a great deal for plumbing, streets, and streetlights.

Colonias continue expanding to the south and southwest of San José. As land has become scarce and expensive, row dwellings of up to four stories have been built. One gloomy prediction is that San José will always be ringed by slums because as soon as some poor families manage to escape them and move into a *colonia*, others take their place; new housing does not keep pace with population growth. And under structural adjustment cutbacks, even the public-sector banks have curtailed loans to low-income Ticos. Invasions of vacant lots and steep riverbanks are still the simplest way for the poor to acquire land.

Health and Longevity

Asked what they value most in life, Ticos are likely to mention health as well as work, a decent house, and their families. Anthropologist Setha Low notes that "Costa Ricans worry more about their health than about their economic status."[2] This preoccupation is reflected in the traditionally high prestige of physicians—five of whom have served as president—and, more recently, in the large numbers of health-related newspaper articles and TV programs, medical offices, laboratories, and pharmacies and in the size of the CCSS, or Social Security Fund, the country's largest formal organization.

Greater prosperity, peace, and education have long made Ticos healthier than other Latin Americans; those born in 1900 could expect to live seven and a half years longer than the regional average.[3] Still, life expectancy of those born in 1927 was only about forty years. By contrast, Ticos born in 1996 could expect to live, on the average, to age seventy-six, a figure comparable to that for highly industrialized countries.

Costa Ricans are now far more likely to die of heart disease or cancer, both of which typically strike in middle or old age, than of childhood diseases or malnutrition. (Accidents are now the leading cause of death of those under fifty.) In 1920, one baby out of every four died in its first year; by 1996 this figure had dropped to one in eighty-five—the second lowest (after Cuba) in Latin America.

A former health minister, Dr. Juan Jaramillo, attributes much of the improvement in Costa Ricans' health and longevity to preventive public health measures: vaccinations, purified piped water, improved sewage disposal, and health education. These, he asserts, have resulted from political choices, not simply from increases in the GNP. Infant mortality did not rise during the economic crisis of the early 1980s, since many public health programs remained in place. In fact, between 1980 and 1993 it fell from 19 to less than 14 per 1,000, and life expectancy at birth rose from 73.5 years to 75.3 years. Costa Rica is, he says, healthy without being wealthy.[4]

The picture is not all bright. Along with improvements in some aspects of health, Ticos in recent years have experienced a marked decline in physical activity, mostly due to more sedentary jobs, TV, and motor transport. Stress, obesity, and alcoholism have all increased. Although starvation is now rare even in the poorest regions, malnutrition remains a major concern.

Public Health Programs

Long a direct cause of death, malnutrition also increased the risk of death from diarrhea and measles. Between 1970 and 1976, infant deaths attributed to malnutrition fell by 70 percent. A government program that offered two free daily meals to schoolchildren, their mothers, and their preschool siblings was largely responsible.

So was the expansion, after 1970, of the state's decades-old rural health services. These were designed to compensate for the fact that hospitals and doctors, both public and private, were concentrated in large urban centers (as they still are). Paramedics trained in the rudiments of vaccination, nutrition, prenatal care, and simple medication were expected to visit every home in their area, averaging about 150, every six weeks, to take a health census and to counsel people on health, hygiene, and family planning. Covering their territories by jeep, motorcycle, boat, horseback, or foot, they referred urgent cases to the nearest hospital if no doctor was due on a routine visit to the local clinic. The drop in deaths from communicable diseases is one indication of the program's success.

The program did not stop with paramedics and free meals. For food to be properly absorbed, children must be cured of parasites and prevented from contracting them again. Therefore other government agencies helped communities achieve a good water supply (which also lowers the incidence of hepatitis and typhoid) and provided free latrines to those willing to install them. Mothers were taught elementary hygiene and food preparation at the nutrition centers. Teachers were encouraged to organize school gardens. Dentists from the Ministry of Health made annual visits to nearly every school, bringing portable drills and other equipment.

Despite setbacks, many public health programs continue in both city and countryside, and the very low incidence of cholera in the 1990s—a major concern elsewhere in Latin America—demonstrates their value. A state agency provides potable water in most communities. The Ministry of Health uses billboards, free pamphlets, TV spots, newspaper articles, and school lessons to warn about the symptoms and causes of cholera and to outline means of its prevention and cure. Another such campaign urges the use of condoms (and, perhaps less successfully, sexual monogamy) to prevent HIV transmission (930 cases of full-blown AIDS were reported between 1982 and 1996). One important vector in the spread of AIDS is HIV-infected prostitutes. Although nearly all prostitutes have monthly medical checkups, as required by law, the requirement that their clients use condoms has not been so easy to enforce.

Since the early 1980s, however, health programs have suffered from spending cuts, and many rural clinics now treat only small children and pregnant women. Says a Ministry of Health dentist, "Fifteen years ago we didn't have to ask schoolchildren's parents for donations—good thing too, as almost all of them had cavities. Now our budget is so tight that we must ask." And whereas schoolchildren in many areas were given two full meals at government expense in the 1970s, by 1994 many got only one small sandwich a day—if local raffles and fairs generated enough income. The Health Ministry found an increase in the incidence of moderate malnutrition between 1987 and 1990 and in 1995 reported that one out of five children under age six was malnourished. The percentage of babies born underweight rose from 3 percent in 1980 to 6.5 percent in 1992. The 1990s saw a resurgence of malaria, tuberculosis, intestinal parasites, and diarrhea as well as an outbreak of dengue fever after half a century of no reported cases.

One reason for such setbacks, say some physicians, is the transfer of many public health programs and all community hospitals from the Ministry of Health to the Social Security Fund, the Caja Costarricense de Seguro Social (CCSS), which stresses cure rather than prevention. Ironically, although PAE-III (the 1996 loan contracts with the World Bank and Inter-American Development Bank) requires the Health Ministry to take the lead in health care, the ministry's budget was cut by 70 percent in that year, and the new rural health clinics established by the Figueres Olsen administration, which were supposed to function like those of the 1970s, were run by the CCSS. It was no surprise, then, that a 1996 study of these centers by the Guild of Physicians and Surgeons found that they emphasized cure, not prevention, and that they seldom treated the uninsured.

The Social Security System

Before the CCSS was established in 1942, and for a long time afterward, most medical care was either private or charitable. Hospitals had an air of the old European pattern of convent care and charity. In each provincial capital a committee of clergy and laymen administered a hospital financed by lottery ticket sales. Large coffee planters as well as the United Fruit Company, faced with a scarcity of workers, paid doctors to treat their peons. Indigents were treated free of charge but feared hospitals as places where one went to die.

President Rafael Angel Calderón Guardia (1940–1944), a physician, conceived of social security as a plan to ensure national health standards rather than merely to provide pensions. Doctors, druggists, and employers opposed the plan from the outset. It covered, at first, only the lowest-paid urban workers. Little by little the ceiling on wages was raised, each step accompanied by complaints that socialization would eliminate private medicine and business.

By 1990 the Seguro, as Ticos call the CCSS, claimed to provide 89 percent of Costa Ricans with insurance for sickness, accidents, dental problems, disability, maternity, old age, and unemployment. Even in 1997, however, some lived too far from any clinics to use them except in emergencies. Others, including many self-employed Ticos, bought medical insurance from the government monopoly, the National Insurance Institute; this allowed them access to far better treatment by private practitioners than that provided by Seguro clinics. Still others, perhaps one in six salaried workers, were not covered, as required, by their employers.

The Seguro, one of the oldest autonomous institutions, has been called the strongest formal organization in the country. Not only does it—by law, at least—enjoy administrative autonomy but it also has de facto legislative power, for all rules and regulations set by its board of directors are mandatory and universal. It has the public sector's biggest budget—nearly $1 billion in

1995, and 27,000 employees. The power of its employees' unions is rivaled only by that of teachers' unions. Four out of five doctors, as well as most nurses, work for CCSS. (About half of all doctors also have private practices, though most appreciate the guaranteed income of a public-sector job.) It now runs nearly all hospitals and clinics, and most newborn Ticos enter the world in a Seguro hospital. It produces and distributes great quantities of medicine and other supplies. Between 1986 and 1990, 6.6 percent of the GNP was spent on health care; 72 percent of this went to CCSS versus only 20 percent for the government's preventive programs.

The Seguro has also been, since the late 1950s, the biggest single source of income for the central government, in the form of defaulted loans and unpaid premiums for government workers and the indigent, as well as government bonds the Seguro is obliged to purchase. According to Diputado Otto Guevara, this "looting" of the agency amounted to over $2 billion by 1998, or two-thirds of its revenue.[5] This debt, along with deadbeat private-sector employers and overbuilding of hospitals in the 1980s, has kept it chronically short of funds; it has had to close many operating rooms and cut down on services and even on such basic supplies as medications and linens.

The system is often criticized as wasteful, expensive, and dehumanizing. A common complaint is that except in emergencies, appointments are scheduled for weeks or even months in the future and that patients must often wait for hours past their scheduled times. A physician laments that even if the typically hasty examination—averaging five minutes—discloses a tumor, the patient must wait three months for another appointment; by then the problem may have become incurable.[6] Some doctors contend that such waits are due to the many unnecessary visits by hypochondriacs or by lonely housewives who want adult attention. "They figure, 'I'm already paying for the service, why shouldn't I use it?'" says one doctor, adding that such patients make everyone else wait longer. But Seguro hospitals sometimes suspend services for an employees' strike or a major soccer game, requiring hundreds of patients to reschedule appointments for up to six months later, though some have already waited that long. And doctors commonly show up late and leave hours early with impunity, many attending to their private practices during their scheduled Seguro hours. (Doctors often use their CCSS posts as a *trampolín* to aid their own private practices, telling a patient, perhaps, "I can't see you here again for probably two months, but you can come to my own office tomorrow." Many patients resort instead to bribing doctors for faster or better attention.)

A farm overseer tells a story we have heard dozens of times:

> I went to a Seguro clinic very early one morning and waited hours with crowds of others. I saw a doctor for five minutes, then had to wait another hour and a half for pills and vitamin B6. Nurses and secretaries just stood

around talking. The doctor took no tests—not even blood pressure—and gave me no clear diagnosis. What shall I do when I run out of those pills? Waste another day or spend two days' pay on a private doctor?

Some employers prefer to send sick workers to private doctors even though they must still pay CCSS premiums. (The thousands of U.S. citizens who come to Costa Rica every year for heart or cosmetic surgery in private hospitals find the quality of care at least as high as that in their own country.)

Rather than accept red tape, delays, and cursory examinations, those who cannot afford a private doctor may ask a private pharmacist or relative for medication or try herbal and folk remedies. Says a ranch hand, "A Seguro doctor gave me tranquilizers for my lower back pain [a common complaint among farmers and ranchers]. How stupid, especially since I'm a recovering alcoholic! But they prescribe tranquilizers to everybody, it seems. So I went to a *sobador* [a kind of folk massage therapist] and he cured me right away."

Patient care has suffered, says Jaramillo, not only from the Seguro's budgetary problems but also because medical personnel lost prestige as the agency expanded and they came to be seen more as bureaucrats than as professionals; this, plus low salaries and an increase in malpractice suits, accounts for a shortage of physicians and an even more acute lack of nurses, who are likely to seek jobs in the United States. Furthermore, the CCSS's authority is so centralized that employees rarely make independent decisions.[7]

Doctors and patients alike laud the Seguro's response in emergencies. A forty-two-year-old *pulpería* owner told us when we visited him in his small private room in a major hospital's coronary unit, "When I had chest pains, a Red Cross ambulance took me to the hospital's emergency ward, and a big team of Seguro doctors worked on me at once. If the hospital staff decides you don't have a serious problem, that's when you get an appointment months in the future."

On balance, however, the increased size of the Seguro may well have harmed general health by diverting funds from more cost-effective prevention programs. One indication of the change: Many Seguro patients are now sent to Colombia for eye surgery; at the same time, the eyesight of many thousands of children is threatened by vitamin A deficiency, a problem that could be prevented very cheaply. And in the early 1990s, even as doctors took pride in the first heart and liver transplants performed in Costa Rica, school lunches were including more animal fat (in cheap bologna and sausage)—a major cause of heart disease, now the nation's leading killer. Jaramillo comments that the diseases increasingly typical of Costa Rica's aging population are so expensive to treat that education programs in healthy living have become even more important. Unfortunately, he adds, medical, pharmacy, and dentistry schools—like the Seguro most graduates work for—still emphasize treatment, not prevention.[8]

Psychological Disturbances and Substance Abuse

In the 1990s we heard far more complaints of stress and depression than in earlier decades. A Health Ministry study in 1994 concluded that two out of three women, mostly those between ages twenty-two and forty-four, were depressed, fifteen times the rate among men. The study cited as causes an excess of obligations, poverty, unhappy relationships, and the cultural acceptance of physical and psychological abuse of women.

Psychologist Henning Jensen adds that loneliness is a growing problem among Ticos. "People feel more and more alone. 'The other' becomes a potential enemy, and social relationships are more aggressive than before."[9] This and other forms of malaise may be reflected in a doubling of the per capita suicide rate—from 2.5 to 5 per 100,000—between 1950 and 1994. Unemployed men are the most frequent victims; the Christmas season, the most common time. Three children, ages nine, ten, and thirteen, killed themselves in separate incidents in one month of 1995; suicides of children had been almost unheard of. The education minister, concerned that children's stress inhibited learning, urged teachers to begin each day with a "harmonious circle"—a ten-minute period of discussion and physical exercise.

Eighty-three percent of the 879 beds in the Seguro's psychiatric hospital were occupied in 1995, some of them by patients who go out to work by day. Many outpatients come for psychological counseling and chemical and occupational therapy. Psychiatrists and psychologists say that they are increasingly sought out, and priests less so, by people with emotional problems and that the great majority of their patients are now self-referred.

Still, says psychiatrist Francisco Jiménez, Costa Ricans prefer to avoid facing painful issues. "They think one shouldn't cry or suffer, so they seek substances to reduce the pain."[10] A Seguro employee confirmed what many Ticos had told us: that tranquilizers are prescribed to over half of Seguro patients.

Alcoholism is widely acknowledged as a major problem. It has deep roots: Three eighteenth-century Heredians complained that "the vice of *aguardiente* [cane liquor] is so widespread in this town that even youths and women drink it like water."[11] A 1991 study by the public-sector National Institute on Alcoholism and Drug Dependency (IAFA) identified 6.3 percent of the population over fifteen as alcoholic, an increase from 5 percent in 1982. Although heavy drinking by women is still frowned on, especially in rural areas, one out of three "problem drinkers," according to the IAFA, is a woman as compared to one in twenty in 1982.

The anxiety of which many complain—some of it stemming, no doubt, from rapid social change—may be one reason for increased drinking. Another may be easier access to money as Costa Rica has industrialized. Anthropologist Jorge Amador, in his study of plantation workers who became tunnel workers for the Costa Rican Institute of Electricity, says that their increased incomes enabled them to drink far more.[12] And a teetotaling seventy-year-old farmer says he stopped his youthful binges after going broke.

Drinking—today mostly of beer rather than cane liquor—has become firmly embedded in the culture, a social ritual surrounding many leisure activities. Sociologist Marlon Yong says that Costa Ricans use alcohol "to ease the integration of the individual into the group—that is, it facilitates reciprocity, solidarity, spontaneity, sincerity."[13] It also lowers the need to *quedar bien*, and Ticos are far more ready to express anger and resentment when intoxicated than when sober.

Opportunities and pressures to drink exist everywhere. Twelve thousand bars were reported to exist in 1992. Drinking is common even at adolescents' parties, and young buyers are seldom asked for proof of age. Boys of ten or twelve are often given drinks at parties and wedding receptions, and half of the male alcoholics in one study reported that they began drinking at this age. Since heavy drinking is identified with manliness, abstinence is sometimes considered a sign of immaturity or effeminacy.

Alcoholics Anonymous groups are found even in small towns. There are also religious and private treatment programs, including inpatient clinics. In 1976 police were told to stop imprisoning drunks; alcoholics were officially recognized as sick rather than criminal and were to be turned over to the IAFA. Still, said the institute's director in 1995, "Doctors seem to be prepared to do their job once the patient is bleeding or having seizures, but want no part of attending to the early stages of something that they (like almost everyone else) think could be avoided by the application of just a little 'will power' or 'moral fiber.'"[14]

The fact that alcohol—much of it distilled and sold by a public-sector agency or else taxed—has long been a substantial source of government revenue may help account for the scanty funding of the IAFA's prevention and rehabilitation programs. (A similar conflict of interest existed in colonial times, when royal authorities enjoyed a monopoly on legal liquor distillation and sales but professed concern about excessive consumption.)

Other psychotropic drugs, both legal and illegal, are widely used. Ticos have one of the world's highest rates of caffeine consumption, perhaps one reason for the *nervios* of which so many complain. Cigarettes, like alcohol, were long heavily advertised. Health officials now use TV notices and billboards to warn against smoking. They have convinced the legislature to prohibit tobacco advertising and to place restrictions (largely ignored and unenforced) on smoking in public places. They assert that the number of Costa Ricans who smoke—most of them men—fell from 35 percent in 1980 to 20 percent in 1993.

Although women drink and smoke more than they once did, they are much more likely to use tranquilizers for emotional problems and insomnia and to become addicted to them; tranquilizer use is less stigmatized and more easily concealed. A Health Ministry study found that Costa Ricans consumed twice as many tranquilizers in 1996 as in 1993 and that 30 percent of the population self-medicates with tranquilizers.

Illicit drugs—the most popular are marijuana and cocaine—are less widely used than alcohol or tranquilizers but far more deeply feared by many Ticos as threats to health and morality, and as causes of crime. Cocaine was once perceived as a rich person's drug; its street price, in the form of crack (now processed locally), plummeted in the early 1990s, and police attributed the rising number of muggings largely to crack addiction. Heroin use, uncommon for seventy years, also increased in the 1990s.

Alternative Medicine

Costa Ricans of all classes draw on a broad spectrum of cures and healers. Some are supernatural—saints, spirits, and God. Others have empirical referents—doctors, midwives, pharmacists, and, until recently persons who gave injections in their own homes, catering to a belief in the almost miraculous powers of the needle. Forms of "alternative" medicine vary from age-old practices such as herbal cures, now enjoying renewed popularity, through homeopathy, practiced in Costa Rica for a century (one out of four Ticos has consulted a homeopath), to newly imported practices such as acupuncture and chiropractic.

Most Ticos share to some degree what anthropologists call "popular medicine"—a complex of ideas, facilities, and practices regarding the cause and cure of illness that may only partially coincide with those of orthodox medical specialists. Many use both traditional healing or preventive methods and new ones advised by health professionals or advertisers. The working-class adolescent mothers studied by anthropology student Grettel Kooper followed doctors' advice in not cutting off the stub of a baby's umbilical cord but also rubbed lard or coffee on it to prevent infection, as their mothers had done.[15] A heart patient told us he was soaking garlic in alcohol and then taking eighteen drops daily "to clean out my arteries." Afro-Caribbeans "do not completely trust 'white man's medicine' and, for many ailments, prefer 'bush medicines.'"[16]

Although they describe menstruation and pregnancy as illnesses, Ticos take colds, stomach upsets, and aches and pains more or less for granted as part of the natural order of things. Many ascribe more serious illnesses to God's will (though not necessarily as punishment for misdeeds) or to an evil spell cast by a witch hired by an enemy. They may scrub with disinfectants, water, and lemon juice to ward off illness; this practice often stems from belief in countermagic against evildoers rather than from knowledge about microbes. Individual or group prayers (by members of the family or church) are common responses to serious illness.

Nervios is a common complaint, especially among working-class and adolescent females. Its main symptoms are a desire to cry and to run away. A female doctor we spoke to dismissed *nervios* as a psychosomatic disease usually diagnosed by the patient herself, but anthropologists Carole Hill and Lisa Cottrell see it as a result of women's stressful and restricted roles.[17] CCSS sociologist Leda Montoya concurs and attributes women's *nervios* to their lack of a feeling of being in control. "It's like headache and backache," she says. "Women, especially housewives, suffer most from these indicators of stress; men, especially bosses, least." Body functioning can also be disturbed by a *susto,* or emotional shock. The penal code, reflecting the prevalence of this belief, prescribes punishment for anyone who shocks another person in delicate health—a pregnant woman, for example.

Almost everyone knows and uses some herbal remedies. Medicinal plant lore may come from parents and grandparents, from herb vendors in municipal markets, or even from the mass media. Many bars offer herbal hangover remedies. A farmer lauded the use of several local herbs "for the liver," an organ that preoccupies Ticos as the heart does North Americans or the stomach, Germans. Asked how he had learned about these herbs, he replied, "From TV." Friends, coworkers, and neighbors all will tell one which herbs to get for a cold, an ulcer, arthritis, or almost any other ailment that human flesh is heir to and how to use them. Herbal cures became especially popular in the 1990s not only as a consequence of price hikes in patent medicines but also, admits a drug company executive, because they are coming to be seen as safer and often more effective than commercial drugs and are now taken seriously by many professionals.

For decades a familiar panacea—for colds, stomach upsets, fatigue, hangovers—has been Alka-Seltzer. We have seen Ticos take a couple of tablets after a big restaurant meal simply as a precaution against indigestion.

Self-medication is encouraged by the ease with which both patent medicines and prescription drugs may be obtained. Says the drug company executive, "Patients often insist on getting a prescription from a doctor no matter what the problem. Then they often take several times the prescribed dose, reasoning that more is better—or they take less to stretch out their supply until their next visit."[18] Researchers in one rural area found that 80 percent of homes had medicine cabinets with expired prescription drugs. Family members would often take these indiscriminately when feeling ill or give them to others who felt ill.

The expansion of social security has somewhat reduced self-medication—except with herbs—but it continues in part because it is not as time consuming as getting attention at the local clinic and because many are convinced that Seguro medicines are inferior and that the same drug, usually aspirin or a tranquilizer, may be prescribed for many unrelated illnesses. Perhaps the chief reason, however, is that "historically, the community pharmacist established the therapeutic relationship that was the focus of primary care."[19] Although they do no medical tests, pharmacists frequently diagnose and prescribe, and many Ticos address a pharmacist as "Doctor." In remote hamlets the *pulpería* owner has a license from the Ministry of Health to sell medicine; although he has no pharmaceutical (let alone medical) training, he, too, often diagnoses and prescribes.

Among traditional healers are *curanderos* and *sobadores*. *Curanderos* insist that the patient have faith in them and prescribe herbs and special diets, often accompanied by special prayers. *Sobadores* massage specific parts of the body—the arms, for example, to expel a *pega*, a wad of undigested food that is seen as a source of stomach disorders. A nurse who is also a *sobadora* showed us the technique while massaging a colleague who had become ill at lunch. It involves pressure on specific points, similar to Japanese shiatsu.

To sum up: Though Ticos have always respected orthodox physicians and their prescriptions, few rely entirely on modern medicine for diagnosis and healing; they prefer to combine herbs and Alka-Seltzer, prayers and prescriptions, magic and medicine.[20] And they tend to agree that the crucial ingredient in healing is faith, whether in herbs, saints, or doctors.

Daily Routine

The rhythms of everyday life vary considerably from farm to city, among social classes, and from one stage of family life to another. Routines were, until a few decades ago, more predictable: It was safe to assume, for example, that most Ticos rose and retired very early. Today one had best be careful about telephoning a city friend before 9 or 10 A.M. as he or she may work or study late at night. And some of the same things—television, for example—that changed urban patterns in the 1960s are now affecting rural life as well.

Still, *campesinos* say, "God helps those who rise early." Their workdays start early to minimize exposure to both midday heat and afternoon rain; even in the rainy season mornings are usually clear and sunny. Outdoor activity is restricted during the rainy season, and farmers in newly deforested areas often have little work in the dry season. "There is no rain from December to May, so we don't plant crops, but go to the banana zone to work, or spend a lot of time visiting," says a young man in arid Acosta canton.

So attuned to sun time are rural people that when the government, in an effort to economize on electric current during water shortages, decreed daylight saving time in 1973 and again in 1980, many complained of disrupted sleep and digestion. Rural peons, expected to work from 6 A.M. to noon, refused to start work in the dark and continued to go by the sun. Both times, the government soon nullified its decree. But since schools, buses, television, and radio—which announces the time every few minutes—have become part of rural life, many *campesinos* now wear watches. A rural high school student told us, "The sun wakes me, and then I look at my watch to see if it's time to get up."

By 4 or 5 A.M. an electric light or candle is already burning and a radio playing in the kitchen of the rural peon or small farmer, whose wife and older daughters rise early. After a cold shower or quick sponging with soap and cold water, they prepare breakfast.

They pour boiling water through a cloth bag full of powdered coffee, perhaps homegrown, and then sit awhile with a cup of the strong sweetened black brew and bread or commercial tortillas and sour cream and perhaps a fried-rice and bean dish called *gallo pinto* (spotted rooster). Then they prepare the lunches a child will take to the men for their nine or ten o'clock break: tortillas or white bread, cold black beans and rice, a bottle of raw-sugar water, and perhaps some sausage, meat, or eggs.

Before their own breakfast the men slip on cotton pants and shirts, denim aprons, canvas hats, and sheathed machetes, which they may use to clear weeds and brush from cropland or pasture. All members of the family wear rubber boots during the rainy season, when roads and trails become muddy and fast-growing weeds may hide snakes. They save their shoes for mass and trips to town.

Schoolchildren may be wakened by six and served a breakfast like that of their parents, including coffee, which is thought to be nourishing and is given even to toddlers. If their classes are in the afternoon, they may be allowed to sleep a little longer. Many need an hour or more to walk to school; others ride a bicycle or horse.

Meanwhile their mother and older sisters make beds, feed chickens, milk any cows they may have, and sweep the dirt or plank floor, perhaps using a homemade broom of small branches. They wash clothes with cold water and a bar of laundry soap, rub them in one section of the concrete sink, rinse them in another, then lay them on the grass or bushes or hang them on a barbed-wire fence to whiten in sun and rain for a day or so. In areas without piped water, the nearest stream serves for laundry. Since 87 percent of rural homes had electricity by 1995, they are likely to press the clothes with electric irons rather than the old flatirons heated on the woodstove. Even on Sundays the women may do laundry, for Ticos highly value clean, unwrinkled clothing. Schoolgirls wash and iron the blouses of their uniforms daily.

In late morning the women and children lunch on rice, black beans, fried plantains, chayote squash or chopped raw cabbage, commercial tortillas or bread, and fresh fruit juice mixed with water and sugar or, for the children, a little milk. Families of fishermen also eat fish, though rarely with much enjoyment. Foods are prepared the same way every day. A little after noon, the men may return from a six-hour workday and eat a second lunch or perhaps only coffee with bread. Others will knock off after eight hours of work; peons who are paid by the job rather than the hour—for example, those under contract to clear a pasture—may work until dark or until it rains. Fishermen have a much more erratic work schedule, depending on tides and weather; many also work on their own or others' small farms.

Though all may sit awhile after the noon meal, they will probably not nap. Nor will the women lie down until they retire for the night, although they sit for brief respites. Many sell eggs or homemade ice cream or do paid work such as sewing at home. Peggy Barlett found that women in a farm village in Guanacaste in the late 1960s worked, on an average, about 44 percent of the time; men, less than 27 percent.[21] A 1986 Planning Ministry study revealed that rural women worked an average of eighteen hours a day.[22] In many rural areas, water shortages caused by deforestation oblige women and children to spend several of these hours carrying water from a distant creek. And half of all rural women, according to a study conducted between 1992 and 1994, spend five or more hours a day cultivating, storing, or processing crops on their own or other people's land.

If the family has a bit of land, the men may work it during the afternoon. Favored crops for home use are beans, corn, and chayote; many also still grow cash crops such as coffee and sugarcane or some of the newer "nontraditional" crops, especially oranges (whose juice is now a major export). Boys aged eight and up are expected to help when they are not in school. Their sisters may begin household chores and baby-sitting at about age six. Until the 1950s, a peon spent most of his afternoons working his plot or making rude furniture for the house. Fewer peons today have any land of their own, and most now buy furniture as well as food. Many spend their afternoons looking for odd jobs to bring in money, chopping firewood, playing with the children, listening to the radio, or talking with other men at a nearby *pulpería* or village street corner. Boys and young men devote many hours to impromptu soccer games.

Women spend the afternoon finishing their farmwork and housework and boiling beans for the coming day, meanwhile listening to Latin American dance and pop music and Mexican or Venezuelan soap operas on the radio or TV. Children run occasional errands to the store on weekdays, though parents buy most necessities on Saturdays at a local *pulpería* or a town market.

As in the city, everyone has a cup of coffee with bread or pastry at about three o'clock. Supper, often identical to lunch, is eaten between four and five. During the coffee harvest, Central Valley *campesinos* may spend their extra money for cheese, sausage, or *olla de carne,* the traditional stew made with beef, yuca, potatoes, corn, plantains, squash, and other vegetables.

After supper the women wash dishes and put younger children to bed, sometimes saying a prayer with them, then iron or sew while other family members drink coffee and listen to the six o'clock news on radio or TV. Older children may watch television for several hours, at home or with neighbors, while the younger men talk or play soccer with friends. The family may say a rosary, a vanishing practice even in the countryside. A cup of coffee, cocoa, or raw-sugar water is taken just before retiring, and most members of the family are asleep by ten; younger men may come in an hour or two later.

The daily life of a somewhat wealthier small farmer's family differs only slightly. He and his older sons may drive a pickup truck to a field where they work alone or with kinsmen or friends. They eat lunch (often while watching TV) with their own families at eleven or twelve o'clock unless they are working on a distant piece of their often widely scattered holdings. Their meals are likely to include more eggs, meat, milk, and vegetables than those of the landless peon's or *minifundista*'s family.

An urban manual worker may rise at four or five o'clock to be at work by six or seven; he or she may commute up to two hours each way.[23] Breakfast usually includes sweetened coffee with *gallo pinto* and sour cream or an egg or white bread bought each morning by one of the children at a nearby store. The worker may pack some sandwiches or rice and beans for lunch before boarding a crowded public bus, company van, motor scooter, or bicycle. Housework—often a "second shift" facing women who have already worked ten hours at a factory job—varies little from one day to another: making beds, sweeping floors, and washing clothes by hand. If a woman has no refrigerator, she may send a child to a nearby *pulpería* for each day's perishables and purchase staples weekly at the municipal market or a supermarket. Lunch consists of rice, beans, and fruit juice or coffee with little variation in the menu or the way it is prepared.

The men may go to another job after lunch; many hold two or more regular jobs or, like small farmers, spend much time looking for and doing odd jobs. After work a man may stop for drinks at a favorite bar, then play with the children when he gets home. After a five or six o'clock supper—the menu a repetition of lunch—he may watch television while his wife sews, finishes her housework, and chats with the younger children. The older boys are likely to be at night school; talking with friends at a billiard hall, street corner, or bar; or trying to pick up girls. Girls, except for night school students, usually stay home after supper. By ten or eleven most family members are asleep.

Urban and suburban middle-class Ticos with jobs, classes, or children to get ready for school still rise early, perhaps setting a clock radio or alarm for 5:30 or 6 A.M. Their day begins with a shower—perhaps a cold one, which many Ticos say they prefer. As in the working class, they take care to dress in wrinkle-free, spotless clothing. Still, dress codes have relaxed in recent years, and many male office workers and professionals, even those in San José, now forgo a coat and tie, as they always have in hot lowland towns. Their female colleagues, however, still devote much care to dress and makeup.

Breakfast may consist of coffee, packaged cereal, an egg, fruit juice, and fresh bread from a nearby store. An hour-long commute through dense traffic by car, bus, or taxi (often shared with others) may be necessary to arrive at work by seven or eight.

Middle-class families once had live-in cooks and housemaids; many now hire a *doméstica* for a few hours a week. In the days of an ample supply of servants at low wages, a middle-class woman may have done only some cooking and sewing; now she does most of the housework. Once she sent the cook to market and bought milk, produce, and chickens from door-to-door vendors. Now she shops at the supermarket and occasionally at a weekly farmers' market. She is likely to prefer packaged foods; though much more expensive, they take less time to buy and prepare, and "saving time" has become important to the middle class. If she has an outside job—as many do—it is usually her responsibility to take small children to a day-care center or baby-sitter (usually a relative) first and to pick them up after work.

Noon dinner was once the main meal of the day, with most of the family present; then the breadwinner had a two-hour midday break and children were home from school. Now many families can manage that only on weekends; whereas many businesses and local branches of government agencies still close at midday in small towns, few do in the San José area.

On weekdays, adults' lunch is often a light meal brought from home or eaten at a fast-food restaurant near work, or a sandwich eaten at home. When schoolchildren get home, perhaps not until midafternoon, they are served their main meal, which typically includes rice and beans, soup, steak, plantains, bread or tortillas, a salad of lettuce and tomatoes, cooked vegetables and eggs, topped off by fruit and lemonade, milk, or coffee. (In the era of long midday breaks from work and school and before weight control had become a common concern, their parents usually joined them.)

Even if she has no outside job, the mother may leave the younger children with a servant or relative or at a day-care center, freeing her to shop, call on friends, or attend a club meeting. Or she may stay at home and watch television, work on arts or crafts with friends (for fun and possibly profit), or help younger schoolchildren with their homework. After work her husband, like the urban working-class man, may stop for drinks, though at a more elegant bar. Like men in other classes, he spends some time with the children after he gets home.

Supper, served about six, is now the main meal, but middle-class suppers are now much lighter than a few decades ago. Many middle- and working-class Ticos occasionally take their children to the fast-food places that have proliferated in recent years. Or they may have a pizza delivered and share it while watching TV or a video.

Older children, especially boys, may hang out with friends in the evening. Just before exams, high school and university students may study much of the night. Ordinarily, however, most do little studying. Upper-middle-class men may entertain business or professional acquaintances at a restaurant, nightclub, or their own home bar. On most nights family members, except the older boys, who may be out with friends, are asleep by ten or eleven.

The daily life of an upper-class family is similar in many ways. Men of this class, however, are more likely to have independent occupations allowing flexible working hours. Upper-class households also include more live-in servants—typically a maid for cleaning, a nursemaid, and a cook. A chauffeur and gardener may also serve the family. Most upper-class women, even those who do not work outside the home, regard servants as necessities, and the "servant problem" has long been a favorite conversational theme; since at least the late nineteenth century affluent Ticas have lamented, "These days one cannot find an honest, hard-working servant as one could in my mother's day." Servants allow upper-class women to spend much time shopping (often in Miami, a two-and-one-half-hour plane trip from San José); calling on friends; painting or writing poetry; doing volunteer work; and attending teas, card parties, and club meetings. Men of this class spend considerable time working with political parties, economic pressure groups, and business associates (often over breakfast at luxury hotels), relaxing at their professional associations' clubs or playing with their children, and traveling abroad on business and pleasure.

Summary and Conclusion

A growing number of Costa Ricans live in concrete-block houses that vary little in design from one region to another but do differ greatly in size and furnishings among social classes. Government housing programs have only partially remedied a chronic housing deficit stemming from rapid population growth, lack of planning, and the desire of each family to have its own dwelling.

Health, like housing, is a major preoccupation of Ticos. Preventive programs, responsible for raising life expectancy to one of the world's highest levels, have been cut since the early 1980s. The widely criticized Social Security Fund, which emphasizes cure rather than prevention, dominates health care. Many prefer to consult pharmacists and folk healers; those who can afford it consult private doctors. Stress, loneliness, and anxiety are reflected in the widespread abuse of alcohol and tranquilizers.

Costa Ricans' daily routines, like their housing and health practices, vary greatly among social classes. Many Ticos now spend much time moonlighting. Those living in metropolitan San José now spend far more time commuting. As more women work away from home and time for family life and diversion diminishes, home-delivered foods and restaurants—especially fast-food chains—attract those who can afford them.

Notes

1. Julio Cesar Mora Monge, "Análisis del crecimiento urbano del cantón de Alajuelita," Lic. Thesis, UCR, 1993, p. 24.

2. Setha Low, *Culture, Politics, and Medicine in Costa Rica* (Bedford Hills, N.Y.: Redgrave, 1985), pp. 4, 17–18.

3. Juan Jaramillo Antillón, *Salud y seguridad social* (San José: UCR, 1993), p. 32.

4. Ibid., pp. 14, 35, 207. Infant mortality and life-expectancy data from the Bureau of Statistics and Census.

5. "Gobierno saquea a la Caja," *Al Diá*, June 5, 1998, p. 4.

6. Dr. Roberto Ortíz Brenes, "Costa Rica: País de avanzada social," *La República*, June 18, 1992, p. 3A.

7. Jaramillo, *Salud*, pp. 531–542.

8. Ibid., pp. 14, 19, 119, 178–179.

9. Quoted in *Rumbo*, April 18, 1995, p. 15.

10. Quoted in *La República*, June 21, 1992, p. 5A.

11. Eva María Guevara, Raimundo Quesada, Damaris Salazar, Clotilde Banavides, and Afredo Aymerich, "Vida cotidiana en la colonia, 1680–1821," Lic. Thesis in History, UCR, October 1994, p. 271.

12. Jorge Luís Amador Matamoros, "De jornaleros agrícolas a obreros de la construcción de túneles," Lic. Thesis in Anthropology, UCR, 1991, pp. 391–392.

13. Marlon Yong Ch., "Sinópsis de las patologías sociales en Costa Rica," in Juan Manuel Villasuso, ed., *El nuevo rostro de Costa Rica* (Heredia: CEDAL, 1992), pp. 76–77.

14. Steve Kogel, "Costa Rican Doctors Need Enlightenment," *Tico Times*, November 17, 1995, p. W10.

15. Grettel Kooper Arquedas, "Actitudes y prácticas asociadas al autocuidado de la salud," Lic. Thesis, UCR, 1987, p. 184.

16. Carole E. Hill, "National and Cultural Influences on Economic Development, Political Decision-Making, and Health Care Changes in the Rural Frontier of Costa Rica," *Human Organization*, Vol. 53, No. 4, Winter 1994, p. 368.

17. Carole Hill and Lisa Cottrell, "Traditional Mental Disorders in a Developing West Indian Community in Costa Rica," *Anthropological Quarterly*, January 1986, p. 10.

18. Interview by Mavis Hiltunen Biesanz, 1994.

19. Low, *Culture, Politics, and Medicine*, p. 36.

20. Miles Richardson and Barbara Bode, *Popular Medicine in Puntarenas, Costa Rica: Urban and Societal Features* (New Orleans: Tulane University, Middle American Research Institute, 1971), p. 263.

21. Peggy Barlett, *The Use of Time in a Costa Rican Village* (San José: Associated Colleges of the Midwest, 1969), p. 26.

22. Ministry of Planning, "Descripción de algunas características en torno a la situación de la mujer costarricense," September 1986, p. 22.

23. Carlos Sandoval García, *Sueños en la vida cotidiana: Trabajadores y trabajadoras de la máquila y la construcción en Costa Rica* (San José: EUCR, 1997), p. 68.

— 8 —

The Family

COSTA RICANS, LAMENTING WHAT THEY SEE as the breakdown of today's families, idealize those of the nineteenth and early twentieth centuries. Sexual relations, many insist, were restricted to marriage; divorce and desertion were almost unheard of. Unified families of three generations formed the "moral base" of the society, according to a history text used in Costa Rican schools for many decades.[1]

But this view of yesteryear's family is no more accurate than the gloomy picture of current family breakdown. Family ties remain strong—perhaps stronger, by some standards, than a century ago. When middle- and high-income adults in a 1992 survey were asked, "What is most important in life?" 87 percent replied, "Family"—more than mentioned education or religion.[2] Our working-class informants gave the same response. Ticos see home and family as a haven from life's troubles. Close friends often say they are like sisters and brothers.

Colonial and Nineteenth-Century Family Patterns

Spanish family patterns were not carried intact to the Americas. Early exploration and colonization were almost entirely masculine undertakings. For decades few Spanish women made the crossing. Most early colonists mated with indigenous and African women, taking them peacefully or by force. Female servants and slaves were expected to bear many children to augment the wealth of their masters, who often sired the children themselves. Only after three or four generations did Spaniards formally marry "mixed-bloods."

Incest was common in the tiny, widely scattered settlements.[3] Once the clergy's efforts to establish towns around churches had succeeded, it was easier to enforce Spanish family mores, particularly premarital virginity, wifely fidelity to ensure the paternal line, and mutual aid within the patrilineal extended family. Marriages, frequently arranged by parents, required parental approval if either party was under twenty-five.

167

Other "traditional"—that is, patriarchal—ideas of gender roles, however, date back only to the early nineteenth century. As elsewhere in the Western Hemisphere, European women gained status by crossing the ocean. Although they were *mandadas en España* (bossed in Spain), many women became *mandonas en América* (bosses in America). Colonial women of whatever status, historian Tatiana Lobo argues, did not resemble the ideal the church tried to impose. After independence from Spain, however, many women lost much of the freedom and power they had once enjoyed:

> With the [birth of the] Republic there vanishes the *doña* who founded and rented chaplaincies, who belonged to brotherhoods and fraternities, whose dowry papers protected the property she brought to marriage; the slave trader, businesswoman and smuggler [vanishes]. . . . There appears, then, that irrelevant and anonymous figure we know as "housewife" . . . with her civil identity lost in her husband's surname.[4]

A decree issued by Bishop Nicolas in 1813, shortly before independence, says Lobo, heralded this change. Women who wore seductive garments such as transparent veils to church, the bishop declared, were nothing more than prostitutes. This decree was but one signal of increasing restrictions on women's behavior throughout the West, a result of the industrial revolution and the growth of agrarian capitalism. In Costa Rica, the many women artisans' productive roles and independence were further curtailed by the coffee boom and the subsequent massive importation of consumer goods.[5]

Men were seen as naturally superior in anything political, economic, or intellectual; women, in morality and spirituality as well as home life. This contrast justified male power and privilege as well as female weakness and self-sacrifice. A woman was submissive to males, her status linked almost entirely to her relationships with men: An unmarried virgin was a *señorita* or a *muchacha buena* (good girl); if she remained unmarried after age twenty-five or so, she was an old maid doomed to spend her life "dressing saints." A promiscuous woman was a *zorra (*fox*)*. Other single nonvirgins were *mujeres,* or women; the title of *señora* was given only to married women and common-law wives. No such abundance of terms denoted men's sexuality or marital status.

Having learned their role in early childhood, most women were not merely resigned to it but took bitter pride in the suffering that they endured for the sake of their husbands and children and that they described at length to sympathetic listeners. They often called marriage a cross that was woman's highest calling to bear and through which she gained virtue in the eyes of God and society. Members of both sexes criticized overtly dominant wives, quoting the proverb "The rooster sings, the hen only cackles."

Current Family Patterns and Gender Roles

Spanish patterns survive today in the emphasis on family reputation and patrilineal descent. Slights against the honor of family members, including deceased ones, may be punished by recourse to law. According to Spanish tradition, the continuity of blood lines, traced through males, is deemed so important that procreation is considered the primary purpose of marriage, and there must be no doubt about a child's paternity. Women in "respectable" families, therefore, are regarded as creatures whose honor and chastity must be protected.

Laws reflect cultural ideals of mutual aid among kin. Spouses are responsible for supporting each other (though the husband's duty is paramount) as well as their minor or disabled children, and adults are responsible for all members of their immediate family, for example, disabled siblings. A worker insured by the social security system (as most Ticos are) can have parents and even grandparents insured at no extra cost. And a person convicted of murdering a spouse or family member may get a longer prison sentence than one who kills a nonrelative. Orphaned nephews and nieces, relatives who have come to study or work in one's community, and widowed or impoverished relatives of either spouse are often taken into one's home. Nepotism in business and even in government is seldom criticized.

Vestiges of nineteenth-century gender roles are reflected in the many popular songs that depict women as willing to sacrifice everything for a man's love.[6] But women are increasingly challenging double standards, as did the Tica suffragists before 1949. A revived women's movement has flourished since the 1980s, when poverty, which especially affects women and children, began to increase. By 1993, some forty well-established feminist groups existed with goals ranging from bank credit for women to the eradication of domestic violence and gender stereotypes in schooling.[7] Of over 180 delegations to the Fifth International Women's Conference in Beijing in 1995, Costa Rica's was one of only ten that approved the proposed platform for action without reservations.

Feminist ideas appeal mostly to middle-class women freed by their jobs from financial dependence on parents and husbands. Lower-class urban women have long had such independence forced on them by their single status or their partners' meager earnings. The same is true of the many *campesinas* who run their own small farms or hire out as peons.

Males increasingly accept changes in gender roles. We have heard schoolboys disparage "*machista*" attitudes and have stayed with families where boys did much of the housework. We saw many more fathers playing with their children in the 1990s than a decade earlier.

Government now expresses support for gender equality. Men and women, according to the 1949 constitution, enjoy absolute legal equality. The

*Tica business
executive
(Ingrid Holst)*

1974 family code stipulates that husband and wife have equal duties and rights. Husbands no longer have legal control over wives' business affairs. Women can make contracts, take out loans, inherit property, and form corporations on their own. The law also forbids sexual harassment and sex discrimination in hiring and salary. Government agencies and large businesses are required to provide day care for workers' children.

The 1990 Law for Promotion of the Social Equality of Women applies to many areas of life, ranging from political party caucuses to images used in ads. A mother's opinions on childrearing are legally as valid as a father's; if they disagree, a judge can decide. Household responsibilities must be shared by all members without regard to sex. Schools are forbidden to use discriminatory texts such as the old readers that state: "Mother kneads the dough" while "father reads the paper." Violations of antidiscrimination laws, however, are frequent and seldom punished. If both a man and a woman are considered for a high-level job, for example, the man is usually chosen. Even for lower-level jobs, many employers are reluctant to hire a woman who they think is likely to become pregnant because the law not only requires that she be given maternity leave but also that she cannot be fired simply because she is pregnant. Women find it harder than men to get business loans even though they have better repayment records. The government's land-distribution program tends to bypass women. They earn less than men, largely because they are concentrated in lower-paying jobs. But even in jobs demanding equal qualifications and work, women are paid less than men.

Pressure for enforcement of gender-equality laws increases as more women enter the paid labor force. In 1963 only one worker in ten was female; in 1997, one in three. Because professional expertise is at a premium in such developing countries as Costa Rica, women who acquire socially useful knowledge and skills are more likely to get prestigious jobs than are their counterparts in more industrialized societies. And unlike in many countries, Costa Rican women's reported literacy rate (93 percent) is about the same as men's.[8] Female students (many of whom combine a wife-mother role with study) outnumber males in most university departments, and instructors say they are more serious. Women have entered many professions—from airline pilot to zoologist—besides the traditional ones of teaching, social work, nursing, and secretarial work, and in 1992 they accounted for 46 percent of all professionals.[9]

Gays and lesbians have long been subject to discrimination even though private homosexual acts among consenting persons over seventeen are legal. Says historian and gay rights advocate Jacobo Schifter,

> Gays have been able to reach high positions in Costa Rica [but only if] their homosexuality is hidden. The price of acceptance has been conversion, total or halfway, to heterosexuality. This means that the gay politician must marry, the writer deny his [or her] theme, the poet conceal the sex of his or her lover, and the policeman persecute his own companions. All—without exception—must lie about their identity.[10]

Homophobia was less extreme in the 1990s than in earlier decades, and a growing gay rights movement may be in part both cause and effect of this change. Still, harassment has declined only slightly since 1990, when several women hoping to attend an international conference of lesbians were refused entry to Costa Rica. Police continued occasional raids of gay bars in the mid-1990s. A sign in a men's health club reads "Homosexuals and persons with skin diseases may not enter."

Nuclear families—parents and their unmarried children—made up 53 percent of all Costa Rican households in 1996. In four out of five of these families the parents were married; the rest cohabited in *unión libre*, "free union." Female-headed households, mostly single mothers and their unmarried children—and often their daughters' children as well—accounted for 20 percent of all households. Couples without children and one-person households, mostly among the elderly, accounted for about 12 percent. The remaining 15 percent were extended-family households—couples living with at least one of their children and one or more grandchildren or other relatives.

Many free unions are as stable as legal marriages. Though lower in prestige than formalized marriages, they are sometimes called *matrimonios de hecho*—de facto marriages. Recognizing this fact, a 1995 law (passed after much debate) gives cohabitors exactly the same rights and obligations as married couples, including "divorce" after three years with accompanying provisions for child support and division of property.

Since colonial times cohabitation has been especially common among the very poor. Ticos are reluctant to marry when the man cannot support a wife—which public opinion and law deem a husband's duty. A lower-class woman may be a companion to a succession of men, each of whom may refer to her simply as "my woman," beget one or more of her children, and provide little or no support after deserting them.

Female-headed households, too, have long been common among the poor; many women belong alternately to each type of household as men enter and leave their lives. An elderly or middle-aged woman may share a house with her unattached sons and her daughters and their children. Most of these women have been deserted, and the rest have never had an enduring sexual relationship. Eugenia López found such families harmonious—our impression as well—and the women said they would find a man's presence disruptive.[11]

Family Size

Until the late 1960s, the demands of farm life encouraged Ticos to have large families. After living conditions improved and government health programs provided prenatal care, the birth rate reached a world high in 1960—55.4 births per 1,000 population. Then a phenomenon occurred that intrigued population experts the world over: The birth rate dropped to 29.5 per 1,000 in 1975.[12]

Costa Rica is the only Latin American country—and one of very few in the world—in which the birth rate has fallen so sharply. The 25 percent drop between 1960 and 1968 occurred despite church and state opposition to birth control.

Since the 1970s, however, the government has promoted family planning. It offers contraceptive services at social security clinics. It uses TV spots and billboards to encourage smaller families and the use of condoms, although describing the latter primarily as a safeguard against AIDS. Many priests now offer tacit support for family planning.

In a 1994 study, 70 percent of a random sample of married and cohabiting women ages fifteen to forty-nine said that they currently use birth control; nearly all the rest reported having used contraceptives at some time. The most common method, reported by 21 percent, was sterilization—legally restricted but readily available—followed by oral contraceptives, used by 18 percent.[13]

Why is contraception so common now? With improved health conditions, parents can expect most children to survive to adulthood. Small children have long been an economic burden in urban areas, where a higher proportion of Ticos now live, and are so now even in the countryside, where unemployment has increased. Many parents say it now costs an enormous amount to raise and educate children properly and that they want the children they do have to be educated and healthy.

Nonetheless, the trends toward earlier initiation into sexual activity and toward later marriage increased the incidence of out-of-wedlock births from 14 percent of all births in 1970 to 47 percent in 1995. Such births are especially prevalent in rural areas and in the coastal provinces. Public attention has focused on adolescent mothers, but most new single mothers are twenty or older.

Abortion is illegal except to save the mother's life, but it is easily available at private clinics for those who can afford it or from less skilled, less hygienic practitioners for a smaller fee. Rarely are clients or their abortionists jailed. Complications following amateur abortions are now the main cause of maternal mortality. Between 1984 and 1991, according to one study, there was one abortion for every ten live births.[14]

Fertility varies with social class. A 1994 Social Security Fund study found that women ages forty-five to forty-nine at the highest educational and income levels had an average of three children, and those at the lowest levels had five. The trend toward smaller families is also related to place of residence: Mothers between twenty-five and thirty in urban areas average two children; in rural areas, four to six. The total fertility rate in 1993 was 3.1 children per woman.

Despite the sharp decline in the birth rate and family size, the population continues to grow. The main reason is that those born when the birth rate was at its peak and the average family had 7.3 children are now producing babies themselves. Population experts predict a population of 5 million by the year 2025.

Birth, Infancy, and Childhood

Although they prefer smaller families than their parents had, most Costa Ricans say they love children and want two or three. But a 1990 sample of social security prenatal-care patients found that 48 percent were upset when they learned they were pregnant, and 62 percent described their pregnancies as accidental. Those over forty and those who already had several children were especially unhappy to learn they were pregnant, as were unmarried teens.[15] And nearly everyone sees pregnancy as a discomfort and an inconvenience; when a woman gives birth, Ticos say she "gets well."

Except for pregnant teens (who are often reluctant to make their condition public) and women in remote rural areas, most expectant mothers have several medical checkups. Infant mortality is among the lowest in the world: only 12 infants in 1,000 die in their first year.

Until the 1950s childbirth usually took place at home attended by a midwife; today it nearly always occurs in a hospital. Middle- and upper-class women use private doctors and hospitals; most births occur in public hospitals, where anesthesia is usually given only for cesarean sections and where labor-inducing drugs are frequently injected. The father is often present.

A Red Cross ambulance typically takes rural women to the hospital. Rafa, who drove one from 1978 to 1989, delivered over 100 babies himself, most of them to women living in remote rural districts. "Maybe the father had to walk an hour or two to the nearest telephone," he explains; "then it took me several hours to drive and then walk there, to help take her to the ambulance on a stretcher over country trails, and then drive to the hospital." To be sure of medical help, some rural women stay with urban relatives when it is nearly time to deliver.

About half of all babies are delivered by obstetric nurses; only in San José hospitals is a doctor likely to deliver the baby. Boys are circumcised in the hospital soon after birth; girls' ears are pierced and adorned with tiny earrings. Mother and infant are often sent home within twenty-four hours.

If the infant is taken out it is wrapped in a bonnet and shawl even on warm days, as any draft is thought to be dangerous. Neighbors and relatives calling to fuss over the baby bring gifts of clothing, toys, soap, and money, and of food to the very poor or to mothers too ill to cook.

A man and a woman, generally a married couple related to one parent, are asked to serve as godparents. This role was far more important a half-century ago, when children were more likely to be orphaned, and many visited their godparents daily for a blessing and a snack. Baptism makes the child's parents and godparents *compadres* (coparents). *Compadrazgo*, once considered a special bond of friendship and mutual aid, is now, like godparenthood itself, undertaken less willingly, since the Catholic Church now requires godparents to take twelve hours of instruction.

Except in some matrilineal Indian societies, surnames reflect the fact that Costa Ricans, like other Latin Americans, trace descent through both the male and female lines. A child's paternal surname is his *primer apellido;* his mother's, his *segundo apellido.* Thus Victor Manuel, born to Carlos Enrique

Estrada Vargas and Ana María Villalobos Mena, will be known as Victor Manuel Estrada Villalobos, part of the Estrada Villalobos family. His sister, Elena Estrada Villalobos, will keep that name for a lifetime—on legal documents, in medical files, and among her friends—through marriage and divorce or widowhood even though she may add her husband's paternal surname, preceded by *de*, for some purposes. Many Ticos, however, find it more convenient to use only their paternal surnames, particularly if they travel or have many contacts with non-Latins, who find the double surname confusing. And a child of an "unknown" father receives only its mother's paternal surname, often repeated, for example, Walter Luís Sibaja Sibaja.

Until several decades ago, a child's first or middle name was often that of the saint on whose day it was born; religious names such as Jesús, Ezequiel, and Caridad (Charity) were popular. Such names are rare today, and American names such as Cindy, Wendy, William, and Frank are common. First sons are often named after their fathers. Nicknames have been popular for decades; one bestowed by peers in childhood often sticks for life. In small towns many people, especially working-class males, are known outside their families only by a nickname. The city of Alajuela is noted for residents' imaginative nicknames. One Alajuela man whose parents hail from villages translatable as Hot Water and Cold River is called Lukewarm. Another, who often loiters silent and nearly motionless on the sidewalk for hours, is known as Hydrant. An entire family may share a nickname; a talkative family in one small town is known as the Parakeets; another, whose forefathers raised poultry, is called the Turkeys.

Years ago babies were nursed for at least eight months, sometimes for several years, but breast-feeding has declined. Health authorities urge mothers "not to deny our children the best of all foods." Many poor mothers have no choice; they wean the baby after a month and return to work. The Social Security Fund reported in 1992 that although 95 percent of rural mothers nurse their newborn babies, by the fourth month only 35 percent do.

Mothers believe that bottle feeding should end only when the child no longer demands it, and children as old as six are often seen with a baby bottle containing juice, cola, raw-sugar water, or coffee with milk. At one month many parents begin to supplement the bottle with bean broth, mashed banana, or egg yolk. Commercial baby foods are popular; many parents are convinced, thanks to heavy advertising, that they are superior to unprocessed foods. Parents may also give vitamin supplements.

Most children, even unplanned ones, are cherished, and parents take their well-being into account when they make major decisions. The proximity of schools and health centers, for example, affects parents' choice of neighborhood. Settlers in isolated areas often cooperate to bring such services to their community or send their children to live with relatives in towns.

A child's first birthday is a great occasion. *Campesinos* may slaughter a pig and invite relatives and neighbors to celebrate, especially for a first son. Some families pay to have the child's photo in a newspaper.

Until half a century ago, many children died very young, and parents let small children enjoy what might be a brief stay on earth. Infants and toddlers are still allowed much free rein. Their misdeeds are laughed at or ignored or at most punished with a gentle scolding or a soft slap on the leg. Crying children are hushed by attempts to distract their attention, such as insincere promises of candy. Parents like to teach their toddlers cute tricks to perform for visitors; a young shipping clerk had his three-year-old son sing the national anthem for us.

Costa Rican preschoolers' self-esteem, according to a study by three U.S. psychologists, is generally high because "children are highly regarded and much attention and praise is given to the youngest members of each household. Children are valued, not for achievement, but simply because they are loving and cute." When children start school, "the basis for praise and recognition gradually shifts to achievement and to relative standing among peers. . . . [Children] begin to compare themselves and this generally lowers self-esteem," which the researchers found to be much lower among third-graders than first-graders.[16]

For preadolescent children, family relationships take precedence. Preschool children are much more likely to play with siblings or cousins than with unrelated neighbors. In the lower and working classes, a child's older sister, as young as six or seven, and its mother's female relatives play a major role in its upbringing. Although day-care centers and nurseries are increasingly popular, many working mothers see them as a last resort. A YMCA camp, opened in 1989, soon failed, says a frustrated volunteer, because so few parents would let their children sleep away from home.

Very poor couples, widows, and unwed mothers may give a child to its mother's parents or sister, who usually treat the child with great affection. Children typically call these caregivers *papi* and *mami* and address their own mothers by name.

Socialization for gender roles begins early. Girls learn to be coquettish and concerned with their appearance as well as to do "women's work." By age six most are expected to help sweep, wash dishes, and care for younger siblings. By age eight or ten they can perform most household tasks, especially if their mothers work outside the home.

Rural boys begin running errands at age five, often walking long distances to deliver their fathers' and older brothers' midmorning meal. By age eight they are likely, when not in school, to chop firewood, herd and milk cows, and help in the fields, using small machetes of their own. Some also help sweep and mop, though after puberty these are usually regarded as females' tasks.[17]

Poor urban boys may sell papers or flowers on the street, guard parked cars, or bag groceries in supermarkets. Many boys of the upper and middle classes do not help their parents in any way. Girls of all classes, however, are expected to help at home—and to wait on their brothers.

By age five, working-class children are no longer pampered. They win little sympathy by crying, and minor injuries are ignored. Most Ticos believe that children four years of age and older—especially boys, who are considered more impulsive and disobedient than girls—must be punished for misdeeds. Fifty years ago the father was the chief disciplinarian—indeed, until 1948 he had the exclusive legal right to punish his children—and often used his belt or machete sheath to punish an older child for disobedience or lack of respect.

Neighbors and teachers were also expected to punish children for disrespect or laziness and to report to the parents, who might give them a second beating. Grownups believed that severe punishment brought moral and spiritual benefits: "Better to go broken to heaven than in one piece to hell."

Punishment, although still considered necessary to socialization, is less harsh today. A sixty-five-year-old *campesino* is happy that fathers' authority has declined:

> My father once ordered me to work with a dangerous ox at our sugar mill. He held a stick in one hand, and I didn't know if it was to hit the ox or me. Today, if a child doesn't want to do something his father asks, he'll just disappear. And there's much less farm work, so parents aren't as demanding. Besides, kids are in school a lot longer.

Parental control over children is now limited by law. A doctor may perform life-saving surgery on a child over the parents' objections. And the National Children's Protection Institute (PANI) sometimes removes neglected or abused children from their homes.

Although fathers are often referred to as the heads of households, mothers do far more to raise children. An increasing number of mothers work outside the home, but two out of three still do not—including many with advanced degrees. Many fathers, by contrast, give their children little attention even when at home. They may play with the children briefly, especially with the youngest, but regard feeding, cleaning, and dressing children as exclusively women's work. Fathers also depend on their wives and older children to help the younger ones with homework and catechism. Even though the mother holds *papi* up as an authority figure, children tend to run to mothers with their problems, turn over earnings to her, and, like advertisers, pay much less attention to Father's Day than to Mother's Day, which is a public holiday. Nearly all Costa Ricans agree that children have less respect for either parent than they once did, since they have less fear of punishment; but many add that children now feel closer to their parents and better able to confide in them.

The constitution states that "parents have the same obligations to their children born out of wedlock as to those born within." But enforcement is difficult. Since 1933 PANI has threatened to imprison deadbeat fathers. But many women do not file charges, especially in lowland areas where courts and police are few and female-headed families common.

Family members often go their separate ways for work, study, and diversion—even church attendance. Many teens and young adults, especially males, work by day and spend evenings in night school, at parties, or with friends, going home only for solitary meals and sleep. A small-town *pulpería* owner, devoted to his wife and five children, expresses a common frustration: "I often dream of our all eating together, or just sitting down to talk. But something always comes up for me or for some of them." Even when all family members are home in the evening, television and solitary video games have largely supplanted conversation, interactive games, and the evening rosary. Sunday and holiday activities, however, are frequently shared, especially with young children, who join their parents on trips to a zoo, beach, riverbank, restaurant, or amusement park or to visit relatives.

Adolescence

One Tico out of five is between ten and nineteen years old. Until two or three generations ago, adolescence was not considered a distinct stage of the life cycle; working with their parents, many children gradually took on adult roles. Today, many reach puberty while still in school and, in the middle class, long before they begin working; they are now called *adolescentes*.

Two generations ago rural youths, especially males, often remained subject to their fathers' authority even after marriage. Landownership was widespread and all children were likely to inherit. There were few jobs in the towns. Few rural youths today can expect a sizable legacy from their parents, who may own little or no land. Many seek work in a town, a banana plantation, or the United States. Says a nineteen-year-old waiter in a San José cafe: "Most of my coworkers are, like myself, from the countryside. We'd all like to be back there, but there's no work."

Upper-class youths, by contrast, may still be tied to their parents and other kin by hopes of inheritance and a position in a family business or professional firm. Their quest for university degrees often keeps them, as well as many middle-class youths, dependent on parents into their late twenties.[18]

Young women in all social classes are more submissive to their parents and more confined to the home than are their brothers—who often try to "protect" them from boyfriends. Working daughters are more likely to give parents money than are sons, especially if the latter no longer live at home.

An unmarried professional woman is likely to continue living with her parents. But many young women feel hemmed in there, particularly in poor families, where they may share a room with several siblings; they spend as much free time out of the house as they can.

For a girl, high school graduation and legal maturity at eighteen are minor rites of passage compared to her fifteenth birthday, which calls for a special party; in well-to-do families, this is comparable to a debut. No similar transition exists for boys.

Thousands of young women, even in the countryside, commute to coeducational high schools and universities or work in factories, stores, and offices where they meet young men, often from other towns. Whereas their grandmothers had to be home by six o'clock, they are usually allowed to stay out later, though not as late as their brothers. In rural families and a few more traditional urban ones, especially of the middle and upper classes, girls under eighteen are sometimes chaperoned at night.

Ticas tend to dress up and use abundant makeup even at work. (A young foreigner we know is often told by Tica acquaintances that she would be "more womanly" if she wore makeup.) The beauty of young females is celebrated constantly—in "queen" contests, advertising, public girl-watching, and *piropos*. These flirtatious compliments, whispered into a passing woman's ear fifty years ago, are now shouted, often in joking competition with other males: "Wow, what curves, and me without brakes!" To a young woman dressed in blue, "So little blue for so much heaven." "Hi, mother-in-law" and "Your doll got out of her box" may greet a strolling mother and daughter. Older Ticos say their *piropos* were gracious and imaginative, even poetic, whereas today's (perhaps because of greater urban anonymity) are often crudely sexual. Some young women now respond to any *piropo* with withering looks or words. Others feel flattered and return a flirtatious glance, as their mothers and grandmothers probably did. A San José dentist told us that when his middle-aged wife feels depressed and worried about losing her looks, she dresses up and goes downtown to harvest *piropos*, returning home with her self-esteem restored.

Costa Rica, like other industrializing societies, is increasingly youth-oriented. In the 1970s young people often complained that the country was run by old men. Since then, three presidents have taken office while in their forties; José María Figueres took office in 1994 at age thirty-nine. In 1978 the Ministry of Culture, Youth, and Sports was created, and the voting age was lowered to eighteen. The Ministry of Health has a number of new clinics just for adolescents.

Newspapers devote many pages to the interests of young people, from music to sexuality, and report the activities of environmental, religious, and political youth groups. They also report such problems as youth gangs, teen pregnancies, and the disorientation of those who neither work nor study.

Courtship and Weddings

Until the 1950s, the *retreta,* or band concert in town parks, where boys and girls strolled around the square in opposite directions, provided opportunities to look over the opposite sex. Girls' mothers, meanwhile, chatted on a park bench, discreetly watching.

If a boy's interest in a girl was reciprocated, he asked her father (who usually knew him already) for the *entrada,* permission to call on her at times specified by the father. These meetings seldom took place more than once a week and were always chaperoned. Says a farmer married in 1930: "When the boy came to call, he and the girl could not touch each other except for a brief handshake. If it ever reached her parents' ears that she had even talked to him on the street, she'd get a good beating."

Although boys in one remote hamlet told us they still ask for the *entrada* and can't be alone with a girl "unless her mother falls asleep," chaperonage has virtually ended in urban areas. And young people everywhere now have a much greater chance to meet members of the opposite sex.

Flirtear is a favorite pastime. A young man shows his interest in a girl by silently and insistently staring at her. If the stare is returned and he already knows her, he may invite her to a soda bar or a movie or ask to walk her home. If they are strangers he may seek a mutual acquaintance to introduce them, though many now consider this unnecessary. If the pair hits it off, he will ask to see her again, perhaps arranging to meet her at a movie or dance and not visiting her home until they have met several times.

A flirtation may lead to only a brief sexual encounter. Boys go, often in pairs, to dances and country fairs, where pickups are reportedly easy. "All you have to do to get a girl to go into a pasture with you," said a young male at a church fair, "is convince her that you love her."

Though couples seldom explicitly agree to be *novios,* they seal an implicit *noviazgo* by exchanging rings or photos.[19] The relationship is no longer tantamount to engagement, but while it lasts, each expects the other to see no one else. Still, a double standard persists. Juan Carlos, age twenty, who lives in a small highland town, says:

> I'm not really a *machista,* but I'm like most of my male friends: If I had sex with someone other than my girlfriend, I wouldn't feel guilty. If my *novia* found out, she'd probably get angry, but then forgive me. Then I'd tell her how good she is. But I couldn't forgive her if she did the same, because this is a small town and my friends would know and look down on me.

Still, because of this same fear of gossip, many young men confine their skirt-chasing to distant locales where they will not be seen by their girlfriends' acquaintances.

Until the early twentieth century, a peasant suitor was required by his *novia*'s parents to leave three cartloads of firewood at their doorstep as a test of his ability to provide. His parents in turn expected her to grind corn and make tortillas for them. The urban girl learned to cook, sew, and adorn the parlor. Her mother showed her handiwork to potential mothers-in-law.

Although such tests have passed into folklore, in some rural areas a girl's father may watch his prospective son-in-law at work before giving the match his blessing. And working-class girls, asked what qualities they consider most important in a husband, echo their grandparents' attitudes by saying that he should be a good worker and free of vices. Middle-class girls, who perhaps take economic security for granted, reply that he should be affectionate. Mothers of all classes tell their sons to look for a faithful girl who likes home life, and boys' attitudes regarding the ideal wife reflect this advice.

Ten-year-old girls may talk about *novios* and exchange love notes with boys, but usually only at age fifteen or sixteen do they begin going out alone with boys; even then, they may do so mostly in larger groups of both sexes in which few members are paired off. Most marry by age twenty-five after several *noviazgos;* the median age is twenty-two. But whereas in the 1960s Costa Ricans told us that a single woman of twenty-five had "missed the train," fewer do so today. Degrees and careers that did not exist a generation ago are now options for many. Some consider careers to be incompatible with marriage; many more perceive education for a career as insurance in case of a failed marriage. A growing number of young women are so well educated and independent that they see only disadvantages in marriage. Others take care of aging and ailing parents and may turn down a suitor they love, especially if marriage would mean leaving home.

Males feel even less pressure to marry, for they have a longer period of eligibility and, as they see it, less to gain by marrying. But even those who joke, "Why buy a cow when milk is free?" are usually married by their midtwenties, typically to a woman a year or two younger.

Men of all ages and marital status told us, "Husbands should be very responsible." Young men may wait until they have either saved enough money to marry or have spent enough on liquor, women, and wild times to satisfy them before settling down. (And many young husbands today, far from bragging about their extramarital conquests—as was expected of men thirty years ago—do claim to have settled down.)

Saccharine love songs remain popular with both sexes. The AIDS epidemic and the coincidental rise in teenage pregnancies have increased the demand for sex education. *La Nación* frequently publishes sexologists' nonjudgmental responses to young people's questions. But adult experts and high school students note that young people still learn most about sex "in the street." Thus 40 percent of girls in a 1993 study were bewildered by their first menses. Other studies have found that most young Ticos use no contraception during their first intercourse, which now usually occurs, for both sexes, long before marriage—typically at about age fifteen for boys and sixteen for girls.[20]

As in other societies, Ticos' choice of mates is influenced by such factors as social class, laws, and the size of one's local pool of eligible partners. Parental influence on the choice is strongest in the upper class, particularly on daughters, for a couple's class position depends mostly on that of the husband. Rural *novios* are frequently lifelong acquaintances. They are often second cousins because so many local families are related; first cousins, prohibited by church and state from marrying, sometimes live in *unión libre*.

Most weddings are preceded by a formal engagement that may last two or three months, seldom over a year. Elderly *campesinos* say that a rural girl's parents used to urge her to marry a boy if he had courted her more than three months because "otherwise, people would gossip. A boy's father would put pressure on him to marry only if he got her pregnant, which wasn't as common as it is now."

After obtaining the girl's consent, the boy may ask for that of her parents. He and his parents may then call on the girl's family. Relatives and friends may celebrate the engagement with a small party at which the boy gives his *novia* a ring. Broken engagements were once a disgrace for the girl, reducing her chance of finding another desirable suitor; little stigma now attaches to her.

Several organizations attempt to prepare couples for marriage. They invite engaged and recently married couples and their parents to lectures by physicians, social scientists, and clergymen on such topics as dating, marital communication, family budgets, reproductive physiology, birth control, and child raising. Since 1975 couples planning a Catholic wedding have had to attend short workshops led by older couples and intended "to instill a sense of responsibility."

A few days before her wedding, a middle- or upper-class *novia*'s women friends have a tea for her, a "farewell to being single." After she is married she is likely to see less of her single friends than will her husband of his, for her new interests and obligations will differ from theirs more widely than do those of single and married men.

The evening before the wedding, close friends and relatives attend a party at the bride's house. Most bring gifts, which are displayed on a table. Before joining the party the *novio* and his cronies or a hired band may assemble outside to serenade the bride-to-be. Perhaps they will later spend the night on the town—drinking, joking, and visiting a brothel—as they may often have done "on happier occasions, before he was caught." The *novio* is teased that he must renounce the pleasures and liberties of bachelorhood and warned about domineering wives and mothers-in-law.

Until the late nineteenth century, priests married most couples at home; now they do so in a church. The local parish church (or the bride's home for many non-Catholics) is the scene of weddings for the poor; many middle- and upper-class Ticos favor a fashionable church decorated with flowers and candles.

An equal number of persons of each sex serve as witnesses. They are usually relatives and friends, often of the parents' generation, but many couples seek local and national politicians or rich acquaintances likely to give lavish gifts as well as lend prestige. In rural areas even the poor invite local officials, the schoolteacher, and the most prosperous farmers.

Catholic weddings today follow no one standard pattern. Formerly, the groom waited at the altar with his mother, who gave him away. This still sometimes occurs, but it is also common for mother and son to come down the aisle together, followed by the witnesses and the bridal attendants, the bride's best friend on the arm of the groom's best friend, perhaps several bridesmaids, a ring bearer, a couple of flower girls, and another child carrying the traditional *arras*, a gift of thirteen coins (perhaps forming a bracelet) that symbolize the groom's sharing of his material goods with his bride. The bride follows on her father's arm; her white gown and veil provoke loud whispers and head-turning.

Applause breaks out the moment the priest pronounces the couple husband and wife. They then kneel and a long white silken cord (or perhaps a gold chain traditionally used in the bride's family) is draped around their shoulders while the priest blesses their future children. Guests and attendants shower the newlyweds with rice as they leave the church—in some rural areas, with both rice and beans to ensure that they will always have enough to eat.

Among the working and middle classes, the wedding party usually attends a luncheon at the church, the home of the bride's or groom's parents, or a restaurant. After toasting with sparkling hard cider or rum (or, among most Protestants, lemonade) and feasting, perhaps on barbecued pork, they may dance to music supplied by a DJ.

Among the wealthy, after an early evening church wedding, the wedding guests move on to a private club or hotel ballroom. Dancing and drinking of champagne and Scotch continue for two or three hours. At midnight a supper is served while a mariachi band plays. After the cake is cut and souvenirs distributed, the bride, following a newly imported U.S. custom, tosses a bouquet to the unmarried females present, and the groom throws her garter to the unmarried males; the young man who catches the garter puts it on the leg of the girl who catches the bouquet—both often embarrassed by ribald comments. The party may continue through breakfast. But the new couple, amid reminders to eat plenty of seafood (allegedly an aphrodisiac) departs long before then for a honeymoon—perhaps to a coastal or hot-spring resort or to Disney World—that may last several weeks. Even working-class couples often spend a few days at a beach, though some are back at work in a day or two, as their parents were. (One rural couple jokingly referred to their tiny new house as "the beach.")

Civil ceremonies have recently become more common, accounting for two of every five weddings in 1992. Since the Catholic rite is the only religious ceremony that can transform a couple's legal status, non-Catholics may choose to have both a religious ceremony and the civil one that makes their marriage official.

Yet the increase in civil ceremonies has far outpaced even the rapid growth of Protestantism. Among the reasons Catholics give for civil weddings are fear that the marriage might not last ("It's not such a sin to get divorced if you haven't made your vows before God," said one young man), remarriage after divorce (not approved or recognized by the Catholic Church), and unexpected pregnancy (the couple may have no time to comply with church protocol such as posting banns and taking premarital instruction).

The bonds, including expectations of mutual aid, that marriage creates between two families are reflected in such terms as *consuegros* (coparents-in-law of a couple), *cuñada* (sister-in-law), and *concuño:* You and I are *concuños* if, for instance, my sister is married to your brother.

Residence Patterns and Kinship Ties

Costa Ricans have traditionally lived in clusters of close relatives in neighboring houses, newlyweds moving into a house near the husband's parents, often a gift from them. But few newlyweds, even in colonial times, would share a house with anyone else unless poverty compelled it.[21] Ticos commonly cite such proverbs as "Quien casa, quiere casa" (He who marries wants his own house) and "Better to be close by than scrambled together."

Even in towns it is not unusual for several married siblings to live in adjacent houses. Still, many families have dispersed not only because they ran out of land to divide but also because of improved transportation and job prospects throughout the country.

Costa Rica's small size and the concentration of half its population in only one major metropolitan area make it easy for most Ticos to stay in touch with relatives. When parents live less than an hour's bus or car ride away, their adult offspring, with spouses and children, may visit them on Sundays as well as on holidays and special occasions. Many family members, however, are likely to be absent. Some are visiting their spouses' relatives; others, especially young people, would rather be with friends and *novios;* still others live abroad. A forty-two-year-old *pulpería* owner in a small town recalls his childhood, when relatives would visit one another nearly every evening, "not just in my family but in everyone's. Most people here still have kin in town, but they don't see one another as much. That's a big loss." The abundance of telephones, others comment, now makes it easy for relatives to stay in touch.

Asked who belongs to their family, Ticos may include all kin on both the father's and mother's side up to and including third and even fourth cousins. Many admit, however, that they have not even met all of their first cousins.

Extended family ties traditionally were strongest in the upper class. As we noted earlier, family pride and nepotism as well as the hope of an inheritance and other forms of economic aid still give older relatives in this class considerable influence over younger ones. But as family coffee plantations have been sold and their heirs' legacies invested in industries, urban real estate, or education for a profession that may make them financially independent of their relatives, even the bonds among upper-class kin are no longer quite as close.

Kinship ties among rural Ticos remain strong. Two unmarried sisters in their forties, a journalist and a lawyer, work in San José and enjoy its nightlife. But they continue to live with their widowed mother in a village that is now a dormitory suburb of the capital. "Our *campesino* relatives are continually dropping by our house with fresh milk or homemade tortillas. And they expect us to visit them. Years ago, neighbors used to drop off food if, for example, Mother was sick. They don't now; they just say 'Hello' as they get into their cars and go their separate ways. But relatives always come by."

Households are often larger in the upper-middle and upper classes than among the poor, in spite of their having fewer children. Such families are better able to afford live-in servants and to house needy relatives or those who have come to the city for schooling or to keep a widowed aunt company. (These categories may overlap; the poor kinsman may also be a student or companion and is sometimes treated as a servant.)

In both city and country, mutual aid, mostly among kin, is often essential for the poor. Says a resident of a village near San José:

> There are a lot of homeless people in Costa Rica, though most of them don't live under bridges, but with relatives. Some houses here are huge, with lots of relatives constantly moving in and out. Additions are made to the house as people can afford it, while other rooms may fall apart. It's hard to find a house for sale around here, because a few extended families have so many adjacent lots.

Allen Cordero and Nuria Gamboa, studying a San José slum from 1987 to 1990, found that few residents could survive without mutual aid among kin. Parents and children or neighboring adult siblings often pool their earnings. Because employment is unstable and wages low, aid is offered mostly in the form of food or money. The researchers found the greatest solidarity among the neediest.[22]

In 1935 Chester Lloyd Jones commented: "The family continues almost to monopolize social interests."[23] This is still true to some extent. At one middle-class child's birthday party, for instance, all but one of the seventy children were kin. Many Ticos have told us they are wary of friendships with nonkin. Anthropologist Setha Low found that "the majority who report that they have no friends and do not trust outsiders are also those who live in large extended households or maintain the closest kin relationships."[24]

Marital Relations and Gender Roles

Gender roles learned in childhood shape the expectations that men and women bring to marriage: The girl expected to serve her brothers may later see it as natural to wait on her husband. The boy whose father was dominant expects to control the behavior of his wife and children.

Marital relationships are also affected by early sexual experiences and the cultural beliefs in a strong male sex drive and a weak or nonexistent female one. The affectionate demonstrativeness that Ticos learn as children also carries over into marriage. "A lot of Latin attitudes toward women are chauvinistic," writes a longtime North American resident of Costa Rica, "but Latin men, unlike U.S. men, aren't afraid of letting their tender feelings show."[25]

Whereas wives in all classes may use the formal *señor* or *usted* to address their husbands, men commonly address their wives with the familiar *vos;* in many middle- and upper-class marriages, both say *vos,* and both use frequent endearments: "my life," "my heart," *mijito* or *mijita* (my child), and *negrito(a)* ("little black one," regardless of skin color). After children are born, the pair may call each other *mamá* and *papá.* Among their male companions, many working- and lower-class men refer jokingly to their wives as *la media naranja* (the other half of the orange), *la costilla* (the rib), *la cobija* (the blanket), or, less affectionately, as *la culebra* (the snake) or *la peor es nada* (the better-than-nothing—because, says a truck driver, "wives try to stop you from going out and having fun"). Sociologist Robert Williamson noted in the early 1960s that lower-class couples communicated less and had less happy marriages than did middle-class couples;[26] this was our observation as well nearly four decades later.

Although they are more likely than men to refer to the sex act as "making love," many Costa Rican women experience little sexual satisfaction; a 1992 study, for example, found that two out of five had never experienced orgasm. Foreplay is rare; sex is equated with intercourse, and this, says sexologist Mauro Fernández, seldom lasts more than two or three minutes.[27] Premature ejaculation is a problem for 70 percent of sexually active Costa Rican men,

Fernández adds. Many, he says, first experience sex as masturbation; believing it to be shameful, they perform it secretly and quickly. Their first sexual experiences with women also occur under conditions of pressure and anxiety. In general, men over thirty-five first had intercourse with prostitutes, for whom time is money. (Many, we were told, had been taken to a brothel by their fathers to initiate them into "manhood.") Those under thirty-five "experienced sex first in the living room of a girl whose mother had gone to the *pulpería.*" After many such experiences, the man is unlikely to control ejaculation even when he and his partner have plenty of time.[28]

Men—who frequently refer to sex as "using" a woman—are still seen as having far stronger sexual needs than women.[29] A faithful husband's cronies may tease him—one reason, perhaps, that many men do not wear their wedding rings in public. Many Ticos were shocked and mystified by the immediate popularity of the first male striptease shows among upper- and upper-middle-class women in the early 1990s. And since men's sexual desire is believed to be an imperative urge, many men see other men as sexual predators, and women assume their husbands will stray at every opportunity. (A dentist told us how glad many women were when she started to practice. All too often, she was told, male dentists would fondle them and their daughters.) Men often appear at parties without their wives; when women do go along, they are careful not to offend their husbands. A man who notices his wife talking for more than a moment with a male nonrelative may join the two and perhaps tell his wife suddenly that it's time to go home. Young wives whose husbands travel on business are kept under their in-laws' wing; someone invites them for dinner each evening, visits them, and otherwise checks up.

Even so, 87 percent of married and cohabiting women in a 1987 sample survey said they had been unfaithful before age forty-five. Two out of every five wives or widows over age sixty reported having had extramarital affairs at some time in the past. Their main concern was not guilt but fear of being found out.[30] Most of these women, however, reported only a few instances of extramarital sex, which usually occurred, they said, because they did not feel loved or valued. (A *pulpería* owner told us of his brief flings with women who complained that their husbands no longer showed affection. "That's what they want more than anything," he said.)

Most men confine their extramarital sex experiences to brothels or to brief flings with female employees, coworkers, or domestic servants, often patronizing "motels" that do a thriving business catering to clandestine lovers. Fewer men now have the sort of *querida* (mistress) that many did a few decades ago. Says sociologist Francisco Escobar:

> La querida was not the prostitute, the occasional courtesan. . . . She was a decent woman, usually beautiful . . . who surrendered out of love and passion, and often gave him a child. He rented a house for her, paid her ex-

penses and gave her the time left over from his official family life. . . . [Although many such men were wealthy] men of more modest means also had their little *querida* on a more modest scale. Wives chose to pretend absolute ignorance of the matter and settled for being the official favorite of highest status in the harem.

But things have begun to change. The girlfriend has a university degree and a good position. She does not want to be the clandestine "little woman." There is an impasse that has not been resolved. Ticos dream of the past between the sheets of women loved in secret, ignored in public. . . . But now there are no *queridas*.[31]

Men, like their wives, try to hide even the appearance of infidelity from their spouses. "I have to deal with a lot of women in my work," says a thirty-year-old labor contractor. "But my wife would get very jealous whenever a woman called me. So I had the phone moved next door to my mother's house." A divorced woman comments that wives have never been immune to jealousy but that as more get jobs, they no longer resign themselves to their husbands' philandering.

A North American woman reports that she ended a "special relationship" with a Tico because she could not accept "the cultural tendency to use lying as a survival tool or way of pleasing others." Tico couples tacitly understand that each may lie "to get along as best they can and make each other feel better in the process. . . . [They consider lies] not as breaches of morality and trust but acceptable ways to avoid trouble and make each other feel better."[32]

Often juggling jobs, housework, and child care with little help, many women experience severe role conflict. Although a growing number of men do some housework and child care, many refuse to help even if their wives have other jobs, are ill, or have just given birth. They don't think of housework as work and, in any case, consider it a woman's responsibility and fear that they would be considered effeminate if they helped. As a result, a *campesina* told us, "for men Sunday is a day of rest. For women it's just like Monday."

One study found that the more accepting a woman is of her traditional roles as wife, mother, and housekeeper, the more prone she is to depression. And contrary to general belief, women are less likely to suffer depression in their menopausal years, when grown children are leaving home, than in their thirties.[33]

For middle-class Ticos, as we noted in Chapter 7, servants are no longer readily available or cheap. And the female relatives on whom working women long depended for child care may now hold jobs of their own. A growing number of private and public nursery schools have filled the gap. Yet even professional women—two out of three in the private sector—usually leave their jobs when their first child is born, and many do not plan to return. A young married woman working in a clothing factory near Grecia typically quits as soon as she has earned enough to contribute to building her own house and returns to the factory only to show off her first baby.[34]

Said a woman of about thirty who had left her job as announcer for a San José radio station and returned to the highland village where she grew up:

> I loved my work; I didn't do it just for the money. But I could spend hardly any time with my kids. They were being raised by the nursemaid. And city life is so frenetic. One day when I was hurrying my son to get dressed, I realized that this was crazy! So I moved back home.
>
> Papi is building us a house next door; meanwhile, we live with my parents and I worry because the kids make too much noise and bother for them. My husband comes from the capital every weekend.
>
> In the country, you can't earn as much, but you don't need as much either. In the city, you have to work. I was neither a good mother nor a good worker. I couldn't do both well.

That was in 1992. When we revisited her village a year later, we found she had missed her job so much that she returned to work in San José, where her mother-in-law now cared for the children. Such role conflicts are becoming more common and are especially difficult for single mothers and those whose partners earn little. Irma González of PRIEG (Interdisciplinary Program for Gender Studies) describes one such woman:

> She gets up at 4:30 to get everything ready. She leaves on the run to take the children to a day care center where they must wait outside the fence until it opens at six. She worries about them all day, perhaps warding off harassment by some supervisor, and in the afternoon she leaves work, sweaty after ironing her minimum quota of 500 shirts, to get home and work four hours more.[35]

Mothers in many professions opt for part-time work. Says a twenty-year-old woman studying dentistry at the University of Costa Rica: "More than half the students in dentistry, as well as in medicine and pharmacy, are women. Costa Rica is short of professionals in these fields, and I should have no problem getting work. In fact, if I have children, I'll still be able to practice part time; it's easier to get part-time work in these fields than in many others." A practicing dentist says that many of her female colleagues, like herself, have an office at home so they can be near their children, although they would earn more in another location. And a growing number of women start or resume a career in middle age after their children have left home.

But even women in professions are identified mostly in relation to their husbands' jobs. Numerous women's organizations are based on their husbands' shared occupation: lawyers, doctors, diplomats, journalists, pilots, accountants, and so on.

López found in the 1970s, as we did two decades later, that lower-class wives and *compañeras* saw themselves as "just housewives" even when the sewing or laundry they took in was the main source of income.[36] Having a *real* job meant going outside the home. Lowell Gudmundson comments that although a third of all women reported "working" in all nineteenth-century censuses, only one in ten did so in 1927, since "work" by then had come to be equated with earning a wage or salary.[37]

Many Costa Ricans now acknowledge that their self-image as a peaceful people does not apply to domestic relations. Ombudsman Rodrigo Carazo Zeledón estimated in 1994 that physical, sexual, and psychological violence against women and children is common in 40 percent of households. In another study that same year, one of three married or cohabiting women complained of long-term, continuing aggression.[38] Many Ticos believe that domestic violence is a private matter and that the aggressor will stop if the victim changes her ways. But only 15 percent of women in a 1989 poll said that male violence against women is natural; 81 percent said that women need not submit to it even to keep their families together.[39]

Domestic violence is by no means new; Ivan Molina and Steven Palmer point out that battered Ticas sought legal protection even in the eighteenth century.[40] Some social scientists think the apparent increase is a result of growing public awareness and reporting by battered wives and children; others are sure that actual violence is increasing rapidly. Recourse to violence is aggravated by the persistence of *machismo*. "Some men find no other way to demonstrate their masculinity except by means of blows and insults."[41] Although those who complain to the several government and nongovernmental agencies "for defense of women and the family" include wives and companions of lawyers, doctors, and government officials, poor women are most likely to report violence.

Divorce

In 1886 the "liberal generation" established legal provisions for divorce, but for nearly a century there were few divorces because of restricted legal grounds, church pressure, and fear of scandal. Though most Ticos still accept a sexual double standard, a woman is no longer subject to discriminatory divorce laws. Until 1974 she could divorce her husband for adultery only if "open and scandalous concubinage" could be proven, whereas a single act of adultery on her part gave him grounds. Now adultery serves as grounds for either spouse. After a minimum of three years of marriage a divorce can be obtained—often within two months—by mutual consent, which is now the chief grounds.[42] Most couples involved are in their late twenties or early thirties.

The mother is usually awarded custody of minor children; the father is legally responsible for their food, clothing, shelter, and schooling.

In 1996, 4,663 divorces were granted, about one for every 150 married couples; twice as many couples were granted legal separations.[43] About one couple in ten either separates or divorces within five years. Many Ticos see these rates as alarmingly high and cite them as further evidence of the breakdown of the family institution.

Ironically, though, as in many countries, divorce may have increased partly because many now see companionship and emotional support as the main reasons for marriage. These rewards may well be more common now than in marriages of a few generations ago, but the gap between expectation and reality may also have widened. Although *machismo*, for instance, has declined somewhat, wives' resentment of it has probably risen even faster.

Another common source of marital friction and, in many cases, of separation or divorce is men's strong attachment to their mothers. Boys and men are as likely to serenade their mothers as their *novias* or wives, and many wives resent this closeness. A thirty-two-year-old suburban woman is separated from her husband because "he wanted to do things with his mother more often than with me."

Social psychologists Alicia Neuberger and Rodolfo Quirós see this as a common pattern arising from the prolonged nurturing of sons by mothers whose partners are absent physically or emotionally. A grown man separated from his wife is likely to return to his mother's house, where he continues to be coddled.[44] Divorced women, by contrast, typically have no such support. They are likely to blame themselves for the divorce, to worry about their ex-husbands' well-being, and to fear both solitude and gossip.[45]

Still, as divorce becomes more common, such gossip has become less virulent, making it easier to decide on divorce. And women's increased outside employment has made them less dependent on abusive or neglectful husbands.

Low-income couples are especially prone to separation—more often through the man's desertion than through divorce. They must frequently share housing with relatives, which adds tension to their relationships.[46] The most dependent wives and *compañeras* are most susceptible to desertion; they are chiefly uneducated women burdened with many children.

Aging

A Costa Rican born in 1850 could expect to live only thirty years on the average; one who lived to age twenty-five could expect to live thirty more years.[47] In the mid-1990s life expectancy was seventy-one for men and seventy-seven for women. These changes, as well as the decline in childbearing, have made the elderly a rapidly growing segment of the population. Whereas only one Tico in twelve was over age sixty in 1995, the ratio is expected to rise to one in seven by 2025.

Ticos now live longer than ever, but youth is considered the prime of life and aging has mostly negative associations. Help-wanted ads commonly specify, "Must be under 40" or "between 18 and 25." A sign urging citizens to support striking teachers' demand for a lower retirement age asks, "Would you want a sixty-year-old teaching your child?" Most Ticos let adult birthdays pass unnoted, though higher-status men may observe their fiftieth birthdays with big parties. Women do not care to publicize this date, for it is said of a postmenopausal woman that "ella ya jugó"—she has "finished playing" (the sex game). Only on silver and golden wedding anniversaries do most older Ticas acknowledge milestones in their own lives.

Landowning farmers continue to work until well into their seventies, only gradually reducing their activity. But salaried Ticos in both government and the private sector often retire in their fifties or even sooner. Some are political appointees who lose their jobs in a change of administration; others are dismissed by managers who want younger or better-educated employees, such as the ever more numerous MBAs. Many more retire voluntarily, as soon as the law allows them a pension.

Many retirees start a business or become active in politics. Retired civil servants often use their former colleagues as valuable contacts for cutting red tape or gaining political favor. Dread of loneliness and loss of status as well as financial need encourage retirees to find new jobs; totally retired people, even former big shots, are widely seen as has-beens.

Elderly women may spend much of their time in church; men gather in parks, bars, and, in rural areas, *pulperías,* where they recall the past and discuss politics and local news. Many elderly people spend most of their time at home listening to the radio or watching television, reading, baby-sitting their grandchildren, or watching passersby from a window or veranda.

Few clubs or other facilities served the elderly when their numbers were relatively small. Now several government agencies, including the social security system, have special programs for "third age" Ticos. Many meet for exercise, day trips, and lessons in acting and manual arts. They may audit courses at public universities at no charge. Says a seventy-three-year-old woman, "Elderly people today are more concerned with their own happiness than they used to be, and their organizations promote this attitude." Nonetheless, lack of money, loneliness, and boredom are common complaints.

Although youth is increasingly valued and parental authority has declined, most Costa Ricans still feel an obligation to care for parents who can no longer work—an obligation formalized in the family code. Only 30 percent of retirees in 1995 received any sort of pension, and these were rarely adequate. (One-fifth amounted to less than $8 a month.)

Most people over sixty live next door to one of their children or live alternately with different children. Many, however, say they fear "being in the way." These fears are sometimes justified. The two-bedroom, government-subsidized houses in which many low-income Ticos live were designed for small nuclear families. And although daughters often help their aged parents financially and otherwise, sons—especially married sons—help much less even though they profess strong emotional bonds to their mothers.

Several private nursing homes are run for profit. Nearly 100 small nursing homes and day-care centers for the aged are subsidized by taxes, the national lottery, and families' donations. Most full-time residents are those who need special care because of mental or physical disabilities; a growing proportion are placed there by working daughters. Few Ticos like the idea of living in such a place, and in 1994 only about 3 percent of those over age sixty did. In any case, the government, under pressure from foreign lenders to cut spending, stopped building such centers in 1992.

Death and Mourning

When a death occurs, friends and relatives are notified by telephone or wire or by a message read over the radio. Middle- and upper-class families also announce their bereavement in the newspapers—usually after the burial, which by law must be performed within twenty-four hours. Corpses are rarely embalmed unless some mourners need a day or two to arrive for the funeral—from the United States, perhaps.

The open coffin—a cheap wooden box covered with felt or plush for the poor, a metal or precious-wood casket for the wealthy—is traditionally taken to the family living room for a wake enlivened by liquor, coffee, and conversation. In the San José area, if a wake is held at all, it now usually takes place in a funeral home.

After a funeral mass, the mourners (but not the priest), singing and praying in unison, follow the pallbearers to the cemetery—on foot if the cemetery is nearby. A hearse carrying only wreaths and flowers may precede the pallbearers. At the cemetery entrance the coffin is lowered to the ground, where all may take a last look at the face through a glass panel in the top. After the coffin is buried or placed in a mausoleum or niche the mourners leave.

Ticos profess a horror of being buried in the ground, and many are now entombed in small above-ground vaults with niches just large enough for one coffin. Family plots or vaults are preferred, but there is no cultural norm decreeing which relatives should be interred together. In any case, Ticos prefer to avoid the subject of death, and many make no plans for interment. One-person vaults may be hurriedly built only as needed. Thus as a cemetery fills up, the remains of parents, spouses, siblings, and young children, who may of course die many years apart, often lie in different parts of a cemetery or in different cemeteries.

The poor are still commonly buried. Says a thirty-year-old Guanacaste ranch hand, "Even in death, people are treated differently depending on money. If you have money, you'll be entombed above ground, in a mausoleum that takes many hours to build. But a poor person is buried, as we say, 'so he can't get out again.'"

Still, in urban cemeteries, the poor often do get out again. The bereaved may lease a niche in a wall, and if they don't renew the lease after five years, groundskeepers transfer the remains to a common grave. A San José undertaker says few leases are renewed for more than twenty years.

Though funerals are simple and rapid, numerous ceremonies follow. Friends and business associates of the deceased and bereaved who can afford it, as well as their guilds, companies, and clubs, buy space in the newspapers to express condolences; the more prominent the person, the larger and more numerous these are.

Among Catholics, each evening for nine days a rosary for the departed soul is said at home before a makeshift altar decked with flowers. Mourners then chat over liquor and coffee. On the last day a rosary is led by as many as nine professional mourners depending on the family's means and desire to *aparentar*. An elaborate mass is said at the church, followed by a meal at home for all who attend. A monthly mass and rosary usually mark the date of death for a year, followed by a special meal on the first anniversary of death.

In 1942 anthropologists found that mourning customs had become less strict in the preceding decade:

> Black was traditionally worn two years for a parent, husband, or wife, one year for brothers, sisters, or parents-in-law, three months for an uncle or an aunt, a month and a half for a cousin. If one's parent died, the curtains of the house were kept drawn, pictures and adornments were covered in black for one year, and the family left home only to attend mass. . . . Now, one mourns only about half as long as formerly.[48]

Many men now wear no mourning even for a close relative. Women, especially old women, are stricter; a few widows wear black the rest of their lives. Yet many women, sometimes still in black, now attend parties a few weeks after the death. A combination of black and white, called "half mourning," is a transition to brighter colors. For funerals and memorial services, most mourners dress informally.

A rosary and sometimes a mass are said on the anniversary of the death for another decade or two or until the immediate relatives themselves have died. Old women like to recall, "Next month it will have been thirty-seven years since Fulana died"; relatives and friends may have a poem or eulogy published in the newspaper on the anniversary, perhaps with a picture of the departed and an invitation to a memorial mass. It is illegal to defame the memory of a dead person and thus the family honor. Every year on the Day of the Dead (November 2), as well as on Mother's Day (August 15), and increasingly on Father's Day (the third Sunday in June), Costa Ricans lay flowers on family graves. Thus the dead continue, for a time, to be members of their families.

Summary and Conclusion

Costa Ricans speak of the breakdown of the family as a phenomenon obvious to all, comparing today's families to the harmonious ones they believe were once typical. They lament the rapid rise in divorce and the frequent news articles about out-of-wedlock births, unwanted children, and domestic violence.

Yet divorce has increased in recent decades partly because it is now easier to obtain and less stigmatized; nonetheless, most married Ticos remain together. Female-headed families and out-of-wedlock births have been common for centuries. And domestic violence may be reported more frequently than in the past simply because it is less tolerated.

The role of the family in child care and socialization has indeed become less prominent; television, day-care centers, and schools increasingly perform these functions. Church attendance has increased, but family prayer has declined. Doctors, pharmacists, and psychologists have largely supplanted the family's role in health care. Both church and state have created agencies to help victims of abuse and abandonment; to strengthen existing families; and to educate childen and young people, especially those contemplating marriage, in sexual and family responsibility. Feminists' protests about gender discrimination have helped change many laws, though enforcement lags far behind intent.

Economic development and modern health services have dramatically increased longevity and reduced infant mortality and family size. Modernizing trends have thus increased the amount of attention each child gets and have made it possible for more Ticos to enjoy their grandchildren and great-grandchildren. They have also made companionship and emotional intimacy more commonly accepted criteria of a good marriage.

Most Costa Ricans are deeply attached to their families. They prefer to live near close relatives and to spend most of their leisure time with family members. They freely show their affection for one another. Despite changes and problems, the family is still seen, as the constitution describes it, as "the natural basis of Costa Rican society."

Notes

1. Carlos Monge Alfaro, *Geografía* (San José: Imprenta Universitaria, 1942), p. 23.

2. Demoscopia survey cited in *Rumbo,* February 9, 1993.

3. Victor Sanabria Martínez, *Genealogías de Cartago hasta 1850,* Vol. 1, 1957, republished in *Población de Costa Rica y origenes de los costarricenses* (San José: ECR, 1977), pp. 155–214.

4. Tatiana Lobo, *Entre Diós y el Diablo* (San José: EUCR, 1993), pp. 11–12.

5. Lowell Gudmundson, *Costa Rica Before Coffee: Society and Economy on the Eve of the Export Boom* (Baton Rouge: Lousiana State University Press, 1986), pp. 99–101.

6. Sandra Castro Paniagua and Luisa Goncalves, "Women and Love: Myths and Stereotypes in Popular Songs Broadcast in Costa Rica," in Ilse Abhagen Leitinger, ed., *The Costa Rican Women's Movement* (Pittsburgh: University of Pittsburgh Press, 1997), pp. 262–268.

7. *Mujeres latinoamericanas: Costa Rica* (San José: Instituto de la Mujer, Ministerio de Asuntos Sociales de España y Facultad Latinoamericana de Ciencias Sociales [FLACSO], 1993), p. 45. For a detailed description of this diverse movement by feminist activists, social scientists, and artists, see Leitinger, *The Costa Rican Women's Movement.*

8. Silvia Lara, Tom Barry, and Peter Simonson, *Inside Costa Rica* (Albuquerque: Resource Center Press, 1995), p. 103.

9. Ibid., p. 38.

10. Jacobo Schifter Sikora, *La formación de una contracultura: Homosexualismo y SIDA en Costa Rica* (San José: Ediciones Guayacán, 1989), pp. 30, 46.

11. Eugenia López de Piza, *How Costa Rican Women of Low Economic Status Face Economic and Sex Discrimination* (San José: UCR, 1977), pp. 73, 151.

12. For an account of the history of the decline in the birth rate, see Luís Rosero B., *Impacto del programa oficial de planificación familiar en la fecundidad, Costa Rica, 1960–1982* (San José: Comité Nacional de la Población), March 1978.

13. Luís Rosero, "Conocimientos y práctica anticonceptiva," in Victor Gómez, ed., *Actualidad demográfica de Costa Rica: 1994* (San José: Fondo de Población de las Naciones Unidas, April 1995), p. 7.2.

14. Isabel Brenes, "El aborto inducido en Costa Rica," in Gómez, *Actualidad demográfica de Costa Rica,* p. 8.1.

15. Johnny Madrigal et al., *Factores relacionados con el embarazo no deseado en Costa Rica* (San José: Asociación Demográfica Costarricense, November 1990), p. 3.

16. Mary Jane Richardson, Jean Pyfer, and Claudine Sherrill, "Self Concepts of Costa Rican Elementary School Children," in *Perceptual and Motor Skills,* June 1990, Part 2, pp. 1331–1334.

17. López's comment is, nonetheless, still true of many poor families such as those she studied in the 1970s: "As soon as a girl can walk, a broom is put in her hand; a boy is sent out to play." See López, *Costa Rican Women of Low Economic Status.*

18. Alicia Neuberger and Rodolfo Quirós, "Ambiguedad, conflicto y vida cotidiana," Paper presented at Second Congress of Social Psychology, San José, September 1992. Cited in Maria Montero, "Alicia en el país de las evasiones," *Rumbo,* November 27, 1995, pp. 44–46.

19. *Novio* means both boyfriend and groom; *novia,* both girlfriend and bride. Likewise, one's *suegros* are one's parents-in-law or the parents of one's sweetheart. But *noviazgo* no longer implies a probability of marriage.

20. Victor Gómez and Helena Ramírez, "Nupcialidad y actividad sexual prematrimonial," in Gómez, *Actualidad demográfica de Costa Rica*, pp. 5.2–5.4.

21. Gudmundson, *Costa Rica Before Coffee*, p. 90.

22. Allen Cordero and Nuria Gamboa, *La sobrevivencia de los mas pobres* (San Pedro: Editorial Porvenir, 1990), p. 10.

23. Chester Lloyd Jones, *Costa Rica and Civilization in the Caribbean* (New York: Russell & Russell, 1967), p. 126. First published in 1935.

24. Setha Low, *Culture, Politics, and Medicine in Costa Rica* (Bedford Hills, N.Y.: Redgrave, 1985), pp. 10–12.

25. Kate Galante, "Latinos Are Less Afraid to Show Affection," *Tico Times*, July 22, 1994, p. 39.

26. Robert Williamson, "Variables of Middle and Lower Classes in San Salvador and San José," *Social Forces*, Vol. 41, No. 2, December 1962, pp. 195–207.

27. Cited in Mariana Lev, "Maripepánico," *La República*, July 30, 1992, p. 20A.

28. Ibid.

29. Male prisoners have long been allowed brief conjugal visits by wives, girl-friends, or prostitutes—not as a reward for good behavior but as a necessity almost as imperative as food. Female prisoners have no such privilege.

30. *La República*, December 13, 1992, p. 1B.

31. Francisco Escobar, "La querida," *Rumbo,* July 12, 1994, p. 4.

32. Kate Galante, "'Little Lies' Haunt Special Relationships," *Tico Times*, July 26, 1995, p. 37.

33. May Brenes Marín, Sandra Castro Paniagua, and Roxana Pinto López, *Mujer y depresien* (San José: Producciones Creativas, 1990), pp. 163–164.

34. Sandra Shaw, "Gringa in Costa Rica," unpublished journal, 1995. Courtesy of the author.

35. Irma González in *Rumbo,* March 16, 1993, p. 16.

36. López, *Costa Rican Women of Low Economic Status.*

37. Gudmundson, *Costa Rica Before Coffee*, pp. 101–103.

38. *Aportes,* October-November, 1994.

39. Ana Carcedo, "Violencia y salud mental de la mujer," in *Mujeres, violencia y poder* (San José: CEFEMINA, 1990), p. 17. Also Edda Quirós R., "Violencia familiar: Un problema de salud mental," in *Mujeres, violencia y poder,* p. 4.

40. Ivan Molina and Steven Palmer, *Costa Rica 1930–1996: Historia de una sociedad* (San José: Porvenir, 1976), p. 40.

41. Editorial, *La República,* February 22, 1996, p. 12A. See also Joyce Zurcher de Carrillo, "Cuestiones de género," *La Nación,* March 1996, p. 15A.

42. Other grounds are an attempt by either one on the life of the other or their children; the attempt to force one's spouse or child into prostitution; the legally declared disappearance of a spouse; an attempt to corrupt the spouse; mental or physical cruelty or abuse; legal separation for at least a year.

43. This ratio is our rough estimate using other census data; current official figures of the number of married couples were not available.

44. Neuberger and Quirós, "Ambiguedad."

45. Tatiana Soto Cabrera, "The Law and Women's Lives: Contradictions and Struggles," in Leitinger, *The Costa Rican Women's Movement,* p. 108.

46. Carlos Sandoval García, *Sueños en la vida cotidiana: Trabajadores y trabajadoras de la máquila y la construcción en Costa Rica* (San José: EUCR, 1997), p. 200.

47. Gudmundson, *Costa Rica Before Coffee*, p. 94.

48. John Biesanz and Mavis Biesanz, *Costa Rican Life* (New York: Columbia University Press, 1944), pp. 105–106.

— 9 —

Education

WE HAVE MORE TEACHERS than soldiers," Ticos bragged when they still had an army. "We have the highest literacy rate in Central America," they still boast. The 1949 constitution makes elementary education obligatory, and schooling from preschool through high school "free and paid for by the Nation." In 1992, the new constitutional court added that schooling is a fundamental right of citizens rather than a concession by the state.

Ticos' largest common enterprise, the school system involves more than a fourth of the population as teachers and students. Uniformed schoolchildren greet visiting dignitaries, march on patriotic holidays, and carry banners during presidential inaugurations. Parents may move to a larger community so that their children can get better schooling. Costa Ricans, it would appear, still regard education as a high priority. But a 1994 UN study revealed discomfiting statistics:

1. The average Costa Rican adult, with only 5.7 years of school, had not finished the six years of primary school. (In Panama, the average is 6.6; in Trinidad-Tobago, 8.4; in Colombia, 7.5; in Cuba, 8.)
2. Costa Rica currently invests less money per capita in education than do most other Latin American countries.
3. A smaller percentage of students go on from primary to secondary school than in most other countries of "medium development," and both primary and high school teachers have larger classes.
4. A much smaller share of the gross national product goes to higher education than in other moderately developed countries (0.7 percent as compared to the 1.6 percent average for countries in the middle range outside of China).[1]

Thus the many Ticos who are highly critical of today's schools have good reason for concern, especially since the demand for academic degrees is greater than ever. A glance at history may help us understand why the system is faltering.

Education Before Independence

The indigenous peoples of precolonial Middle America offer one clear lesson for our time, says philosopher Jacinto Ordoñez: how to live in harmony with nature. One of the area's dominant societies, the Nahuatl, who used different temples for specialized instruction in war, religion, and poetry, expressed in their myths the idea that the universe is in permanent movement and seeks equilibrium to prevent a future catastrophe. The society must be ruled by the laws of this movement and this equilibrium, and human beings are as responsible as their gods for observing them so that there can be life.[2]

The colonists, steeped in Spanish Catholic tradition, failed to heed this message. Not until the present generation has it had any impact on schooling.

Formal education, like other institutions, was even less developed in isolated and impoverished Costa Rica than in neighboring colonies. Artisans learned their trades through formal apprenticeships. The chief purpose of the few primers—mostly written by priests—was to teach Catholic doctrine, although they also included lessons in writing and simple arithmetic. Colonial governors were hard pressed to find literate persons to help administer the colony. One of the few literate laypersons of the late colonial era is described by her grandson:

> My grandmother was a teacher of "first letters," and taught reading with a primer, counting and subtracting with the fingers, and Christian doctrine with a catechism written by a Jesuit of the time of Philip II. She also taught geography. The world for her consisted of Guatemala, Spain, Rome, Jerusalem, and Heaven—neither more nor less.[3]

Small wonder, then, that when independence was declared there were only six people in Alajuela, for example, who could read and write.

The Development of Public Education

In the republic's early years many officials were teachers who believed strongly that education could ensure democracy, though an 1828 law requiring school attendance was seldom enforced. The few public schools were jointly controlled by local governments and the Catholic Church.

A few women taught cooking and sewing along with the rudiments of literacy and Catholic doctrine to small groups of girls. But during most of the nineteenth century, as in colonial times, most pupils were boys and most teachers were priests or laymen trained by priests. Since "letters enter with blood," slow learners were often struck with spiked boards or made to kiss their classmates' feet or to kneel on dried corn, a stone in each outstretched hand.[4]

Poverty and illiteracy hampered the schooling that was supposed to eradicate them. Most new teacher-training institutes were soon closed for lack of funds. According to one estimate, less than 10 percent of the population in 1864 had attended any school, and only 11 percent was literate.[5] Subsequently school enrollment steadily increased, thanks largely to wealth from coffee exports. In the 1860s and 1870s, high schools patterned after French lycées were opened in major towns. The 1871 constitution made Costa Rica one of the first nations in the world to declare that education should be free, obligatory, and tax-supported. (In some ways, as we shall see, this provision has not yet been fulfilled.)

The anticlerical "liberal generation" specified, in an 1886 law, that public education must also be secular. In 1888 Santo Tomás University, the pride of the nation since its establishment in 1814, was closed (except for the Law School, where, until the 1940s, many of the country's leaders studied) on the grounds that it was too tied to the church and that funds would be better spent on the new high schools.

Although both primary and secondary schooling were indeed upgraded, it once more became necessary for anyone who aspired to master any field other than law to become self-educated (as many Costa Rican intellectuals have been) or to study abroad—usually in France or Belgium—which required either official favor or family wealth. Separate schools of fine arts, pharmacy, teacher education, and agriculture were founded after 1888, but no university was established until 1940.

The education of the few who earned a high school diploma was roughly comparable to two years of college today. In 1923, a Costa Rican was admitted without question to the Sorbonne on presentation of his diploma.

The great gap between this tiny elite and the poorly schooled majority disturbed leaders imbued with the ideal of Costa Rica as a democracy of *culto*—cultured—people. As we will see, a similar, and widening, breach disturbs many Ticos today.

The Quantitative Revolution

After the watershed year of 1948, government development programs created new demands for skilled workers, technicians, civil servants, and business managers and thus reduced the importance of being *culto*. Economic growth as well as easy international credit made spending on schools possible. People whose parents had studied only a few years began to see education as *the* means to jobs, income, and status. The result, enhanced by a baby boom in the 1950s and a sharp decline in infant mortality in later decades, was mass education.

As the middle class grew, so did its aspirations for its children. Whereas less than a fifth of the 1943 government budget went for education, by 1978 nearly a third of a budget some fifty times larger was allotted to schools. A study of the urban middle class (1988–1990) suggests the relationship of education to class: Those in the sample averaged a tenth-grade education, whereas 58 percent of the nation's labor force had not gone beyond some level of primary school.[6]

Rural communities also demanded schools—and helped build them. A sixty-five-year-old farmer in a mountain village recalls,

> When I was a boy, fathers didn't encourage kids to go to school, at least not past sixth grade. A boy might say, "Papi, I want to go to high school," and the father would answer, "I'll get you a pen." Then he'd give the boy a machete and say, "Here's your pen; now get to work." Not today. There are parents here who suffer hunger in order to send their children to school. We don't want our children to live through all the hardships we did.

Budgets and Shortages

Many Ticos blame the current problems of public schools on the budget cuts of structural adjustment. In 1978, 6.2 percent of the GDP was spent on schooling; in 1992, only 2.7 percent. In the same years, the school system's share of the central government budget dropped from 31 percent to 18 percent. Meanwhile, population growth has spread these budgets ever thinner. The population grew by more than 29 percent in the 1980s, but per capita spending on public education declined by 35 percent.

Not surprisingly, then, few schools have had maintenance or repairs in recent years, and few new ones have been built. Some parents take their six-year-olds to the nearest school on opening day only to find that they must go on a waiting list until space is somehow found. Some children now must bring their own chairs to school.

Teaching materials, too, are in short supply. More than 98 percent of the Ministry of Public Education (MEP) budget goes for salaries, including those of the MEP's own 4,000 employees. Some teachers, especially those in remote rural areas, buy chalk and paper out of their own slim paychecks or do without. "We work with our fingernails," say many teachers.

Shortly before school opens each year, the ministry announces in newspapers a list of supplies required for each grade: uniforms, notebooks, pens, colored pencils, knapsacks, and so on. In 1993, parents found they had to scrape up about 10,000 colones per child, roughly a third of a month's pay for the many parents earning the minimum wage. Uniforms, intended to cut down on display and thus democratize schools, often have the opposite effect: They are beyond the means of the poorest families, and children not in uniform stand out. In 1994 the ministry told teachers not to insist on uniforms.

Textbooks are supposedly required, and teachers may choose among alternatives approved by the MEP. But few parents can afford them, so teachers photocopy selected pages. Most teachers also ask parents for "registration fees" or voluntary donations for classroom supplies, perhaps calling a parents' meeting to agree on the amount. Many organize raffles. "I couldn't photocopy assignments for all my students if they didn't sell raffle tickets," said a small-town teacher.

Plenty of teachers apply for positions in the better schools and neighborhoods. Urban slums and remote rural communities are likely to have *aspirantes*—students working toward a teaching certificate—or no teacher at all. Says the teacher in a one-room school, "It's uncomfortable living in the country. Almost no one wants to teach there unless they have to. Many *aspirantes,* since they expect to stay in such schools only until they get the certificate, do nothing to improve conditions there."

A short school year and short school day leave little time for the formal teaching-learning process. At the beginning of the twentieth century the school year was 240 days long. By 1967, after teachers' unions achieved an end to Saturday classes, it had dropped to 208. In 1981 President Carazo, in the face of crises in energy and the economy, cut it to 177 days.

By 1993 the school year was one of the shortest in the world—officially, 176 days; holidays, patriotic celebrations, festivals, interschool soccer games, and teachers' seminars and union meetings cut the real number to 120. Nationwide teachers' strikes, which occur every year or two, shorten the school year even more. A 1995 strike for an improved pension fund lasted a month.

Eight-year-old Rolando told us he had no school the day we met him because his teacher had a meeting with the principal. He attends a two-room school; one of the two teachers also serves as principal. Some *aspirantes* take off as many as four days a month to take courses toward a certificate at a regional university. Others take advantage of the rarity of supervisors' visits. When Richard accompanied a school inspector into one remote hamlet, the teacher was absent and had not held classes for several days.

For many primary students, especially those in poor areas, the school day is also short. More children and fewer classrooms mean that the day is divided into two five-hour shifts or even three three-hour shifts to accommodate all local children.

Organization by Grades and Curricula

Children as young as three, especially those in urban areas, may attend a private preschool or one run by the Ministry of Health. Most parents, however, believe that "no one is as good as Mama," or at least some other close relative, in caring for small children.

In 1995, 70 percent of five- and six-year-olds, many of them with working mothers, attended kindergartens, most of them within public primary schools. The uniformed children, between twenty and thirty to a group, attend for three hours each weekday morning. A female teacher leads singing, supervises painting and play, lectures, and reads stories—activities intended to develop the sensory-motor and social skills needed in elementary school.

The first nine years of formal schooling, divided into three cycles of three years each, are considered to provide "basic general education." After finishing the third cycle—the first three years of high school (*colegio*)—students may choose as a fourth cycle either a two-year academic track leading to a diploma and possible university admission or the three-year vocational track. Some, desiring both a diploma and a vocation, continue in both. In some areas only vocational high schools are available, offering courses in agriculture and animal husbandry, industrial arts, secretarial work, and accounting.

Primary Schools

The six-year-old entering first grade encounters a curriculum much the same as fifty years ago. Through all six primary grades the same basic subjects are taught: Spanish, mathematics, social studies, and science. And except in urban schools, agriculture is also part of the curriculum and involves work in a school garden—the source of some lunchroom food. (In some towns and villages, children are instead expected to work in a home garden, which teachers may check on.) Programs for each subject come from the MEP, and each teacher draws up her own lesson plans accordingly. Children in the first cycle may have the same teacher for all subjects all three years; second-cycle students have a new teacher every year.

In 1988, computers donated by IBM, MIT, and other foreign organizations were introduced into some kindergartens and primary schools, and by 1996 nearly a third of all primary schools had computers. Children working in pairs use them for two forty-minute periods a week. Says Clotilde Fonseca, the prime mover behind their use, "The main purpose is not to turn out computer experts but to help children learn to think step-by-step, in logical fashion." Children are enthusiastic about computers. "My seven-year-old daughter begs me to buy her one," says an electrician.

In urban schools, specialized instructors impart two weekly lessons each in "home and family," religion (from a Catholic perspective), art, and music. In many rural schools the only special subject is religion, taught by the regular teacher. In 1994 English and French were introduced in some schools with plans to offer them as well as computers in all eventually.

A student who fails one of the four basic subjects must pass a makeup exam or repeat the whole year. "This is not as unfair as it sounds," one teacher

Computer class in a public primary school (Julio Laínez)

told us; "A child who fails one subject usually does poorly in all of them." Most students pass the makeup exams. And although 30 percent of sixth-grade students failed one or more of the three-hour final exams in each subject in 1995, 99 percent were promoted.

Most urban primary schools have an ungraded classroom for mildly retarded and learning-disabled children. Because of budget cuts, the special public schools for physically disabled children were closed in 1997 and their 20,000 students assigned to mainstream schools.

Secondary Schools

By law the central government must provide facilities for nine years of schooling in every canton and every town of 5,000 or more. (Since 1997, students in a few smaller, more isolated communities, unable to attract high-school teachers, have gathered in the local *Salón Comunal* to watch educational videos in an MEP distance-learning program.) Many courses are required in high school. In the third cycle (seventh to ninth grades), thirty-five forty-minute class periods totaling twenty-four hours a week are devoted to Spanish, English, French, social studies (with emphasis on Costa Rica), math, general science, religion, civics, family life, industrial arts (shop), plastic arts, music, and physical education.

The fourth cycle—tenth and eleventh grades—includes most of these same subjects; adds philosophy and psychology; replaces general science with separate courses in physics, chemistry, and biology; and offers a choice of English or French. This ambitious curriculum belies the frequent charge that secondary schooling is simply a continuation of primary schooling. But there are not enough classrooms or trained teachers for so many subjects in so many schools. Any one subject can be explored only superficially at best.

A university psychologist believes, nonetheless, that Costa Rican high school students learn far more than do those in some more-developed countries. A recent high school graduate from a small mountain town agrees. "When I was in the U.S., I was appalled by how little the students there know about world geography or even their own country's government. We live in such a small and vulnerable country, we *have* to know such things."

A requirement added in 1995 was that eleventh-graders perform thirty hours of community service. Working in small groups, they may choose among tasks as diverse as planting trees in a watershed; teaching soccer to elementary school children; and helping out in a local post office, day-care center, or senior citizens' home.

The high school day is much longer than the three-to-five-hour day of urban primary schools. Particularly in the fourth and fifth years, when they are preparing for the dreaded *bachillerato* exam, students may be in school from 7 A.M. to 2:35 P.M. with a half-hour lunch break. Even so, students in many schools attend only four days a week because of shortages of teachers and classrooms.

The Quality of Education

Recalling his schooling in the 1930s, a *campesino* wrote over forty years later: "Back then, there were many teachers without titles; now there are many titles without [competent] teachers, and consequently many illiterate graduates. Before, they called a school an *escuela* (seven letters). Now you must say *centro educativo* (fifteen letters)."[7]

Measured by the time, energy, and money devoted to it, education is no longer a high national priority. Experts and laypeople agree that the quality of teaching and learning has fallen disastrously low. A 1983 study of 400 high school students, still often cited in the press a decade later, found that eleventh-graders were no more likely to solve seven logic and math problems than were seventh-graders.[8]

Some critics say curriculum content is too thin and is repeated from year to year. Others blame faulty teaching methods. In 1968 a rural schoolteacher blamed both: "The students must memorize all sorts of things that have nothing to do with their lives, and these are not learned in a practical way but almost entirely out of books and lectures."

Almost twenty years later, Humberto Pérez, a leading authority on Costa Rican education, wrote:

> Learning to learn: this is rarely taught in our schools. We often see primary, secondary, or university students copying information from a notebook or an encyclopedia, only to repeat it later in an exam without analysis or question. Our education continues to be bookish and by rote. It is believed that to read books *about* biology or history is to study biology or history.[9]

The MEP urged reforms in the 1970s to reduce rote learning and to involve students more actively in the learning process. Many teachers, however, find it easier to teach the way they were taught—asking fourth-graders, for instance, to copy the numbers from 1 to 2,000 and giving multiple-choice and true-false tests but few essay exams. One teacher adds, "The ministry tells us not to make the kids memorize facts. But when they take a national exam—made up by that very ministry—and find they are expected to know dozens of facts, would they forgive us for having made them spend their class time 'more creatively'?"

The problem, some critics argue, is not memorization but the wrong kind—of trivia devoid of context. Sixth-graders are asked, on the ministry's year-end exam, to name all the presidents but not to explain important events or trends. A priest complains that students who ask him for help with their religion homework are assigned such questions as "What are the Pope's parents' names?" The nationwide *bachillerato* exams have included such questions as "Who was Gaspar's sweetheart?" (in a subplot of *Don Quixote*) and "What was Braulio Carrillo's most identifiable characteristic on his strolls in San José?" (Answer: his ebony cane.) One frequent consequence is that students' only mode of participation in class is answering teachers' questions, often in chorus. We observed, likewise, an eighth-grade civics class in which four students elected by the class were urged to voice and solve problems involving the whole class. The teacher asserted she should be considered just another class member but in fact regulated who talked and when and suggested most of the solutions.

Concentration is impeded by heavy rain on the metal roof, by noise from neighboring classrooms, and by restless classmates. Much time is spent copying from the blackboard and writing texts from dictation. While a teacher lectures or helps individuals at their desks or hers, other students talk, walk about the room, fidget, carve on their desks, and show every sign of boredom. Her frequent calls for silence often go unheeded. (Observers in the 1940s noted the same behavior: "The monotony inevitably produced by the lecture method in high school results in lack of attention and discipline in many classes. Students who know they can copy someone else's notes after class whisper, knit, read, or study other lessons.")[10]

Except perhaps for charts of her own making, the teacher lacks visual aids to illustrate lessons. Even in science classes, experiments and direct observations are few, for not only do most schools lack equipment but teachers often fail to take advantage of local resources. "The only thing our chemistry teacher uses is the blackboard," says a high school student. Homework often consists of neatly recopying a lesson dictated in class, and many teachers seem to regard a tidy notebook as evidence of understanding. Students seldom study until just before exams; if they fail, they know they can take a makeup test later.

We have seen some change in teaching methods. Many teachers follow such ministry suggestions as seating the pupils in small groups—supposedly to discuss an assignment, though often only to share the few textbooks. During the 1990s, many primary school classes spent a few hours in state reforestation projects. Students also aided in the removal of mosquito breeding grounds to prevent the spread of dengue fever. High school students, alone or in small groups, can often be seen taking notes in art galleries, parks, and other places, a rare sight before the 1990s.

Says a domestic servant living in a small town near the capital:

> My eleven-year-old son, in fifth grade in a public school, is expected to go on field trips with a small group of classmates, for example to museums in San José. He has to learn to use libraries without teachers along, and to bring plants and other things to discuss in class. I favor these new policies, although they involve more work for me, such as showing him how to use the bus and attending more parents' meetings.

The School in Social Context

Despite such innovations, the same criticisms—largely valid ones—have been made for decades. Why is the system so resistant to improvement? Centralization, bureaucracy, political influence, lack of long-range policy, and the growing breach between those who must go to public schools and those whose parents can afford private schools—all these impede change.

Centralization and Government Control

Unlike some other government services, the school system was highly centralized even before 1949; the MEP has long controlled everything from supplies to syllabi in public schools throughout the land.

The education minister, appointed by each incoming president, heads the hierarchy. Many staff members, protected by civil service regulations, stay on through changes of administration, but a new minister usually replaces top officials with friends or political partisans. He or she heads the Superior Council of Education (CSE), which makes both general policy and specific decisions on curricula, texts, allocation of funds, teacher qualifications, and supervision of teachers.

In practice a forceful minister can easily control the CSE, a control resting largely on "the paternalistic tradition in which each subordinate solves his problems in private conversation with the minister."[11] The minister usually has only four years in which to make any changes and, if there has been a change of party, is likely to discard previous programs and perhaps "erase with the elbow what his predecessor did with the hand."[12]

Neglect of school computers during the Calderón Fournier administration (1990–1994) illustrates this last point. Columnist Julio Rodríguez wrote in 1992 that the 127 computer centers established in 1988–1990 in rural and slum areas had "injected vigor and life" into a crumbling school system "and opened to our children—above all, poor children—an unsuspected panorama of science, of excellence, of a desire to live and be somebody." Many such centers languished not for lack of resources, which came from foreign foundations, but for lack of support by the new minister.[13] (The next minister restored and extended computer education.)

When a new minister almost ritualistically announces plans to reform curricula and methods, teachers, who have heard it all before, are likely to stick with familiar methods. This regular turnover and disparagement of earlier policies, says Carlos Cortés, perpetuates teachers' pattern of improvising from day to day rather than developing long-range goals.[14]

Eduardo Doryan, minister from 1994 to 1998, decentralized the system in some ways. He divided the country into nine regions and 150 circuits; each sponsored workshops for teachers, and the scores of each circuit's students on national tests were announced to local teachers so that they could improve weak areas. Still, most major decisions continued to be made by ministry officials. This centralized control remained so strong that, as one teacher complained, "The curriculum hardly takes regional or rural-urban differences into account. Even teachers in Talamanca [a thinly populated mountainous district], for instance, are supposed to teach traffic safety." And the MEP-approved blueprint for school buildings nationwide reflects San José's highland climate, so even schools in hot lowland areas have metal roofs and little ventilation.

Socioeconomic Inequalities

Social class has affected Ticos' access to schooling since colonial times. The founding fathers and numerous administrators have always declared that education must be free and obligatory. But there has always been a wide breach between the uneducated many and the educated few. Although this gap narrowed somewhat after 1948, it has widened again since 1980.

Despite the quantitative revolution, the system continues to favor the urban well-to-do, who attend private schools or the best public schools. Three youths in a small town told us why they commute an hour to a public high school in the capital: "We went to the local school for two years, but the teachers here are terrible." Their parents could afford the extra supplies demanded by teachers in the San José school. Many others cannot. The owner of a small fruit stand in the same town is the mother of an exceptionally bright ten-year-old. "My son's teachers said he should be in the public school for gifted children in San José," she told us, "so I had him take the admissions test and he did well. But I wondered how I could afford it so I didn't enroll him."

Then, too, poor parents need their children's economic help. "I know I'm supposed to enforce truancy laws," a rural canton official told us in 1968. "But my own parents took me out of school each year in November to pick coffee. And anyway, I have to live here and don't want everybody angry at me." Since the early 1980s, increasing numbers of poor children work at odd jobs to help the family or leave home for the streets. In 1996, half of all twelve- to seventeen-year-olds were not enrolled in school. A high school director comments, "The law now requires attendance through the third year of high school. But it's not enforced at all."

"When I was in school," say many older Ticos, often in almost identical words, "the shoemaker's son shared a desk with the son of the doctor or lawyer." Although private schools have always existed, today's professionals are far more likely to send their children there; shoemakers—and their modern-day counterparts such as factory workers—go to public ones.

Private schools, attended by one student in five, have a longer year (by forty-five days) and a longer day (by two or three hours) than do public schools. Classes are smaller—an average of twenty-five children versus forty in public schools. Buildings, equipment, and libraries are far superior. (An MEP official calculates that one private school in San José has the funding of all thirty-two public vocational high schools combined.) Content is much richer; not only are art, music, dance, theater, and sports usually offered even in primary grades but they may be part of the standard curriculum. Many require some knowledge of English, useful in many fields today. Standards of teaching and study in most are strict; salaries and tuition are correspondingly high. Says a teacher in a top-ranked private school:

> As a student twenty-five years ago I enrolled in a private school after four years in a rural public school and had no problems. I felt at home. But now private schools don't accept transfer students from public schools. They can't adapt. They don't know English. They aren't used to the heavier demands for study and reading. It hurts to see public primary school kids going home at 10:30 in the morning because they've covered the four basic subjects and there's nothing more to do—no manual activity [shop], no garden, no music, no library.

> Public education suffers from a frightening lack of planning. They built schools for a population of two million, and went to sleep, not thinking ahead to three million and more.[15]

Results are evident in the comparative grades on the *bachillerato* exams at the end of high school: In 1990, only 49 percent of public high school students passed the exam and got a diploma; in private ones, 85 percent. Acknowledging private schools' success, the Constitutional Court ruled in 1992 that the Superior Council of Education has the right only to inspect such schools, not to regulate them. Their high exam scores, however, probably also reflect other advantages of their students: They are better nourished and healthier than many public school students and more likely to have a favorable study environment at home.

The elite typically send their children to a private, bilingual "American" school where all courses except Spanish are taught in English; Presidents Arias, Calderón Jr., and both Figuereses enrolled their children in the private Lincoln School. Many middle-class parents make the financial sacrifice lest they sentence their children "to an intellectual and job leprosarium," says Fernando Durán, former rector of the University of Costa Rica. Thus they help perpetuate a vicious circle: Public schools are so bad that upper- and upper-middle-class parents wouldn't dream of sending their children there; since these parents are the ones with political clout, their lack of interest in public education is reflected in government neglect. The increasing gap in quality and prestige between private and public education then widens class inequalities even further. Cultural differences among Ticos thereby increase in other ways as well: The University of Costa Rica's weekly paper denounces private schools as profit-making enterprises that charge in dollars and downgrade the nation's culture—by ignoring Costa Rica's Independence Day, for example.[16]

Minister Doryan, upset by this widening breach, made "equal opportunity" a top priority. In 1994 the ministry donated uniforms, shoes, and school supplies to 21,000 poor students, revitalized school breakfast and lunch programs, and established special programs for schools attended mostly by children from poor families. Dropouts from such schools, he says, declined by 7 percent in 1995.

School and Community

Despite the centralization of public education, each school reflects not only a community's degree of wealth but also the level of cooperation among its adults. Each community has a board of directors for its primary school(s) and another, called the administrative board, for its high school(s). A school board's chief duty is to allocate the funds assigned by the Ministry of the Treasury on the basis of enrollment. Many boards complain that because these payments are often delayed by three or four months, schools often cannot pay their utility bills and their electricity, phones, and water are cut off. Parents, especially mothers, help with schools much more than they did before the 1990s—serving lunch, cleaning buildings, supplying food for parties, speaking to classes about their jobs. The MEP now encourages parents to sign their children's homework and to confer with teachers. Many teachers arrange conferences with all parents as often as every two weeks—too often, say many working parents, particularly the many mothers who have outside jobs. (Fathers rarely attend.)

Subsistence farmers in peripheral areas and squatters in urban slums typically request government help in building a school soon after they settle in a new locality. Neighbors and local businesses may donate lumber, a building site, labor, and possibly money and supplies, and the MEP sends a carpenter and standard blueprints. Usually, after a school is built, more people settle in the area. Without a school there is usually little community organization.

Rural schools, including those with all six grades, are allotted only one teacher until enrollment passes fifty (unlikely today with rural populations declining). Although many rural teachers are simply marking time while working for a certificate, an MEP curriculum adviser says that many others "have developed teaching practices that are more participatory, more active, more motivating, and more in accord with the reality the students face" than have those in larger urban schools. A standard practice, one now encouraged by the ministry, is to ask older pupils to help younger ones.

We spent several hours with a young teacher in his one-room school; he apparently loves to teach and uses imaginative methods. He writes out a copy of lesson objectives tailor-made for each pupil. He built a microscope and asked parents for money to buy a globe, although neither is required for ministry programs. When one child saw an insect larva while doing a lesson, the teacher did not scold him for being distracted but described the insect's life cycle. He sometimes takes the children for a short walk, perhaps down to the river, for a science lesson that he thinks would benefit them all. "But," he told us, "I could do such things more often if I had only one grade."

Cultural Acceptance of Mediocrity

Although parents value schooling, many raise their children in ways that hinder learning. The *pobrecito* ("poor thing" or victim) complex fosters a reluctance to work and study hard, even in adults who sign up for private lessons. "They want the prestige of knowing English," says a tutor, "but they are lazy and expect to be spoon-fed everything." Ticos are reluctant to admit even obvious mistakes and resent having them called to their attention, particularly if others are present. Teachers are also hesitant to criticize or, as we saw, to fail students, just as anthropologists noted in 1942.[17] Many teachers will pass an academically deficient student not only because failures make the teacher look bad but also, perhaps, because the *pobrecito* has to work after school or has an unhappy home life. Consequently, the quality of teaching tends to fall to the level of the lowest common denominator—the most *pobrecito* of all.[18]

A critic adds that very successful students are envied but not admired by their classmates and even by their families and teachers. "Our ideal of equality has actually become mediocrity."[19] A fifty-five-year-old businessman agrees. "This has even affected students in private schools. When I went to a private high school in the late 1950s, the better students were admired by their classmates. Today, my daughters tell me, such students are considered nerds."

Reading and Study Habits

Census figures show that the literacy rate among those over age ten rose from 11 percent in 1864 to 93 percent in 1984. But these figures are based on simple tests such as the ability to sign one's name. Thus many functional illiterates who have forgotten skills acquired in school are officially classified as literate. A columnist reports that telephone operators are swamped with calls from the many people too unfamiliar with alphabetical order to use directories.[20]

Many Ticos believe that illness and even insanity afflict those who read and study too much and commiserate with the *pobrecito* who is expected to write a paper or pass an exam. A retired university professor, warned by his doctor that reading worsened his anxiety attacks, reluctantly gave up reading.

Many critics blame television viewing—an average of six hours a day among young Ticos—for short attention spans and lack of interest in reading and thinking. A librarian in a small town says patronage began to decline as soon as local people began acquiring TV sets.

A nation of readers bespeaks a nation of good schools. And Costa Rican schools do not encourage reading. Even teachers, says an education specialist, prefer workshops to correspondence courses "because workshops don't usually require reading." A 1992 ministry memo indicates the dimensions of the problem: Teachers were asked to set aside *fifteen minutes a day* for reading.

Another obstacle to reading is the high cost of books. Perhaps even more fundamental is an aversion to solitude; rather than take a book or magazine along to a doctor's waiting room or the long line at a bank or government office, a Tica usually asks a friend or relative to accompany her and help pass the time in conversation.

Goals of Education

Many employers now require a high school diploma even for guards and messengers. Legal minimum wages depend not only on the job category but also on the jobholders' academic degrees. So important is *titulismo* (credentialism) that cheating on exams and homework is now common, and students frequently interrupt lectures to ask, "Will this be on the exam?"

Two criteria determine hiring and placement of public employees, says Gerardo Esquivel: political pull and academic degrees. "The consequences of this dictatorship of the *titulocrácia* are well known: it has displaced the knowledge and experience of the self-educated. . . . The ironic sign seen in some offices is still true: 'Here the person who knows how to do things does them, the person who doesn't is boss.' "[21]

From the 1880s until the 1948 civil war the official goal of Costa Rican schools was to produce "cultured" citizens of a democracy, though historian Astrid Fischel insists the elite wanted only their own children to become *cultos* and those of peons to achieve just basic literacy, numeracy, and patriotism.[22] After the war, as we saw earlier, the growth of industry, business, and government shifted the focus to education as a public investment in economic development. Increasing Costa Rica's supply of skilled workers, for example, is the purpose of the semiautonomous National Institute of Apprenticeship (INA). Founded in 1965, INA, with 48,000 students in 1993, has largely replaced the less formal apprenticeship of yesteryear, in which a boy might learn a trade by working for a relative or neighbor.

The system has, however, not kept pace with social change: New ministry officials complained in 1994 that the high school curriculum, unchanged in fifteen years, was geared to an industrial society, not the emerging "technological" one.

The stigma of manual labor remains so strong that even when other options are open, most prefer the academic track, not necessarily because they want to be *cultos* but because they want the prestige of white-collar jobs and professional titles. Many students settle for a vocational school simply because it is the only high school nearby, but they keep their sights on professional degrees. A survey of students at one such school found boys in a cabinet-making class hoping to study law, engineering, chemistry, and architecture; girls in a sewing class wanted to study medicine, psychology, and biology.

Whatever their failures, Costa Rican schools succeed in producing patriots through constant celebration of the country's virtues. Schools convince children that Costa Rica is the best country in the world. Although MEP authorities often declare that schooling must reflect "the national reality," texts depict an idyllic country without poverty, unemployment, conflict, broken homes, or crime. Most show middle-class nuclear families: The father is always there. Boys are shown as active outside the house and girls, at home—both doing sex-stereotyped jobs. There is no mention of single-parent families or of mothers who support their children by farming, factory work, or domestic service. There is no hint of industrialization or class differences.

(Anthropologist Trevor Purcell agrees but sees a contrast with the state-supported universities: "At the lower levels, education presents the social system as ideal, while at the higher level it serves the unintended function of helping to expose the contradictions and provide the basis for critique.")[23]

Students hear that other peoples, burdened with armies, admire and envy Costa Rica. They spend many hours preparing for and celebrating holidays commemorating historical events and, even in primary school, for student government elections, which, they are told, train them for adult participation in Costa Rican democracy. Because children thoroughly "absorb the values, beliefs and world views of the dominant class," says Fischel, Costa Rica's elite, unlike those in such countries as Guatemala, needs no army to exert social control.[24]

Novelist and columnist Alberto Cañas argues that despite all these observances, the system does not produce public-spirited citizens. "What they want is to be legislators, and then ambassadors or agency directors in order to raise their pensions."[25] Humberto Pérez agrees, blaming the "hidden curriculum" that is the antithesis of the official one, which

> tries to form citizens who love their country, are conscientious about their duties and rights, with a profound sense of responsibility. . . . However, this is not achieved; and indirectly but effectively students are taught negative attitudes, habits and values that constitute the hidden curriculum. The school, for example, teaches its students [unintentionally, through its failure to correct such habits] to arrive late, to copy, to push, not to study, to deceive, to have no discipline, to improvise, and to pass the grade without learning or doing anything. . . . The student . . . is not interested in learning, but in getting a diploma that permits him to get a job or to go on studying.[26]

A professor of teacher training objects that this diatribe exaggerates the faults of the system. Still, it seems clear that many students, especially older ones, hate school. All but 4 percent of high school students polled in a 1995 study said school is a waste of time and they learn very little.[27] When teachers announce that classes are canceled because of a teachers' strike, for instance, students cheer.

Adult Education

Despite the deficiencies of public schools, many adults take evening courses in them as well as in private institutions, usually hoping to get a degree to improve their job prospects. Over 100 public and private schools offer adults elementary or high school diplomas or certificates for completing two- or three-year programs in such diverse fields as languages, computers, insurance, interior decorating, occupational health, secretarial skills, bookkeeping, soil conservation, and nutrition. These shorter programs appeal especially to those unable or unwilling to take a university degree or to finish high school. Many evening students are factory workers, clerks, and domestic servants; some are housewives. Course loads are heavy, especially for those with day-time jobs, and about a third drop out each year.

Thousands of adults also take noncredit courses, often simply for plea-sure. During vacations the University of Costa Rica offers courses at nominal fees in subjects ranging from guitar, cooking, word processing, and etiquette to feminism and political theory. Many public autonomous institutions offer short courses—often of a week or less—in such skills as accounting and bookkeeping. Increasing numbers of adults take private, small-group lessons in philosophy, literature, painting, or psychology from retired or moonlight-ing professionals—often merely out of curiosity. Some elderly Ticos audit courses free of charge at the state universities.

Several programs take advantage of widespread radio ownership. *The Teacher in Your House* broadcasts primary and secondary school lessons in Spanish and several Indian languages from twelve small, noncommercial ra-dio stations. Since the Costa Rican Institute of Radio Education was founded in 1973, thousands of farmers living in isolated areas have enrolled in corre-spondence courses leading to certificates of completion. The institute, di-rected by the Ministry of Education, is funded by several foreign govern-ments. Beamed by radio to all of Central America and Mexico is *School for Everyone,* founded in 1965 by private individuals. Its staff answers letters asking about everything except politics. The school is now a public semiau-tonomous institution.

The Status of Teachers

Rural teachers were once expected to lead prayers, give medical advice and treatment, write or visit public officials requesting favors for the community or for individuals, and play a prominent role in all community activities. But even in hamlets where they are the only government employees, they are no longer the only literate adults. And Ticos now have other sources of knowledge. Says a woman who has taught for seventeen years in rural schools, "People now learn so much from TV they don't ask you for advice as they once did."

Although their unions are among the country's strongest, teachers are among the poorest-paid professionals, possibly because most are women (78 percent of elementary school teachers and 54 percent of high school teachers in 1991). Teachers say it is impossible to support a family adequately on their salaries.

Salary and placement are based primarily on civil service ranks that re-flect training and experience, though placement is still sometimes affected by

Teachers striking for an improved pension plan, July 1995 (Julio Laínez)

political pull. "A certified teacher cannot be fired and has benefits and a pension," says a teacher in both private and public schools who keeps her status as a public school teacher because of this security. "In private schools, you can be fired for incompetence." Since teachers are paid according to the number of hours they work, many, especially high school teachers, work in two or three schools and spend much time commuting.

Teachers are often accused of being interested primarily in their short workdays, three-month vacations, salaries, and pensions—motivations considered normal in most occupations but beneath the dignity of this calling. Such charges make many teachers furious. Says a high school teacher:

> Our easy jobs, short days, and long vacations are a myth. Our work is supposed to end in November; it doesn't really end until about December 20. Then we're called back to work in February to be ready for the opening of school in March. Many of us are truly dedicated; why else do we keep working when we may not even get paid for eight months? A young teacher in charge of forty kids must love kids a lot to stay on.

Teachers may retire at age sixty; until 1995 they could retire after twenty-five years' service—twenty in remote rural areas—and some did so in their midforties. Most teachers defend early retirement, saying their work is exhausting. The noise level in classrooms is one likely reason for this, as are the consequent throat problems many teachers report. Says a fifty-year-old teacher in a working-class urban school, "I don't know how I can last another ten years. Classes are much bigger than when I started twenty years ago and kids are spoiled at home now. No one listens to the teacher, and with the laws passed in the late 1980s, she can't do anything when a child misbehaves. And the kids know it!" Teaching is surely all the more tiring in a culture in which reading and studying are widely thought to overtax the brain.

Most of the country's 27,000 teachers pay dues to ANDE, the National Association of Educators, founded in 1941. It provides loans, legal help, and recreation as well as sponsoring seminars and literary contests. Most high school teachers also belong to the Association of Professors of Secondary Education, APSE. Many members insist that these organizations are not *sindicatos* (unions), a term smacking of manual labor and communism. A smaller union, the Syndicate of Costa Rican Educators (SEC), is so active that rural teachers are often approached by a recruiter long before an MEP representative comes around. SEC has organized most teachers' strikes, which other unions then support.

Though strongly opposing a longer school year, teachers refused to hold union conferences during vacations when that was suggested by the MEP. A journalist found that in every threatened or actual strike—nine in all—between 1974 and 1994, teachers' demands were eventually granted.[28] A 1995 strike protesting changes in the retirement age and teachers' lack of control over their pension fund was, however, unsuccessful.

Unions may also work to improve education. They often collaborate with the MEP in sponsoring seminars and workshops. And in 1996, officials from APSE and the MEP agreed that students' absences should lower their grades, as they currently did not.

Teacher Training

Although governments from the 1880s until 1940 sent many aspiring high school teachers to Chile for training, most teachers were trained in the prestigious Escuela Normal Superior in Heredia or in the few high schools. After public universities were established, they took over teacher training. The two biggest, the University of Costa Rica and the National Autonomous University, as well as several private universities, offer three-year programs leading to a primary school teaching certificate and four-year programs for high school teachers. Each university sets its own curriculum, methods, and standards, which are then subject to approval by the Superior Council of Education.

Teacher-training curricula, like those in secondary schools, once consisted of a great many subjects treated rather superficially. As in the schools they came from and those in which they would work, the future teachers made few independent observations or experiments, read little, and spent most of their time memorizing lectures and cramming for exams. When graduates were abruptly plunged into teaching with little or no guidance or follow-up training, the easy and natural thing was to teach as they had been taught.

Our observations suggest that this has changed considerably in recent years. In a typical class, aspiring teachers now take turns presenting lessons they have devised, using materials they have made, to their classmates. Class participation is encouraged and usually forthcoming. Small groups of students may plan a lesson they will later present in a nearby school. "These students really have to think, not just memorize," says a sociologist at one university. And several education departments, such as that of the private Universidad Panamericana, require each education student to observe and assist teachers in several regions of the country. "Our professors want us to be sure we have a vocation to be teachers," says a third-year student.

Many teachers complain that the MEP gives them little help with their work. "The ministry," says a teacher, "suggests that we attend science workshops. But they don't even pay bus fare, let alone lunch. So do you think they really want better teachers?" Rural teachers especially resent the lack of guidance and appropriate books for one-room or other combined-grade schools; even more than urban teachers, they have to improvise constantly. Teachers say that the leading newspapers are more helpful than the ministry. They publish weekly supplements that most primary school teachers use in class. Says one teacher, "We'd be lost without *La Nación*, because the ministry doesn't send us such good material. A language specialist paid by *La Nación* visits schools to help us learn how to use the paper. Maybe we take an ad and make a math problem. Or we look for regular verbs."

Higher Education

After going without a university since 1888, Ticos hailed the establishment of the University of Costa Rica in 1940. Easier high school graduation requirements and the growth of the state bureaucracy in the 1950s and 1960s swelled demand for admission. But many applicants were rejected as unqualified. This, plus a conviction that the UCR had become "too academic" and elitist, led President Pepe Figueres to inaugurate the National Autonomous University (UNA) in Heredia in 1973. Its detractors objected that it imparted little more than degrees and leftist ideology. A former UNA professor of cooperative management told us that in the late 1970s he was about

University of Costa Rica (Richard Biesanz)

to give some lectures on methods of accounting when his superior told him that accounting was technical and therefore "not part of the national reality." He resigned.

Such ideological disputes have given way to acceptance of both universities, along with recognition that UNA, despite its lower prestige, is more accessible and in closer touch with Costa Rica's economic and social conditions. For example, an epidemic of porcine fever was quickly identified at UNA's College of Veterinary Medicine. Says a UNA agronomy graduate: "As a requirement for one course, I had to live in a remote region for several weeks—not because I'd learn more about plants, but so I'd get used to the mud and other hardships an agronomist must deal with." UNA faculty say their promotions, unlike those at UCR, are based partly on whether they have done research into practical problems and applied it to their teaching.

Helping correct the tendency to train unneeded professionals while losing needed ones to more industrialized countries is the state-run Institute of Technology near Cartago, whose first class was graduated in 1975. Offering intermediate levels of technical-professional training, it serves as a bridge between highly skilled labor and university-trained engineers; for example, its construction engineering degree fills the vast gap between construction foremen and civil engineers. Industrial production, industrial maintenance (a most important specialty, since nearly all equipment is imported), electronics, and highway construction are among the subjects offered. The program is not purely technical; it also includes liberal arts courses. So does the State University at a Distance, founded in 1978, which offers credit courses via television as well as tutoring each week by professors who commute to its tiny but widespread offices. Most of its 12,000 students are adults.

The state, not student tuitions, pays most costs of the four public universities—79 percent of UCR's 1993 costs, for instance. These costs accounted for a quarter of the MEP's 1994 budget. As in primary and secondary schools, nearly all funds went to pay salaries; little was left for textbooks or lab equipment. Since few students can afford books—primarily translations of U.S. authors—teachers may assign only photocopied key chapters. Says a young psychology professor, "The shortage of texts was actually a good thing for some of us when we were undergrads. We discussed the ideas in the text or photocopies we shared and learned a lot that way."

Tuition is charged on an eleven-point scale according to family income, and about one student out of four pays nothing. Even those in the highest bracket pay very little compared to the cost of the private high schools most attended. But wealthy students are few. Says one longtime UCR professor, "Most of my students are from the lower-middle class. The few upper-class students I've had complain that many professors jeer at them as 'rich brats' as soon as they learn their surnames. That's one reason most upper-class kids study in the United States or the leading private university."

A 1991 proposal to reduce the state subsidy was followed by the biggest public demonstration the country had seen in twenty years. Students and faculty from the state universities, joined by high school students, immobilized San José for hours. The proposal was shelved.

The UCR is generally regarded as the best university, public or private. Plaques outside many professionals' offices boast "UCR graduate." High-school graduates usually try first for admission there. Teaching, business, and engineering students predominate; most of the remainder major—in decreasing order—in the social sciences, literature, medicine, accounting, agronomy, pharmacy, architecture, dentistry, microbiology, journalism, philosophy, and fine arts. Each department limits its enrollment, and many qualified students are unable to enter the program of their choice.

UCR's general-studies program—a liberal arts core required of all students and generally taken during their first two years—includes sociology, math, "the national reality," sports, a fine arts elective, and a team-taught course combining Spanish, philosophy, and Western history. The requirement, instituted in 1957, was at first hailed as a means of ensuring well-rounded, "cultured" graduates with a knowledge of the humanities, even in specialized careers. Today, it is more often justified as a remedy for the deficiencies of secondary schools.

As at lower levels, *titulismo* reigns in universities. Most students are interested primarily in obtaining grades high enough to earn a prestigious degree and corresponding jobs. Because of the proliferation of university degrees, however, and because of structural adjustment pressures to cut public-sector jobs—once the main source of graduates' employment—since 1993 there have been more graduates than professional jobs. This may well have accelerated the "brain drain," already evident for several years, of physicians, nurses, and other professionals, especially to the United States.

The emphasis on credentials affects hiring within the universities as well as outside. Comments a professor, "The great journalist José Marín Cañas taught in the UCR School of Journalism. But he didn't have a degree, so eventually he was fired and one of his own students was put in his place."

After the BA a student may take two or more years of coursework (often financed by a government loan) and write a thesis that will enable her to put "Lic." (*licenciada*) before her name. (Joint theses are fairly common. Whereas most have only two or three coauthors, we read an excellent 1994 history thesis coauthored by five students, the maximum allowed.) Many students go on for a master's degree. Engineers study a total of six years. The UCR's departments of medicine, history, philosophy, agronomy, and education offer doctorates, though foreign doctorates still confer more prestige. The College of Medicine at UCR is considered by far the best in Central America.

Just as at lower levels, lectures and memorization characterize university teaching. But field research and oral presentations are increasingly required, even of first-year students, who often work in teams of three or four.

Graduates of public schools are at a particular disadvantage at universities. A 1995 MEP study found that of entering freshmen who had studied at public schools, fewer than one-fifth could identify the main ideas in an essay and only one out of ten was accustomed to reading. A business professor told us he gave his students, all public school graduates, two essays with opposing theses. "Not one student noticed that the authors disagreed," he says.

Students in turn complain that they take too many courses to have much time to study; besides, most work at least part time. But the *pobrecito* appeals that may have ensured passing grades in high school rarely work. "You're on your own at the university," says one student. "It's not like high school. Here no one makes sure you pass or tells you how to organize your time." In part, perhaps, because many are unprepared for such responsibility, over half of those who enroll never graduate.

For years most professors taught part time and gave their main efforts to their professional practice, such as law. They taught because they enjoyed the prestige and warm, friendly contact with young people afforded by university teaching, which was (and still is) poorly paid. Many still are adjuncts but even most adjuncts are now exclusively teachers, some at two or more universities. One-third are women.

Costa Rica's constitution guarantees academic freedom. During the 1960s and 1970s, many professors at the public universities espoused with impunity views far to the left of most Ticos. One sociology professor used only four texts: by Marx, Engels, Lenin, and Mao. Although as another UCR sociologist said in 1991, "the red flag has finally been lowered at this school," this has not been due to any overt pressure on Marxist professors. The collapse of communist governments in Eastern Europe and the Soviet Union is one likely reason. Another is students' increased conservatism. "Students today are simply bored when a prof talks about the need to redistribute wealth," says one longtime UCR professor.

But frank criticism between professors and students, and even among colleagues, is rare, as it is among Ticos generally. "We haven't learned how to express disagreement," says a UCR department chairperson. Whether because or in spite of this, the atmosphere in a typical university classroom is relaxed (though much less noisy than in elementary and high schools), and students and teachers—both often clad in jeans—engage in much friendly banter.

Professors now publish far more than did those of a generation ago. Although publications are considered by the peer committees that decide on promotions and tenure, they are not required, and tenure is usually granted after three years of full-time teaching. Research is often unremunerated, and many professors say its major goal should be social betterment. Thus, for instance, a UCR anthropologist hopes that her research on traditional folk arts will encourage their revival.

This action orientation—typified by UNA but part of the ethos of all four state universities—is evident in scholarly publications as well as graduate theses, which usually cite the social problems that motivated the research as well as possible solutions suggested by the research findings. Sociologist Daniel Camacho, in the keynote address to a 1991 convention, defended this approach, arguing that a scientist, like a soccer player, must be objective—aware of reality—but cannot and should not be neutral, that is, unconcerned with whether or how that reality can or should be changed.

State universities offer many nonprofit services ranging from literary projects and free music lessons to free advice for farmers and gardeners and investigation of patent applications to determine whether an invention is socially useful. And students in many programs at both UCR and UNA must perform up to 300 hours of community service related to their specialties. Dental, medical, and agronomy students may spend several weeks working in a rural area; philology students may edit government publications.

Science long had a low priority in Costa Rica (where scientists are popularly stereotyped as insane). The UCR's two-year-long liberal arts requirement includes no experimental or laboratory science. Several annual prizes are given in fine arts and literature but only one in science. In recent years, this picture has begun to change as some Costa Rican scientists have won international recognition. A Spanish foundation awarded a prize in 1995 to the National Institute of Biodiversity for its work in environmental science and conservation. A joint U.S.–Costa Rican research team in 1996 identified a possible genetic link to manic depression. The demanding curricula and teachers of the four public science high schools as well as the Costa Rican Institute of Technology are highly respected. Much of the scientific and technological research in Costa Rica today is done in the public universities, often under contract with multinational firms. Most research has practical goals, and most involves veterinary medicine and agronomy, human health, or social services.

Amid charges of elitism, the first private university was opened in 1976—the Autonomous Central American University (UACA). Founded by a group of UCR professors who resented department heads' power, it had about 5,000 students on its several campuses in 1995. It is organized into autonomous colleges on the British plan. Though tuition is far higher than at UCR, there are scholarships and loan programs. Professors have small classes and considerable freedom in methods; a tutorial system encourages a long, close relationship between students and teachers. Says a medical student who transferred from UCR, "The profs here treat their students like their own kids." A great deal of reading is assigned, and reports on assigned themes are presented and discussed in groups. Many students are transfers from the big universities and say—somewhat paradoxically—that they are attracted both by UACA's lack of a general studies (liberal arts) requirement and by its academic excellence.

Forty-two private institutions, mostly very specialized and small, enrolled about one in five university students in 1998. Some Ticos regard the competition they represent as a healthy stimulant and note that at least one, the tiny Universidad de Diseño (design) is highly respected both in Costa Rica and abroad, far more so than the much larger School of Architecture at the UCR.

Critics reply that this competition has diverted resources from state universities and lowered their standards: Private universities will admit anyone who will pay, and the public universities, in response, have eliminated some degree requirements. Most private universities, they add, are unworthy of the name because they offer degrees in only a few fields. Many have scanty libraries and laboratories or none at all, and their faculty do little research. Says a UCR agronomy professor, "They are run strictly as businesses—not for the public good—and research isn't profitable to them." A growing number of professional guilds, such as the Lawyers' Guild, concerned with the low quality of some private universities, no longer automatically admit anyone with a degree but demand that prospective members pass a qualifying exam.

Private universities meet some needs not answered by state ones: training in some newly available careers, for example. An architecture student at UACA lists other advantages:

> I can get my degree in four or five years rather than seven because we study all year with no long vacations. I can also hold down a job because my classes are all in late afternoon and evening. At UCR I might be assigned to a morning class and a late-afternoon class one term and another schedule next term; it would prevent me from working. Once I enrolled in a specific field at UCR I would be on a track I could not deviate from without losing all my credits.

Summary and Conclusion

Costa Ricans have long linked education with such values as peace, democracy, and "culture." Before 1948, however, poverty restricted most to only a few years of schooling. Increased prosperity, a baby boom, and changes in employers' demands led to a proliferation of schools and universities beginning in the 1950s.

The quality of this mass education has become a major concern. The traditional emphasis on memorization rather than on thinking has continued. Materials, classroom space, and well-trained teachers are lacking. These issues are hardly new, but modernization has made them more apparent and reforms, more urgent. At the same time, budget cuts have made solutions more difficult.

Other longstanding problems persist. The school system remains highly centralized with little allowance for regional differences. It also remains highly politicized with little continuity from one administration to the next. Old cultural patterns, such as the toleration of mediocre work and the belief that reading impairs health, continue to impede learning.

New concerns emerged as the school-age population grew faster than the state's resources, teachers' unions gained power, and the school year and school day shrank alarmingly. And social class differences in educational and life opportunities have grown with the deterioration of public schools and the increase in private ones.

Few Costa Ricans acknowledge any bright spots, but they do exist. Imaginative new teacher-training programs are increasing. Special attention was given—during the 1994–1998 administration, at least—to one-room rural schools and urban slum schools, and the ministry made computer classes available to many and revived its nutrition program. Students have become involved in community service. Many parents are now, with ministry urging, interacting far more with their children's teachers. Public university professors show great concern for helping solve Costa Rica's problems. And thousands of teachers remain dedicated to their work despite the many problems they face.

Notes

1. Manuel Delgado, "Desarrollo sin rostro humano," *Rumbo*, November 1, 1994, pp. 28–31.

2. Jacinto Ordoñez, "El aporte del pensamiento educativo precolonial," *La República*, October 23, 1992, p. 19A.

3. Manuel Echeverría, "Medio siglo atrás," in Lilia Ramos, ed., *Júbilo y pena del recuerdo* (San José: ECR, 1965), p. 259.

4. Joaquín García Monge, "El moto," in *Obras Escogidas* (San José: EDUCA, 1974), pp. 401–440.

5. Luís Felipe González Flores, *Historia del desarrollo de la educación pública*, Vol. 1 (San José: Imprenta Nacional, 1945), p. 4.

6. Gabriel Coronado and María Eugenia Pérez, *La clase media costarricense* (Heredia: EUNA, 1992), p. 79.

7. *Autobiografías campesinas*, Vol. 1 (Heredia: EUNA, 1979), p. 159.

8. Zayra Méndez, C. Chaves, and Ana C. Escalante, *Estudio de razonamento lógico-matemático en liceistas del area metropolitana de San José* (San José: EU-NED, 1983).

9. Humberto Pérez Pancorbo, *Ensayos sobre educación* (San José: Ediciones Guayacán, 1987), p. 56.

10. John Biesanz and Mavis Biesanz, *Costa Rican Life* (New York: Columbia University Press, 1944), p. 122.

11. George R. Waggoner and Barbara Ashton Waggoner, *Education in Central America* (Washington, D.C.: U.S. Deptartment of Health, Education and Welfare, Office of Education, Bureau of Research, June 1969).

12. Historian Astrid Fischel suggests that such erratic changes were already common in the nineteenth century. "Desenvolvimiento estatal y cambio educativo," in *Historia de Costa Rica en el siglo XX* (San Pedro: Porvenir, 1991), p. 10. John and Mavis Biesanz noted the same pattern in the 1940s; see *Costa Rican Life*, p. 110.

13. Julio Rodríguez, "En vela," *La Nación*, May 29, 1992, p. 15A.

14. Carlos Cortés, "Sr(a). ministro(a):," *La Nación*, January 16, 1994, p. 14A.

15. Katia Arraya, interview, July 1993.

16. *Universidad*, September 11, 1992, p. 15.

17. Biesanz and Biesanz, *Costa Rican Life*, p. 124.

18. Pierre Thomas Claudet, *La cultura del pobrecitico* (San José: EUCR, 1992), p. 23.

19. José Alberto Briceño, "Educación y 'corronguera,'" *La República*, April 28, 1994.

20. Cecilia Valverde B., "Analfabetismo," *La Nación*, July 8, 1996, p. 15A.

21. Gerardo Esquivel Monge, "Burocrácia y educación," *Universidad*, September 3, 1993, p. 16.

22. Astrid Fischel, Paper presented at International Women's Conference, UCR, February 1993.

23. Trevor W. Purcell, *Banana Fallout: Class, Color, and Culture Among West Indians in Costa Rica* (Los Angeles: Center for Afro-American Studies Publications, Regents of the University of California, 1993), p. 97.

24. Astrid Fischel, *Consenso y represión: Una interpretación socio-politica de la educación costarricense* (San José: ECR, 1990), p. 202.

25. Alberto Cañas, "Chisporroteos," *La República,* February 17, 1993, p. 15A.

26. Pérez, *Ensayos sobre educación,* p. 54.

27. Milena Fernández M., "Estudiantes creen inútil secundaria," *La Nación,* February 13, 1995, p. 8A.

28. Ivannia Varela Quirós, "Educadores . . . siempre ganan lo que piden," *La República,* July 22, 1995, p. 6A.

— 10 —

Religion

SOME FOUR OUT OF FIVE Costa Ricans say they are Catholic. But their Catholicism has long been blended with indigenous, occult, and secular beliefs and practices. This blend reflects not only the accidents of history but also Ticos' inclinations toward fatalism, their insistence on individual freedom, their indifference to authority, and, perhaps most of all, Ticos' desire to *quedar bien*—to get along with others.

The Colonial Period

Pre-Columbian aborigines practiced a nature-oriented religion. Earth, sun, moon, winds, and ocean were major deities. Creator gods lived in families from which a child or grandchild would come to earth to teach human beings. (Many of today's Indians see this teacher as a lone, benevolent creator god, probably as a result of five centuries of Christian influence.) There were many lesser gods, good and evil, everywhere. Shamans cured sickness with chants and herbs.

The Spanish monarchs regarded the conversion of the Indians to Catholicism and the preservation of the faith among the colonists as an integral part of Spain's mission in the Americas, allied with the quest for wealth and empire.[1] Colonial sermons were often long exhortations to love and obey the Crown and its representatives. Costa Rica's clergy were named by the Crown; most were trained in the seminaries of Nicaragua, Guatemala, and Mexico. Their early attempts to convert the Indians seldom involved force but were often ineffective; the first missionaries, for example, considered the mere sight of a crucifix enough to convert the most stubborn heathen. Later missionaries often helped grow food, taught literacy as well as Catholic doctrine, and sometimes served as judges. Because of these labors, as well as intermarriage between Indians and Spaniards and the declining size and power of the indigenous population, by the end of the sixteenth century most Indians in the territory practiced a mixture of Catholicism and their own older rites.

As we noted in Chapter 2, on a rare pastoral visit to the isolated colony in 1711, the bishop of León, Nicaragua (whose diocese included Costa Rica), was appalled by Costa Ricans' low church attendance and failure to pay tithes. He ordered them to build a chapel in each parish within six months under pain of excommunication and forbade marriages and burials without prior payment of fees. When he found no change on a visit three years later, he decreed the excommunication of all rebellious and disobedient colonists. But the decree had no effect and was soon rescinded.

The Nineteenth Century

Clergymen were active in politics in the early years of the republic. Five of the nine members of the first governing junta, including the president, were priests, no doubt because, says historian Ricardo Blanco, "the clergy was the nucleus of the educated elite of the era, as well as those the people most trusted."[2] The first constitution declared Catholicism the state religion "to the exclusion of any other." Nonetheless, the church remained poor and subordinate to civil authority.

Scouting Central America in 1825 on behalf of North Americans who hoped to settle there, John Hale found the clergy of Costa Rica to be much more tolerant of Protestants than were priests in neighboring countries.[3] In 1853, by which time freemasonry and liberalism had strongly influenced many teachers and political leaders, two devout German Catholics noted:

> The majority of Costa Ricans are good believing Catholics, customarily going to confession at least once a year; their belief is not fervent, however, and they attend church more from hereditary custom than from individual impulse. They are not intolerant, and the rich class is indifferent, caring nothing about philosophy. They respect the ignorant and unlettered clergy, but accept neither Jesuits nor the intervention of priests in secular affairs. And above all, they do not want to give much money to the church.[4]

Inventories at the University of Santo Tomás and a major bookstore in the late 1850s found far more scientific, political, legal, economic, and literary books and fewer religious works than in private libraries thirty years earlier.[5]

By the 1880s such ideas—largely a result of foreign travel and the immigration of non-Catholic teachers and businessmen—had influenced most Costa Ricans with any pretensions to being modern or enlightened. During that decade, as we saw in Chapter 2, the government secularized cemeteries and permitted divorce and civil weddings. It also abolished religious instruction in public schools, though this was once again permitted in 1890. In 1884 the British-educated president, Próspero Fernández, expelled the Jesuits, the most "fanatical" order of priests, and denied admission to Costa Rica to members of any religious order. When Bishop Thiel protested, he too was briefly exiled. But the church retained its special constitutional status and token subsidies. And one inaugural rite for each administration continued to be a ceremony in the cathedral. Philip Williams argues that anticlericalism was never strong in Costa Rica, whose clergy had few economic interests that might have been threatened by liberal governments' promotion of such activities as coffee growing and road building.[6]

The confrontation of Bishop Thiel's Catholic Union Party and the Liberal Party in the early 1890s was another conflict between clerical and secular power. But President José Joaquín Rodríguez's electoral manipulations kept the bishop's party aligned with a weak presidential candidate and thus, said a later president, saved the country from "the bloody battles inevitably provoked by a clerical government."[7]

The Early Twentieth Century

Most of Rodríguez's successors until 1940 were freethinkers but not overtly antichurch. Ricardo Jiménez, an atheist, was elected president three times, perhaps because even "the most recalcitrant Catholics felt very much at ease [with Jiménez], who knew how to maintain liberalism *a la costarricense,* that is, a balanced liberalism, extremely compliant with all religions and political views."[8]

Anticlericalism among intellectuals and politicians declined even further after President Calderón Guardia (1940–1944), a devout Catholic, worked with an unusually progressive archbishop, Victor Sanabria, and communist leader Manuel Mora to institute his landmark social reforms. Protest was therefore minimal when Calderón and the legislature repealed the 1884 laws that had banned Jesuits and monastic orders from the country and when Calderón reestablished religion classes as part of the primary school curriculum.

The Catholic Church Today

Catholicism permeates Costa Rican culture. The capital as well as hundreds of towns and villages are named for saints; in many the patron saint's fiesta is the high point of the year. Most Ticos are baptized, married, and blessed before interment by Catholic priests. Crucifixes and saints' pictures are prominent in homes, schools, government offices, and motor vehicles. Shrines to the Virgin are common in public buildings, parks, and front yards. News media cover church events from Vatican Councils to parish fairs. Politicians and columnists frequently attack or defend a program by citing papal encyclicals or "Christian principles." Before a new commercial or government building is opened it is customarily blessed by a priest, as are many private homes and new fleets of taxis and buses. Many pedestrians and drivers cross themselves each time they pass a Catholic church, cemetery, or roadside shrine, and many passengers in a plane or long-distance bus do so before departure.

Everyday speech is salted with phrases and proverbs out of Costa Rica's Spanish Catholic tradition. Although visitors no longer announce themselves by shouting "Hail Purest Mary!" predictions, hopes, and appointments are still qualified with "God willing." Relatives and friends departing on a journey or even an errand are told, "May God go with you," and a common reply to inquiries about one's health is "Fine, thank God." Beggars thank donors with "May God repay you."

Though far weaker and poorer than that of many other Latin American countries, Costa Rica's Catholic Church is, in the absence of an army, the strongest traditional organized institution after the state. It is also among the most respected. Eighty-seven percent of the respondents in a 1992 poll had a favorable opinion of the church; only the Supreme Electoral Tribunal was rated higher. Priests, trusted by both sides, often act as mediators in disputes between the government and squatters or strikers.

Roman Catholicism is still the official religion. The 1949 constitution provides that "the Catholic, apostolic, Roman religion is that of the State, which contributes to its support, without impeding the free exercise in the Republic of other religions that do not oppose universal morality nor good customs."

Far from abolishing religious education in primary schools, the National Liberation Party extended it in 1949 to high schools, where a prayer read over the intercom starts each day. Women's suffrage (also in 1949) strengthened the church's political position, as women had long been the most fervent Catholics. The president and cabinet ministers attend special holiday masses. Each government agency has a patron saint, and many public buildings have chapels or shrines built by employees' donations. The Catholic marriage ceremony, as we noted in Chapter 8, is the only religious one recognized by the state; non-Catholics married by their own clergy must also be wed in a civil ceremony.

Despite its official status, the church receives less than 1 colón in 10,000 of the central government's budget. Church-owned land is no longer tax-exempt, and some priests complain that "the state takes away more from the church than it gives." Local churches are financed almost entirely by parishioners, whose offerings and fund-raising events barely suffice, in most cases, to keep them open and pay priests. Just as Moritz Wagner and Karl Scherzer noted in the 1850s, most parishioners contribute little.

The church is small as well as poor. Although a seminary has trained Costa Rican youths for the priesthood since 1863, it has never attracted many students. In 1850 there was 1 priest per 1,600 Catholics; the ratio in 1995 was about 1 per 4,000. Although this ratio is somewhat higher than fifty years ago and is high for Latin America, priests complain that their small numbers help account for lukewarm Catholicism. Yet, although some urban churches have several pastors, in contrast to many rural areas where one priest says mass once a month in each of ten or fifteen churches, rural Catholics tend to be most fervent.

Nearly 1,000 nuns of various religious orders do social work among the poor, run the women's prison, teach school, and work in hospitals. Catholics in some rural communities are served exclusively by nuns, who baptize, visit homes, and give communion. Monks, less numerous, do most of these same things.

Vatican II resulted not only in services in Spanish rather than Latin but in far greater participation in the mass by laity and the formation of lay Bible study and discussion groups. Since 1979 priests have trained lay deacons to preach, baptize, lead prayers, and give communion to the sick, particularly in remote areas where priests seldom visit. At first restricted to married men over age thirty-five, such authority is now vested in persons of both sexes, who may be single and as young as twenty.

In many respects the church has gained influence since 1940. As school enrollment has grown, both the number and the percentage of children who receive the two weekly catechism lessons has also increased. (These are taught by lay teachers trained in a state institute or by priests, monks, or nuns. In remote schools the regular teacher assumes this responsibility.) Women also catechize children in their parishes for their first confessions and communions, between ages six and nine. The local priest periodically reviews their progress, and the children's mothers or grandmothers help them memorize the catechism. Says a small-town priest, "At one time, the lessons lasted only three months; now it's three years. And about twenty years ago, babies were commonly confirmed a week after being baptized. Now one gets instruction first, and is usually confirmed about age fifteen or so." These changes, he says, have made many Catholics more attached to their faith.

Many Ticos, including ministers of education, consider classes in Catholic doctrine essential to the formation of "the Costa Rican character." Many high school teachers of philosophy, a required subject for tenth-graders, were trained in the Catholic seminary, and their teaching reflects this. (We heard one teacher tell a class that philosophy rejects myth in search of truth—as a way to know God.)

Since 1965 thousands of adults have attended the church-sponsored Small Courses of Christianity. These intensive three-day retreats, led by laypersons, include emotional sermons, prayer and meditation, doctrinal instruction and discussion, and an effort to create ties of love. Many who have attended report that the courses helped them practice their faith "out of conviction rather than tradition."

The 1949 constitution retained the 1871 constitutional provision that "neither clergy nor laymen may make political propaganda of any sort by invoking religious motives or by taking advantage of religious belief." But clergy can exert political influence in other ways. Padre Benjamin Nuñez was active in the PLN until his death in 1994. A prime mover behind the party's declaration of social democratic ideology, he served as negotiator of the 1948 peace accords, minister of labor, ambassador to Israel, and major labor organizer. Many graduates of the private high schools run by priests and nuns become the nation's political and economic leaders.

One writer charges that the Catholic Church has become "a State within a State," the fourth power of the government. He regards its official status as a violation of the liberty of conscience supposedly guaranteed by the constitution. Taxes paid by non-Catholics help support it. Thanks to government policies since the 1940s and to the clergy's "constant reprimands, admonitions and social pressures on the members of the three powers of the Republic," its power is evident in all aspects of public life. He cites as one example the publication of sex-education booklets for public high schools, held up year after year during the late 1980s and early 1990s while the Ministry of Education allowed church authorities to make changes.[9]

But the church has seldom opposed government policies. Archbishop Carlos Humberto Rodríguez, notes Williams, "affirmed the principle of divine origin of [secular] authority" during the 1962 inauguration of President Francisco Orlich, "thereby implying that Orlich was president by divine right."[10] Bishops (with rare exceptions, such as Monseñor Sanabria) have expressed far more concern with communism and Protestantism than with economic injustice. They see the primary social role of the church as one of providing charity, often in collaboration with state welfare agencies. This, says Williams, has kept them more isolated from the poor than are the clergy in countries where the church developed its own welfare programs to compensate for governments' comparative neglect of the poor. So has their role as teachers in Catholic schools, which cater to the middle and upper classes.[11]

Many priests, tired of hearing bishops urge moral reform and charity as well as more preaching of the gospels as the only solutions to poverty and other social ills, are active in community projects. They work to establish cooperatives, craft shops and markets, and lay organizations and workshops to improve family life or to teach skills needed in the business world. Some are active in the labor movement, Scouts, reforestation, and agrarian reform. A few report success in getting parishioners to tithe (to donate a tenth of their income) to support such projects. But those activists who openly support strikers or squatters or who denounce growing inequality may be rebuked or transferred by their bishops; therefore, such actions are often clandestine.[12]

We listened in 1991 to three seminarians singing about the lack of bread on many tables and asked them what would put that bread there. "Social justice," said one, and the others agreed. What can a priest do to help bring about social justice? "He can do many things, but he has to be careful not to offend anyone; otherwise he might, for example, be considered a communist." All three said they support liberation theology, "but one that combines spirituality with social action." Said one, reflecting a typically cautious attitude, "Liberation theology was developed mainly in countries where there is much less social justice than in Costa Rica, so some of its spokesmen sound like extremists here. We have to adapt it to our conditions, not accept it as a package."

Catholicism, Tico Style

Belief and observance vary greatly among Catholics. A few speak proudly of their "blind faith." At the other extreme are young, educated urbanites who deny any religious belief and government officials who put in an appearance only on important occasions of church and state.

Most Ticos fall somewhere in between. Theirs is the easy and lukewarm Catholicism noted by Wagner and Scherzer almost 150 years ago. "I'm a Catholic, but not a fanatic," many say. A Venezuelan told us, "In my country, when one says he is a Catholic or a communist, he *really* is. Not here." A Spanish priest, in Costa Rica two years, agrees: "Ticos' thoughts and positions are not well defined. They try to get along with everyone."

A San José taxi driver in his midthirties expresses both a characteristic desire to *quedar bien* and a typical wariness of close relationships: "A good Catholic is one who stays on the good side of God and doesn't get too involved with anyone, especially in discussions of religion, which may lead to arguments." Like many other men he sees those who are too openly pious as hypocrites—an attitude also evident in the numerous jokes about sexual liaisons between priests and nuns.

Likewise, many professing Catholics question the authority of the clergy, whether the parish priest or the pope. Observers noted a similar pattern in the 1940s: "Costa Rican Catholics appear to be individualists first and Catholics second. 'Oh, I don't believe in that,' they will say of some church doctrine. Those interviewed did not hesitate to attack church doctrine, to disagree about some point, or to find fault with the priests or church policy. 'I'm a Catholic, but . . .' is a common beginning."[13]

Many of today's Ticos who call themselves "very Catholic" say, "I hardly ever go to mass." They doubt the existence of heaven or hell—except in this life as a consequence of one's deeds. They insist on freedom to decide for themselves how many children they should have: "If the *padre* wants me to have more, let *him* feed them." A young, newly married *campesino* told us, "The pope preaches that birth control is a sin, but I think he's mistaken in that."

Even clergy are often selective in their acceptance of church doctrines. Another young rural man told us that in the prematrimonial classes he and his wife attended, "the priest said we'd all probably use birth control no matter what he said, and added that we should use our own judgment. He probably favors birth control, as my wife and I do, but doesn't want to get in trouble with his superiors by saying so openly."

Reactions to the Vatican's 1992 catechism, which is especially critical of antisocial sins such as tax evasion, corruption, exploitation of employees, and drunken driving, reflect this attitude toward authority. A nun who teaches the catechism insists that it, too, must be adapted to Tico ways: "The new catechism won't change anything. The catechism we use is the national one; we work with national values. The directives that come from Rome must be adapted to the country in which we live, because Costa Rica isn't the same as Rome, or as Nicaragua."[14] Six priests interviewed by *Rumbo* magazine agreed that Ticos "don't confess sins that destroy society . . . that they evade taxes, deceive voters, or underpay their employees. . . . Instead they bring up individual errors [such as masturbation, profanity, and drunkenness] rather than social ones, and probably don't consider the more serious ones as sins."[15] Several priests we interviewed agreed. Said one, "We Ticos are individualists to the point of egotism. 'Each in his own house and God in everyone's,' people say."

Many Catholics believe "El que peca y reza empata" (He who sins and prays, balances his accounts). They feel free to pick and choose among points of Catholic doctrine as elements of individual faith and to adopt beliefs and practices that to many priests smack of Protestantism and even witchcraft. Hundreds of Costa Ricans, rural and urban—most of them Catholics—describe their abductions by visitors from other planets. Some meet regularly in fellow abductees' homes, where they compare their experiences, interpreting them in a broadly Christian framework: God sent the visitors, as He sent Christ, to save us.

Catholicism Tico style is markedly fatalistic. Costa Ricans of all social levels, says sociologist Luis Barahona, "accept the will of God in such a way that it is pagan fatalism more than Christian resignation."[16] One Huetar Indian's reliance on faith is combined with resignation and fatalism when things go wrong. "Faith is needed for you even to attempt anything. If I plant a field of beans, it's because I have faith that they will grow. But I also have faith that if they don't grow, it's because God didn't think it was good for me that they grow."

Sickness and death bring out both faith and fatalism. A thirty-eight-year-old housewife says she prays when a family member is ill. "Then God will heal the person or, if not, at least help me to resign myself."

Illness also reveals Ticos' highly personal, syncretic approach to religion. One woman who lives many hours' walk from the nearest church usually watches Sunday mass on television. "Once I hurt my hip badly. The next Sunday, when the priest raised the Host for God's blessing, I silently asked God to bless the glass of water in my hand, then drank it. The next day I was much better."

Belief and practice vary according to sex, age, and place of residence. Elderly people and those with less education are least likely to join revival groups but most likely to attend mass and the elaborate, solemn Holy Week processions. Urbanites, despite greater opportunity, attend mass less often than villagers; those who can afford to are likely to spend Holy Week drinking and dancing at a beach resort. In many rural districts, by contrast, when the priest makes one of his rare visits, some *campesinos* will walk an hour or more to be present.

Lowland regions—where, unlike in the highlands, few communities are named for saints—have always had the fewest clerics. A Central Valley businessman who had moved to Guanacaste observed in 1975, "On the Meseta the first thing people want in a village is a church. In Guanacaste, it's a school." In a 1996 Demoscopia survey, 63 percent of Catholics in highland Cartago Province reported attending mass at least three times a month versus only 29 percent in coastal Puntarenas Province.

Women are regarded as more spiritual than men. Many men, even among the generally devout *campesinos*, never enter a church after childhood except in their wedding finery and their burial caskets. John and Mavis Biesanz noted in 1942:

> From a social standpoint religion offers little to men which they cannot obtain elsewhere. Women, on the other hand, have few diversions outside the home, to which tradition confines them. Churchgoing gives them an opportunity to leave the house, see and talk with other women, get completely away from their household cares for a time—and they can do all this not only without subjecting themselves to gossip but even gaining merit in the eyes of others.[17]

Although such gender differences are still evident, we have observed, and many Ticos report, that both urban and rural men participate far more in church rites than they did before the 1970s. More now attend mass and take communion, and no longer do most cluster around the entrance or stand against the back wall. Many become deacons. A small-town priest comments, "This change is due to the decline of *machismo*. Men used to think church was for women. Now they're not afraid they'll be criticized if they're too devout." Such changes are perhaps most evident among married men. Says a twenty-four-year-old single man, a small-town video store clerk, "Girls are more attached to the church than boys are. But when a man marries, his wife often gets him involved in church activities."

Two or three generations ago, families commonly said grace before each meal and a rosary before retiring. Prayer is now mostly an individual matter. When family members do pray together it is normally an evening rosary, perhaps a weekly rite led by an elderly grandmother. A family may hire a *rezador*, usually an elderly man or woman known as devout and experienced in leading prayers and hymns, on the ninth day after a death—or on more festive occasions such as someone's saint's day or the Christmas season.

In rural communities where priests seldom visit, group prayer and other practices help satisfy the desire for religious observance. A saint's image with an attached collection box for alms for the poor may circulate among twenty or thirty households, remaining in each for a day. Usually women are in charge; some invite neighbors and relatives for prayers and supper.

A newer, quite popular rural practice is lay preaching. A young man describes its origin in his highland village:

> A group of seven of us guys about the same age were curious about the charismatic movement. We went to San José and met a man who later came here and helped us organize regular meetings for prayer, singing, and Bible study. It was all Catholic, but the parish priest was a little upset, saying we were acting like Protestants. Then Marcos, a quiet young local man, asked if he could say something. That was his first sermon.

The priest, he went on, was impressed and now advises Marcos and others in their new role as lay preachers. "We know the villagers better than the parish priest does. The priest is never a local man. He comes to our church only once a month and is replaced every four years anyway," says Marcos.

In 1991 we heard Marcos preach during the village's pre-Christmas *posadas*, a Mexican custom recently introduced by priests in many Costa Rican communities. For nine successive evenings, groups of villagers with lanterns and candles went from house to house, accompanying two children who portrayed Mary and Joseph seeking shelter. They stopped at a different house each night to sing, pray, and hear a sermon. At the first *posada*, Marcos preached against gossip. "Just as Adam blamed Eve for offering him the apple," he said, "so a man today might blame a friend's visit for his own gossiping."

At the second *posada*, Marcos's theme was "love of God through loving our neighbor"—perhaps a stranger asking for a night's shelter or a Protestant wanting to tell others about his beliefs. "It could be that the Protestant is mistaken. But it could also be that *we* are mistaken in what it means to be a Catholic." Says a local youth: "Marcos is a third-grade dropout, but you'd think you were listening to an intellectual. Every Sunday during Lent when the priest couldn't come, he preached and dispensed communion. And unlike many priests, he's very clear. He'll finish making a point before going on to the next; he doesn't jump around and confuse you."

Devotion to the Saints

No matter how fatalistically they say they accept the will of God, most Costa Rican Catholics ask a saint—often one with special powers—to intercede for them when they want to conceive a child, cure an illness, find a lost object, or pass an exam: For toothache, they appeal to Santa Apolonia; for fever, Santa Genoveva; for protection of a farmer's pigs, San Antonio Abad.

The *santo* may be a canonized saint or, less commonly, some aspect of God such as the Sacred Host or the Sacred Heart of Jesus. Or he or she may be an uncanonized "popular saint" such as two deceased Costa Ricans who many believe have miraculous powers: Marisa died of a brain tumor in 1954 at age twelve after she dedicated her suffering to the Lord in return for her father's reconversion from Protestantism. Dr. Ricardo Moreno Cañas, a charismatic surgeon, was murdered, possibly for political reasons, in 1938. Believers report visions and cures associated with them.

Rituals associated with devotion to a saint are often idiosyncratic. A forty-year-old housemaid says,

My favorite saint is San Martín de Porras, the patron of the poor. I always pray on Tuesdays, but when my son was very ill, I prayed with special devotion at the little St. Martin shrine in my house. Sometimes I pay an Indian *rezadora* to pray with me either at home or in the church. Why? Because my thoughts are easily distracted and my prayer may not be effective, while she knows many prayers, and she concentrates and has special powers to direct the prayer straight to heaven.

Certain rituals are often recommended as accompaniments to given prayers or as means to a desired end. Bookstores and street vendors offer pamphlets of prayers and rituals for particular saints. Prayers for health addressed to Dr. Moreno Cañas, according to one leaflet, should be accompanied by a glass of water covered with a handkerchief, a burning candle, and, if possible, a white flower placed before his portrait. The supplicant should ask Dr. Cañas to bless the water and to use it to cure the illness, then recite a Hail Mary and the Lord's Prayer, expecting the doctor to come in the night and cure the patient, even to perform surgery.[18]

A saint's picture or statue in one's bedroom or living room and a smaller image on a medallion or card carried on one's person or on the dashboard of a car are believed to bring luck. Some devotees pray before an image of the saint at home or in church, also lighting a candle as a "down payment" on a favor desired or as recompense for one already granted. If the favor is urgently desired—recovery from an illness, for example—the believer may make a vow, usually not just to be good or to give up some vice but to carry out some devotional act. A woman in distress, for example, may promise to wear the brown robe of the Virgin of Carmen for a certain num-

After mass (Ingrid Holst)

ber of months or years and to observe the ban on drinking and dancing this promise involves.

The Virgin Mary is especially revered, to a degree unusual even in Latin America. In many churches, images of the Virgin are as large as the central crucifix. Shrines to her abound, and many towns have one in each *barrio,* where neighbors gather for occasional masses and prayer meetings. Devotion to the Virgin and to the country are blended in a popular song: "So lovely is my Costa Rica that when the Virgin of the Angels descended and saw its beauty, she never returned to heaven."

On her special day, August 2, some 700,000 pilgrims from all over Costa Rica—over a fifth of the population—journey long distances to the basilica in Cartago that houses her shrine to ask a favor or thank her for granting one. Many walk, beginning the previous day (even earlier if they live far away), continuing all night to arrive at dawn, and proceeding up the long nave of the church on their knees. Many carry bottles to fill with holy water flowing from the outdoor grotto. Many leave emblems of a promise fulfilled in a special room, its walls hung with thousands of tiny silver hearts, legs, eyes, and other symbols of healed body parts. A young artist says, "I never attend mass. But I went to the Basilica when a friend was about to have brain surgery. That's *muy tico*—first we go to the Social Security clinic if we're ill, then to a private doctor if we're still sick. And if all else fails, we turn to the Virgin."

In 1992 a teenage boy in rural Sarapiquí claimed to see a Virgin he named "the Queen of Love." She appeared in the sun the first day of each month and finally spoke and asked him to proclaim her message: love, tolerance, religious faith, and spirituality. Crowds continue to travel to the site at the appointed times. Some believe they see her; a few damage their retinas because they think they can look directly at the sun and behold her with no risk. As with other such sightings, church authorities have declared the "apparition" a phenomenon that has no supernatural meaning and cautioned—without being heeded—against visiting the site.

Why is devotion to the saints so strong and widespread? Saints seem closer and more personal than God, who is most often described in terms of power. Says a twenty-four-year-old woman, a clerk in a Catholic bookstore, "We keep pictures of the saints in our homes for the same reason we keep pictures of deceased family members—to remind us these were real people who once walked the earth."

Even those who are aware of the church doctrine that they should pray to God and ask the saints only to intercede with him on their behalf prefer an intermediary. At mass in 1994, the young priest, after describing Mary as "the mother of us all—even of non-Catholics and atheists," said one should pray to her "so that God will act in our favor." Just as Ticos use connections to get something mundane accomplished—going to a friend in a government office for a job or a way around bureaucratic red tape, for example—so they seek a saint who has special "pull" with God.

Whatever the request of whichever saint, nothing will happen, devotees say, unless one has faith and lives a good life. If the favor is not granted, then lack of faith, a sinful life, or the fact that one asked too late is to blame.

Occultism and Witchcraft

Occultism is rarely discussed, and the practice is often secret. But belief in the occult—in supernatural powers other than God and the saints—and in ways of manipulating such powers, is widespread among Costa Ricans, including agnostics and intellectuals as well as many who consider themselves good Catholics. (In the 1996 Demoscopia survey of Catholics, 46 percent admitted to belief in witchcraft or magic.) Many believe that certain people have psychic, magical, or supernatural powers for good and evil. The accompanying beliefs and practices are of mixed indigenous, Spanish, and (in Limón) African origin.

The combination of medicine and magic called *curanderismo* (curing) is the main indigenous contribution. Shamans were traditionally chosen and trained very young by older shamans, often their own fathers. Many non-Indian *curanderos* as well as tribal shamans now combine centuries-old indigenous rituals with prayers to Catholic saints, both canonized and popular. The practice of *obeah,* or sorcery, is still found in Limón among descendants of Afro-Caribbean immigrants. Many Ticos who are neither Indian nor black patronize shamans or obeahmen.

There is little agreement about what to call practitioners other than shamans and *curanderos*. Psychics, spiritists, and diviners who read the future with cards, tea leaves, coffee grounds, crystal balls, or palmistry merge into the amorphous category of *brujos* (witches) who specialize in casting harmful spells or removing them from clients harmed by other *brujos*. Some practitioners charge a fee; others do not. Although the penal code prescribes short jail terms for those who practice "witchcraft, sorcery, or any other cult or belief contrary to civilization or good customs," few are charged with breaking this law, and some practitioners advertise in newspapers. Some communities, notably Escazú (now a San José suburb), are famed as centers of occult practices; anthropologists May Brenes and Mayra Zapparoli found them to be widespread in the entire San José metropolitan area, the focus of their study.[19]

To what extent do Ticos believe in the occult? In this as in other things they tend to be fence-sitters, says anthropologist María Eugenia Bozzoli.[20] Just as their speech is heavily qualified with "maybe," "more or less," and "Who knows?" so their consensus on witchcraft is "Probably it's true, probably not." There are things one cannot explain, and the safest policy is "Neither believe nor cease to believe." Even a woman who at first denied belief in witches finally shrugged and told Brenes and Zapparoli, "De que vuelan. . . . Vuelan!" ("They say they fly. . . . It's true—they do fly!")

Just as different saints are believed to have specialized powers, so too almost anyone can tell one where to find an occult practitioner for a specific problem ranging from skin diseases and depression to unrequited love or the desire to harm an enemy or a faithless lover. Few, however, admit to having dealt with any, particularly with those who work black magic. Practitioners themselves deny that they ever cast evil spells but say there are those who do. Like favors from saints or remedies from a *curandero*, countermagic against such spells is said to work only if the victim has faith; thus if it fails, it is one's own fault.

The flourishing commerce in things prescribed by practitioners, whether *curanderos*, witches, or diviners of various kinds, indicates that they attract many clients. Several shops specialize in such ingredients: pomades, perfumes, candles for fumigation, incense, leaflets of prayers, cards, pins, animal skins, plants, herbs, bones, sulfur, mercury, and spices. A pamphlet, *How to Recognize and Combat Evil Spells,* describes ritual cures for arthritis, asthma, and other maladies. Writes a reporter who observed a shop near a large urban hospital:

> The number of people who came into La Arcana during the hour we were there was incredible; mostly women with prescriptions from their witches. Some wanted to attract a specific man, while others wished to discourage a boss who had been harassing them sexually. . . . One very beautiful woman of about 23 asked for the seven perfumes to attract a lover, as well as some mercury. The clerk told me, "That young man will be at the altar in the wink of an eye; if he wants to get out of it he must find a super-witch."
> The shop opened in the late 1970s with a stock of 132 perfumes, and now its shelves hold more than 1500, with suggestive names like Harmony, Good Luck, Seven Perfumes, Seven Machos, Road Opener, Get Away from Me and Rain of Money. To keep a husband from straying it offers Stay at Home, to be rubbed on the soles of his shoes.[21]

Many practitioners think they have a *don*—a gift from God. Some told Brenes and Zapparoli that they were at first reluctant to acknowledge and use it but decided it was their duty. Said one, "My papa and brother had the *don*, like me, and were born with a cross in the roof of the mouth. We are chosen by God to carry out this work for the love of God."[22]

Among those interviewed was doña Gertrudis:

> More women come to me than men, most often because their husband has a girlfriend. Or they have problems with their children, or health, or nerves, and come to me almost crazy, unhinged. I give them advice and orientation, with medicinal plants, including the seven herbs, which I use a lot, and give them spiritual help. Faith has a lot to do with it; it's like when you go to a

doctor and have faith, you will be cured by the first medication he prescribes.

I am very Catholic, but I also have faith in Dr. Moreno Cañas, in that esoteric pentagram behind the door, and in that picture of the Archangel St. Michael, who protects us from thieves. But the truth is, Jesus Christ is everything to me; one does nothing without the will of God. Thanks to Him, my work is very important. I am a counselor; I have a lot of patience for listening.[23]

Another practitioner, doña Sofia, also says she is very Catholic: "But what the church says is one thing and what the Bible says is another, for the church is moralistic and tries to keep people within what it wants."[24]

The fear of evil spells reflects the proverbial mutual distrust among Ticos, as it does in many other societies. Of more than 100 clients she interviewed, Bozzoli found that all claimed to be victims rather than aggressors and that those who take witchcraft most seriously are people who constantly have problems finding and keeping jobs, money, or lovers or have an incurable illness or frequent misfortune. Some go from one practitioner to another and attribute all their problems to evil spells worked by enemies. Thus they explain failure or misfortune by blaming it on envy.[25]

"There are people who will make friends with you just to get an item of clothing, a strand of your hair, or a photo; but you must be careful because it can be used for black magic by a jealous person," says the wife of a prosperous coffee planter. Many rural people were unwilling to let us take their pictures. Explains a young *campesino*, "They're afraid you might want to harm them with sorcery."

One can avoid exciting envy and evil thoughts by being humble, discreet, and modest. Practitioners in turn are controlled to some extent by the belief that if they use their talents for evil ends, they will be punished.

Witches, says Bozzoli, "reduce anxiety, restore tranquility and cure some psychosomatic ailments."[26] Brenes and Zapparoli believe the "so-called witches" perform an important social function as popular psychologists because they talk to people in their own language, use easily understood terms, and, most of all, listen to complaints and answer questions about health, money, love, luck, and the future.[27] A sociologist and a historian, after telling us that they themselves sometimes consult fortune-tellers, suggested that Costa Rica's economic problems since the early 1980s have spurred interest in both the occult and in evangelical Protestantism.

Protestantism

Costa Rica's Catholic majority more or less tolerates non-Catholic religions, from the staid old Episcopal Church through many evangelical missions and two synagogues right up to today's Krishna Consciousness dancers and Children of God passing out pamphlets on San José streets. It was not always so, as some early-nineteenth-century visitors reported.

Tolerance of Protestant religious groups increased after the coffee boom, reflecting the growing role of Europeans and North Americans in commerce, industry, and education and the increasing liberalism and anticlericalism of *cafetaleros* who had studied in Europe. In any case, the construction of an Anglican church in 1865 aroused little hostility because it was not a mission church but was meant to serve resident foreign Protestants. Nor were the Episcopal, Baptist, and Methodist churches of the West Indian immigrants seen as a threat; their members were considered alien and different—and safely isolated on the Caribbean coast.

But Catholic clergy and many laymen fiercely resented the fundamentalist Protestants who began to arrive from the United States in 1891 to "save" the Ticos. These missionaries "saw the local Catholic population as legitimate objects for conversion, as far from the true Christian faith as tribesmen in the interior of Africa. Latin American Catholicism was condemned as utterly debased and idolatrous."[28]

The missionaries' aggressive tactics aroused resentment that erupted in stoning and other incidents. Bishops instructed priests to preach against the missionaries and to strengthen veneration of the Virgin Mary, under attack from the newcomers, by promoting religious festivals. Some priests threatened to excommunicate those who helped the missionaries in any way, such as renting houses to them. Although the government refused to expel them, by 1910 it had forbidden them to preach publicly, advertise meetings, or establish Protestant schools. In 1912 missionaries could claim a total of only 150 baptized converts, fewer than in any other Central American country.

Perceiving the missionary effort as a failure, the Catholic clergy paid little attention to an evangelical campaign that began in 1921 until seminary students from other Latin American countries arrived to enroll at the Bible Institute and began to preach in Spanish. In 1925 priests tried to collect and burn the Bibles the missionaries distributed. In 1927 Harry Strachan, the Institute's British founder, was beaten by a crowd in Heredia.[29]

After President Jiménez upheld missionaries' right to hold public meetings, such violence declined. The Catholic clergy counterattacked instead with publications, sermons, and political pressure. During the 1920s and 1930s and even when Costa Rica was nominally an ally of the United States in World War II, many priests proclaimed that Protestant propaganda was really designed to open the road to Yankee imperialism. They insisted that converts had been bad Catholics and even bad people before they left the Catholic Church.

Nonetheless, by 1960, Protestants numbered 60,000, up from 23,000 four years before. By 1963, encouraged by Pope John XXIII's reforms and by the conciliatory efforts of local Episcopal priests, the Costa Rican *Eco Católico* had begun to refer to Protestants not as heretics but as "separated brethren." Missionaries in turn now emphasized the virtues of Protestantism rather than the defects of Catholicism, and most no longer used "Christian" and "Protestant" as synonyms. Priests lectured at the Protestant seminary and language school; missionaries wrote occasional articles for *Eco Católico*. Catholics and Protestants, clergy and laity, joined forces not only in distributing Bibles but in social action such as prison reform and the Goodwill Caravans that brought medical, agricultural, and educational aid to poor rural areas.

In 1996 Protestants composed an estimated 11 percent of all Costa Ricans. They belonged to about 100 sects and denominations and met in 1,500 churches and homes throughout the country. As elsewhere in Latin America, most are members of small evangelical and fundamentalist sects. Most emphasize salvation through faith in Jesus. It is these sects that most concern the Catholic clergy; the Catholic charismatic movement is partially a response to their success.

The anxieties produced by geographic mobility make migrants to cities open to conversion. Converts long came almost entirely from the lower class, whose members, says sociologist and missionary Clifton Holland, "look for a sense of security in the modern world, and some find it in the evangelical churches."[30]

Few upper-class Ticos become Protestants; they are typically more satisfied with things as they are, and Ticos of any class have a more secure social status as nominal Catholics or freethinkers than they would as Protestants. Still, the rapid change and growing insecurity of recent years may account for the rise in middle-class conversions.

Believing that the roots of all social problems are in unsaved individuals' sins, evangelicals rarely support political change. Says one, "What we can do is pray for the authorities, because God has put them above us." Movements for social justice, he argues, deal with things of this world: "We Christians are of another world, another citizenry; we are merely passengers here. We must take care not to become victims of political manipulation." Every *evangélico* member of Guápiles's banana workers' union quit the union when it called a strike.[31]

Many converts report a far greater sense of community in their tiny new congregations than in their former Catholic parishes. Members participate freely and frequently in the highly emotional services, dancing and clapping while singing hymns set to a salsa beat. They help make policy decisions. Pastors, often part-time lay preachers, typically stress the promise of God's love and happiness rather than the threat of damnation. (Few Ticos, of whatever faith, relish hellfire-and-brimstone preaching; Protestantism, like Catholicism, reflects dominant cultural values and beliefs.)

Says a Protestant convert, a premedical student:

I was Catholic as a child, but later I read the Bible. I now attend a Pentecostal church. Except for the Jehovah's Witnesses and the Mormons, who go outside of what the Bible says, all the Protestant churches are very similar in being Christ-centered; we sometimes have big interdenominational prayer meetings. We think you should pray to God through Christ, not through saints as Catholics do. Also we believe in spontaneous prayer, not everybody reciting a formula together.

Catholics object especially to the idea that veneration of the Virgin Mary is idolatry. "I think they are wrong in concentrating on Christ. He came from his mother, didn't he?" says a farmer. Many also denounce the persistent proselytizing of certain sects and post signs on their front doors announcing that their family is Catholic. When Karen and Richard moved to San Isidro de Heredia in 1968, many villagers were at first reluctant to talk, thinking they were Protestant missionaries, as were the only other *gringos* who had once lived there. After his distrust had vanished, one villager explained, "They say those people pester you until they've got you."

Some Catholics, though attracted to Protestantism, remain uncommitted, fearing conversion would weaken their social ties. Others—even devout Catholics—listen to Protestant radio programs. A fifty-two-year-old retired schoolteacher who is a Catholic lay preacher and gives out communion says he enjoys listening to translated sermons by Jimmy Swaggart on the radio. "Maybe he's not such a good man, but he's a good preacher. It doesn't matter that he's a Protestant; he's still a Christian." Others sometimes attend mass, sometimes Protestant services.

Such fence-sitting may help prevent conflict within a family where some members have become Protestants. When one member of a family, especially a parent, converts, however, others commonly follow suit. Even if they do not, their religious differences seldom cause serious family problems. A rural Catholic woman, age thirty-seven, told us several of her relatives had become Protestants, but of these, only one aunt naggged others to convert. "I tell her, 'Look, we worship the same God, don't we?'"

Although converts are seldom ostracized by their Catholic friends, they are likely to see much less of them as they become active in the affairs of their new church, form new attachments there, and, very probably, give up drinking—a mainstay of many friendships among Catholic males. A resident of an island in the Nicoya Gulf bemoans the conversion of three-fourths of his 2,000 fellow islanders for this last reason: "The party's over."[32]

A priest acknowledges that many converts to Protestantism may have felt like mere numbers in the impersonal Catholic service and that "we have sometimes been very moralistic—'this is bad; that is a sin'—without realizing that people come to mass tired from a week of work and struggle. They must find in the church a message of hope and enthusiasm that gives them a positive attitude." Many priests, impressed by the joy and participation they see in Protestant churches, have introduced changes such as small Bible-study groups, guitar music, and having laypeople read the Epistles aloud and help dispense communion. Since the early 1970s many priests have conducted masses that feature "the gifts of the spirit"—speaking in tongues, prophesying, clapping, swaying, and shouting amens and alleluias; they ask massgoers to shake hands or pat shoulders and wish one another peace and to link hands while saying the Lord's Prayer.

Nonetheless, says Padre Walter Howell of Escazu, "Laymen have always been more enthusiastic about the charismatic movement than have priests—they'll meet in private homes, or go on retreats, usually without the priest." Sociologists studying the movement in 1990 found that charismatics outnumbered other Catholics. The economic crisis of the early 1980s, they say, had much to do with the growth of the charismatic movement, both Protestant and Catholic: "Many hoped to gain 'symbolically' what they couldn't achieve materially."[33]

Charismatic gatherings often involve unrelated people as well as kin of the host family. Says a taxi driver, "Doctors gave my father three months to live; he was riddled with cancer. Then a group of charismatics prayed over him. He saw Jesus telling him he was healed. The doctors couldn't find a trace of cancer. This was seven years ago and he's still healthy."

Visiting a farm family near the central Pacific coast in 1993, Richard and another visitor, a young local man, were invited to stay for the evening rosary. The local man, a charismatic Catholic, suggested instead a session of spontaneous prayer and songs of praise. The family enjoyed the evening and asked the young man to return soon with his guitar.

In 1993 several Catholic and evangelical churches collaborated on a program in which church-affiliated schools taught about sex from a religious perspective and about AIDS from a medical and scientific one. This unprecedented joint action, a response to pleas for ecumenical action from the World Health Organization, was hailed as "a clear symptom of the profound changes occurring in Costa Rican society."[34]

At the same time, leaders of many Protestant denominations were campaigning for "equality rather than tolerance." Said one, "In Costa Rica there is tolerance but not freedom of worship. We tolerate something we don't like but cannot avoid. Tolerance implies a certain contempt. When the state supports a certain religion it goes against the human rights of Costa Ricans of other faiths."[35] Protestants complain that many public school teachers ignore their requests to excuse their children from religion classes. They admit that some Protestant churches' amplified services annoy neighbors (a common epithet for Protestants is "tambourine beaters") but ask why police sometimes close such churches rather than loud discos or why the law prohibits bars within 400 meters of *Catholic* churches.

Other Faiths

Although non-Christian religious organizations abound in Costa Rica, few have more than a few hundred members. Two San José–area synagogues serve some 2,500 Jews. One is used by descendants of the Orthodox Jews who migrated from Europe in the 1920s and 1930s. (See Chapter 5.) The other serves Reform Jews, mostly Canadian and U.S. citizens. There is also a nascent Chabad Lubavitcher group of less than two dozen families. Like their Catholic and Protestant compatriots, Orthodox Jews are selective in the rules they follow: Most, for example, keep their businesses and professional practices open on the Sabbath and even on Rosh Hashanah.

Although many Ticos of Chinese descent have become Catholics, others practice a melange of Confucian and Buddhist rites. Foreigners and Ticos mingle on the International Society for Krishna Consciousness farm-cum-ashram near Cartago, as well as at small Bahai, Quaker, and Masonic meetings. Masons, now primarily a philosophical and philanthropic group, are no longer as active in politics as were those of the late nineteenth century, including presidents Tomás Guardia and Bernardo Soto, who secularized schools and cemeteries. Nor are Catholic Masons excommunicated as they once were. But Masons are still widely suspected of anti-Catholic and even satanic leanings.

The Theosophical Society has attracted small numbers of intellectuals for over a century. A variety of heavily filtered Hindu and Buddhist ideas influence the thousands of Costa Ricans who take classes in yoga, tae kwon do, and karate or who eat at the popular Vishnu vegetarian restaurants in the capital. Few of these Ticos are affiliated with a Hindu or Buddhist organization; most are at least nominal Catholics, though many blend Catholic or other Christian ideas with some of Asian origin. A high school philosophy teacher describes the high state of consciousness one feels when Christ enters the *atman* (a Sanskrit term for the individual soul) and enthuses, "Before, one's aura extends out only a few meters. With Christ, it embraces kilometers."

Summary and Conclusion

Their faith may be no less important to the Catholic majority of Ticos than in any past era. Priests complain that materialism is now greater than Catholic devotion. But Catholic Ticos' faith has always been tempered by fatalism, indifference to authority, and, paradoxically, both an insistence on individual freedom and a desire for community approval; thus a Catholic may feel little or no guilt about consulting a witch but would probably not mention it to others.

Increased urbanization and economic stress help to account for the rapid growth of evangelical Protestantism. The Catholic Church, in response, has adopted such Protestant practices as Bible study and lay participation. These may have strengthened its position in Costa Rica. The decline of *machismo,* moreover, may have helped stimulate men's involvement in Catholic rituals and study groups. Nonetheless, one can make few predictions about an individual Costa Rican's belief or behavior by simply learning his or her religious affiliation.

Notes

1. Much of this section draws on Ricardo Blanco Segura, *Historia eclesiástica de Costa Rica: Del descubrimiento a la erección de la diócesis (1502–1850)* (San José: ECR, 1965), especially ch. 2.

2. Ricardo Blanco Segura, "Intervención de la iglesia en la independencia de Costa Rica," *Revista de Costa Rica,* No. 5, 1974, pp. 79–96.

3. John Hale, *Six Months Residence and Travels in Central America,* translated in Ricardo Fernández Guardia, *Costa Rica en el siglo XIX,* 2nd ed. (San José: EDUCA, 1970), p. 29.

4. Moritz Wagner and Karl Scherzer, *La República de Costa Rica en la América Central* (San José: Ministry of Culture, 1974), p. 253.

5. Ivan Molina Jiménez, "'Azúl por Rubén Darío. El libro de moda,' la cultura libresca del Valle Central de Costa Rica 1780–1890," in Ivan Molina Jiménez and Steven Palmer, eds., *Héroes al gusto y libros de moda* (San José: Porvenir, 1992), pp. 137–138.

6. Philip J. Williams, *The Catholic Church and Politics in Nicaragua and Costa Rica* (Pittsburgh: University of Pittsburgh Press, 1989), p. 100.

7. Carlos Monge Alfaro, *Historia de Costa Rica* (San José: Trejos, 1976), citing President Iglesias.

8. Mario Alberto Jiménez, *Obras completas,* Vol. 1 (San José: ECR 1963), p. 35.

9. Hugo Mora Poltronieri, "Estado y religión oficial," *Universidad,* January 17, 1992.

10. Williams, *The Catholic Church,* p. 127.

11. Ibid., pp. 121–166. See also Silvia Lara, Tom Barry, and Peter Simonson, *Inside Costa Rica* (Albuquerque: Resource Center Press, 1995), p. 98.

12. Maritza Delgado G. and Yalile Jimenéz M., "El papel social del movimiento de renovacien carismática en la Iglesia Cattlica costarricense," Lic. Thesis in Sociology, UCR, 1990.

13. John Biesanz and Mavis Biesanz, *Costa Rican Life* (New York: Columbia University Press, 1944), pp. 211–212.

14. "Confesionario," *Rumbo,* December 8, 1992, pp. 8–14.

15. Ibid.

16. Luís Barahona Jiménez, "Cristianismo a la tica," in *El gran incógnito* (San José: ECR, 1975), pp. 146–150.

17. Biesanz and Biesanz, *Costa Rican Life,* pp. 208–209.

18. Cited in Eduardo Oconitrillo, *Vida, muerte y mito del Dr. Moreno Cañas* (San José: ECR, 1985).

19. May Brenes Marín and Mayra Zapparoli Zecca, *De que vuelan . . . Vuelan!* (San José: ECR, 1991).

20. María Eugenia Bozzoli de Wille, "No creer ni dejar de creer," *Revista de Costa Rica* (Ministerio de Cultura), No. 1, November 1971, pp. 75–84.

21. Luís Fernando Mata, "Brujas," *Revista Perfil,* November 1992, pp. 21–29.

22. Brenes and Zapparoli, *De que vuelan,* p. 99.

23. Ibid.

24. Ibid.

25. Bozzoli, *"No creer,"* pp. 35–84.

26. Bozzoli, "'Maleficio': A Rational Principle Behind an Irrational Practice," Unpublished paper, University of Georgia, 1974. Courtesy of the author.

27. Brenes and Zapparoli, *De que vuelan.*

28. Richard L. Millett, "Protestant-Catholic Relations in Costa Rica," *Journal of Church and State,* Vol. 12, No. 1, Winter 1970, pp. 41–57.

29. Ibid.

30. Interviews with Clifton Holland, May 6 and August 23, 1976. See also his "A Profile of Evangelical Churches in Costa Rica," *In-Depth Evangelism Around the World* (San José: Indepth), Vol. 2, No. 4, January-March 1975, pp. 59–64.

31. Jaime Valverde, *Las sectas en Costa Rica: Pentecostalismo y conflicto social* (San José: Departamento Ecuménico de Investigación [DEI], 1990), pp. 69–70.

32. "Isla Chira," *Contrapunto,* November 1992, p. 30.

33. Any Pérez and Cristina Arias, "Los ticos al filo del XXI," *Rumbo,* February 9, 1993, pp. 11–16. Poll by Demoscopio.

34. *La Nación,* November 22, 1993, p. 1B.

35. Ana Orozco, "Queremos pasar de la tolerancia a la igualdad," *Aportes,* August 1993, pp. 9–10.

— 11 —

Leisure

WITH A SHORT SCHOOL DAY and school year, a five-day work week, and numerous holidays, many Costa Ricans have abundant leisure time. Even at work, many spend part of each day *matando la culebra*—killing the snake—a classic explanation idle banana peons once used when irate foremen asked what they had been doing.

The demands of modern urban life, the resurgence of the private sector, and, for many Ticos, increased poverty threaten this easygoing approach to work. Many find it hard to adapt to the schedules and supervision of modern business and industry. They resent clocks and whistles announcing the start and end of factories' coffee breaks. Others—the many underemployed— spend much time looking for odd jobs. Although most Ticos enjoy modern diversions such as television and shopping malls, many are nostalgic for the preindustrial era, when leisure time, though less abundant, was inseparable from family, church, and community ties.

Until well into the twentieth century, most Ticos spent free time with family members and neighbors. After an early supper they gathered on wide verandas to chat and tell stories. They celebrated religious holidays with community festivals that originated with Spanish colonists and African slaves. The Indians living among the colonists soon shared and contributed to these customs. Thus festivals—a mélange of bullfights, drinking, marimba music, and dance—evolved as "a fusion of Indian, African and Spanish elements . . . which were a cultural heritage to *mestizos* of succeeding generations." They endure, with modern touches, to this day.[1]

Nineteenth-century literature depicts a life of hard work punctuated by plenty of merrymaking. As the coffee economy increased the complexity of their society, Ticos' diversions came to vary by social class. Upper-class families exchanged invitations to evenings of parlor games, poetry, taffy pulls, skits, and music and attended performances of touring European opera companies. On Sundays they often rode horses or took oxcarts into the countryside for picnics. In January many retired to their country houses or took the eight-day oxcart journey down to the Pacific port of Puntarenas, where they waited out the dusty months of the highland *verano*. Men (and, to a lesser extent, women) met frequently for *tertulias*—sessions of conversation, readings, and poetry recitals. After the National Theater—a "jewel in a mudhole" according to one visitor—was opened in 1897, debutante balls were held on the orchestra floor raised to stage level.

Rural parties were spontaneous. If musicians dropped by, word spread, someone brought cane liquor, and neighbors came to sing and dance. Until the mid-twentieth century, wakes for "little angels," too young to have sinned and hence in heaven without delay, were occasions for joyful celebration. The local *pulpería*, often including a bar and billiards table, was the social center for village men, who gathered to drink and gossip after work and on Sundays. The week's high point for many men was a Sunday trip to town to attend mass, stroll around, shop, and converse. Women often stayed home except to attend mass but did join in the coffee harvest and in church fairs, welcome occasions to flirt and chat.

Until the 1950s, people of all ages and social classes gathered at the central parks of larger towns on Sunday mornings and several evenings a week to gossip and flirt while the local brass band played marches, waltzes, and mazurkas. Religious processions, too, provided a welcome change from daily routine.

As the population has grown and transportation has improved, ties to community and kin have weakened and outside diversions—as well as more solitary ones—have become more abundant, more commercial, more avidly sought. It has become easier to escape into urban anonymity at cinemas, restaurants, dance halls, clubs, brothels, bars, and sports events that fit many tastes and pocketbooks. Ownership of dogs has boomed in recent years, especially in urban areas, where they provide companionship as well as protection. As women and adolescents gain more liberty, many are spending more leisure time with friends, less with family. Television may unite family members for several hours each evening but, like many video games, affords much less interaction than did the parlor, veranda, and kitchen of yesteryear. And today's Ticos increasingly travel for pleasure both within their country and abroad.

Informal Socializing and Friendship

Foreign visitors find Costa Ricans gracious and sociable. Villagers salute even a passing stranger with an "Adiós!" or "Amigo!" Ticos use the word *amigo* freely and greet acquaintances with handshakes or embraces, as well as inquiries after their health and family, as we saw in Chapter 1. Men call male acquaintances *maje* (buddy) or '*mano* (*hermano*, or brother).

Nonetheless, many Ticos still say they spend most leisure time with family and visit only relatives. Mario Sancho noted in the 1930s:

Costa Ricans' sociability is purely formal and is undone as easily as it is formed. . . . It is rare to find cases of neighboring families that maintain close contact. . . . There are many, many families that live next door to one another for years, separated only by walls which allow voices and noises to pass, but that, nonetheless, have no more relations among their members than a friendly greeting.[2]

Many Ticos remain wary of intimate friendship. Says a thirty-five-year-old private guard, "I don't have or want any friends. Friends will use confidences against you. Women are even worse. I only trust my own *huevos* ['eggs'—testicles], and not always those, because they've got me in a lot of trouble." A small-town clothing vendor, a thirty-two-year-old woman, says, "My father taught me not to be involved in other people's affairs, but to keep to myself; he often quoted a proverb, 'The lone ox takes good care of itself.' "

Newcomers are puzzled by—and Ticos joke about—the insincerity of many invitations. Face-to-face, an acquaintance will say, "I'll call you and we'll have dinner at my house on Sunday." Frequently, no call ever comes. Or one may accept a definite invitation and never show up or call, possibly thinking the invitation meant as little as one's own. Psychologist Pierre Thomas Claudet suggests that such behavior stems in part, ironically, from Ticos' desire to *quedar bien*, especially in face-to-face situations.[3] Ticos see most invitations as simply gestures, ways of expressing friendliness without a desire for intimacy.

Much of the reluctance to visit and be visited stems from fear of being known as a gossip and of being gossiped about. Privacy is valued as a means of avoiding problems. (One is taught from childhood to say "with permission" upon entering another's house, even after being invited in, and to announce one's presence with a shouted "Upe!" when approaching an isolated rural house.) Yet in all classes, "eating people"—gossiping—remains a favorite pastime as well as a major form of social control. This is especially true in small communities, whose residents cite the Spanish proverb "Small town, big hell."

Novelist Carmen Naranjo offers another explanation. Many Ticos, she told us, try to give the impression that they are more prosperous than they really are, and a visit from an acquaintance would destroy the facade.

Despite their wariness of close friendship and preference for quiet homes and neighborhoods, most Ticos abhor solitude. They enjoy crowds and noise away from home, and one of the highest recommendations of a beach resort or nightspot is not that it is "undiscovered" but that "everyone goes there."

A great deal of socializing, however brief, goes on outside the home. In impersonal settings Ticos of both sexes easily strike up conversations with strangers; a common icebreaker is a search for mutual acquaintances. Workers, particularly civil servants, construction workers, and coffee pickers, chat during coffee breaks and often during working hours. Gossip and jokes punctuate men's discussions of soccer and politics and women's talk of romance magazines, soap operas, and their own dreams. Many Ticos ride buses or collective taxis to work, and their long commutes, where they often see the same people each day, encourage conversation to pass the time. The village *pulpería* is still a favorite hangout of rural men. Those that don't sell beer or *guaro* lose business to bars, where men sometimes linger for hours of drinking, joking, and televised soccer games. Few rural women have a comparable gathering place. They often stop to talk at stores, after church, or along the sidewalk near home.

Humor

Besides providing sheer fun, jokes are a safety valve for frustration and envy—an important outlet in a society whose members are anxious to *quedar bien*. Men, in particular, enjoy jokes and teasing on almost any occasion and in any setting. Office workers fax or e-mail jokes or their own cartoons to friends; good ones spread rapidly. Frequent jokes enlivened the Legislative Assembly committee meetings we sat in on. When a landslide stalled a bus for four hours, the Ticos aboard vied to make the wittiest remarks about their plight and to swap jokes in their repertoires. Even in the heat of a demonstration by street vendors protesting police harassment, the banter never stopped.

Ticos have words for various kinds of jokes. A *chiste* is a story, a pun, even a funny nickname. A *chile* is sexual or scatological. An *ocurrencia* is a wild, funny fantasy. A *broma*, a practical joke, is typified by a Holy Saturday tradition in small towns: Adolescents steal neighbors' belongings and leave them in the central plaza. A *bomba* is a short, funny verse recited or improvised by a folk musician, dancer, or onlooker during a pause in the music. *Mentirosos* (liars) are prized for their tall tales and jokes, skillfully delivered with exaggerated voices and gestures.

In a San José suburb at a Friday night barbecue party for coworkers, the hostess, a social security administrator, regaled her guests with an improvised *ocurrencia* of her contacts with extraterrestrials. Amid much laughter, the guests made ribald comments about what happened next, and she used the most promising of these in developing the story.

Ticos also prize quick wit and skill at repartee. The word *vacilón* may connote a lazy person, but it is most often a complimentary description of one skilled at casual, improvised jokes. When we asked a shoeshine man in San José's Central Park why there no longer are young shoeshine boys around, he replied, "We all grew up." Similarly, when we gave our hosts in a mountain village an imported chocolate bar, the mother, age fifty-one, asked her son to translate the English label. He pretended to read it with great care: "Consumption of this product by anyone over forty is strictly prohibited." In both cases, bystanders howled with laughter and said of the joker, "¡Que vacilón!" The public health campaign promoting condoms during the 1990s provided a rich new source of jokes. Columnist Edgar Espinoza describes the embarrassment of a man at a supermarket checkout. A very young female clerk held up the package of condoms he'd tucked under groceries and called to the manager, "How much are these balloons?" It was a busy Friday evening, and a couple of his friends were also in line. One called, "Economize, Pepe, buy the reversible ones." Another said, "Put those back. You don't need the large size."[4]

A Tico party is often one long round of joke-swapping. Perennial themes are politicians, Nicaraguans, sex (including the escapades of priests and nuns and, in 1998, Viagra), parrots' revelations of their owners' foibles, and embarrassing questions asked by a naive schoolboy named Pepito.

No president escapes. Ticos concentrate on one theme for each. One was supposedly overly proud of his intelligence; another so stupid that he ordered two water glasses for everyone at cabinet meetings—one full glass in case a minister was thirsty, the other empty in case he was not. Still another was targeted as a hick who, invited to a concert in the National Theater, urged his wife to hurry dressing. When they finally settled in their seats, the conductor announced Beethoven's Ninth Symphony. "I told you to hurry," grumbled the president. "We've already missed the first eight!"

Bureaucrats are another favorite target. A jobseeker in the postal customs office was puzzled by an item on the application form. "Physical defects? I can't think of any, except that I have no testicles." Replied the personnel manager: "Oh, that's no problem. In that case, you don't have to come to work until nine o'clock. Everyone else comes in at eight and just scratches his *huevos* for an hour."

Fairs and Other Community Diversions

Crowds and noise abound at the *turnos* (street fairs) that raise money for churches, clinics, old-age homes, schools, and other causes; at the year-end *fiestas cívicas* in Zapote, a San José suburb; and at towns' annual patron saints' festivals.

"This country was built by *turnos*," says Carmen Naranjo. In small towns and villages they evoke as much community spirit as soccer matches. For weeks in advance committee members visit local households, usually receiving contributions such as lumber, cash, a chicken, a sack of corn, a few eggs, a block of raw sugar, or a promise of labor. The municipality may donate electricity. Volunteers put up wooden stalls on the plaza. Perspiring women prepare beef stew, chop suey, fried pork skins, tamales, Salvadoran *pupusas* (filled tortillas), tripe soup, rice cakes, and other special dishes. Announced by loud rocket bursts each day before dawn, a *turno* normally lasts all weekend; a patron saint's fiesta, a week or more. Except for a mass and a procession around the plaza when the patron saint is being honored, these fairs are completely secular. Beer and liquor flow freely. Riders put fancy-stepping horses through their paces. Clowns on stilts, wearing immense papier-mâché heads, parade in the streets. Ferris wheels and other carnival rides, video games, roulette, and a greased-pole climbing contest are typical highlights. The local wind ensemble and a mariachi, marimba, salsa, or rock band alternate with recorded music. A neighboring village may send a team for a soccer game. Local people may donate used clothing and household items for a rummage sale. The main money-raisers are raffles, bingo, and lotteries. Bull- and bronco-riding are favorite *turno* events in such cattle-raising areas as Guanacaste and San Carlos; horse races in which riders try to grab ribbons strung on an overhead line are popular in all rural areas. Young men display their rodeo skills in hopes of praise and, perhaps, a sexual conquest.

Some fairs—notably the popular ten-day *fiestas cívicas* in Zapote—feature a characteristically Tico form of bull-baiting. Hundreds of young men, many quite drunk, tease a small bull in a ring for a few minutes. Then the animal is lassoed and replaced by another. These events serve as comedy acts as well as displays of skill or daring. Although the animal is never killed, many denounce the spectacle as barbaric.

Invariably a queen is chosen from among teenagers whose swimsuit-clad figures may have graced the newspapers for days ahead; she is crowned at a special dance on the final evening. A fireworks display closes the festivities.

Time and Seasons

Many Ticos complain of their compatriots' *vagabundería* (laziness) and cite long weekends (skipping work on Friday or taking off early), the many public holidays, and "Tico time"—the flexible attitude toward schedules and appointments. (European visitors to mid-nineteenth-century Costa Rica, says Meléndez, "were exasperated by the low value . . . put on time, the lack of haste and urgency.")[5] Others take pride in what they see as their people's ability to relax and enjoy life far more than do the compulsive drones of more industrialized countries. We found Ticos in most settings willing to stop whatever they were doing to chat with unexpected visitors.

Campesinos and urbanites have different perceptions of both time and work. Asked what they do for fun, small farmers are likely to smile and say, "Work." Many do seem to enjoy their work, especially that done on their own land. Although they (men, at any rate) do less work on Sunday, the demands of animals, crops, and housework make the concept of weekends less relevant to them than to city folk. Professionals and office workers often see weekends as an escape from the tensions of work, a time to "get crazy"—to drink, dance, joke with friends—as well as to see relatives and sweethearts. On Fridays, especially paydays, many wear jeans to work, ready for the weekend. Female factory workers are more likely to prepare for weekend fun by dressing up on Fridays.

Sunday is the liveliest day in villages and, except at the soccer stadium, the quietest in towns and cities. Although many Ticos find Sunday boring, many others consider it the high point of the week. It's a day to spend with family members, to dress up, attend mass, stroll, window shop, eat ice cream and big midday meals, enjoy a live or televised soccer game, watch the planes at the airport, go to a zoo, picnic at a beach or riverbank, or lunch at McDonald's. Teenagers may see a movie or video with friends, attend a pop concert, or go to a dance hall (often connected to a bar).

Eleven public holidays were observed in 1998. Secular and religious holidays alike are increasingly occasions for private relaxation or merrymaking. "For the Tico," says a journalist, in defense of the growing custom of celebrating Thanksgiving, "everything serves as an excuse for a party. Any holiday will do for drinking, carousing and eating, no matter where it originated or what it means."[6]

Business and government leaders' pleas to curtail the number of holidays are strongly resisted. And special holidays are often added when a group—especially a public employees' union—petitions the Legislative Assembly. On the Day of the Postal Employee, for example, post office functions come to a full stop.

Any attempt to reduce spending and partying at year's end would probably fail completely. One Tico journalist suspects that Costa Ricans "are more infected with the Christmas spirit than any other people."[7] Plastic snowmen, tinsel, and Santa Claus appear in stores in mid-October. Early in December, extra income from the coffee harvest or year-end bonuses (equal to a month's pay) in their pockets, shoppers crowd the stores, stopping along the streets to see if a lottery vendor has their desired number for the "fat" Christmas drawing. They swamp the postal system with cards. Children write to the Christ Child asking for presents to be delivered by his messenger, Santa Claus.

Most families assemble a *portal* (Nativity scene) on a carpet of moss in a corner of the *sala*. This tableau mixes sacred and secular objects; besides figures of the Holy Family, shepherds, angels, and wise men, it may include miniature houses and churches, jet planes, oxcarts, plastic soldiers, twinkling lights—whatever the family's taste and pocketbook may suggest. The family may also decorate a cypress tree in the living room and string colored lights in bushes near the house.

Campesinos retire as early on Christmas Eve as on any other night. In towns, by contrast, relatives visit each other to eat the seasonal *tamales*, drink, dance, and exchange gifts. At midnight the Christ Child is placed in the *portal*'s manger and the children are sent to bed. The adults may attend midnight mass, then resume partying till dawn, going to bed about the time the children get up to see their gifts.

Asked if her pharmacy would be closed on Christmas Day, a small-town pharmacist said, "Oh, no, impossible! That's our busiest day. People stream in with hangovers and upset stomachs."

Merrymaking is even more boisterous on New Year's Eve. The Christmas season is not over until February 2, when the pope blesses all the world's crèches and Costa Ricans finally dismantle theirs. One reason the season is celebrated so enthusiastically is that it falls near the start of *verano*, when spirits are high from sunshine and people can at last step outside without fear of getting wet or muddy. Many families now spend Christmas week at a favorite beach. The same is true of the once-solemn Holy Week, near the end of *verano*, now mostly a time for fun.

Parties and Dances

Holidays are favorite occasions for parties as well as trips. Surprise birthday bashes are common, as are farewell and welcome-home parties, especially among the upper-middle and upper classes, who may hold them at home, a social club, or a hotel ballroom. To raise money, schools and clubs hold dances, often including a queen contest. At many working- and lower-middle-class parties—often held at the local community development center—guests help defray the host's expenses.

Costa Ricans, even preschoolers, love to dance. Wedding guests and youths in small-town dance halls enjoy *discomóviles*—vans carrying sound-and-light apparatus on which DJs play recorded music at high volume. Spanish-language rap, reggae, heavy metal, and techno are popular among young Ticos, even those in remote rural areas, who tune in MTV. Their parents prefer salsa, merengue, cumbia, and 1950s rock.

Live bands at urban dance halls attract crowds even on weeknights. Most, even many traditional marimba ensembles, use a combination of electric and acoustic instruments. A type of calypso trio popular in Limón uses African-derived acoustic instruments—a banjo, a conga drum, and a *quijongo*, a one-string bass with a wooden box as resonator. Though still numerous, live bands are gradually being replaced by *discomóviles*.

Jones observed in the early 1940s that "most adult social events, especially among the 'social' class, have a certain stiffness and formality. . . . An

*Most Ticos love
to dance
(Fernando
Acuña)*

all-powerful fear of what people will say robs social intercourse of spontaneity."[8] He considered this reserve atypical of Latin America. "We are much
merrier than Costa Ricans," Panamanians and Colombians have told us. The
comparison may be valid, but most Tico parties we have attended, aside from
formal receptions, have been lively enough. Journalist Miguel Salguero says,
"When Ticos are in groups, they change completely. They are boisterous."
This is especially true when partygoers begin to drink. Joking then begins in
earnest. So does dancing—"moving the skeleton" or "shaking off the rust."
Or a guitar is passed around, and merrymakers take turns leading popular
Latin American love songs.

Drinking is closely associated with fun and celebration and with relief
from loneliness and boredom. Says a nondrinking Methodist, "Alcohol is the
basis of social life in Costa Rica. If you don't drink, you're socially dead." "I

don't have any close friends because I drink very little," says a retired university professor, "and for many males it's practically a requisite of friendship." An architect designing an upper-middle-class home usually assumes there will be a bar.

Many parties are sex-segregated. Higher-status women attend teas, showers, luncheons, and card and bingo parties. Men—and a growing number of women—of the elite attend numerous luncheons and banquets connected with their jobs or service clubs. Even when they go to parties together or gather for visits, people of all social classes tend, when not dancing, to gravitate to those of their own sex. When conversation does occur in a mixed group, men do most of the talking.

Except for family get-togethers, urban working- and lower-class diversions are usually confined to people of the same sex. Men cite drinking, parties, and dances as their favorite diversions; women name talking with neighbors, friends, and, above all, family.

Gambling

Gambling has been popular since colonial days; only its form has changed. In the mid-1800s Wagner and Scherzer noted a "powerful passion" for gambling at the weekly cockfight—a government monopoly, like sales of liquor, tobacco, and fireworks.

Cockfights are now illegal, but police often ignore the law, charging the organizer "a tax for charity." Where bribery fails, organizers may shift to one secret location after another in urban neighborhoods—something harder to do in villages.

Raffles play a large part in the growing "informal economy." Businesses, clubs, schools, and even private individuals often raffle a car, a watch, or a cash prize and have little trouble selling tickets. A journalist writes that from morning to night she is pressured to buy a "number" for some good cause. The neighborhood guard approaches her first, then the parking guard, then the man who brings employees their midmorning snack. She dares not offend any of them by refusing. A coworker offers a ticket for another drawing; the writer wants to *quedar bien* and buys one. In the evening her children insist she buy several chances on a school raffle. Even at political party meetings and in church, she is considered legitimate prey.[9]

Upper- and middle-class women's bridge and canasta games are enlivened by the hope of winning a few colones. Many men bet on billiards as well as card and domino games and soccer matches, including their own pickup games. In towns of all sizes, weekend bingo games attract even small children.

The national lottery is immensely popular, especially with the poor, who part with a few colones every week. When Ticos express a cherished but expensive desire, they often add that they will satisfy it "when I win the lottery." Some consult fortune-tellers to learn the lucky number. Illegal lotteries, which pay more, have become a big business, involving more money collectively than the national lottery.

The Mass Media

Movies, radio, and television compete with participatory diversions. Nearly every small town once had a cinema; larger towns had several. Television and video rental stores have driven most out of business, though they still flourish in San José.

For decades Ticos have been avid movie fans; until recently a popular term for children's allowances was "movie money." Most moviegoers are under twenty-five. Groups of boys pack theaters showing war and crime movies; couples and groups of girls are attracted to those with romantic themes. Most are U.S. films with Spanish subtitles, as are the most popular videos (often pirated).

Radios abound in homes, workplaces, buses, and cars. A housewife or maid may keep the radio on all day while she goes about her work ("to feel less lonely") and even while she talks with others.

Some 130 radio stations crowd the airwaves. Popular music from Latin America and the United States predominates. DJs emphasize how new a tune is and what a hit it has become. News and soccer games (both announced at top speed), soap operas, and strident commercials fill most other airtime. Some stations specialize in Catholic or Protestant sermons, jazz, or classical music.

Television antennas sprout from even the humblest homes. Nine out of ten households have TVs. In the few rural areas lacking electric current they are powered by diesel generators or car batteries. Bars and restaurants typically have both TV and radio on. Many Ticos leave the set on even when they aren't watching or when a visitor arrives. By age sixteen, according to one study, Ticos have spent, on the average, 18,000 hours in front of the "electronic baby-sitter."[10] A 1996 study by the Panamerican Health Organization and University of Costa Rica psychologists found that those between fifteen and twenty-five watched an average of six hours a day. Asked how she handles her six small children, a working-class mother says, "They're no trouble. They watch TV from morning till night."

Cable networks and satellite dishes bring dozens of channels to urban homes. Many of the same programs are available in San José, Costa Rica, as in San Jose, California. Cable networks have added Spanish news and South American programs to their menus (and thus changed some Tico speech patterns; folklorist Miguel Salguero laments, for instance, the increasing use of *tu* rather than *vos* as the familiar form of "you").

Local stations offer soccer games, popular music, giveaway shows, newscasts, slapstick comedy, religious and medical counsel, and demonstrations of gardening, cooking, and needlework. Politicians campaign via television; officials defend their policies; charges and countercharges of corruption and incompetence fill the screen. Popular taped programming includes Spanish-dubbed sitcoms, MTV, cartoons and movies from the United States, and soap operas from Mexico and Venezuela.

An elderly resident of a mountain hamlet describes the impact of TV, which arrived on the heels of electric current in the 1980s: "Children stopped playing with tops and marbles. They didn't visit one another as much, and they spent less time outdoors. People now stay up later and get up later, mainly because of TV." Adds a small-town librarian:

> When I started this job in the late seventies, you still used to see lots of kids in the street playing tag, jumprope, jacks, and so on. Not now—they're all watching TV. And at night the only time they'll listen to a story is during a power failure. People of all ages read for pleasure a lot less than they once did. And TV doesn't even bring family members together. If they can afford it, they have a set in each room. So some may be watching on their sets while another is playing Nintendo on his.

Children's and Adolescents' Diversions

Children of all classes play—or watch TV—mostly with siblings until puberty. Seldom do those of any age play alone. Little girls enjoy tag, hide-and-seek, jacks, "house," "doctor," and dolls. School-age girls also jump rope and bat balls. Small boys like to run, kick soccer balls, play with toy cars and skateboards, and hang around the fringes of older boys' groups. They seldom play organized games until about age twelve. Rural boys have long delighted in pilfering fruit from orchards and swimming in rivers. Both boys and girls enjoy imitating television heroes and riding bicycles.

After entering school at age seven, boys and girls usually play apart, and boys are teased if they play with girls. But age differences between preadolescent playmates are often as much as five years.

Poor children have few commercial toys but some homemade ones; a small boy, for instance, may tie a plastic soda bottle to a string and kick it in lieu of a soccer ball as he walks along. Children of affluent families play with a wide variety of imported toys.

Unlike many U.S. children, according to a study of fourth- and sixth-graders in both countries, Costa Rican children regard their parents as more important even than their best friends. As in the United States, girls are more likely than boys to cite a best friend as important to their lives.[11]

On weekends, San José–area families with young children and groups of young people flock to the Metropolitan Park in La Sabana. In the 1970s the Ministry of Culture planted this former pasture-cum-airport with trees and made paths and reflecting pools, basketball and volleyball courts, soccer fields, and a small lake and provided picnic tables. There children can swim, ride bikes or rented ponies, fly kites safely, and see greener vistas and breathe purer air than in most of their neighborhoods. A commercial amusement park outside San José is designed to appeal mostly to children.

The Ministry of Culture sponsors frequent performances in large towns, often tailored to local traditions, by clowns, musicians, dancers, and story-tellers, as well as lessons and contests for children. The ministry also tries, through workshops and exhibits, to revive the games and toys of past genera-tions. Says the director of this effort, José Edwin Araya, "Modern electronic games are usually played alone and indoors. Traditional games are played outdoors in groups and stimulate creativity. They are healthier and cheaper. They also permit more family interaction; grandparents can teach them to kids." He attributes the decline of such games to urbanization: "We used to play in pastures and coffee groves and race our hoops when we were sent on errands." As cities have grown, fewer children live near such spaces. And for fear of traffic and crime, many middle- and upper-class urban children are not allowed outdoors without adult supervision.

A columnist writes that his young children frequently complain of bore-dom during the long school vacations. One day he decided to entertain them:

> I ran to a bookstore to buy them books to read and color, paints and educa-tional games. I invited them to eat ice cream. We went to a movie. We prac-ticed soccer, had a pillow fight, painted an old piece of furniture, relaxed with modeling clay, turned somersaults, climbed to the roof, broke a win-dow, played guessing games, walked the dog—and I went to bed, ready for intensive care.
>
> When they repeated, "We're bored!" I talked with other parents and found that they, too, were concerned with their children's boredom and powerless, because of their work, to do much to entertain them.
>
> . . . I discovered with some surprise that neither they nor I had ever been bored as children. Quite the contrary. We had to be dragged into the house for meals, chased after in the bushes to be given our spoonful of med-icine. And when it got dark, we reluctantly gave up the beat-up old soccer ball we knocked around in the street. We wanted morning to come so we could go outdoors to roll hoops, spin tops, toss beanbags or play hide-and-seek, and we hated nightfall and bedtime.
>
> But oh! irony of destiny! Now that technology has filled our homes with the most sophisticated electronic games, from TVs to Nintendos with

remote control, computers, pregnant dolls, Walkmans, laser guns and even story books that read themselves—now is when our children are unhappy. All this, dear parents and my colleagues in these modern social misfortunes, is summed up in one simple sentence: We have lost freedom.[12]

Rural adolescents, too, often complain of boredom. On a trip to five small communities in 1977 with Minister of Planning Oscar Arias Sánchez, we noted that one invariable request was for recreational facilities—sports grounds, a community hall, a library—"to help keep our young people from leaving for the city." In a remote hamlet of eight families we visited in 1992, two sisters, ages thirteen and fifteen, told us that if there were a road, more people would come. "How many?" "The more the better." "As many as in San José?" "That would be great." "Have you been to San José?" "Yes." "Do you like it?" "YES!" "What did you see there that you'd like to see here?" "A dance hall!"

Asked about their favorite diversions, adolescents of both sexes cite dancing, TV, listening to music, visiting, and movies. Males also enjoy playing and watching soccer. In large towns, they crowd video arcades. Those with access to cars sometimes drag race in town late at night. Young teens prefer to go out in small groups of the same sex, especially to Sunday dances and concerts. By age sixteen, these groups are more often mixed.

Among wealthy families a girl's fifteenth birthday traditionally marks her debut into "society," and the celebration, marked by a special mass and party, is almost as formal as a wedding. Like a bride, the birthday girl dances the first waltz with her father; fifteen couples of her friends circle the pair, then join the dance. After a late supper, identical souvenirs are passed out to the guests and will join mementos of similar occasions on knickknack shelves. Working-class families have also begun to celebrate this occasion, though quite modestly.

Most Ticos see adolescence as the prime time for fun. Working-class men often told us that the wild times they had enjoyed as youths ended with the responsibilities of marriage and children. Middle- and upper-class Ticos agree that one should have fun in youth but—in moderation—throughout life as well.

Sports

At almost any daylight hour, all over the country, one can join *mejengas*, informal *futból* (soccer) games open to all. Many towns also have regularly scheduled *mejengas*, perhaps every Wednesday at 2 P.M., and opponents bet on the outcome. Boys, and male factory workers on a break, play in the street or in any vacant flat space; fishermen play on a beach while waiting for the

Soccer mejenga *(Julio Laínez)*

tide to turn. Youths in towns and cities organize *barrio* teams. In the 1960s, men over age twenty-five told us they were too old to play; today men up to thirty-five or forty join *mejengas*. And the first all-female teams appeared in the 1990s, mostly in small communities.

Introduced early in the twentieth century, soccer is played mostly by young working-class males, who begin kicking a ball around at age two. The first artifact in a new hamlet is a centrally located soccer field—"so the men can have fun while they build the school," one settler explained. Among the things a settlement must have to qualify as a political district is a soccer field—no matter if the goalposts are simply bamboo poles.

Village teams solicit money for equipment and uniforms, broadcast challenges over the radio, and usually find a taker every Sunday. When cattle trucks full of cheering players and fans arrive at a rival village, spectators of all ages and both sexes crowd the edges of the plaza.

In the 1970s leading soccer teams began to take on the look of profit-making businesses. Teams were organized into leagues, leagues into divisions of various levels of professionalism, and divisions into FEDEFUTBOL, a federation with a director and a board. Wrote sociologist Mayela Cubillo in 1986: "Every weekend, five teams of the first division [major league] attract between 25,000 and 30,000 people to the stadiums." In the previous ten years, she continued, the state gave heavy subsidies to first-division clubs and passed laws to benefit them. Half of all state aid to sports in 1979 went to professional soccer, mainly to first-division clubs. The government, then, "helps professional soccer, spectator soccer, soccer as a business."[13] This remains true despite these clubs' mounting debts to the Social Security Fund, to municipalities that host games, and to other public agencies.[14]

Soccer, from *mejengas* through World Cup games, has no rival as a spectator diversion. About half of the front-page photos in major newspapers depict recent matches. A Tico's portable radio may be tuned to a major national or international game on Sunday even while he or she watches another game on TV or in a stadium or village plaza.

Soccer has been called the best therapy in the uphill struggle of life. It is a safety valve, "a functional alternative to the violence of more militaristic peoples," a source of national pride, and a secular religion on a par with politics.[15] Says a small-town storekeeper, "No matter how tense or worried you are, there's nothing like watching a good soccer game to take your mind off your troubles."

Few Ticos show strong emotion except when soccer is involved. Cheering fans of the winners throng streets, honk horns, wave banners. Soccer rivalries are generally good-natured but can arouse more rancor, especially among men, than do political disputes. A taxi driver told us that to avoid arguments with passengers he does not discuss politics, religion, or soccer. In

1993 Cartago fans stoned the bus carrying Heredia players, fought police, and tore down the stadium's fence.

During World Cup games most Ticos are glued to TV sets; in 1994 a small-town dentist divided his attention between Richard's teeth and the TV in his office. When a 1990 wedding in one village conflicted with a World Cup game between Costa Rica and Scotland, says columnist Mitzi Stark, "nobody showed up except the bride and groom, and even they hurried home to catch the end of the game."[16]

Many other sports occupy, collectively, almost as much space as soccer in newspapers' large sports sections. Bicycle racing has many working-class fans and participants. Boxing and wrestling are two favorite spectator sports for men of this class. Most Ticos prefer to fight only vicariously; they pride themselves on their peaceable natures and do not even like to argue, although a combination of alcohol and political or soccer rivalries sometimes overcomes these inhibitions. Even children seldom strike one another. Young working-class males gathered on a street may relieve their boredom by brief impromptu mock boxing, but blows are light and seldom lead to serious fights.

Basketball and volleyball are popular among teenage boys and girls of all classes; tennis, among upper- and upper-middle-class youth, who often play at their private high schools. Their parents, even those in their sixties and seventies—an age working-class Ticos consider ridiculously advanced even for amateur sports—play tennis and golf at private clubs. Billiards, popular among men for over a century, is played in fly-specked *pulperías* as well as in the exclusive Club Union. Baseball teams are sponsored by large private companies, and there is a large stadium. The sport has long been popular in Limón. The Ministry of Culture, Youth, and Sports employs a woman to teach baseball to boys between four and eight years old; they have competed in Japan and Mexico.

Horse, auto, and cross-country motorcycle races attract spectators from all social classes. Some wealthy men and women ride show horses in parades. Young Ticos have adopted surfing from foreigners enthusiastic about the waves on both coasts. Men of all classes fish and hunt, often illegally—some for sport, others for food.

Young Tica swimmers have excelled in international competition including the Olympics; in 1995 Claudia Poll set a world record for the 200-meter free-style race; she won a gold medal in the 1996 Olympics and others in international meets in 1997. Swimming in rivers and oceans is popular in the dry season, and many wealthy families have pools.

In the 1850s, Wagner and Scherzer observed that Ticos, especially women, exercised as little as possible.[17] (Very likely they were referring only to upper-class Ticas; most women did a great deal of physical work.) In the early 1940s, exercise was still considered harmful for women.[18] And as late as 1976, a male runner in training was jailed in a small village; the local policeman thought he must be crazy.

But as more Ticos work in sedentary jobs and worry about weight gain, school curricula have incorporated physical exercise, and direct involvement in sports has climbed for both sexes. Many middle- and upper-class women swim, play tennis and golf, or work out at health clubs. A common suburban sight around dawn is pairs of women in shorts or sweatsuits walking briskly along a road. A growing number of men study karate or tae kwon do, cycle, lift weights, jog, and climb mountains for fun and exercise. Says a forty-eight-year-old teacher we met hiking with his ten-year-old son, "I like to ride my bike and play soccer, too. I want to be healthy until I die."

Clubs and Organizations

Although they have always disliked solitude, most Costa Ricans have traditionally not been joiners. In the early 1940s observers found that "the often-remarked individualism of the Costa Rican has kept him from forming many clubs and from doing much to keep them going once they are formed."[19] A 1988–1990 study of middle-class urbanites found that few belonged to any sort of voluntary association.[20]

Even so, many such associations have been formed in the past few decades—a common trend in "developing" societies, where many new wants arise and where older means of satisfying basic needs, including the need for social interaction, have become less adequate. Rural high school boys and working-class youths in large towns are likely to join soccer clubs. Popular civic clubs for young people include Boy Scouts; the National Youth Movement, whose members help maintain national parks; and, in rural areas, 4-S Clubs, similar to 4-H and encouraged by government and U.S. advisers. Many teens solicit contributions from drivers for the prestigious Red Cross.

Business and professional men's Rotary and Lions Clubs sponsor dances and civic projects. Many men's groups have women's auxiliaries whose members meet for bingo, cards, and teas where they plan charitable fund-raisers. The women's groups also do volunteer work in hospitals, orphanages, and nutrition centers. Numerous church organizations help the needy, organize processions, and promote group study of the Bible and church doctrine.

Ecological activist groups are now popular among middle- and upper-class adults as well as high school and university students of both sexes. There are numerous self-help and twelve-step groups as well as mutual aid societies and a few neighborhood-watch groups.

The Arts

Compared to Latin American countries with large indigenous or African populations, Costa Rica retains few very old traditions in arts and crafts. Even the elaborately painted oxcarts that have become a symbol of Costa Rica date back only to the early twentieth century.[21] In most Spanish colonies, observes art historian Carlos Francisco Echeverría, indigenous and Hispano-Arabic artistic traditions blended into a new culture with its own life and identity. This, he claims, never happened in Costa Rica.[22] On the contrary, says José Ramírez, former director of the Ministry of Culture's folklore department: "Many of today's dances, songs, poems, and stories are based on oral traditions with pre-Columbian and African as well as Spanish roots, though most have only recently been revived after long neglect."[23]

During the first century of independence, European influences prevailed: Italian and Spanish companies dominated theater, and the most popular novelists were French and Spanish. French and Italian artists designed the National Theater—a small-scale replica of the Opéra Comique in Paris—and many patriotic monuments as well. San José's General Cemetery is full of marble angels sculpted early in the twentieth century by Costa Ricans who studied in Italy. Today U.S. influence is strong in the arts as in so much else. (This has been true for decades. Several wealthy Ticos built mansions in the 1940s inspired by Tara in the movie *Gone with the Wind*.)

Imitative rather than creative, Ticos' tastes, many critics charge, are shaped by advertising and are evident not only in decor—plastic flowers, knickknacks, predictable furnishings—but also in literature, architecture, and other arts. In a review of an art exhibition, one critic says, "Costa Rican painting is the candy of a lazy, passive, and saccharine sensibility."[24] In a small country where most people want above all to *quedar bien,* such frank criticism was rare until recently. Praise for conventional efforts is still lavish in less public forums. A Tica who started writing short stories while living in the United States recalls the writers' workshop she attended upon her return in the early 1990s: "I expected the writers to be tough on one another, as they were at workshops in San Francisco. Not at all! The most godawful poems and stories got the same response as the best ones: 'Oh, how lovely!'"

The beliefs that everything foreign is better and that art can be appreciated only by an elite, the popular suspicion that male artists are effeminate, the indifference to creativity in public schools, and the unlikelihood of any economic return long discouraged artistic innovation. In the 1930s, for example, when many of his countrymen sneered at his blocky stone figures, sculptor Francisco Zuñiga left Costa Rica in disgust to live in Mexico, where his growing fame finally brought him recognition at home.

In recent decades, however, the *bellas artes* (fine arts) have flourished to such a degree that some Ticos speak of a "cultural revolution." One evening in the city of Heredia we saw a private oil-painting class that was full of enthusiastic beginners ages ten to thirty, an exhibit of high school students' paintings, and classes in several instruments. We watched a music teacher in a highland town conduct a recorder-and-keyboard orchestra of twenty-eight children, all his private students. The government-subsidized House of the Artist has offered free lessons in painting and sculpture since 1951, and many well-known artists got their start there. Many others—musicians, dancers, painters—were trained at the state-subsidized Conservatorio Castella, an arts school for children and youth founded in 1953. State support for the arts increased with the establishment of the prolific Editorial Costa Rica in 1959 and with Pepe Figueres's institution in 1970 of the vigorous Ministry of Culture, headed by playwright-novelist Alberto Cañas. At first the ministry was generally dismissed as a frill, but the work of Cañas and other innovative directors has earned it great respect. As its functions expanded, its title was changed to the Ministry of Culture, Youth, and Sports. It sponsors Sunday performances of music, dance, and storytelling in cities and towns as well as an annual two-week-long International Arts Festival and many workshops for children.

The National Symphony Orchestra presents the most dramatic example of the boom in the arts. Until 1971 a small ensemble played ten or twelve poorly rehearsed concerts a year, often to very small audiences. Then don Pepe, who had said earlier, "It is necessary to consider the quality of life as well as the standard of living," asked, "Why should we have tractors if we lack violins?" The orchestra was revitalized. Many young foreigners were hired, their contracts stipulating that each would also teach an instrument to youngsters; thus began a second orchestra—the only state-subsidized youth symphony in the Western world. Its performances have been vigorously applauded at the White House, the United Nations, and on several European tours.

Internationally famous soloists often appear with the National Symphony. The ensemble—now mostly Ticos trained in the Youth Orchestra—frequently plays for enthusiastic audiences in small-town churches and plazas and often includes works of Costa Rican composers. Its chamber groups frequently play at the German, French, Spanish, Mexican, and U.S. cultural centers in San José as well as at hotels and private parties.

Theater and dance have also boomed since the early 1970s. On many an evening during the rainy season up to a dozen plays are presented in San José. They may include translated works by Sophocles, Brecht, Pinter, and Shakespeare, though most are slapstick comedies with broad sexual humor by Costa Rican playwrights. In productions of foreign comedies, Tico slang expressions and allusions to current national events are often worked into the script in order, says one director, to help audiences identify with the characters. Much of the impetus for theater has come from immigrant Argentine and Chilean playwrights and actors.

Despite Ticos' love of social dancing, disdain for exercise and display of the body long hampered the growth of ballet and modern dance. These attitudes are rapidly being overcome, as seen in growing enrollment in private and university dance classes and companies and a government-sponsored National Dance Company, which emphasize modern dance choreographed by Costa Ricans. Several new state-subsidized folk-dancing groups have shed the longtime Panamanian and Mexican influence on the costumes and repertoires of authentic Costa Rican art.

The upsurge in dance, music, and theater shows that the proverbially individualistic Costa Ricans can cooperate effectively and creatively. The national orchestra, chorus, and dance company join forces to perform an annual opera. Alumni of several high schools have formed brass bands to represent their alma maters at fairs and civic events.

Only after 1920 did Costa Rican painters and sculptors begin to break away from European influence. The favorite theme of Teodórico Quirós and Fausto Pacheco was the rural adobe house set amid trees and mountains. Their paintings portrayed the individualistic *campesino* as isolated even from his neighbors.[25]

Since the late 1950s many painters have favored abstract styles, dismissing their elders' obsession with "little houses." But human figures as well as their settings appear in the lyrical watercolors of Margarita Bertheau, the dramatic oils of Luisa González de Saenz, and the stylized murals of César Valverde. Although no uniquely Costa Rican styles are evident, the most successful painters do have distinctive styles or themes of their own: Isidro Con Wong's shimmering "magical realism"; Francisco Amighetti's strong woodcuts; Rafa Fernández's mysterious women in misty surroundings. Some of the more than 300 professional sculptors, like several painters, now make a living entirely from their work. Countless amateur sculptors shape human and animal figures from wood and clay.[26]

One means of keeping up artists' morale has long been such groups as Los Amigos del Arte, whose members meet to discuss their projects informally, and the Association of Costa Rican Painters and Sculptors, whose main goal is to "deofficialize" art, to free artists from total dependence on government support. Even rural women, the most neglected of Ticos, now sometimes gather to study painting. Says a young artist who teaches such women, "Ticos generally, especially rural women, are very reluctant to express emotion, even their likes and dislikes. At first, they won't even admit they like one color more than others. Many really blossom in these groups." Women in the remote village of La Unión de Monterrey asked a Peace Corps volunteer to teach them drawing and painting. She enlisted the help of

Sculptor carving coffeewood figures of campesinos *(Julio Laínez)*

painters Ana Barrientos and Fernando Páramo, who encouraged the women to paint specific experiences, memories, and dreams. The women named their group Valiant Hearts because they continued painting even though their husbands ridiculed them. In 1995 half a dozen continued to meet once a week as a co-op while their small children played or watched. One woman says, "It is very important to have free time, to do something for myself"; another, "It shows me I can do something besides wash clothes." The group's paintings and note cards sell locally to foreign tourists and in U.S. galleries, and the co-op has used the money to buy appliances since electricity arrived in 1993.[27] Benita Pérez, president of a similar co-op in Bahia Drake, accessible only by water, reports similar success—and more support from husbands. "They built the place where we meet," she told us while making change for tourists buying members' T-shirts and appliqué wall hangings.

Costa Rica's many museums are mostly new. The principal ones are in buildings transformed from their longtime purposes: An army barracks is now the National Museum; the original National Liquor Factory, the National

Center of Culture; the old airport terminal, the Museum of Costa Rican Art; an old prison, the National Museum of Science and Culture, primarily for children. The ornate pre-Columbian artifacts in the Gold and Jade museums attract thousands of visitors a year. The elegant century-old National Theater, reinforced after a 1991 earthquake, is a museum in itself. Other museums commemorate goldmining, the Atlantic Railroad, or nineteenth-century rural life; still others display insects and other nature specimens. All over the country, smaller museums preserve items of folk history, painting, and sculpture.

Increasingly, since the early 1980s, private businesses have sponsored classical concerts, theater, and art exhibits.[28] Still, the state, through the Ministries of Culture and Education, remains the chief promoter of folk art as well as the fine arts.

Some attempts to rescue artistic traditions put them in very different contexts than their original ones: folk dances presented in a huge theater for a paying audience of foreigners; miniature oxcart wheels or sales-oriented indigenous crafts bought by tourists to hang on their walls at home; state-sponsored contests for the best Nativity scene; folk songs taught in schools.

Says an eighteen-year-old student, "Some professors came to our school to tell us about Costa Rican folklore. But old folks like my grandfather tell great stories that can go on for two hours. Some are probably lies, but they sound true. Others are probably true, but embroidered. Anyway, they sound a lot better than what the professors told us." And a small-town high school music teacher told us that her students find her renditions of rural folk songs hopelessly corny; they'd much rather listen to rock, rap, and techno.

Today, far from rejecting nonconformist artists, museums and private galleries exhibit work of all kinds, and state agencies as well as private collectors purchase it. And although the state seeks to encourage authentic Costa Rican art, it does not try to impose any official aesthetic or ideological view. On the contrary, its facilities make it possible for Ticos, especially young people, to express themselves freely; the University of Costa Rica, for instance, has sponsored graffiti contests. (This tolerance has limits. In 1992, for instance, police broke up a heavy metal concert; the minister of public security condemned its slam-dancing and "satanic" atmosphere.)

Literature

Despite a high official literacy rate, most Costa Ricans enjoy reading only newspapers and magazines; even these are comparatively scarce outside the Central Valley. All wide-circulation newspapers are printed in San José. Most emphasize national rather than foreign events, though they include several syndicated columns and cartoons from other countries and foreign news— mainly about the United States, Europe, and Latin America. Sports news, horoscopes, and pages devoted to crimes and accidents are especially popular. Venezuelan and Spanish *fotonovelas* (like TV soaps in print and photos) as well as fashion and romance magazines appeal to many lower-middle-class women. Among readers of all social classes, women's magazines (which claim four-fifths of magazine readership nationally) and the Spanish edition of *Reader's Digest* are especially popular.

Publishing was long a risky venture. Traditionally writers paid to have their work printed and often failed to recover the cost. Since the state-subsidized Editorial Costa Rica printed its first book in 1961, however, it has provided great stimulus to writers, as has EDUCA, the Central American university press.

The Ministries of Culture and Education, the state universities, and a growing number of private firms also publish books; their lists include inexpensive editions of world classics as well as Latin American and national authors. Weekly newspaper supplements include poetry, stories, essays, reviews, and interviews with writers. Literature prizes are given regularly by the government, *La Nación,* and private organizations. But aside from salaried journalists and advertising copywriters, no Ticos make a living solely by writing.

Costumbrismo—local color—has been a main ingredient of Costa Rican writing since the 1890s. The stories and prose poems of that era depict the ways of different social classes in the developing coffee civilization. Aquileo Echeverría's century-old *Concherías* is the best-known example; its humor, emotion, and exaggerated rural dialect still appeal to readers.

Other still-remembered writers of the early twentieth century were essayists, fiction writers, and poets concerned with both local political and social life and universal themes. Masters of the essay were Roberto Brenes Mesén and Joaquín García Monge, editor of *Repertorio Americano,* which was well known in all of Latin America. Carmen Lyra wrote such still-popular children's books as *Cuentos de mi Tia Panchita.* Adela Ferreto wrote children's versions of Bible stories. (In Costa Rica being a communist, as she was, has not necessarily meant being an atheist.) Her husband, Carlos Luís Saenz, wrote "grandfather stories" as well as lyrical poems. Essays continue to be, as elsewhere in Latin America, a major form of intellectual and artistic expression, appearing daily in newspapers.

In the 1930s and 1940s many novelists protested the exploitation of peasants and peons by wealthy landowners and foreign companies. Carlos Luís Fallas's classic *Mamita Yunái* depicts the plight of banana workers. Other classic protest novels of that era are Fabian Dobles's *Ese que llamen pueblo* and *Puerto Limón,* by Joaquín Gutierrez (who has also translated some of Shakespeare's plays and written a children's book, *Cocorí,* which has been translated into several languages). Of universal appeal are the very short stories of Carlos Salazar Herrera, depicting the powerful emotions of poor people in remote areas when faced by a crisis. His books are standard reading in public schools.

Today's writers, although still challenging class oppression, foreign domination, and other social injustices, take a broader view of evolving social and cultural patterns. Social climbing and status competition, bureaucracy, racism, sex discrimination, and foreign cultural influence are pervasive themes. In *Los molinos de Diós* (1992) Alberto Cañas traces 130 years of social and political history through six generations of a *cafetalero* family. Poet and storyteller Alfonso Chase also turned to historical fiction in 1996 with a novel based on the political events of 1889, *El pavo real y la mariposa*. Quince Duncan writes scholarly books and essays as well as fiction based on the black experience in Costa Rica. Internationally acclaimed novelist Carmen Naranjo often dwells on the absurdity of modern urban life.

Several novels that appeared in the 1990s broke new ground. Linda Berrón's *El expediente* describes how a compulsive womanizer is eventually stymied by modern women's rejection of double standards. Anacristina Rossi's *La loca de Gandoca*, a novelized polemic against the real-life destruction of an idyllic Caribbean beach environment by greedy foreign hotel builders assisted by corrupt bureaucrats, went through several printings in a few months. Tatiana Lobo's *Asalto al Paraíso*, which describes the adventures of a refugee from the Spanish Inquisition in colonial Costa Rica, was hailed as a major work and in 1996 was translated into English and French. Daniel Gallegos's *El pasado es un extraño país*, casts light on today's society by recalling the Tinoco era.

In *Aquél fue un largo verano*, a devastating novel about petty bureaucrats, Jaime Fernández Leandro depicts the employees of a state agency in a Guanacaste village. The agency's function remains hazy; the employees are mostly concerned with drinking, sex, and surviving or rising within the bureaucracy. Fernando Contreras's *Única mirando al mar* portrays the lives of scavengers at the metropolitan garbage dump; both there and in *Los peor* (1995), which features a sheltered cyclopean boy, an eccentric former monk, and a group of prostitutes, he finds expressions of the universal human condition.

Participants in the *tertulias* of a century ago often read their own poetry; such gatherings still occur in a few upper- and middle-class homes. Much poetry is written and published today; some Costa Ricans have won international prizes. As in fiction, women now share and even dominate the field; among them are Julieta Dobles, Mia Gallegos, Ana Istarú, and Emilia Macaya.

Among today's children's writers are Delfina Collado and Marilyn Echeverría (pen name Lara Rios). Echeverría told us she finds it difficult to write truthfully for and about teenagers without offending some Ticos, particularly priests, whom she consulted before publishing *Pantalones largos* (1995), written from the point of view of a middle-class high school boy. She also wrote *Mo*, the first children's book about today's Indians, from a young Indian girl's point of view.

Summary and Conclusion

As free time has become more abundant, its uses have changed. Community entertainments such as town band concerts as well as chats in the neighborhood *pulpería*, shoemaker's shop, or barbershop have vanished from daily life in areas that have become urbanized and increasingly divided by class, whereas private clubs and often-solitary diversions such as TV and video games have grown more appealing.

Still, few Ticos are loners; most also enjoy parties, dancing, and beach outings with family or friends. Nearly everyone relishes conversation, especially gossip and jokes. Politics and sex are favorite topics. So is sports—especially soccer, which working-class boys and young men enjoy playing and which provides emotional release as well as group identification for many spectators and fans.

Interest in the arts has boomed in recent decades. Theater and dance attract mainly young performers and audiences. Encouraged by the state through the Ministries of Culture and Education, the boom is not confined to an elite but is typified by the visits of the National Symphony Orchestra to rural churches full of enthralled villagers, by working-class women's painting and crafts cooperatives, and by thousands of amateur poets, painters, and sculptors.

Notes

1. Eugenia Ibarra, "Corridas de toros, fiestas y bailes," *La Nación,* December 27, 1995, p. 14A.

2. Mario Sancho, *Memorias* (San José: ECR, 1961), p. 39.

3. Pierre Thomas Claudet, *La cultura del pobrecitico* (San José: EUCR, 1992), pp. 51–52.

4. Edgar Espinoza, "Al grano," *La Nación,* August 2, 1992, p. 15A.

5. Carlos Meléndez, *Historia de Costa Rica* (San José: EUNED, 1991), p. 104.

6. Dino Starcevic, "Mr. Thanksgiving," *La República,* November 25, 1993, p. 22.

7. Yehudi Monestel in *Tico Times,* December 13, 1974.

8. Chester Lloyd Jones, *Costa Rica and Civilization in the Caribbean* (New York: Russell and Russell, 1967), p. 129. First published in 1935.

9. Marcela Angulo, "Las rifas, economía sumergida," *La Nación,* November 11, 1992, p. 14A.

10. Carlos Rivera, "La niñera electrónica," *Contrapunto,* December 1990.

11. Melissa E. DeRosier and Janis B. Kupersmidt, "Costa Rican Children's Perceptions of Their Social Networks," *Developmental Psychology,* Vol. 27, No. 4, July 1991, pp. 656–662.

12. Edgar Espinosa, "Al grano," *La Nación*, January 19, 1992, p. 15A.

13. Mayela Cubillo Mora, *El futból: Una perspectiva sociológica* (San José: UCR, Editorial Alma Mater, 1986).

14. Brian Harris, "Soccer Subsidies Under Fire," *Tico Times*, December 1, 1995, p. 1.

15. José Marín Cañas, *La Nación*, July 11, 1974.

16. Mitzi Stark, "Sunday Soccer—Complete with 'Pachos,'" *Tico Times*, January 22, 1993, p. 20.

17. Moritz Wagner and Karl Scherzer, *La República de Costa Rica en la América Central* (San José: Ministerio de Cultura, 1974), Vol. 1, p. 130.

18. John Biesanz and Mavis Biesanz, *Costa Rican Life* (New York: Columbia University Press, 1944), p. 200.

19. Ibid., p. 178.

20. Coronado and Pérez, *La clase media costarricense*, p. 95.

21. See Constantino Láscaris and Guillermo Malavassi, *La carreta costarricense* (San José: Ministry of Culture, 1975), and J. Ramírez Saízar, *Folclor costarricense* (San José: Imprenta Nacional, 1979). The wife of a cart maker in San Ramón is said to have designed the first decoration, which quickly caught on. Many drovers painted their own carts in bright geometric designs—notably the mandala-like wheels—and stylized motifs based on flowers, leaves, and vegetables. Some such carts are still in use, although jeeps, trucks, and planes have taken over most of their work. In the San José suburb of San Antonio de Escazú, the Day of the Oxcart Driver is celebrated every year with a parade of working carts. Carts are also made in smaller sizes for toys, decorations, and home bars, and many tourist brochures and souvenirs use the traditional motifs.

22. Carlos Francisco Echeverría, *Historia crítica del arte costarricense* (San José: EUNED, 1986). See also Ricardo Ulloa Barrenechea, *Pintores de Costa Rica* (San José: ECR, 1974), p. 13.

23. Interview, May 2, 1993.

24. Klaus Steinmetz in *La Nación*, May 5, 1992, p. B4.

25. Echeverría, *Historia*, p. 63.

26. Luis Ferrero, *Escultores costarricenses* (San José: ECR, 1992).

27. Anne Newton, "Art Flourishes in an Isolated Township," *Costa Rica Today*, March 3, 1994, pp. 10–11.

28. Twenty-six short stories by Costa Rican writers appeared in English translation in 1994. Barbara Ras, ed., *Costa Rica Traveler's Literary Companion* (San Francisco: Whereabouts Press, 1994).

—12—

Continuity and Change *a la Tica*

A RETURNING COSTA RICAN who has lived abroad since 1948 hardly recognizes the country of his youth. It does not look as green or feel as peaceful as he remembers it. There are now four times as many Costa Ricans as when he left, and more than half of them live in towns and cities. He notices far more North Americans and Europeans—many obviously tourists—than in his youth. He sees mostly Nicaraguans picking coffee—an activity that was long a primary symbol of Costa Rican identity. He can hardly recognize the village where he was born and spent his childhood; no longer surrounded by coffee groves and little farms, it merges into the greater San José metropolitan area. The children and grandchildren of farmers he knew work in government and multinational corporate offices, factories, hospitals, supermarkets, hotels, and tourist agencies or as doctors, lawyers, teachers, engineers, bus or taxi drivers, or construction workers. Many, such as the Electrical Institute tunnel workers interviewed by anthropologist Jorge Luís Amador, "have spent half their lives immersed in one world and the other half in a totally different one, a transition from oxcarts to microcomputers."[1]

Small Protestant churches are everywhere. In Catholic churches mass is said in Spanish rather than Latin, and sometimes women and children read parts of the service. Men are more likely to attend than their grandfathers were.

State employees, most of them working for agencies the returned expatriate never heard of, now deliver babies, build hydroelectric dams, teach computer programming, play in symphony orchestras, and make the government's presence felt at every turn. He observes that many more women now work outside their homes. He sees pregnant teenagers everywhere, most of them unmarried. Parents, especially fathers, have less authority than he recalls but are often more intimate with their offspring than were their own fathers.

His old schoolmates often yearn for times free of the continual anxiety and stress that so many complain of today. Decades ago, they insist, people

281

worked harder; children played safely in the street and obeyed their elders; a hair from a man's mustache, rather than an unreadable legal contràct, sealed a bargain; teachers thought more of forming their pupils' minds and character than of shorter school years and larger pensions. People were happier despite or because of their simpler, more frugal lives.

Now cars, planes, and interurban buses, telephones and fax, radio, television, and the Internet link all parts of the country and bring ideas, news, things, and people from abroad. The returning Tico misses the sociability of the old corner *pulpería* and barbershop and the gatherings of neighbors and kin on the roofed verandas that once faced a quiet, unpaved street. Instead, his relatives invite him for a drink at their living room bar and fill him in on the decades he missed.

During the 1950s, 1960s, and 1970s, government jobs were easy to get and a couple needed only one paycheck or their own small farm to live decently. Progress was in the air; life was full of promise and of more and more things to buy; schooling, even public schooling, and an academic title were magic keys to an ever brighter future. Infant mortality fell dramatically while life expectancy rose, thanks largely to government spending on potable water, sewage systems, nutrition programs, and a nearly universal system of health insurance. Much of this progress was financed by huge foreign loans. The recession of 1979–1982 prompted international banks to withhold further loans unless Costa Rica agreed to streamline government bureaucracy, privatize the economy, and encourage foreign investment and open competition in a global marketplace. "Overnight," the returning Tico is told, "our salaries bought only about half as much as before, and the colón kept losing its value—as it still does. The government has been forced to sign structural adjustment pacts to qualify for more loans."

His friends disagree about the effects of these pacts. Some say that it was high time to trim government and make the economy more competitive, that inflation has been kept within reasonable limits, and that the GDP is growing once more. Others insist that the rich have become richer, the poor, poorer and more numerous, and that government services in health, education, and welfare have deteriorated sharply because of budget cuts.

Although the middle class is far larger than in 1948, he may see the gap between rich and poor as deeper and more obvious. High-rises and Miami-style shopping malls stand not far from shantytowns; BMWs zoom past crowded buses. Most poor children now finish primary school, but they no longer share classrooms with those from more affluent families, who attend private schools of far higher quality. The rural poor, especially those living in the coastal provinces, feel particularly neglected—with good reason; the country's development, they point out, remains focused, as always, on the Meseta Central.

The promise and reality of upward mobility have shrunk since the crisis. Today it is harder to achieve and maintain middle-class status. The traditional subsistence farmer has virtually disappeared, and small- and medium-sized farmers have less access to credit and technical assistance than do big agroindustries. Urban jobs require ever more advanced degrees, and even these no longer guarantee a good government job. The cost of living rises faster than most salaries.

As in 1948—and much earlier—Ticos blame the government as a whole, corrupt public officials, and above all the president. So many Ticos see government as ineffective in controlling street crime and domestic violence, environmental pollution, and the deterioration of the health and educational systems that it has lost much of its legitimacy. Government agencies, many say, will remain unable to solve these problems as long as they have no concrete goals other than serving the interests of their employees and of the party in power. Although most Ticos continue to take pride in their democracy, its meaning has become increasingly limited to their honest elections. Even so, they deplore the unending electoral campaigns, the essential similarity of the two major parties, and the partisan bickering that slows down decisions on important issues in the Legislative Assembly.

Many of those—including ourselves—who blame a bloated, uncoordinated government bureaucracy for much of the nation's malaise are nonetheless leery of structural adjustment as a solution. That bureaucracy, for all its defects, provided a safety net for many poor Costa Ricans, promoted public education and health, and made social responsibility one criterion for government investment. All this has helped keep Costa Rica at or near the top among Latin American countries in the UN's quality-of-life indices.

Nor does across-the-board privatization of public corporations guarantee greater economic progress or national self-determination. Although banks were nationalized and autonomous institutions established to replace the old hated foreign monopolies, many Ticos now fear renewed domination by foreign interests.

Selectivity

Even a century ago, some Costa Ricans lamented their people's receptivity to everything foreign. A character in Maximo Soto Hall's 1899 novel *El problema* complains, "We have disdained everything that was our own in favor of anything foreign. We have shaped ourselves to the pattern of those who want us to be like them." Many critics today echo these charges and cite, in particular, the fondness of many Ticos for Big Macs, MTV, Halloween, and other elements of U.S. popular culture.

But since colonial times—indeed, since long before the Spanish con-quest—the region that is now Costa Rica has been affected by outside influ-ences. These accelerated with the coffee boom in the mid-nineteenth century, an era widely imagined today as one of authentic, homegrown traditions. Thanks to coffee profits, say cultural historians Ivan Molina and Steven Palmer,

> the German sofa appeared alongside the creole bench, and the rustic melodies of the guitar were displaced by the works of Chopin played on the salon piano by a young lady. Lamps illuminated the sacred images, and clocks measured the movement of the sun. Well-to-do urbanites now could refuse the cane liquor of the country and enjoy champagne, port, and sherry; mix ordinary fruits with almonds, raisins and nuts; feast on Westphalia ham and Dutch cheeses; dress in silks and cashmere, and walk about the city in French shoes. . . .
> Instead of lamenting the loss of a supposed authenticity, corroded by the penetration of foreign products, tastes, behavior, and feelings, it would be worthwhile to remember that, to cite just one example, without the grow-ing importation of basic grains, which began in 1850, today *gallo pinto* [the national breakfast dish of rice and black beans] would be unknown.[2]

Nonetheless, Costa Ricans, like other peoples, have been selective in appro-priating foreign ideas and products, ignoring many while modifying others to fit their own needs, values, and customs. Soon after the coffee trade began, the value they had long placed on equality made them receptive to Chilean and British writers' ideas on human rights. Today a Caribbean-coast fisher-man may use fiberglass to line his dugout canoe (made with a chainsaw as well as an ax and adze) not because it is modern but because it will make the dugout, which is still cheap and practical, last much longer. The *pupusa*, filled tortilla introduced by Salvadoran immigrants, is now standard fare at *turnos* and at restaurants offering "typical" Costa Rican cuisine—no doubt because of its resemblance to older Costa Rican dishes. ("Chapsui," a *turno* staple of Chinese origin, has a similar history.) Though we observed students marching in a 1992 protest to "Yellow Polka Dot Bikini," the tune was modi-fied to a salsa beat. And a teacher at the protest commented, "In most coun-tries, the students would have thrown rocks. Our students are singing." The U.S. military marches long played by Costa Rican town bands carry no mar-tial associations for musicians or listeners.

Closer ties to other countries have greatly increased Ticos' chances to judge themselves against others and to accept, reject, or modify foreign ideas. Even those who complain of their country's combination of shortages and too-rapid modernization may insist that they have not allowed either to de-stroy what is most valuable in their way of life. A young Tica married to a German says: "Germans and North Americans are robots. They do everything according to rules. There's no emotion. But here in Costa Rica there are 3 million people who somehow manage to survive without turning into machines, who take the time to talk to one another or at least acknowledge each other's presence." A young San José cabdriver echoed her: "I hope Costa Rica never becomes too industrialized. Many people who have traveled to those countries say that the people there are always busy, that they have no time to talk." And an artist recently returned from a conference in Finland reports that although she admires Finnish design, she developed a stronger sense of what she likes about her own country:

> The Finns were annoyed when we Latinos weren't all ready to break for coffee at exactly 10 A.M., perhaps because we were really involved in discussing some point. Why should a clock regulate our lives? They enjoyed watching us dance but didn't join us. And while we Ticos do favors for one another on an informal basis, in Finland you have to go to the proper specialist for everything. That's not for me!

Ticos have long insisted that foreign influences be evaluated carefully as to whether they fit into "our idiosyncrasy." Such pleas have become more urgent with structural adjustment, cable TV, and the tourism boom. In 1987 President Arias, while bowing to foreign creditors' pressure for a more privatized economy, cautioned that such changes should be introduced "gradually . . . *a la tica* . . . so that social stability will never be threatened." And privatization of state functions, note sociologist Silvia Lara and her coauthors, has proceeded slowly, since Ticos "derive a certain sense of security from the services offered by the state as well as pride for some of its stellar institutions."[3]

Rejecting or accepting innovations according to this criterion, the Costa Ricans have to some extent controlled the degree and direction of change to create their own version of a modern society. A report to the Inter-American Development Bank on the country's options for the twenty-first century suggests that the high-technology firms such as Intel currently investing in Costa Rica may reduce the importance of agriculture and agroindustry even further. But, the report adds, they can also contribute greatly to development if these investors understand the country's history and culture and if Ticos strengthen their own traditional allegiance to such values as equality, education, and democracy. Adherence to such values will enable Costa Rica to "join the world market as a small and efficient country."[4]

Continuity

Reading *Costa Rican Life* more than fifty years after it was published, we find many of its observations still valid. Ticos' *idiosincrácia*—their way of doing things—is deep-rooted indeed. Even a Methuselah who had last been in Costa Rica before its independence might note familiar attitudes and values in the Costa Rica of the late twentieth century.

Ticos stubbornly—though passively—refuse to obey rules and orders that interfere with their own inclinations. In colonial days, subsistence farmers ignored their bishop's orders to move from their widely scattered hamlets to form towns around churches. The Catholic majority is still reluctant to accept many church doctrines: Many do not believe in an afterlife and have no qualms about practicing contraception or consulting witches and fortunetellers. When they go to confession, if at all, they confess only what *they* see as sins. Their fondness for risqué jokes about priests, nuns, and even the pope reflects not only their historic ambivalence toward the clergy but also an old practice of "lowering the floor" under those who presume to tell others what to do.

This resistance to authority is also evident in the public school system, where students ignore teachers' calls for order, just as teachers ignore many Ministry of Education directives. Distrust of concentrated authority is reflected in the abolition of the army; in irreverent jokes about the president, even by his supporters; in the common fear that a more professional police force would be, in effect, an army; in the many checks and balances provided for in the 1949 constitution; and in the complexities of the bureaucracy developed in the following three decades.

Other longstanding cultural patterns linked to this antiauthoritarian attitude also shed light on recent social changes. Ticos are proverbially distrustful of others—one reason they fear concentrated power. Columnist Cecilia Valverde notes that when, early in the twentieth century, a private citizen offered to plant trees along the state rail line to Puntarenas at his own expense, suspicions that he had hidden motives were so widespread in both government and the general public that his offer was rejected. She adds that this "typically Costa Rican" distrust explains the unpopularity of the 1995 Calderón-Figueres pact. Even though this bipartisan agreement was intended to mollify a public disgusted with partisan wrangling, most Ticos believed that the "real"—private—negotiations must have involved personal interests at the expense of the common good.[5]

Likewise, furor over the government's 1996 arms purchase from Israel was provoked less by the caliber of the weapons—essentially replacements for police agencies' older ones—than by the secrecy of the deal. Distrust of others is also a likely reason that even though many voluntary associations have been formed in recent years, few last long. Many Ticos instead seek expensive private solutions to collective problems: Rather than join with others to demand better bus service, they may buy a car or a motorcycle; reluctant to cooperate with neighbors to prevent burglaries, they may instead hire private guards and buy guns; rather than work to improve public schools, they may send their children to private ones, or hope to someday, as a way of retaining or gaining middle-class status. Political scientist Olivier Dabene concluded in 1992 that national unity was one of the country's greatest achievements, but this unity has eroded as distrust and social inequality have grown.[6] The 1994 report to the Inter-American Development Bank insists that Costa Rica needs a national project discussed and shared by all.[7]

Ticos' disdain for authority, which might doom any such project if it were perceived as originating with a high official, also reflects a belief that despite differences in wealth, income, and education, all Costa Ricans are equal in worth. This belief may stem from colonial times, when even high officials were not isolated in regal mansions but were encountered daily by the humblest residents of the tiny capital and most colonists were subsistence farmers with land of their own, not peons on large plantations. It may explain why both cabinetmakers and cabinet ministers may describe themselves as middle class and why a person of high status takes care to act humble in public. The common perception of some recent politicians as arrogant is often cited as a reason for their low popularity despite their admitted competence, and since such perceptions can spread quickly in the television era, many now usually appear in public without coat or tie in an effort to look more folksy.

Faith in equality as well as a sense of national unity have long been strained by the political and economic preeminence of the Central Valley, particularly the San José metropolitan area. Lowlanders complain about Meseta dwellers' arrogance and disproportionate access to employment, roads, certified teachers, and state-sponsored art events.

It may seem odd that recent presidents have shown so much concern with their standing in the now-frequent opinion polls, since the president is barred for life from serving again. But this concern reflects a strong desire, not unique to presidents (or to Costa Ricans), to *quedar bien,* a pattern Ticos themselves usually describe as their love of peace. This desire, many Ticos believe, is tied to the national habit of fence-sitting, of maintaining at least an appearance of neutrality wherever opinions may vary; to "wait until the clouds of the day disperse" before declaring a decision; and to the emphasis on consensus rather than debate. Along with the attitudes toward the clergy noted previously, this propensity may account for the common statement "I am a Catholic but not a fanatic" and for the refusal of many other Ticos even to label their own religious affiliation. It may also explain why many laws are unenforced where police or inspectors are not bribed; enforcement would require confrontation, which Ticos dislike.

"Costa Ricans," John and Mavis Biesanz noted in the 1940s, "criticize themselves rather unsparingly" except when comparing their country to others.[8] Half a century later, 43 percent of those responding to an opinion poll blamed the country's problems on "the way Ticos are." José Ricardo Chaves, returning after a long absence, noticed this tendency:

Ticos like to speak ill of themselves and want to explain their problems and defects by citing the national character. They don't do so in a tragic way. Far from it. They do it from laugh to laugh, from joke to joke, like the most amusing thing in the world. The magic wand that immobilizes everything is "You see, that's the way we Ticos are."[9]

Into the Third Millennium

Given their deep-rooted cultural values and patterns, such as their dislike of planning and even of change itself, are Costa Ricans prepared for the increasing pace of global change? Those who would answer no believe that acting *a la tica* means indecision, delay, and acceptance of symbolic, improvised, and slipshod solutions to problems, of mediocrity rather than excellence. Traffic jams, potholed roads, and urban sprawl, they insist, are clear evidence. Although the early introduction of computers into primary schools indicates awareness of the dawn of the information age, the reluctance of teachers' unions to lengthen the world's shortest school year is only one clue that Costa Rica may not be prepared to participate fully when the clouds disperse. In any case, if the social breaches between the center and the periphery of the country, between the well- and the poorly educated, the rich and the poor, continue to grow, only the few will be ready.

Many of Costa Rica's problems cannot be addressed without some sacrifice of traditional values and norms. Deforestation cannot be halted unless the new restrictions on landowners' longstanding right to fell trees on their own property are enforced. Further improvements in health probably cannot occur without changes in the preferred diet—high in saturated fats, sugar, alcohol, salt, and caffeine. Crime may remain high until the country has well-trained career police, unlikely as long as this change is equated with militarization. Even then, crime and corruption, as well as the government's high internal and foreign debts, are unlikely to abate much as long as Ticos equate the good life with consumerism and tax and credit structures favor the rich. Without more attention to women's reproductive rights and employment opportunities, changes many Costa Ricans resist, the problem of overpopulation—more evident every year—may well prove insoluble. (At the 1996 annual growth rate, the population will increase from 3.5 million to 5 million by 2025.) Finally, many needed changes, according to a growing number of Costa Ricans, are blocked by the current constitution, which was based largely on that of 1871; it is high time, many say, to adopt one more appropriate to changing conditions.

To what degree will Costa Ricans of the late twenty-first century resemble those of today or of earlier eras? Given their country's limited voice in the global political economy, the answer depends largely on decisions made in foreign capitals and multinational companies' boardrooms and only partly on the choices Ticos themselves make as citizens, neighbors, producers, consumers, and family members.

But some aspects of their culture have shown remarkable persistence despite centuries of foreign influence. It is likely that whatever changes occur in this tiny Central American country during the first century of the new millennium, many will still occur *a la tica.*

Notes

1. Jorge Luís Amador Matamoros, "De jornaleros agrícolas a obreros de la construcción de túneles," Lic. Thesis in Anthropology, UCR, 1991, p. 6.

2. Ivan Molina Jiménez and Steven Palmer, eds., *Héroes al gusto y libros de moda* (San José: Porvenir, 1992), pp. 208, 210.

3. Silvia Lara, Tom Barry, and Peter Simonson, *Inside Costa Rica* (Albuquerque: Resource Center Press, 1995), p. 37.

4. German W. Rama, "A la búsqueda del siglo XXI: Nuevos caminos de desarrollo en Costa Rica," in *Report of Pilot Mission of the Program of Social Reform of the Interamerican Development Bank,* 1994. Cited and quoted by Gabriel Macaya Trejos, "Nuevos caminos para Costa Rica," in *La Nación,* January 25, 1997, p. 15A.

5. Cecilia Valverde B., "Acérrima desconfianza," *La Nación,* June 5, 1996, p. 15A.

6. Olivier Dabene, *Costa Rica: Juicio a la democrácia* (San José: Facultad Latinoamericana de Ciencias Sociales, 1992), p. 120.

7. Rama, "A la búsqueda del siglo XXI."

8. John Biesanz and Mavis Biesanz, *Costa Rican Life* (New York: Columbia University Press, 1944), p. 228.

9. José Ricardo Chaves, "San José revisitada," *La Nación,* April 14, 1993, p. 14A.

Selected Bibliography

Most of the following Spanish-language sources are available only in Costa Rica and only in a few bookstores. Libreria Macondo, near the University of Costa Rica, has one of the widest selections.

Ameringer, Charles D. *Democracy in Costa Rica.* New York: Praeger, 1982.

Bell, John Patrick. *Crisis in Costa Rica.* Austin: University of Texas Press, 1971.

Biesanz, John, and Biesanz, Mavis. *Costa Rican Life.* New York: Columbia University Press, 1944.

Blake, Beatrice, and Becher, Anne. *The New Key to Costa Rica.* Berkeley: Ulysses Press. (Updated annually.)

Claudet, Pierre Thomas. *La cultura del pobrecitico.* San José: EUCR, 1992.

Creedman, Theodore. *Historical Dictionary of Costa Rica.* Metuchen, N.J.: Scarecrow Press, 1977.

Dabene, Olivier. *Costa Rica: Juicio a la democrácia.* San José: Facultad Latinoamericana de Ciencias Sociales, 1992.

Edelman, Marc, and Kenen, Joanne, eds. *The Costa Rica Reader.* New York: Grove Weidenfeld, 1989.

Gudmundson, Lowell. *Costa Rica Before Coffee: Society and Economy on the Eve of the Export Boom.* Baton Rouge: Louisiana State University Press, 1986.

Hall, Carolyn. *Costa Rica: A Geographical Interpretation in Historical Perspective.* Boulder: Westview, 1985.

Janzen, Daniel H., ed. *Costa Rican Natural History.* Chicago: University of Chicago Press, 1983.

Jaramillo Antillón, Juan. *Salud y seguridad social.* San José: Universidad de Costa Rica, 1993.

Jones, Chester Lloyd. *Costa Rica and Civilization in the Caribbean.* Madison: University of Wisconsin Studies in the Social Sciences and History, No. 23, 1935. Reprint; New York: Russell and Russell, 1967.

Lara, Silvia, Barry, Tom, and Simonson, Peter. *Inside Costa Rica.* Albuquerque: Resource Center Press, 1995.

Leitinger, Ilse Abhagen, ed. *The Costa Rican Women's Movement.* Pittsburgh: University of Pittsburgh Press, 1997.

Low, Setha. *Culture, Politics, and Medicine in Costa Rica.* Bedford Hills, N.Y.: Redgrave, 1985.

Meléndez, Carlos. *Historia de Costa Rica.* San José: EUNED, 1991.

Molina Jiménez, Ivan, and Palmer, Steven. *Historia de Costa Rica.* San José: Editorial de la Universidad de Costa Rica, 1997.

Molina Jiménez, Ivan, and Palmer, Steven, eds. *Héroes al gusto y libros de moda.* San José: Porvenir, 1992.

Purcell, Trevor W. *Banana Fallout: Class, Color, and Culture Among West Indians in Costa Rica.* Los Angeles: Center for Afro-American Studies Publications, Regents of the University of California, 1993.

Ras, Barbara, ed. *Costa Rica Traveler's Literary Companion.* San Francisco: Whereabouts Press, 1994.

Villasuso, Juan Manuel, ed. *El nuevo rostro de Costa Rica.* San José: CEDAL, 1992.

Williams, Philip J. *The Catholic Church and Politics in Nicaragua and Costa Rica.* Pittsburgh: University of Pittsburgh Press, 1989.

Wilson, Bruce M. *Costa Rica: Politics, Economics, and Democracy,* Boulder: Lynne Rienner, 1998.

Index

About the Book

Written with the perspective of more than a half-century of firsthand observation, this unparalleled social and cultural history describes how Costa Rica's economy, government, educational and health-care systems, family structures, religion, and other institutions have evolved and how this evolution has affected—and reflected—people's daily lives, their beliefs, and their values. The authors are particularly concerned with change and continuity since the economic crisis of the early 1980s and the structural adjustment that followed.

Providing a comprehensive introduction to a country they know well, the Biesanzes also contribute astutely to an understanding of the reciprocal influence of structural adjustment and national culture.

Mavis Hiltunen Biesanz is author (with John Biesanz) of *Costa Rican Life* and *The People of Panama* and (with Richard and Karen Biesanz) *The Costa Ricans.* Her publications also include multiple editions of *Modern Society: An Introduction to Social Science* and *Introduction to Sociology.* She has been a resident of Costa Rica since 1971. **Richard Biesanz** is professor of sociology and anthropology at Corning Community College. **Karen Zubris Biesanz** writes on Costa Rican society.